Cognition and Intractability

Intractability is a growing concern across th   .... many models of cognition can describe and predic   ....an behavior in the lab, it remains unclear how these models can scale to situations of real-world complexity. *Cognition and Intractability* is the first book to provide an accessible introduction to computational complexity analysis and its application to questions of intractability in cognitive science. Covering both classical and parameterized complexity analysis, it introduces the mathematical concepts and proof techniques that can be used to test one's intuition of (in)tractability. It also describes how these tools can be applied to cognitive modeling to deal with intractability – and its ramifications – in a systematic way. Aimed at students and researchers in philosophy, cognitive neuroscience, psychology, artificial intelligence, and linguistics who want to build a firm understanding of intractability and its implications in their modeling work, it is an ideal resource for teaching or self-study.

Iris van Rooij is a psychologist and cognitive scientist at the Donders Institute for Brain, Cognition and Behaviour and the School for Psychology and Artificial Intelligence at Radboud University, the Netherlands.

Mark Blokpoel is a computational cognitive scientist at the Donders Institute for Brain, Cognition and Behaviour at Radboud University, the Netherlands.

Johan Kwisthout is a computer scientist at the Donders Institute for Brain, Cognition and Behaviour and the School for Psychology and Artificial Intelligence at Radboud University, the Netherlands.

Todd Wareham is a computer scientist at the Department of Computer Science at Memorial University of Newfoundland, Canada.

Cognition and Intractability

A Guide to Classical and Parameterized Complexity Analysis

IRIS VAN ROOIJ
Radboud University Nijmegen

MARK BLOKPOEL
Radboud University Nijmegen

JOHAN KWISTHOUT
Radboud University Nijmegen

TODD WAREHAM
Memorial University of Newfoundland

CAMBRIDGE
UNIVERSITY PRESS

CAMBRIDGE
UNIVERSITY PRESS

University Printing House, Cambridge CB2 8BS, United Kingdom

One Liberty Plaza, 20th Floor, New York, NY 10006, USA

477 Williamstown Road, Port Melbourne, VIC 3207, Australia

314–321, 3rd Floor, Plot 3, Splendor Forum, Jasola District Centre,
New Delhi – 110025, India

79 Anson Road, #06–04/06, Singapore 079906

Cambridge University Press is part of the University of Cambridge.

It furthers the University's mission by disseminating knowledge in the pursuit of
education, learning, and research at the highest international levels of excellence.

www.cambridge.org
Information on this title: www.cambridge.org/9781107043992
DOI: 10.1017/9781107358331

First published 2019

Printed and bound in Great Britain by Clays Ltd, Elcograf S.p.A.

A catalogue record for this publication is available from the British Library.

Library of Congress Cataloging-in-Publication Data

Names: Rooij, Iris van, 1973- author. | Blokpoel, Mark, 1984- author. |
    Kwisthout, Johan, 1976- author. | Wareham, Todd, 1963- author.
Title: Cognition and intractability : a guide to classical and parameterized
    complexity analysis / Iris van Rooij (Radboud Universiteit Nijmegen), Mark
    Blokpoel (Radboud University Nijmegen), Johan Kwisthout (Universiteit
    Leiden), Todd Wareham (Memorial University of Newfoundland).
Description: Cambridge ; New York, NY : Cambridge University Press, 2019. |
    Includes bibliographical references and index.
Identifiers: LCCN 2018057971| ISBN 9781107043992 (hardback : alk. paper) |
    ISBN 9781108728973 (pbk. : alk. paper)
Subjects: LCSH: Computational complexity. | Decision making. | Probabilities.
Classification: LCC QA267.7 .C64 2019 | DDC 511.3/52–dc23 LC record available at
    https://lccn.loc.gov/2018057971

ISBN 978-1-107-04399-2 Hardback
ISBN 978-1-108-72897-3 Paperback

Cambridge University Press has no responsibility for the persistence or accuracy
of URLs for external or third-party internet websites referred to in this publication
and does not guarantee that any content on such websites is, or will remain,
accurate or appropriate.

Contents

Part I Introduction

Part II Concepts and Techniques

Figures

Tables

Preface

P.1   Why This Book?

Intractability has been a growing concern in cognitive science: many theories of cognition can describe and predict human behavior in the lab, but it remains unclear how these theories can scale to situations of real-world complexity given that they postulate intractable (e.g., NP-hard) computations. Unbeknownst to many cognitive scientists, there exist complexity theoretic tools for dealing with the problem of intractability. These methods have been developed over the last decades in theoretical computer science. This book aims to make those methods visible and accessible for a broad cognitive science audience, in effect growing the community of researchers that will have these complexity theoretic tools as part of their standard theoretical toolkit. With this, we believe cognitive science will be in a significantly better position to tackle one of its key theoretical problems – namely, how can cognition in its full richness and complexity be computationally tractable?

In addition, we hope to contribute to the unification of otherwise discon-nected work in the cognitive science literature. At the end of this book, you will find a compendium of computational-level theories, together with their known complexity results. These theories come from different content domains (decision-making, analogy, reasoning, vision, language, action, etc.) and fall under different theoretical frameworks (e.g., symbolic, neural network, prob-abilistic, dynamical, logic, robotic, and heuristic models of cognition). It is our experience that researchers from different areas often are not aware that from a formal perspective these (superficially distinct looking) models and their computational complexity are in fact closely related. By bringing these models together in one place and by highlighting their common and distinct structure, we hope to generate new and more general ways of thinking about computational-level theorizing in cognitive science and the associated problem of intractability. We hope that our compendium, not unlike the compendium of NP-complete problems in Garey and Johnson's classical book of 1979, will become invaluable as both a reference for existing work and an aid to future work.

P.2   For Whom Is This Book?

The book is written for advanced undergraduate students, graduate students, and researchers in cognitive science and its affiliated disciplines. Among these disciplines we count computational- and psycholinguistics, cognitive psychology, artificial intelligence, cognitive neuroscience, computer science, logic, and philosophy of mind, science, and computation.

The book assumes an inherently interdisciplinary perspective. It is written primarily for cognitive scientists interested in developing and assessing computational explanations of natural cognition. This will likely include cognitive psychologists and cognitive neuroscientists, but also artificial intelligence researchers interested in emulating natural cognition in artificial systems. The book may also be of interest to computer scientists who wish to apply complexity theoretic methodology to cognitive theories. Finally, philosophers of cognitive science may find the meta-scientific considerations laid out in this book of special interest. We hope the book will inspire interesting and productive interdisciplinary collaborations.

In an attempt to give the reader a firm grip on the notion of intractability, we will cover many more formal details than is common in the cognitive science literature. We believe that a proper understanding of tractability, its formalizations, and its role in cognitive science, demands more than a superficial understanding of the mathematical theory of computational complexity. To make these formal details accessible for a broad audience of cognitive scientists we include in our textbook many informal explanations, simple examples, and practical exercises. See also the Section P.5 Guide to the Reader.

P.3   What Not to Expect

Both cognitive science and complexity theory are vast fields of study. We cannot possibly cover everything about these fields in this book. Even if we could, it would detract from our main points. This book focusses on a specific interface between complexity theory and cognitive science: the *intractability* of *computational-level* theories of cognition. Even doing justice to this focus requires us to cover a substantial amount of material in a coherent fashion. Consequently, this book will not cover many topics one may otherwise expect in a computer science book on complexity theory or in a cognitive science book on computational modeling.

For instance, we will not cover complexity classes that distinguish between different types of highly efficient computations (such as the classes inside P). Also, we largely ignore many of the classes that contain NP, because most relevant problems for cognitive science live in NP (or parameterized or probabilistic analogues of NP), and even where they don't it is hardness for NP that matters ultimately for intractability (not membership in any of the other classes that contain it). Although we mention classes such as PSPACE, EXP, etc. in passing, students who become interested in knowing more about the polynomial-time hierarchy and more advanced complexity classes may do well to seek out other, more specialized theoretical computer science sources. In later chapters, we do mention some other classes, such as BPP and BQP for as far as they are relevant for philosophical discussions about the tractability constraint on computational-level theories of cognition.

We also will be relatively silent about the many important advances in algorithmic-level modeling in cognitive science and how these interface with neuroscience research to inform implementational-level explanations. Instead, we will focus on computational-level theories and consider algorithmic- and implementation-level constraints only insofar as they bear on understanding the constraints under which computations postulated at the computational level can or cannot be tractable. As we explain in the more conceptual chapters in this book, this will be largely without loss of generality.

P.4   Organization of the Book

This book is written as a set of technical chapters sandwiched between more conceptual chapters. We start with an accessible introduction to the topic of *Cognition and Intractability* in Chapter 1. We use the problem of selecting pizza toppings as a running example to illustrate the key concepts. We also briefly review conceptual foundations of intractability and computational explanation to lay the groundwork for understanding the need for learning the concepts and proof techniques in Chapters 2–7. The first three of these Chapters (2–4) cover the classical theory of computational complexity, built on notions such as polynomial versus non-polynomial (e.g., exponential) time; polynomial-time reduction; the classes P, NP; and the notions of NP-completeness and NP-hardness. The latter three (Chapters 5, 6, and 7) cover parameterized complexity theory, built on notions such as parameterized problems, fixed-parameter tractability, parameterized reduction, and parameterized complexity classes such as FPT and W[1]. The technical chapters are followed by two chapters that contain conceptual reflections and philosophical elaborations on how the techniques from Chapters 2 to 7 can be used to deal with the problem of intractability as it arises in cognitive science. The first of these (Chapter 8) considers different ways in which cognitive scientists have been trying to deal with intractability and assesses their validity. The second (Chapter 9) presents a set of 14 common objections to complexity analyses and tractability constraints for models of cognition. By considering each such possible objection one by one we aim to make insightful that many objections vanish upon closer inspection because they are typically built on misunderstandings or incorrect suppositions. Next, Chapters 10–12 illustrate the use of the concepts and techniques from Chapters 2 to 7 for computational-level theories in three distinct cognitive domains: constraint satisfaction theory of coherence, structure-mapping theory of analogy, and Bayesian inference theory of communication.

The book also contains a set of Appendices. Appendix A gives primers on mathematical concepts, definitions, and notation that is assumed throughout the book. Readers who miss some of this background are advised to carefully study this Appendix before reading Chapters 2–7. Appendix B presents an alphabetically ordered list of *all* the computational problems referenced in illustrations, practices, and exercises in this book. Appendix C presents a compendium of existing classical and parameterized complexity results for a set of computational-level theories in cognitive science, spanning a variety of cognitive domains, such as perception, planning, decision-making, language processing, and higher-order thinking and reasoning.

P.5   Guide for the Reader

Whether you are a student or otherwise, we believe that the material in this book is best learned when taking an active approach to learning. We stimulate this in three distinct ways: (1) Stop-and-think boxes, (2) Practices, and (3) Exercises.

1. **Stop-and-think boxes** sometimes appear in the text where the reader is invited to contemplate an idea, topic, or a problem before continuing reading. After such a reflection, we always describe the main message that we think the reader should take away from these reflections and explain how and why.
2. In **Practices** we leave it to the reader to find a way to successfully perform those practices. The build-up of practices throughout the book is such that

a reader should be able to perform them – possibly with non-negligible effort – after having studied and mastered all the material up to that point. Especially practices that require the reader to come up with a proof can take some effort. This should not be taken as discouragement, but it can be seen as a natural consequence of the fact that coming up with proofs is a creative process. Acquiring this competence requires regularly trying to come up with proofs and then learning from your mistakes and successes. In our experience, this learning experience can benefit from peer and teacher feedback on written proofs. A good understanding of the material in this book does not require that one is able to perform all practices. Whether you are a student, teacher, or other reader, you can make a wise selection depending on your interests and the challenges you may have in understanding the material.

3. At the end of each chapter, we include **Exercises**. These are not unlike Practices, but are made available as additional ways for students to quiz themselves about the material and as inspiration for teachers as examination questions.

We think all readers will benefit from reading the chapters in the order that they appear in the book, with the exception of the Appendices (which are best referred to on a need-to basis), the starred subsections in Chapters 3, 4, and 6 (which consist of advanced optional material), and Chapters 8 and 9 (in Part III, Reflections and Elaborations). It is our experience that especially readers with a prior cognitive science training and background may have all kinds of concerns when reading Chapter 1 about how "intractability" is relevant or irrelevant for cognitive science. For instance, they may be concerned that intractability is not a real issue for real brains as it is for computers, because brains are very different from Turing machines or contemporary neural network models. Similarly, they may be concerned that human cognition does not typically operate by exact, serial, or deterministic algorithms but rather adopts all kinds of heuristics, approximate, parallel, and probabilistic computations. Although these concerns are understandable, they need not arise once one has a proper understanding of the formal foundations of intractability. Therefore, Chapters 8 and 9 can probably best be appreciated after having rigorously studied the concepts and techniques in Chapters 2–7. Nevertheless, readers may find it useful to occasionally have a peek at Chapters 8 and 9 whenever concerns arise, so that they can hopefully see that these conceptual issues will be dealt with in due course. Moreover, it is our hope that given the knowledge in this book, the reader may even be able to address concerns that are not present in this book. If you do, then please write us about them!

P.6   Reuse of Materials

The book as it lies before you has grown from the collective effort of four authors, each with their own styles, focus, and expertise. Besides lecture notes that we had developed over the years, the text in this book builds on some of our previously published work. This is most visible in Chapter 9, which reiterates a substantial part of section 6 of van Rooij, I. (2008). The Tractable Cognition thesis. *Cognitive Science, 32*, 939–984. This paper also formed the basis of Section 1.2.2 in Chapter 1 and parts of Section 8.2 in Chapter 8, and its appendix was reused and updated to form Sections A.1 and A.3 in Appendix A.

In other chapters reuse of materials is more implicit, as ways of phrasings and footnotes have been reused from some of our collaborative papers in an integrated manner. Here we give a complete list of which materials this includes.

- Some footnotes in Chapter 1 have been adapted from: van Rooij, I. (2003). *Tractable cognition: Complexity theory in cognitive psychology.* PhD thesis, University of Victoria, Canada.
- Parts of Section 8.2 in Chapter 8 have been adapted from: van Rooij, I. (2015). How the curse of intractability can be cognitive science's blessing. In Noelle, D. C., Dale, R., Warlaumont, A. S., Yoshimi, J., Matlock, T., Jennings, C. D., & Maglio, P. P. (Eds.). In *Proceedings of the 37th Annual Meeting of the Cognitive Science Society.* Austin, TX: Cognitive Science Society.
- Parts of Section 9.14 in Chapter 9 have been adapted from: van Rooij, I., Wright, C., Kwisthout, J., & Wareham, T. (2018). Rational analysis, intractability, and the prospects of 'as if'-explanations. *Synthese, 195*(2), 491–510.
- Parts of Section 8.2.3 in Chapter 8 have been adapted from: van Rooij, I., Wright, C., & Wareham, H. T. (2012). Intractability and the use of heuristics in psychological explanations. *Synthese, 187*, 471–487.
- Parts of Chapter 12 have been adapted from: Blokpoel, M., Kwisthout, J., Wareham, T., Haselager, P., Toni, I., & van Rooij, I. (2011). The computational costs of recipient design and intention recognition in communication. In L. Carlson, C. Holscher, & T. Shipley (Eds.), *Proceedings of the 33rd Annual Conference of the Cognitive Science Society* (pp. 465–470). Austin, TX: Cognitive Science Society.

Where figures and tables are used or adapted from previously published work this is indicated in the captions.

P.7   Acknowledgments

This book would not have come into existence without the help, support, inspiration, and enthusiasm of many people.

First off, we would like to thank our students for having been willing participants in our experimental approach to teaching the materials in this book. The very first version of a course on this topic was taught by Iris in 2008, with several guest lectures from Todd. The course had only three enrolled students (one of the students was Mark, now a co-author of this book). Over the last decade, the group of students has grown to a yearly group of 20–40 students. This is excepting those students and researchers that we have taught in guest lectures, workshops, and tutorials. We thank the Cognitive Science Society, the International Conference for Computational Modeling, and the Interdisciplinary College for funding and hosting tutorials and workshops for international audiences in the period 2012–2013. We also thank Frank Jäkel for hosting a three-day block course on the topic of this book for Bachelor, Master, and PhD students at the University of Osnabrück, Germany, in 2012 and Daniël Lakens for hosting a workshop for PhD students from across The Netherlands at Eindhoven University of Technology in 2013.

From all students we have learned invaluable things – both what works and what doesn't when teaching computational complexity to cognitive science students with little background in complexity theory or to complexity theorists with little background in cognitive science. We have also learned what are typical concerns or misunderstandings to be prevented or fixed. We hope that we have been able to transform those learning experiences into a book with helpful illustrations, practices, and exercises that take the learner step by step through the conceptual foundations of intractability and computational modeling in cognitive science to the concepts and proof techniques from classical and parameterized complexity.

We next would like to thank our departments and institutes – the Department of Artificial Intelligence and the Donders Institute for Brain, Cognition and Behaviour at the Radboud University (Nijmegen, the Netherlands) and the Department of Computer Science at the Memorial University of Newfoundland (St. John's, Canada) – for their generous support of the time needed for writing this book. The Internationalisation fund of the Radboud University has furthermore made it possible to fund yearly visits by Todd to the Radboud University to co-teach and collaborate with Iris, Johan, and Mark and further develop our ideas for this book. We also thank our teaching assistants, Tobias Winner and Nils Donselaar, for helping us evaluate and develop practices over the years.

In the final phases of writing this book we had the pleasure to be supported by excellent proof readers. We thank Antonina Kolokolova and Mesam Timmar for their careful reading and useful feedback on early versions of the book, and we thank Iris van de Pol and Ronald de Haan for checking and contributing to some entries in the compendium. Special thanks goes to Nils Donselaar whose rigor on many dimensions far surpasses ours, which has taught us some invaluable lessons in humility. We are indebted to him for helping us fix numerous mistakes and oversights in earlier versions of this book. We remain, of course, solely responsible for any remaining errors.

Last but not least, we thank our families – in particular Denise, Ilaij, Zinzi, Steffie, Judith, Koen, and Linda – for their loving support.

Part I

Introduction

1 Introduction

In this chapter we introduce the motivation for studying *Cognition and Intractability*. We provide an intuitive introduction to the problem of intractability as it arises for models of cognition using an illustrative everyday problem as running example: selecting toppings on a pizza. Next, we review relevant background information about the conceptual foundations of cognitive explanation, computability, and tractability. At the end of this chapter the reader should have a good understanding of the conceptual foundations of the Tractable Cognition thesis, including its variants: The P-Cognition thesis and the FPT-Cognition thesis, which motivates diving into the technical concepts and proof techniques covered in Chapters 2–7.

1.1   Selecting Pizza Toppings

Imagine you enter a pizzeria to buy a pizza. You can choose *any* combination of toppings from a given set, e.g., {*pepperoni, salami, ham, mushroom, pineapple, . . .* }. What will you choose?

According to one account of human decision-making, your choice will be such that you maximize utility. Here utility, denoted by $u(.)$, is to be understood as the subjective value of each possible choice option (e.g., if you prefer salami to ham, then $u(salami) > u(ham)$). Since you can choose combinations of toppings, we need to think of the choice options as subsets of the set of all available toppings. This includes subsets with only one element (e.g., {*salami*} or {*olives*}), but also combinations of multiple toppings (e.g., {*ham, pineapple*} or {*salami, mushrooms, olives*}). On this account of human decision-making, we can formally describe your toppings selection problem as an instance of the following computational problem:

GENERALIZED SUBSET CHOICE
Input: A set $X = \{x_1, x_2, ..., x_n\}$ of n available items and a value function u assigning a value to every subset $S \subseteq X$.
Output: A subset $S \subseteq X$ such that $u(S)$ is maximized over all possible $S \subseteq X$.

Note that many other choice problems that one may encounter in everyday life can be cast in this way, ranging from inviting a subset of friends to a party or buying groceries in the grocery store to selecting people for a committee or prescribing combinations of medicine to a patient.

But how – using what algorithm – could your brain come to select a subset S with maximum utility? A conceivable algorithm could be the following: Consider each possible subset $S \subseteq X$, in serial or parallel (in whatever way we may think the brain implements such an algorithm), and select the one that has the highest utility $u(S)$. Conceptually this is a straightforward procedure. But it has an important problem. The number of possible subsets grows exponentially with the number of items in X. Given that in real-world situations one cannot generally assume that X is small, the algorithm will be searching prohibitively large search spaces.

Stop and Think

These days pizzerias may provide for 30 or more different toppings. How many distinct pizzas do you think can be made with 30 different pizza toppings?

If n denotes the number of items in X, then 2^n expresses the number of distinct possible subsets of X. In other words, with 30 toppings one can make $2^{30} > 1,000,000,000$ (a billion) distinct pizzas. Of course, in practice pizzerias typically list 20–30 distinct pizzas on their menus. But consider that some pizzerias also provide the option to construct your own pizza, implicitly allowing a customer to pick any of the billion pizza options available.

Stop and Think

Imagine that the brain would use the exhaustive algorithm described earlier for selecting the preferred pizza. Assume that the brain's algorithm would process 100 possible combinations, in serial or parallel, per second. How long would it take the brain to select a pizza if it could choose from 30 different pizza toppings? What if it could choose from 40 different toppings?

You may be surprised to find that the answer is 4 months. That is the time it takes in this scenario for your brain to consider all the distinct pizzas that can be made with 30 toppings in order to find the best tasting one (maximum utility). If the choice would be from 40 toppings, it would even take 3.5 centuries. Evidently, this is an unrealistic scenario. The pizzeria would be long closed before you would have made up your mind!

There is an important lesson to draw from our pizza example: Explaining how agents (human or artificial) can make decisions in the real world, where time is a costly resource and choice options can be plentiful, requires algorithms that run in a realistic amount of time. The exhaustive algorithm that we considered in our pizza scenario does not meet this criterion. It is an *exponential-time* algorithm. The time it takes grows exponentially with the input size n (i.e., grows as c^n for some constant $c > 1$). Exponential time grows faster than any polynomial function (a function of the form n^c for some constant c), and is therefore also referred to as non-polynomial time. Another example of non-polynomial time is factorial time (grows as $n!$). An example of a factorial-time algorithm would be an algorithm that exhaustively searches all possible orderings of n events or actions in order to select the best possible ordering. Consider, for instance, planning n activities in a day: going to the hairdresser, doing the laundry, buying groceries, cooking food, washing the dishes, posting a letter, answering an email, watching TV, etc. Even for as few as 10 activities, there would be 3.6 million possible orderings, and for 20 activities there would be more than 10^{18} possible orderings. Planning one's daily activities by exhaustive search would be as implausible as selecting pizza toppings by exhaustive search.

Table 1.1 illustrates why non-polynomial time (e.g., exponential or factorial) algorithms generally are considered *intractable* for all but small input sizes n, whereas polynomial-time algorithms (e.g., linear or quadratic) are considered *tractable* even for larger input sizes. Informally, intractable means that the

Table 1.1 Illustration of the running times of polynomial time versus super-polynomial time algorithms. The function $t(n)$ expresses the number of steps performed by an algorithm (linear, quadratic, exponential, or factorial). For illustrative purposes it is assumed that 100 steps can be performed per second.

Input size	Polynomial time		Non-polynomial time	
n	$t(n) = n$	$t(n) = n^2$	$t(n) = 2^n$	$t(n) = n!$
5	50 ms	250 ms	320 ms	1 sec
10	100 ms	1 sec	10 sec	10.1 hr
20	200 ms	4 sec	2.9 hr	7.7×10^6 centuries
30	299 ms	9 sec	4.1 months	8.4×10^{20} centuries
40	400 ms	16 sec	3.5 centuries	2.6×10^{36} centuries
50	500 ms	25 sec	3.6×10^3 centuries	9.6×10^{52} centuries
100	1 sec	1.7 min	4.0×10^{18} centuries	3.0×10^{146} centuries
500	5 sec	41.7 min	1.0×10^{139} centuries	4.0×10^{1124} centuries
1,000	10 sec	2.8 hr	3.4×10^{289} centuries	1.3×10^{2558} centuries

algorithm requires an unrealistic amount of computational resources (in this case, time) for its completion. This intractability is the main topic of this book. In this book we explore formal notions of (in)tractability to assess the computational-resource demands of different (potentially competing) scientific accounts of cognition, be they about decision-making, planning, perception, categorization, reasoning, learning, etc. Even though brains are quite remarkable, their speed of operation is limited, and this fact can be exploited to assess the plausibility of different ideas scientists may have about "what" and "how" the brain computes.

For illustrative purposes, Table 1.1 assumed that the listed algorithms could perform 100 steps per second. To see that this assumption has little effect on the large difference between polynomial and non-polynomial running times perform the next practice.

Practice 1.1.1 Recompute the contents of Table 1.1 under the assumption that the algorithms can perform as many as 1,000 steps per second.

Let us return to our pizza example. We saw that the exhaustive algorithm (searching all possible subsets) to maximize utility of the chosen subset of toppings is an intractable algorithm. Does this mean that the idea that humans maximize utility in such a situation is false? Possibly, but not necessarily. Note that the trouble may have arisen from the specific way in which we formalized the maximum utility account of decision-making for subset choice. In the GENERALIZED SUBSET CHOICE problem we allowed for any possible utility function u that assigned any possible value to every subset X. As a result, there is only one way to be sure that we output a subset with maximum utility: We need to consider each and every subset.

The situation would be less dire if somehow there would be regularity in one's preferences over pizza toppings. This regularity could then perhaps be exploited to more efficiently search the space of choice options. For instance, if subjective preferences would be structured such that the utility of a subset could be expressed as the sum of the value of its elements (i.e., $u(S) = \sum_{x \in S} u(x)$), then we could change the formalization as follows:

ADDITIVE SUBSET CHOICE
Input: A set $X = \{x_1, x_2, ..., x_n\}$ of n available items and a value function u assigning a value to every element $x \in X$.
Output: A subset $S \subseteq X$ such that $u(S) = \sum_{x \in S} u(x)$ is maximized over all possible $S \subseteq X$.

If the pizza selection problem would be an instance of this formal problem, then the brain could select a maximum utility subset by using the following simple linear-time algorithm: Consider each item $x \in X$, and if $u(x) \geq 0$ then add x to the subset S, otherwise discard the option x. Since each item in X has to be considered only once, and the inequality $u(x) \geq 0$ checked for each item only once, the number of steps performed by this algorithm grows at worst linearly with the number of options in X. As can be seen in Table 1.1, such a linear-time algorithm is clearly tractable in practice, even when you have larger numbers of toppings to choose from.

The maximum utility account of decision-making would thus be saved from intractability, if indeed real-world subset choice problems could all be cast as instances of the ADDITIVE SUBSET CHOICE problem. But is this a plausible possibility?

Stop and Think

Consider selecting pizza toppings for your pizza using the linear-time algorithm described earlier? Why may you not be happy with the actual result?

If you would use the linear-time algorithm to select your pizza toppings, you would always end up with all positive valued toppings on your pizza. Besides that this may make for an overcrowded pizza, it also fails to take into account that you may like some toppings individually but not in particular combinations. For instance, each of the items in the set {*pepperoni, salami, ham, mushroom, pineapple*} could have individually positive value for you, in the sense that you would prefer a pizza with any one of them individually over a pizza with no toppings. Yet, at the same time, you may prefer {*ham, pineapple*} or {*salami, mushrooms, olives*} over a pizza will all the toppings (e.g., because you dislike the taste of the combination of pineapple with olives). In other words, in real-world subset choice problems, there may be interactions between items that affect the utility of their combinations. This makes $u(S) = \sum_{x \in S} u(x)$ an invalid assumption. From this exploration, we should learn an important lesson: Intractable formalizations of cognitive problems (decision-making, planning, reasoning, etc.) can be recast into tractable formalizations by introducing additional constraints on the input domains. Yet, it is important to make sure that those constraints do not make the new formalization too simplistic and unable to model real-world problem situations.

A balance may be struck by introducing the idea of pair-wise interactions between k items in the choice set. Then we can adapt the formalization as follows:

BINARY SUBSET CHOICE
Input: A set $X = \{x_1, x_2, ..., x_n\}$ of n available items. For every item $x \in X$ there is an associated value $u(x)$, and for every pair of items (x_i, x_j) there is an associated value $\delta(x_i, x_j)$.
Output: A subset $S \subseteq X$, such that $u(S) = \sum_{x \in S} u(x) + \sum_{x,y \in S} \delta(x, y)$ is maximum.

If situations allow for three-way interactions, this model may also fail as a computational account of subset choice. It is certainly conceivable that three-way interactions can occur in practice (see, e.g., van Rooij, Stege, and Kadlec, 2005). Leaving that discussion for another day, we may ask ourselves the following question: Would computing this BINARY SUBSET CHOICE problem be in principle tractable? It is not so easy to tell as for GENERALIZED SUBSET CHOICE, because the utility function is constrained. But is it constrained enough to yield tractability of this computation? Probably not. Using the tools that you will learn about in this book, you will be able to show that this problem belongs to class of so-called NP-hard problems. This is the class of problems for which no polynomial-time algorithms exist unless a widely conjectured inequality $P \neq NP$ would be false. This $P \neq NP$ conjecture, although formally unproven (and perhaps even unprovable), is widely believed to be true among computer scientists and cognitive scientists alike (see Chapter 4 for more details). Likewise, we will adopt this conjecture in the remainder of this book.

1.2   Conceptual Foundations

In our pizza example we have introduced many of the key scientific concepts on which this book builds. For instance, we used the distinction made in cognitive science between explaining the "what" and the "how" of cognition, the notion of "algorithm" as agreed upon by computer scientists, and the idea that "intractability" can be characterized in terms of the time complexity of algorithms. In this section, we explain the conceptual foundations of these concepts in a bit more detail.

1.2.1   Conceptual Foundations of Cognitive Explanation

One of the primary aims of cognitive science is to explain human cognitive capacities. Ultimately, the goal is to answer questions such as: How do humans make decisions? How do they learn language, concepts, and categories? How do they form beliefs, based on reasons or otherwise? In order to come up with answers for such "how"-questions it can be useful to first answer "what"-questions: What is decision-making? What is language learning? What is categorization? What is belief fixation? What is reasoning?

This distinction between "what is being computed" (the *input-output mapping*) and "how it is computed" (the *algorithm*) is also reflected in the influential and widely used explanatory framework proposed by David Marr (1981). Marr proposed that, ideally, theories in cognitive science should explain the workings of a cognitive system (whether natural or artificial) on three different levels (see Table 1.2). The first level, called the *computational level*, specifies the nature of the input-output mapping that is computed (we will also refer to this as the *cognitive function*).[1] The second level, the algorithmic level, specifies the nature of the algorithmic process by which the computation described at the computational level is performed (*cognitive process*). The third and final level, the implementation level, specifies how the algorithm defined at the second level is physically implemented by the "hardware" of the system (or "wetware" in the case of the brain) performing the computation (*physical implementation* of the cognitive process/function).

Hence, in David Marr's terminology, the description of a cognitive system in terms of the function that it computes (or problem that it solves)[2] is called a *computational-level theory*. We already saw examples when we discussed the pizza example: i.e., GENERALIZED, ADDITIVE, and BINARY SUBSET CHOICE were three different candidate computational-level theories of how humans choose subsets of options. Since one and the same function can be computed by

---

[1] We should note that Marr also intended the computational-level analysis to include an account of "why" the cognitive function is the appropriate function for the system to compute, given its goals and environment of operation. This idea has been used to argue for certain computational-level explanations based on appeals to rationality and/or evolutionary selection – i.e., that specific functions would be rational or adaptive for the system to compute. The intractability analysis of computational-level accounts as pursued in this book are neutral with respect to such normative motivations for specific computational-level accounts, in the sense that tractability and rational analysis are compatible, but the former can be done independent of the latter (see Section 8.5).

[2] Since the words "function" and "problem" refer to the same type of mathematical object (an input-output mapping) we will use the terms interchangeably. A difference between the terms is a matter of perspective: the word "problem" has a more prescriptive connotation of an input-output mapping that is to be realized (i.e., a problem is to be solved), while the word "function" has a more descriptive connotation of an input-output that is being realized (i.e., a function is computed). The reader may notice that we will tend to adopt the convention of speaking of "problems" whenever we discuss computational complexity concepts and methods from computer science (e.g., in Chapters 2–7), and adopt the terms "function" or "computational-level theory" in the context of applications and debates in cognitive science (e.g., in Chapters 8–12).

Table 1.2 Marr's levels of explanation: What is the type of question asked at each level, what counts as an answer (the explanans), and labels for the thing to be explained (explanandum) per level.

Level	Question	Answer	Label
Computation	What is the nature of the computational problem solved?	An input-output mapping $F: I \rightarrow O$	Cognitive function
Algorithm	How is the computational problem solved?	An algorithm A that computes F	Cognitive process
Implementation	How is the algorithm implemented?	A specification of how the computational steps of A are realizable by the relevant "stuff" (e.g., neuronal processes)	Physical implementation

many different algorithms (e.g., serial or parallel), we can describe a cognitive system at the computational level more or less independently of the algorithmic level. Similarly, since an algorithm can be implemented in many different physical systems (e.g., carbon or silicon), we can describe the algorithmic level more or less independently of physical considerations.

David Marr, in his seminal 1981 book, illustrated this idea with the example of a cash register, i.e., a system that has the ability to perform *addition* (see Figure 1.1). A computational-level theory for a cash register would be the Addition function $F(a, b) = a + b$. An algorithmic-level theory could, for instance, be an algorithm operating on decimal numbers or an algorithm operating on binary numbers. Either algorithm would compute the function Addition, albeit in different ways. The implementational-level theory would depend on the physical make-up of the system. For instance, different physical systems can implement algorithms for Addition: cash registers, pocket calculators, and even human brains. An implementational-level theory would specify by some sort of blueprint how the algorithm could be realized by that particular physical system.

Practice 1.2.1 Study the cash-register example in Figure 1.1. Can you come up with different computational-, algorithmic- and implementational-level

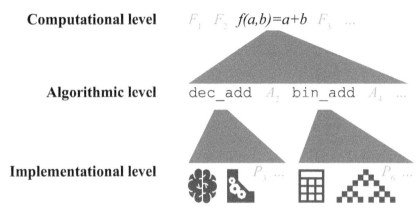

Figure 1.1   An illustration of the three levels of analysis by Marr, using Addition.

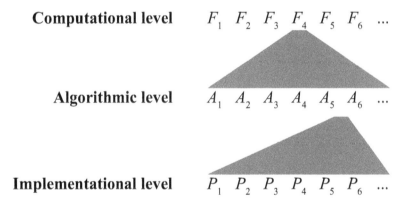

Figure 1.2   An illustration of the underdetermination of lower levels of explanation by higher levels of explanation in the Marr hierarchy.

theories for another example? For example, for the pizza topping example or for the example of scheduling activities throughout the day.

Stop and Think

Study the relationship between the levels of Marr in Figure 1.1. Why is it that a given computational-level theory can, in principle, be consistent with different algorithmic-level explanations? And why can a given algorithmic-level explanation be consistent with different implementational-level explanations?

Note that in Figure 1.2 there is underdetermination of lower-level explanations in the Marr hierarchy by higher-level explanations. By this we mean that even if a cognitive scientist hypothesizes a particular computational-level theory F, he or she can remain agnostic about the nature of the exact algorithm A by which the system under study computes F. What the scientist does need to commit to is that, in principle, there can exist an algorithm that computes F. Similarly, hypothesizing a particular algorithmic-level explanation A for function F, the scientist can remain agnostic about the nature of the exact implementation P,[3] but she will have to commit to the in principle possibility of realizing and running the algorithm on the relevant hardware or wetware. Figure 1.2 gives the general picture.

David Marr argued for the usefulness of top-down analyses for purposes of reverse engineering natural cognitive systems. The idea of such a top-down approach is that it is best to start by developing a computational-level theory and then work down toward the algorithmic- and implementational-levels theories. He believed this was the best way to make progress in cognitive science, because in his opinion:

> an algorithm is likely to be understood more readily by understanding the nature of the problem being solved than by examining the mechanism (and the hardware) in which it is embodied. (Marr, 1981, p. 27; see also Marr, 1977).

This book is written to help cognitive scientists interested in adopting this top-down approach by providing useful formal tools for computational-level theory development.[4] This is not to say that we think other approaches are not to be pursued as well. In fact, we think that cognitive science can benefit from pluralism in approaches, including bottom-up approaches (starting at the implementational level) and middle-out (starting at the algorithmic level). This book merely aims to add useful formal tools to the cognitive scientist's toolbox, not to promote one approach over the other.

---

[3] We use P for *P*hysical implementation instead of I for *I*mplementation to not confuse with our notation for inputs I.

[4] Even theories that are often seen as being formulated at the algorithmic level – such as connectionist or neural network models (e.g., McClelland, 2009) – are not free from computational level considerations (Klapper et al., 2018; McClelland, 2009). Also for neural networks it is of interest to study which functions they can and cannot compute (Parberry, 1994). For instance, neural network learning is a computational task: A neural network is assumed to learn a mapping from inputs to outputs by adjusting its connection weights. Here the input of the learning task is given by (I) all network inputs in the training set plus the required network output for each such network input, and the output is given by (O) a setting of connection weights such that the input-output mapping produced by the trained network is satisfactory. This learning task, like any other task in the more symbolic tradition, can be analyzed at the computational level (Blum and Rivest, 1992; Judd, 1990; Parberry, 1994).

1.2.2 Conceptual Foundations of Computability and Tractability

Given that our focus will be on the top-down approach, it's vital to realize that there is also another type of underdetermination at play. Namely, the computational-level theory itself is underdetermined by empirical observations (see Figure 1.3). By this we mean that given observations about the behavior of a system one cannot deduce the function that it computes. At best, one can abduce it, i.e., make an inference to the best explanation. The problem of underdetermination of theory by data is not specific, of course, to cognitive science but applies in general to all empirical sciences.

Stop and Think

Consider a system that computes a function $F: I \rightarrow O$, where both I and O denote sets of binary strings. Now imagine you could input different strings to the system and observe for each input the string that the system outputs. Why would this information not be sufficient to deduce the function $F: I \rightarrow O$ that the system is computing?

Coming up with computational-level theories for human cognitive abilities – such as decision-making, categorization, learning, etc. – is a creative scientific process. It is not possible to deduce theories from observations of a system's behavior for several reasons:

1. Any finite set of input-output observations is consistent with infinitely many different functions.
2. Inputs and outputs are usually not directly observable.
3. Psychological data are noisy (due to context variables not under the control of the experimenter).
4. Commitment is usually to the informal theory, not the specific formalization.

All four points can be illustrated with our earlier pizza topping example.

Let's say we give a person 20 different sets of toppings to choose from and observe which pizza toppings they choose per set. Then there will be, in principle, multiple set-to-subset functions consistent with the observations, each making a different prediction about what the person would choose if we would make a new, 21st topping, and add that to the set of toppings for them to choose from (point 1 in the previous list). Note, furthermore, that if our computational-level theory is based on the idea that human decision-makers maximize utility, then both the choice options and the final choice set must

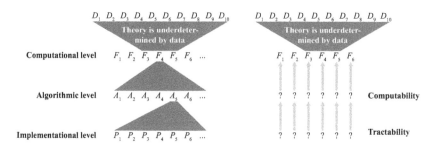

Figure 1.3   An illustration of the underdetermination of computational-level theories by data (left) and the lower-level constraints on computational-level theories (right).

have associated utilities. These utilities are aspects of the input and output that are not directly observable; they are a property of the person's inner mental states, in this case preferences (point 2). Furthermore, even if we would be able to devise procedures to try and estimate those unobservable states, then our measurements would always have some noise and measurement errors that we cannot fully control as scientists. Hence, if the observed behavior of the person would not match exactly with the predictions made by our theory we do not know for sure that it is the theory that is incorrect or that we may have misestimated the person's utilities (point 3). Lastly, even if based on the noisy and partial input-output observations so far, we would be able to rule out some particular Subset Choice functions that may not be sufficient to falsify the idea that human decision-makers are utility maximizers, because there could exist functions based on alternative formalizations of this informal idea that could be consistent with the observations made to date (point 4).

It seems, thus, that it would be useful if cognitive scientists could appeal to some theoretical constraints on the type of computational-level theories they could come up with. If we reconsider the Marr hierarchy we can see that indeed such constraints are available. Namely, a cognitive scientist postulating a particular F as a candidate hypothesis for the "what" of some aspect of cognition is committing that there exists some physically feasible "how"-answer. In other words, the function should be computable and tractable – *computable*, because there should be at least one algorithm A that can compute F; and *tractable*, because it must be possible to run A using a realistic amount of resources (time and space) on a physical mechanism P. We will refer to the first requirement as the "computability constraint" and the second requirement as the "tractability constraint" (see Figure 1.3).

In order to be able to assess which functions meet the computability constraint, a precise definition of *computation* is required. Informally, when we say a system computes a function or solves a problem, $F: I \rightarrow O$, we mean to say that the system reliably transforms every $i \in I$ into $F(i) \in O$ in a way that can be described by an algorithm. An algorithm is a step-by-step finite procedure that can be performed, by a human or machine, without the need for any insight, just by following the steps as specified by the algorithm.

In 1936, Alan Turing presented his machine formalization as a way of making the intuitive notions of "computation" and "algorithm" precise. Turing proposed that every function for which there is an algorithm – which is intuitively computable – is computable by a Turing machine (for more details on this machine formalization we refer the reader to Appendix A). In other words, functions that are not computable by a Turing machine are not computable in principle by any machine. To support his thesis, Turing showed that his formalization is equivalent to a different formalization (λ-calculus), which was independently proposed by Church (1936). The thesis that both Turing's and Church's respective formalizations capture the intuitive notion of algorithm is now known as the Church-Turing thesis. Further, Turing's and Church's formalizations have also been shown equivalent to all other accepted formalizations of computation (such as based on neural networks, cellular automata, and even quantum computers), by which the thesis has gained more support.[5] The Church-Turing thesis has a direct implication for cognitive science: Computational-level theories of cognitive abilities are theoretically constrained to be Turing-computable functions (see Figure 1.4).

Even though the computability constraint can help rule our computationally infeasible computational-level theories, for practical purposes it seems like a too liberal constraint. For instance, we saw that GENERALIZED SUBSET CHOICE could be computed by an exhaustive search algorithm, hence the problem is computable. Yet, such an algorithm seems to be intractable. Here, like computability before Turing and others' formalization of the term, the term "intractability" is an informal notion in need of formalization if we are going to use it to constrain computational-level theories. In this book we will pursue two possible formalizations of tractability: one grounded in what is known as classical complexity theory and one grounded in what is known as parameterized complexity theory.

---

[5] Note that the Church-Turing thesis is not a mathematical conjecture that can be proven right or wrong. Instead the Church-Turing thesis is a hypothesis about the state of the world. Even though we cannot prove the thesis, it would be in principle possible to falsify it; this would happen, for example, if one day a formalization of computation were developed that (a) is not equivalent to Turing computability, and that, at the same time, (b) would be accepted by (most of) the scientific community. For now the situation is as follows: Most mathematicians and computer scientists accept the Church-Turing thesis, either as plainly true or as a reasonable working hypothesis. In this book, we will also adopt the Church-Turing thesis.

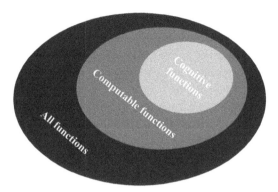

Figure 1.4   According to the Church-Turing thesis, cognitive functions are a subset of all computable functions.

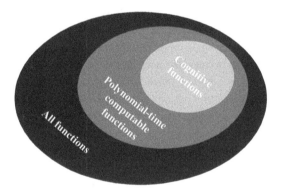

Figure 1.5   According to the P-Cognition thesis, cognitive functions are a subset of the polynomial-time computable functions.

In classical complexity theory a function F is considered tractable if there exists an algorithm A that computes F and A runs in so-called polynomial time (i.e., time that grows on the order of n^c when n is the input size and $c \geq 1$ is some constant). Given this formalization of the notion of "tractability," the tractability constraint would prescribe that computational-level theories are constrained to be polynomial-time computable functions. This thesis is called the P-Cognition thesis (see Figure 1.5).

The classical definition of tractability as polynomial-time solvability is widely adopted in computer science (to be reminded of its merit, you may want to revisit Table 1.1). For instance, Garey and Johnson write the following:

> Most exponential time algorithms are merely variations on exhaustive search, whereas polynomial time algorithms generally are made possible only through

the gain of some deeper insight into the nature of the problem. There is wide agreement that a problem has not been "well-solved" until a polynomial time algorithm is known for it. Hence, we shall refer to a problem as intractable, if it is so hard that no polynomial time algorithm can possibly solve it. (Garey and Johnson, 1979, p. 8)

Accordingly, many cognitive scientists have adopted the P-Cognition thesis, leading them to reject functions that cannot be computed in polynomial time (such as NP-hard functions) as viable computational-level theories. For instance decision-making reseacher Gigerenzer and colleagues write:

> The computations postulated by a model of cognition need to be tractable in the real world in which people live, not only in the small world of an experiment with only a few cues. This eliminates NP-hard models that lead to computational explosion (...). (Gigerenzer, Hoffrage, and Goldstein, 2008, p. 236)

The emphasis in this quote that tractability should hold beyond the small world of an experiment is to underscore that real-world inputs cannot generally be assumed to be small enough to make non-polynomial time algorithms feasible. Recall, for instance, that even though selecting a maximum utility pizza using exhaustive search from five possible toppings could be done within a few minutes, it would take months or centuries when selecting from 30 or 40 toppings. The polynomial-time requirement hence seems to be no luxury for real-world decision making.

Despite the widespread adoption of the P-Cognition thesis in cognitive science, an argument has been made that the thesis may be a bit too strict as a formalization of the tractability constraint on computational-level theories. For instance, van Rooij (2008) noted that the P-Cognition thesis:

> (...) overlooks the possibility that exponential-time algorithms can run fast, provided only that the super-polynomial complexity inherent in the computation be confined to one or more small input parameters. (van Rooij, 2008, p. 973)

This concern is based on an important insight from the newer branch of complexity theory called parameterized complexity theory. That is, the insight that some NP-hard functions can be computed by algorithms that run in so-called *fixed-parameter tractable* time (formally, a time proportional to $g(k_1, \ldots, k_i)n^c$, where g can be any (computable) function of the parameters $k_1, \ldots, k_i$). In fixed-parameter tractable algorithms the non-polynomial time complexity is confined to a function g depending solely on the parameters and *not* on the overall input size n. Since the running time is polynomial in n, albeit non-polynomial in the parameters, fixed-parameter tractable algorithms can run fast even for large inputs, provided only that the parameter remains relatively small. To see this for yourself, perform Practice 1.2.2.

Practice 1.2.2   Reconsider Table 1.1, and add two new columns to the table for the function for the function $2^k n$, with $k = 8$, one time assuming 100 steps per second and one time assuming 1,000 steps per second.

In fixed-parameter tractable algorithms the bulk of the time-complexity depends on the parameters, whereas the size of the input has much less effect on the overall complexity of the running time. For an illustration, perform Practice 1.2.3.

Practice 1.2.3   Reconsider the two new columns you made in Practice 1.2.2. What happens when you increase n from 5 to, say, 100? What would happen if you would increase k from 5 to 100?

Fixed-parameter tractable algorithms generally run considerably faster for a parameter $k \ll n$ than algorithms that require more than fixed-parameter tractable time (e.g., on the order of n^k steps). For an illustration, perform Practice 1.2.4.

Practice 1.2.4   Reconsider the new columns from Practices 1.2.2 and 1.2.3, and now add two new columns for the function n^k, one assuming 100 steps per second and one assuming 1,000 steps per second, with $k = 8$.

Given that cognitive input domains are typically characterized by many different input parameters of widely varying ranges, the younger branch of computation theory—called parameterized complexity theory—may better serve cognitive scientists in characterizing the computational resource requirements of different computational-level theories than classical complexity theory. Reconsider, for example, the pizza topping selection problem again. In real world settings, the number of toppings we may be able to choose may simply be bounded by our budget. If each topping adds an additional $1 to the cost, then on a fixed budget we may be able to not add more than, say, eight different toppings. This does not reduce the overall input size of the problem, which may still contain 40 different toppings to choose from. However, it would matter a lot for the time needed to find a maximum utility pizza within this budget constraint if we can find it using an algorithm that runs in a time proportional to, say, $2^k n$, as opposed to having to search all n^k subsets.

In general, functions that are fixed-parameter tractable are efficiently computable when the relevant parameters are constrained to relatively small sizes. If the parameters $k_1, \ldots, k_i$ are small then the resource demands of computing the (potentially exponential or worse) problem F does not explode and hence the function can be computed effectively in polynomial time. Under parameterized complexity, the set of computationally plausible cognitive theories

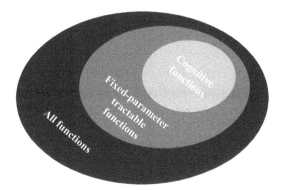

Figure 1.6   According to the FPT-Cognition thesis, cognitive functions are a subset of all fixed-parameter tractable functions.

is a subset of all fixed-parameter tractable time computable functions (see Figure 1.6). This thesis is called the FPT-Cognition thesis.

With the FPT-Cognition thesis we do not mean to argue that NP-hardness results are of no significance to cognitive science. On the contrary, the FPT-cognition thesis, like the P-Cognition thesis, recognizes that an NP-hard function F cannot be practically computed in all its generality. If the system is computing F at all, then it must be computing some "restricted" version of it, denoted F'. The crux is, however, what is meant by "restricted." The P-Cognition thesis states that F' must be polynomial-time computable, whereas the FPT-cognition thesis states that F' must have problem parameters that are in practice "small" and that F' must be fixed-parameter tractable for (a subset of) those parameters.

On the one hand, the FPT-Cognition thesis loses in formality by allowing an undefined notion of "small" parameter in its definition. On the other hand, this allowance is exactly what may bring the FPT-Cognition thesis in closer agreement with cognitive reality. In practice, real-world cognitive inputs seem to have parameters that are of qualitatively different sizes. Ignoring these qualitative differences, and treating the input always as one big "chunk," would risk making complexity analysis in cognitive science practice vacuous. The FPT-Cognition thesis, then, should not be seen as a simple litmus test for distinguishing feasible from unfeasible computational-level theories. On the contrary, the FPT-Cognition thesis is probably best seen as a stimulans for actively exploring how the inputs of computational-level theories are parametrically constrained in order to guarantee tractability in real-world situations.

The following chapters will cover proof techniques for assessing whether or not a given function (or problem) F is computable in polynomial time and/or fixed-parameter tractable time. These techniques can then be used to assess whether or not a given computational-level theory meets the tractability constraint, be it formalized as the P- or FPT-Cognition thesis.

1.3   Exercises

In this chapter you learned about the conceptual foundations of the tractability constraint on computational-level theories of cognition. To consolidate your newly gained knowledge you can quiz yourself with the following exercises.

Exercise 1.3.1   We used Subset Choice as a running example. Consider now a cognitive capacity of special interest to you. Imagine going through the same process of first defining the most general input-output mapping for this capacity and then working toward one that may be tractable. What kinds of input-output mappings would you come up with?

Exercise 1.3.2   Different cognitive scientists have a preference to start theorizing at one or more of Marr's levels of explanation. What benefits and drawbacks do you see for starting at the computational level, the algorithmic level, or the implementational level? Try to come up with at least one benefit and drawback for each option.

Exercise 1.3.3   Search for a few cognitive science articles that use the word "intractability." What is the meaning of the word used in those articles? (Hint: the term "intractability" is often used informally in the cognitive science literature. Regularly, it means "computational intractability," as we use it throughout this book, but not always. For instance, sometimes it means something like unmanageable, uncontrollable, very difficult, or analytically unsolvable.)

Exercise 1.3.4   Just as the Church-Turing thesis provides a definition of computability independent of the Turing-machine formalization, both the P-Cognition and FPT-Cognition thesis intend to use definitions of tractability that are independent of the Turing-machine formalization. This is afforded by the so-called Invariance thesis, which states that two reasonable computing machines can simulate each other with at most polynomial-time overhead. Read the Turing-Machine Objection in Chapter 9, and answer the following question: Why does the Invariance thesis, if true, guarantee that the P-Cognition and FPT-Cognition theses apply to computational-level theories regardless the nature of brain computation?

1.4   Further Reading

The Tractable Cognition thesis and its formalizations in the form of the P-Cognition thesis and the FPT-Cognition thesis were first coined by van Rooij in her PhD thesis in 2003. She built, however, on pioneering work of Edmonds (1965), Cobham (1965), and Frixione (2001). Edmonds and Cobham formulated a polynomial-time variant of the Church-Turing thesis, now known as the Cobham-Edmonds thesis. Frixione translated the Cobham-Edmonds thesis to the cognitive domain: He argued that tractability—conceived of as polynomial-time computability—is a constraint that applies to computational-level theories of cognition in general. This thesis, proposed by Frixione, is what van Rooij coined the P-Cognition thesis. Prior to 2000 the P-Cognition was already tacitly entertained in several subdomains of cognitive science, for instance, in work by

- Cherniak (1986) and Levesque (1989) in the domain of reasoning
- Tsotsos (1990) in the domain of vision
- Simon (1988, 1990) and Martignon and Schmitt (1999) in the domain of decision-making
- Thagard and Verbeurgt (1998) and Millgram (2000) in the domain of belief fixation
- Oaksford and Chater (1993) and Oaksford (1998) in the domain of common-sense
- Parberry (1997) in the domain of knowledge

Work exploring the FPT-Cognition thesis is much younger, given that it was not conceived prior to 2003. The compendium in Appendix C gives an overview of fixed-parameter (in)tractability analyses of computational-level theories to date.

Part II

Concepts and Techniques

2   Polynomial versus Exponential Time

In this chapter we explain how to analyze the time an algorithm takes to solve a given problem, and specifically, whether it takes polynomial or exponential time. We consider a variety of well-known problems from computer science to illustrate polynomial-time versus exponential-time algorithms. In these analyses, we build on a common distinction between three types of problems: optimization problems, search problems, and decision problems. While the first two are most commonly adopted in cognitive science, the last one is widely used for computational complexity analyses. As we will explain in subsequent chapters, the distinction is overcome during complexity analyses by understanding the close relationship between these problem types. We will also see that while it is possible to "prove by example" that a problem is of polynomial-time complexity (viz., give an algorithm that solves the problem that runs in polynomial time), proving that a problem does not allow for any such polynomial-time algorithm requires different proof methods.

2.1   Types of Problems: Optimization, Search, Decision

In the Introduction (Chapter 1) we used the problem of selecting pizza toppings as a running example of how one can formalize different candidate computational-level theories by specifying the input, the output, and the nature of the mapping. Such formalizations yield well-defined computational problems. Recall, for instance, the two problems ADDITIVE SUBSET CHOICE and BINARY SUBSET CHOICE:

ADDITIVE SUBSET CHOICE
Input: A set $X = \{x_1, x_2, \ldots, x_n\}$ of n available items and a value function u assigning a value to every element $x \in X$.
Output: A subset $S \subseteq X$ such that $u(S) = \sum_{x \in S} u(x)$ is maximum.

BINARY SUBSET CHOICE
Input: A set $X = \{x_1, x_2, \ldots, x_n\}$ of n available items. For every item $x \in X$ there is an associated integer value $u(x)$ and for every pair of items (x_i, x_j) there is an associated integer value $\delta(x_i, x_j)$.
Output: A subset $S \subseteq X$, such that $u(S) = \sum_{x \in S} u(x) + \sum_{x,y \in S} \delta(x, y)$ is maximum.

Note that both these problems ask for an output structure that is optimized according to some value function; i.e., in this case the output structure is the subset S and the value $u(S)$ is to be maximized. There are also problems for which the value of the output structure is to be minimized according to some value function. Consider, for instance:

BUDGET SUBSET CHOICE
Input: A set $X = \{x_1, x_2, \ldots, x_n\}$ of n available items and an integer m. For every item $x \in X$ there is an associated integer value $c(x)$ that defines the cost of x.
Output: A subset $S \subseteq X$ of size $|S| \geq m$, such that $c(S) = \sum_{x \in S} c(x)$ is minimum.

Maximization problems such as ADDITIVE SUBSET CHOICE and BINARY SUBSET CHOICE and minimization problems such as BUDGET SUBSET CHOICE are also known as *optimization* problems. Solving an optimization problem means returning an output structure (here, a subset of elements) that has an optimal value (either maximum or minimum, depending on the problem definition).[1]

For analyzing whether or not a given formalized computational-level theory is tractable, it turns out to be useful to distinguish two more problem types: *search* problems and *decision* problems. Search problems are problems whose output is a particular structure with some property, e.g., a subset of elements with a certain size ($|S| \geq m$), cost ($c(S)$), or utility ($u(S)$). Hence, all optimization problems are by definition search problems, but not all search problems are optimization problems. Consider, for instance:

ADDITIVE SUBSET CHOICE (search but not optimization version)
Input: A set $X = \{x_1, x_2, \ldots, x_n\}$ of n available items, a value function u assigning a value to every element $x \in X$, and an integer k.
Output: A subset $S \subseteq X$ such that $u(S) = \sum_{x \in S} u(x) \geq k$, if such a subset exists (otherwise output that none exists).

---

[1] Following convention in computational complexity theory, we will use "maximum" and "minimum," and not "maximal" and "minimal," because the latter are in this area often understood as referring to local optima, whereas the former refer to global optima, as we intend.

Note that this search problem is different from, but closely related to, the optimization version of ADDITIVE SUBSET CHOICE. For instance, by solving the search version for various k one can effectively solve the optimization problem as well. Conversely, by solving the optimization problem one effectively solves the search problem for all k.

Decision problems are problems whose outputs are *yes* or *no* answers to a question. Consider, for instance,

> ADDITIVE SUBSET CHOICE (decision version)
> **Input:** A set $X = \{x_1, x_2, \ldots, x_n\}$ of n available items, a value function u assigning a value to every element $x \in X$, and an integer k.
> **Question:** Does there exist a subset $S \subseteq X$ such that $u(S) \geq \sum_{x \in S} u(x) \geq k$?

Solving this decision problem means returning the correct answer (*yes* or *no*), without needing to output a structure that shows that the answer is correct. Note that by solving the search version for various k one can easily solve the decision version: If for a given input the output for the search version is a subset S with $u(S) \geq k$, then the answer to the decision version is *yes*, and otherwise it is *no*. Conversely, this works only partially: If the answer to the decision version is *no*, then the correct output for the search version is "none exists"; if instead the answer to the decision version is *yes*, you only know that a subset S with $u(S) \geq k$ exists, but the output of the decision problem does not specify what this S is. That said, algorithms for solving decision problems are often (though not always) "constructive," meaning that they construct solutions to the search version in the process of solving the decision problem. In those cases, that same algorithm can be used to solve the search version as well.

Practice 2.1.1 Define the search and decision versions of BINARY SUBSET CHOICE and BUDGET SUBSET CHOICE analogous to how we defined the search and decision versions of ADDITIVE SUBSET CHOICE.

We have introduced three different types of problems: optimization, search, and decision. Understanding these types – how they are different and how they relate to each other – is important for computational complexity analyses. In this and coming chapters we will work mostly with graph, logic, and number problems from computer science. Even though many of these problems have no direct relevance for cognitive science, knowing them and their computational complexity will prove useful for analyzing the computational complexity of computational-level theories in cognitive science.

We will now illustrate the distinction between optimization, search, and decision problems using various graph problems (if you are new to graph theory, you may want to read the primer to graph theory in Appendix A.3 before proceeding). Here is an example of each version for a problem called VERTEX DEGREE:

> VERTEX DEGREE (optimization and search)
> **Input:** A graph $G = (V, E)$.
> **Output:** A vertex $v \in V$ such that the degree of v is maximum. (Here the *degree* of a vertex is the number of edges incident to that vertex; see Figure 2.1 for an illustration).

> VERTEX DEGREE (search)
> **Input:** A graph $G = (V, E)$ and an integer k.
> **Output:** A vertex $v \in V$ such that the degree of v is at least k if such a vertex exists (otherwise output that none exists).

> VERTEX DEGREE (decision)
> **Input:** A graph $G = (V, E)$ and an integer k.
> **Question:** Does there exist a vertex $v \in V$ such that the degree of v is at least k?

Stop and Think

Note that the examples are again three different versions of the same problem. Can you spot the differences between the input and output? Can you see how these problems relate to each other?

Practice 2.1.2 Draw an example instance of VERTEX DEGREE. For example, the graph $G = (V, E)$ with vertex set $V = \{a, b, c, d, e, f, g\}$ and edge set

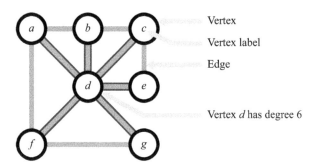

Figure 2.1　Illustration of a graph, its vertices and edges, and its maximum degree vertex.

$E = \{(a,b), (a,c), (a,d), (a,f), (b,c), (b,d), (c,d), (c,e), (d,e), (d,f), (d,g), (f,g)\}$ as in Figure 2.1 or a different, larger one. Next, determine the solution for each of the optimization, search, and decision versions listed earlier for your drawn graph. Determine also if the solution is unique for each version. For search and decision problems, investigate the problem for various values of k.

Practice 2.1.3 Repeat Practice 2.1.2 for all three versions – optimization, search, and decision – of the following two problems (here given in their decision versions).

VERTEX COVER
Input: A graph $G = (V, E)$ and an integer k.
Question: Does there exist a vertex cover $V' \subseteq V$ such that $|V'| \leq k$? (Here a vertex set V' is called a *vertex cover* if for every edge $(u,v) \in E$ we have $u \in V'$ or $v \in V'$. See Figure 2.2 for an illustration.)

DOMINATING SET
Input: A graph $G = (V, E)$ and an integer k.
Question: Does there exist a dominating set $V' \subseteq V$ such that $|V'| \leq k$? (Here a vertex set V' is called a *dominating set* if for every vertex $v \in V'$ we have $v \in V'$ or there is a neighbor u of v such that $u \in V'$; here a vertex u is a *neighbor* of v if $(u,v) \in E$. See Figure 2.3 for an illustration.)

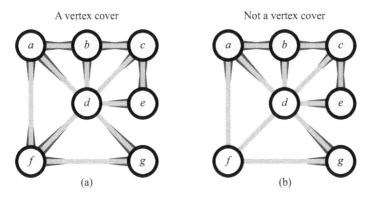

Figure 2.2 Illustrations of (a) a subset of vertices (gray) that are a vertex cover and (b) a subset of vertices (gray) that are not a vertex cover. Note that in (b) the edge (e,d) is not covered, hence the selected selected set of vertices $\{a,b,c,e,g\}$ is not a vertex cover for this graph G.

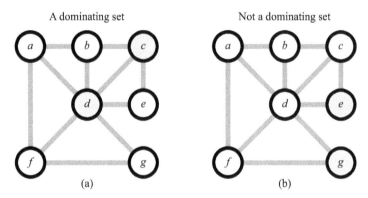

Figure 2.3   Illustrations of (a) a subset of vertices that are a dominating set and (b) a subset of vertices that are not a dominating set. Note that in (b) the vertices a and b are not dominated, hence the selected set of vertices $\{e, g\}$ is not a dominating set for this graph G.

Stop and Think

In Practice 2.1.3 you had to translate a decision problem into a search and an optimization version. How did you do this? Could this be a general approach? Could it also be used to translate search and optimization problems into a decision version?

A formulation of a decision problem like "does there exist an X for which property Y holds" can often be translated to the search problem "*give me* an X such that property Y holds." In case Y is some threshold value (e.g., "give me a vertex cover of size at most k") then it is often possible to translate the search problem into an optimization problem (e.g., "give me a minimum vertex cover"). Reasoning the other way around is also possible: e.g., from "give me a minimum vertex cover" to "give me a vertex cover with size at most k" to "is there a vertex cover with size at most k." Very often search variants of problems may conceptually better match the cognitive capacities we want to formalize, because they output a particular structural solution and not merely a *yes* versus *no* answer. As we will discover in the next chapters, however, most complexity theoretic tools apply to decision problems. Given that the different problem types are related, the results of computational complexity analyses can be translated between different problem variants. Later in Chapter 3 we will prove this formally.

Stop and Think

Even though we cannot yet formally prove how (in)tractability translates between the different versions of a problem, we can informally reason about this now. Let F_o be an optimization problem for which we can quickly compute the output. Let F_d be the decision variant of this problem. Can we quickly compute the output of F_d?

A straightforward way of computing F_d is to *look* at the output of F_o and decide whether it fulfills the criteria (e.g., the size of the minimum vertex cover is indeed k). If we can quickly *verify* that this is the case (more on this in Chapter 4), then we can also compute the output of F_d (viz., *yes* or *no*) quickly.

2.2   Solving Problems with Algorithms

In Practice 2.1.2 and 2.1.3 you found solutions for different versions of VERTEX DEGREE and VERTEX COVER. How did you find the solutions, and how did you know they were correct? For each problem you probably adopted a different method. Can you describe what the method was?

Practice 2.2.1   Describe for each version of VERTEX DEGREE and VERTEX COVER the algorithm that you used for finding the solution. Do you think the algorithm works for all instances? If not, try to construct an algorithm that does.

In this section, we discuss how to describe and analyze algorithms for problems like VERTEX DEGREE and VERTEX COVER. We start with introducing so-called *pseudo-code*.

2.2.1   Pseudo-Code

Pseudo-code can be seen as an "intermediate" way of describing algorithms: It is more formal than natural language, yet not as formal as an actual programming language as C, JAVA, or Python. It can be seen as a high-level description of the *method* employed by the algorithm, without bothering too much about the subtleties of the implementation. Describing an algorithm in pseudo-code has many advantages. It is a compact, platform-independent way of communicating the key concepts and principles behind the algorithm; apart from some elementary programming constructs to direct program flow (such as testing whether a condition is satisfied), the actual statements in the pseudo-code can be fairly detailed or fairly abstract, depending on our focus. For example, when describing a particular sorting algorithm, the focus is on *how* a list is sorted (see, e.g., Algorithm 2.6), and the steps in the pseudo-code will tend to be fairly detailed. In other examples, our focus may be elsewhere and "sorting a list" may be just a trivial subroutine in our algorithm; in the pseudo-code we might just mention as a step "sort list L" as a statement.

Stop and Think

Have a look at the algorithm for VERTEX DEGREE and try to make sense of the different constructs. What would line (4) do? And the **if** ... **then** ... **end if** construction in lines (5–8)? What is the relation between line (3) and line (9)?

Algorithm 2.1 Compute the vertex degree of a graph G with n vertices

VertexDegree(G)

```
 1: d ← 0                    # degree variable
 2: m ← 0                    # vertex with highest degree
 3: for i = 1 to n do
 4:     dᵢ ← degree of vertex i
 5:     if dᵢ > d then
 6:         d ← dᵢ           # d gets updated with new maximum value
 7:         m ← i            # m gets updated with vertex with this value
 8:     end if
 9: end for
10: return m                 # return the vertex with maximum degree of this graph
```

In this algorithm, boldface words (like **for** and **return**) are control flow statements. They are typical constructs that are used in some notation or another in many programming languages, especially languages that facilitate so-called *structured programming*. Typical control flow statements refer to the *selection* of a block of statements, e.g., the **if** *condition* **then** *block 1* **else** *block 2* **end if** construction selects either *block 1* or *block 2* of statements, depending on whether the condition evaluates to *true*. Other control flow statements refer to the *repetition* of a block of statements, like the **for** *start* **to** *end* **do** *block* **end for** construction. Other such constructions may be **do** ... **until**, **for all** ... **do**, **while** ... **do**, etc.

The $d \leftarrow 0$ statements assign values to variables. It should be clear from the context what type of variable is used (e.g., a string, a list, or an integer).

Comments are typically within brackets or using a familiar programming language construct, like // (for the C and JAVA languages) or # (for the Python language). Blocks of statements are often indented to clarify their scope; for example, lines (4) to (8) are indented as they fall within the scope of the **for** and **end for** statements in line (3) and (9). Likewise, lines (6) and (7) are again indented as it falls within the scope of the **if** ... **then** ... **endif** construction. In some pseudo-code dialects, the indentation is the *only* way of determining the scope of control statements, however, we will also use the *end* statements for clarity. Lastly, statements may be a function or subroutine call. For example, in line (4) d_i is assigned the degree of vertex i, without specifying whether this degree is readily available or must be computed by an other algorithm, e.g., $d_i \leftarrow DegreeOfVertex(i)$. We abstracted away here from how the degree of vertex i is obtained and wrote line (4) quite informally. Often, such constructions make the pseudo-code more readable, provided that the more informal construction is unambiguous and its details are irrelevant for understanding the algorithm.

Different authors use different notions in their pseudo-code. For example, assigning a value to a variable, as in line (1) in Algorithm 2.1, can be denoted by $d \leftarrow 0$, $d := 0$, $d = 0$, or even *set d to* 0. However, even when you are accustomed to a particular notation, it will typically not take much time to understand another dialect.

The actual algorithm for finding the vertex degree of a graph is quite straightforward: It initializes the maximum degree counter and vertex number to zero, then loops over all vertices of the graph, finds the degree of that vertex, and if it is higher than the current degree counter, it updates the maximum degree counter and the vertex with this degree is saved in variable m. When all vertices are visited, this variable indeed contains the vertex with the highest degree of the graph; it is returned in line (10).

Practice 2.2.2 Having seen the pseudo-code for the optimization variant of VERTEX DEGREE, now change this algorithm to the decision variant of VERTEX DEGREE that has as input both a graph G and an integer k, and outputs *true* if and only if the graph has a vertex with degree at least k, and *false* otherwise.

VERTEX DEGREE can be solved by a fairly straightforward algorithm. VERTEX COVER is somewhat more involved. Have a look at the following algorithm solving the optimization version of this problem, which uses another function as a subroutine:

Algorithm 2.2 Compute a vertex cover of minimal size of a graph G with n vertices

---

VertexCover(G)

1: $k \leftarrow 0$
2: **while** *true* **do**
3:    $V' \leftarrow$ *VertexCover*(G, k)
4:    **if** $V' = \varnothing$ **then**
5:       $k \leftarrow k + 1$
6:    **else**
7:       **return** V'
8:    **end if**
9: **end while**

Algorithm 2.3 If G has a vertex cover of size at most k, return this, else return $\varnothing$

VertexCover(G, k)

1: **for all** subsets V' of k distinct vertices in G **do**
2:    **if** this subset V' yields a vertex cover of G **then**
3:       **return** V'
4:    **end if**
5: **end for**
6: **return** $\varnothing$

Note that this algorithm quite literally follows a typical "brute-force" way of solving VERTEX COVER:

> Well, let's see, can we make a vertex cover with a single node? What if we select this node? No, that is not a vertex cover. This one then? No. . . . Well, apparently I cannot cover all edges with a single vertex. Let's try it with two vertices. What if I pick these two? . . . And what if pick these two? Let's check whether this is a vertex cover! . . . Hurray, yes, this set of vertices covers all edges. So, this graph has a vertex cover of size 2.

Note that the pseudo-code in this example hides some quite complex stuff. For example, we did not explicitly specify how to *systematically* select all possible selections of k distinct vertices, nor how to decide whether this selection of vertices covers all edges in the graph. This description of a particular algorithm solving VERTEX COVER is thus quite high-level, focusing on *what needs to be done* rather than *how it is actually implemented*.

Practice 2.2.3 Write pseudo-code for the following two (informally described) algorithms:

1. Find the maximum number m in an unsorted list L of n numbers by examining all numbers in the list one by one and keeping track of the current highest number.
2. Sort a deck of playing cards by first making four piles of clubs, hearts, spades, and diamonds and then sort each pile by picking up the cards of the pile one by one and inserting the card at the right position.

2.3 Time-Complexity of Algorithms

In the previous section we discussed algorithms for VERTEX DEGREE and VERTEX COVER. Surely, an algorithm for solving a problem most be *correct*: For every valid input (e.g., a valid description of a graph), the algorithm must correctly compute a correct output, as defined by the problem (e.g., a vertex cover of minimum size). Apart from correct, we also want an algorithm to be *efficient*: It should not take more resources to solve a problem than what is minimally needed. That is, the algorithm should be (asymptotically) optimal in its resource usage.

2.3.1 Measuring Running Times

In the formal analysis of algorithms, we normally focus on the resources *time* and *space*. For many computational problems *time* is the most important resource, as it puts the heaviest constraints on algorithms: Most algorithms will run out of time (i.e., take too much time to be of practical use) before they run out of space. But how do we measure the amount of work that is done by an algorithm? Surely, we can implement and run the algorithm on our desktop computer and use a timer to measure how much time is needed by the algorithm to solve the problem. However, the result is not very informative, as it is hugely machine-dependent. On a different computer, under a different operating system, with different processes running in the background, etc., we are likely to get different results. Furthermore, how can we be sure that we measure the efficiency of the *algorithm*, rather than the *implementation* of the algorithm? Thus, we would strive for a more *analytical* way of measuring the amount of work done by the algorithm.

Typically, an algorithm needs more time for larger inputs. It takes more time to compute 274×731 than to compute 3×2. To really measure the amount of work down by the algorithm, in order to analyze its efficiency (possibly compared to other algorithms trying to solve the same problem), we need to take into account the *size of the input*, for example, the total number of digits in the multiplication.

Practice 2.3.1   Work out both multiplications on paper. Is the amount of work you need to do indeed a function of the number of digits of the numbers? If so, what function?

Now have a close look at the *VertexDegree* algorithm (Algorithm 2.1). We will count the number of instructions done in the worst case as a function of the size of the input. For now, we will take n, the number of vertices of the graph, as the size of the input. The **end** statements are not counted as separate instructions as they limit the scope of the control flow statements only.

Now, lines (1–3), (5), and (8–10) are quite straightforward. We execute lines (3) and (5) once for every value of i, so n times in total. We execute lines (1), (2), and (10) exactly once, and we do not count lines (8–9) as they are part of the control flow statements. Line (6) and (7) are a bit more tricky as it depends on the test in line (5) whether or not these lines get executed. Worst case, however, the degrees of the separate vertices may be in increasing order, i.e., we can encounter an input where the test in line (5) succeeds for every value of i. So, worst case, we execute lines (6) and (7) also n times in total.

--- **Stop and Think** ---

How many instructions does line (4) take? Is the pseudo-code informative enough in this case?

If we have the degree of each vertex readily available (i.e., it can be retrieved using a single instruction), line (4) takes only a single instruction. If we need to do additional work (e.g., in a subroutine) to determine the degree of vertex i, then we need to take that into account as well. Let us (for now) assume that the degree is stored for every vertex, then the algorithm takes $1 + 1 + n + n + n + n + n + 0 + 0 + 1$ instructions, or $5n + 3$ in total.

This result, however, is likely to be *too precise* for our purposes. First of all, in counting instructions we completely ignore that instructions may not all take the same time to execute. And second, for analyzing algorithms, we are really interested in the *order of growth* as a function of the input, rather than the exact number of instructions. Therefore, rather than "merely" counting instructions, our strategy will be as follows:

1. Identify the elementary or "core" instruction that is *fundamental* for the algorithm you want to analyze. Examples of such an elementary instruction might be:

   a. Comparing two elements of an array
   b. Deciding whether two vertices share an edge
   c. Swapping a variable with a list element
   d. Some basic computation, like multiplying two numbers

2. Identify a reasonable measure of the input size. This measure should capture the "size" of the problem instance in a natural way. For example:

   a. The number of vertices in a graph
   b. The number of elements in an array
   c. The number of bits or digits of a large number
   d. The highest degree of a polynomial

3. Count how often the elementary instruction is performed as a function of the input size.
4. Make sure that the total number of instructions that is performed is in the same order of growth as the elementary instruction, i.e., the number of elementary instructions indeed gives a good indication of how the running time increases when the input size increases.

Practice 2.3.2 Apply the four steps in this strategy to determine the complexity of the *VertexDegree* algorithm.

We formally define the *time complexity of an algorithm* as the lowest upper bound on the number of times that the elementary instruction is executed, as a function of the size of the input. Note that the running time of an algorithm is not an absolute number (as it would be when measured with a stopwatch), but is relative to both the input size and the elementary instruction. This is fine, as long as both the elementary instruction and the measure of the input size remain the same when comparing algorithms or methods. For example, take the following SORTING problem.

SORTING
Input: A list L with n numbers $x_1 \ldots x_n$.
Output: A list L' with numbers $x_1 \ldots x_n$ such that for all items x_i and x_j in L', $i \le j$ if $x_i \le x_j$.

Typical sorting methods like *InsertionSort* (see Algorithm 2.8) use arrays as data structures to hold a list of n numbers and define the comparison of two array elements as the elementary instruction, but other methods such as *CountingSort* define the allocation of an array location to an element as its elementary instruction. Thus, caution must be taken when comparing the running times of these algorithms.

2.3.2   Order of Growth

In the previous subsection we argued that, in order to study the complexity of an algorithm, one does not need to count each and every instruction. Instead, we counted the number of times a particular elementary instruction was executed as a function of the size of the input. In practice, however, we tend to be even more abstract in our analysis. When comparing or analyzing algorithms, we are typically only interested in the *order of growth* of the running time as a function of the input size, and discard of constants, lower-range polynomials etc. We will use the so-called Big-Oh notation, $O(.)$, to express the relation between input size and complexity. The $O(.)$ notation is used to express an asymptotic upper bound. Informally, if we state that a function $f = O(g)$ we mean that f does not grow faster than g. The formal definition is a bit more tricky, as we allow for some additional "start-up costs" that make f more costly than g in the beginning: we only require that g "eventually outgrows" f.

DEFINITION 2.1   *A function $f(n)$ is $O(g(n))$ if there are constants $c \geq 0$, $n_0 \geq 1$ such that $f(n) \leq cg(n)$, for all $n \geq n_0$.*

In other words, the $O(.)$ notation serves to ignore constants and lower-order polynomials in the description of a function. For this reason $O(g(n))$ is also called the *order of magnitude* of $f(n)$.

Practice 2.3.3   Determine the order of magnitude of the following functions.

1. $n^4 + n^3 + n^2 + n + 1$
2. $50n^4 + 20n^3 + 10n^2 + 5n + 1$
3. $2^n \cdot n^2$
4. $n^4 + 2^n$
5. $n^4 + n$
6. $1,000$
7. $1,000n$
8. $1,000 \cdot {}^n/_3$
9. $\sqrt{n}$
10. $n + \sin n$
11. $1 + 2 + \ldots + n$
12. $n + {}^n/_2 + {}^n/_4 + \ldots + 1$

DEFINITION 2.2   *An algorithm is said to be of time-complexity $O(f(n))$ if for every input with n elementary operations the number of steps it performs is $O(f(n))$.*

$O(1)$ or *constant-time* algorithms have a running time that is upper-bounded by a constant, i.e., its running time is *independent* of the size of the input (at least from a particular input size n_0 – see Definition 2.1). A (rather trivial) example of such an algorithm might be the following:

Algorithm 2.4 Find the maximum element in a low-to-high sorted array with n values

MaximumSorted($A[1 \ldots n]$)

  1: **return** $A[n]$ # return the last element in the array

---

$O(n^c)$ or *polynomial-time* algorithms have a running time that grows polynomially with the input size. For $c = 1$, $c = 2$, and $c = 3$ these running times are also known as *linear*, *quadratic*, and *cubic*, respectively. For example, the following linear-time algorithm finds the maximum number in an *unsorted* array by looking at all the elements one by one:

Algorithm 2.5 Find the maximum element in an unsorted array with n values

MaximumUnSorted($A[1 \ldots n]$)

  1: $m \leftarrow -\infty$
  2: **for** $i = 1$ **to** n **do**
  3:     **if** $A[i] > m$ **then**
  4:        $m \leftarrow A[i]$
  5:     **end if**
  6: **end for**
  7: **return** m

This quadratic-time algorithm sorts an array by repeatedly finding the maximum number and setting it apart:

Algorithm 2.6 Sort an unsorted array with n values

SelectionSort($A[1 \ldots n]$)

  1: **for** $i = 1$ **to** n **do**
  2:     $m = MaximumUnSorted(A[i \ldots n])$
  3:     $Swap(A[i], A[m])$
  4: **end for**
  5: **return** $A[1 \ldots n]$

Note that there are n calls to *MaximumUnSorted*($A[1 \ldots n]$), with each call taking $O(n)$ time, yielding an $O(n^2)$ time algorithm.

Some algorithms need even more time: $O(c^n)$ or *exponential-time* algorithms have a running time that grows exponentially with the input size. Have a look at the following problem:

GRAPH COLORABILITY
Input: A graph $G = (V, E)$, integer k.
Question: Is there a k-coloring of the graph, i.e., an assignment $V \rightarrow \{c_1, \ldots, c_k\}$ such that no vertices that share an edge have the same color? See Figure 2.4 for an illustration.

The following $O(k^n)$ algorithm solves the GRAPH COLORABILITY problem. It tries to assign a color to all of the n nodes, and checks after each assignment if the (partial) coloring still is valid. If not, it tries to color that node using another color; if all colors are used for that node, it tracks back and tries a different color for the node before. Eventually, the algorithm will halt when all possibilities are exhausted or if all nodes have been assigned a (valid) color. In the worst case, the algorithm needs to try all possible k^n colorings. The elementary operation here is the assignment in line (4).

Algorithm 2.7 Check whether a graph with n nodes can be colored with k colors

$GraphColor(G, k)$

```
 1: V[1 ... n] ← 0
 2: i ← 1
 3: while i > 0 do
 4:     V[i] ← V[i] + 1
 5:     if V[i] > c then
 6:         V[i] = 0
 7:         i ← i − 1
 8:     end if
 9:     if ValidColoring(V) then
10:         i ← i + 1
11:         if i > n then
12:             return true
13:         end if
14:     end if
15: end while
16: return false
```

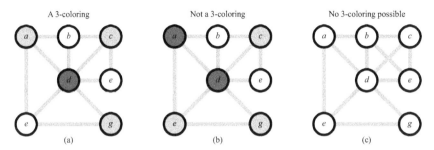

Figure 2.4 Illustrations of (a) a coloring of the vertices in G (white, gray, black) that is a 3-coloring for graph G, (b) a coloring of the vertices in G (white, gray, black) that is not a 3-coloring for graph G, and (c) a graph G' for which no 3-coloring exists.

Observe that we have the following series of increasing orders of magnitude:
$$O(1) \prec O(log(n)) \prec O(n) \prec O(n^2) \prec O(n^3) \prec \ldots \prec O(2^n) \prec O(n) \prec \ldots$$

Practice 2.3.4 Reconsider the algorithms that you considered in Practice 2.2.1 and try to express their time-complexity using the $O(.)$ notation. Determine whether the algorithms are polynomial-time algorithms, or exponential-time algorithms, or neither.

In addition to the $O(.)$ upper bound notation, there is a similarly defined $\Omega(.)$ *lower bound* notation:

DEFINITION 2.3 *A function $f(n)$ is $\Omega(g(n))$ if there are constants $c > 0$, $n_0 \geq 1$ such that $cg(n) \leq f(n)$, for all $n \geq n_0$.*

When a function f is both upper-bounded and lower-bounded by g modulo some constants (i.e., f grows "as hard" as g) we use the following notation:

DEFINITION 2.4 *A function $f(n)$ is $\Theta(g(n))$ if there are constants $c_1, c_2 > 0$, $n_0 \geq 1$ such that $c_1 g(n) \leq f(n) \leq c_2 g(n)$, for all $n \geq n_0$.*

These three notions are illustrated in Figure 2.5. Note that lower and upper bounds can be tight or loose. Assume that $f(n) = 2x^2 + 1$. Now $f = O(g)$ for either $g = x^2$, $g = x^3$, and $g = 2^x$. Furthermore, $f = \Omega(g)$ for $g = x^2$, $g = x$, and $g = 6$. It is implicit in the definition of polynomial-time and exponential-time algorithms that the upper bound on the running time of the algorithm, expressed by the function $O(.)$, is tight. You may also encounter the terms *super-polynomial* time or *sub-exponential* time, referring to algorithms that are $\Omega(n^c)$ for every constant c, respectively that are $O(c^n)$ for every constant $c > 1$. Note that there are algorithms that have a running time that is *both* super-polynomial *and* sub-exponential. An example is the classical algorithm for the

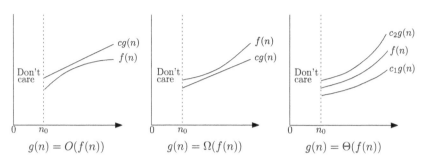

$$g(n) = O(f(n)) \qquad g(n) = \Omega(f(n)) \qquad g(n) = \Theta(f(n))$$

Figure 2.5   Illustrations of $O(.)$, $\Omega(.)$, and $\Theta(.)$.

decomposition of an integer in prime numbers (the INTEGER FACTORIZATION problem defined next), which has a time-complexity of about $2^{n^{1/3}}$.

INTEGER FACTORIZATION
Input: An integer N.
Output: A list of prime factors $p_i, \ldots, p_m$ such that $p_i \times \ldots \times p_m = N$.

Practice 2.3.5   Check that the running time $O(2^{n^{1/3}})$ is indeed both super-polynomial and sub-exponential.

2.3.3   Worst-and Best-Case Running Times

Recall that in Practice 2.2.3 you were asked to find the maximum number of an unsorted list of numbers. Note that, *whatever the list looks like*, you need to examine *all* items on the list to make sure you have identified the highest number, as you cannot know beforehand whether the highest number is at the beginning of the list, somewhere in the middle, or at the end. Moreover, you do not know what the highest number actually is, so you cannot stop when you find it – you only *know* it was the highest number after you have seen all of them. In other words, in *each and every case*, to find the maximum of a list with n numbers you have to look at all n of them.

Practice 2.3.6   Contrast this with the card sorting algorithm you found in Practice 2.2.3. How much work do you need to do in the *best* case? And in the *worst* case?

In the previous section, we studied the complexity of various algorithms on their "worst-case scenario." It can also be interesting to study how much work the algorithm needs to do in the "best possible scenario." We formalize both notions as follows:

DEFINITION 2.5 *We define the worst-case and best-case complexity of an algorithm as follows:*

1. *The algorithm uses* at most $f_w(n)$ *elementary instructions for every possible input of size* n ↔ *The algorithm has* worst-case *complexity* $f_w(n)$.
2. *The algorithm uses* at least $f_b(n)$ *elementary instructions for every possible input of size* n ↔ *The algorithm has* best-case *complexity* $f_b(n)$.

Recall the *SelectionSort* algorithm from the previous section, and compare it to the following algorithm:

Algorithm 2.8 Sort an unsorted array with n values

InsertionSort($\mathbf{A}[1 \ldots n]$)

1: **for** $i = 1$ **to** n **do**
2:      $x \leftarrow \mathbf{A}[i]$
3:      $j \leftarrow i - 1$
4:      **while** $j > 0$ **and** $\mathbf{A}[j] > x$ **do**
5:          $\mathbf{A}[j + 1] \leftarrow \mathbf{A}[j]$
6:          $j \leftarrow j - 1$
7:      **end while**
8:      $\mathbf{A}[j + 1] \leftarrow x$
9: **end for**
10: **return** $\mathbf{A}[1 \ldots n]$

Practice 2.3.7 Assume that the initial array is already sorted low to high. Count the number of array comparisons $\mathbf{A}[j] > x$ required.

Practice 2.3.8 Now assume that the initial array is sorted high to low. Again count the number of comparisons required.

Practice 2.3.9 Recall Practice 2.3.1. What are the worst- and best-case complexity of multiplying two numbers as expressed in the total number of single digit multiplications to be done?

Observe that for every input, *SelectionSort* needed $O(n^2)$ array comparisons. However, while the number of array comparisons for *InsertionSort* is also $O(n^2)$ in the worst case, it can be significantly lower in the best case.

2.3.4 More Fine-Grained Analyses

In Algorithm 2.1 for the VERTEX DEGREE problem we assumed that the degree of each vertex is readily available. If it isn't, we need to calculate it from the graph structure: For any vertex, count the number of vertices it is connected with. Using a so-called *adjacency list* (a data structure representing a graph in the form of a list-of-lists describing for every vertex its neighbors, i.e., the vertices it is connected to; see Appendix A.3), a simple algorithm for counting the degree of any vertex is the following (where v.next indicates the node that is immediately followed by v in the list of neighbors of v, or $\varnothing$ if we reached the last node in the list):

Algorithm 2.9 Compute the degree of a vertex v

Degree(v)

  1: $d \leftarrow 0$
  2: **while** v.next $\neq \varnothing$ **do**
  3:    $d \leftarrow d + 1$
  4:    $v \leftarrow v$.next
  5: **end while**
  6: **return** d

Now, any node in a graph connects to at most $n - 1$ other nodes, so, for a full graph this algorithm would take $O(n)$ time, and, consequently, the *VertexDegree* algorithm takes $O(n^2)$ time. But what if the graph is not full? If the graph is *sparse* (has few connections) rather than *dense* (has many connections), this analysis is too coarse.

Practice 2.3.10   Assume that the graph is a *cycle graph*: a graph in which each node connects to exactly two other nodes. How much time does Algorithm 2.9 take? And the *VertexDegree* algorithm as a whole?

Practice 2.3.11   Now assume that the graph has m edges in total, with $(n - 1) \leq m \leq (n - 1)^2$. What is the *total* time that Algorithm 2.9 takes for all nodes in the graph?

If we describe the running time of the *VertexDegree* algorithm in terms of both the number of nodes *and* the number of edges in the graph, what will then be its running time? To answer that question, we take a closer look at Algorithm 2.1. The **for** loop in lines (2) to (7) ensures that we compute the degree of all vertices d_i. We need $O(m)$ time for the total number of degree calculations. To be more precise: if the time needed to compute the degree of node i equals t_i, then the running time is $\sum_{i=1}^{n} t_i = O(m)$. So, instead of computing $n \cdot \max(t_i)$ (i.e., n times the maximum running time of finding the degree of a vertex), we sum over the running times of all n times we need to find the degree of each of the n vertices. However, we do more work in this **for** loop: we also check whether the thus computed degree d_i is larger than the current maximum degree d and update d if necessary. Worst case, we compute the degree of the vertices in increasing order and need to update d exactly n times. Each comparison and possible update costs $O(1)$, hence, we have total costs $O(m)$ for computing the degrees, and $O(n)$ for updating the maximum degree; in total, the algorithm takes $O(n + m)$ time.

Practice 2.3.12 When asked for the running time of Algorithm 2.1, assume that Bob says that *VertexDegree* takes $O(n^2)$, while Alice insists that *VertexDegree* takes $O(n + m)$. Argue that *both* are right, but that Alice's answer is more precise than Bob's.

2.4 Time-Complexity of Problems

Until now we discussed the complexity of an *algorithm*, i.e., the number of elementary instructions as a function of the size of the instance that is solved by that particular algorithm. While this allows to compare algorithms (and approaches in solving a particular problem), it does not tell us if our algorithm is really as efficient as possible. For example, Algorithm 2.7 checked if a graph with n nodes could be colored with c colors. This algorithm takes time exponential in n; however, we just might have been sloppy in designing this algorithm. There may be a polynomial-time algorithm after all that of which we were unaware. In this section we go a step further and discuss the complexity of a *problem*. We define the complexity of a problem by its "fastest" possible algorithm.

DEFINITION 2.6 *A problem is said to be of time-complexity $O(f(n))$ if the "fastest" algorithms computing the problem are of time-complexity $O(f(n))$.*

How to decide whether we already have found the "fastest" algorithm for a particular problem? We can try to find a *theoretical* lower bound on the running times of algorithms solving such a problem. One proves lower bounds by showing that *any* algorithm needs to do *at least* an amount $f(n)$ of work on the problem. In this section, we will show two proof techniques that allow us to do so: the *input-output argument* and the *counterexample* argument.

The input-output argument gives a lower bound by showing that we need to do $f(n)$ work, simply by reading the input to the problem and writing the output. For example, adding two $n \times n$ matrices will require you to read in every matrix element ($2n^2$ elements in total) and writing a $n \times n$ matrix again, consisting of n^2 elements. So this argument proves that matrix summation of $n \times n$ matrices takes at least $O(n^2)$ time.

The counterexample argument can be used to prove that an amount of $f(n)$ work is needed to be done by constructing a counterexample, where the problem cannot be solved by less work. An example is finding the maximal number in an array of n numbers. Obviously, you need to see all of them to decide which one is maximal, and so we need to do $n - 1$ array comparisons: comparing element $A[1]$ with element $A[2]$, storing the largest in variable *max*, comparing *max* with $A[3]$, and so on. By counterexample, assume that your algorithm has only seen the first $n - 1$ elements of the array A. We now construct arrays B and C by copying A and replacing the last element with a number that is *lower* than A's minimal number in B, and replacing the last element with a number that is *higher* than A's maximal number in C. Now, our algorithm will give the same result for arrays B and C, which is obviously incorrect: In array C the last element is the maximum number, and in array B one of the other elements (but definitely not the last one) is the maximum number.

Likewise, you can show (using the counterexample argument) that to solve a VERTEX COVER problem, you will need to look at all m edges of the graph. Take for example the graph G consisting of four vertices a, b, c, and d, with edges (a,b), (b,c), and (c,d). This graph can be covered with two vertices, e.g., b and d, but not with a single vertex. Now suppose you did not look at the edge (c,d). Now construct the graph H by removing (c,d) and replacing it with (b,d). This graph *can* be colored with a single vertex (namely, b), but G cannot. You really need to examine all edges of the graphs to discriminate between these two situations, hence, the complexity of VERTEX COVER has a lower bound of $O(m)$.

Stop and Think

Make sure you understand this: We are trying to prove *lower* bounds on the *worst-case complexity* of a problem, that is, we want to prove the minimal time needed to solve that problem. What would be the *upper* bound on the worst-case complexity of such a problem?

Finding an *upper* bound on the complexity of a problem is (at least conceptually) easier: The problem definitely needs no more time to be solved than the current fastest algorithm for it! Now, note that there may be a considerable gap between upper and lower bounds for problems. For example, the fastest known algorithm for deciding whether a graph with n nodes has a vertex cover of size k takes exponential time. To be precise, it takes time $O(kn + 1.2738^k)$. It is strongly conjectured, for reasons we discuss in the next chapters, that no sub-exponential-time algorithm exists for VERTEX COVER, which is far from the *proven* lower bound of $O(m)$. On the other hand, adding two $n \times n$ matrices can indeed be done in $O(n^2)$ time, so, its running time is both $O(n^2)$ and $\Omega(n^2)$.

Practice 2.4.1   Reconsider the algorithms that you considered for the problems in Practice 2.2.1, and try to determine if they are of polynomial-time complexity or not. Observe that the time complexity of the three versions are always closely related (e.g., ask yourself the following question: "Could it be that a decision version of a problem is solvable in polynomial time when the optimization version of the same problem is not?").

To finish this chapter, we show how the upper bound on the complexity of VERTEX COVER has converged over time (see Table 2.1). We show here the upper bounds on the running time of the decision version of VERTEX COVER, as a function of the number of vertices n and the maximal size k of the vertex cover we allow in the graph. Note that the algorithms that yielded these upper bounds are highly sophisticated and that the $O(.)$ notation may hide *huge* constants that make these algorithms not very useful in practice. Even so, the increase in performance is only moderate, as you can see: Every running time is exponential in k. Since k can take any value between 0 and n, this is essentially an exponential-time algorithm.

There has been no progress at all in finding a tighter lower bound than $O(m)$, however, from Table 2.1 one may suggest that the upper bound is converging to an exponential limit. This "empirical evidence" suggests that it will be very hard, if at all possible, to come up with a polynomial-time algorithm for VERTEX COVER; however, apparently it is difficult to formally prove the absence of such an algorithm. In Chapter 4, we will indeed show that it is very unlikely that a polynomial-time algorithm for VERTEX COVER exists, but also that it is extremely difficult to actually prove that intuition. What we *can* – and *will* – show is that VERTEX COVER has a comparable lower bound complexity as many other problems, for which it is believed that there do not exist any polynomial-time algorithms. For that we need the notion of a *reduction*; this will be the topic of Chapter 3.

2.5   Exercises

Exercise 2.5.1   Consider the following problems and try to determine if they are of polynomial-time complexity or not. We give illustrations in Figure 2.6 that may help you understand some of the problem definitions better. We advise you to construct such examples for yourself whenever you are having difficulty understanding problem definitions in the remainder of this book.

Table 2.1 Illustration of the development of upper bounds for VERTEX COVER. Depicted are the running time of the currently fastest algoritm, expressed in the size of the graph n and the size of the vertex cover k.

Upper bound	Original paper
$O(kn + 2^k k^{2k+2})$	Buss and Goldsmith (1993)
$O(kn + 2^k k^2)$	Downey and Fellows (1995)
$O(kn + 1.324718^k k^2)$	Balasubramanian et al. (1998)
$O(kn + 1.31951^k k^2)$	Downey, Fellows, and Stege (1999)
$O(kn + 1.29175^k k^2)$	Niedermeier and Rossmanith (1999)
$O(kn + \max\{1.25542^k 2^k, 1.2906^{kk}\})$	Stege and Fellows (1999)
$O(kn + 1.2906^k)$	Niedermeier and Rossmanith (2000)
$O(kn + 1.286^k)$	Chen et al. (2001)
$O(kn + 1.2832^k k^{1.5})$	Niedermeier and Rossmanith (2003)
$O(kn + 1.2738^k)$	Chen et al. (2010)

ADDITIVE SUBSET CHOICE

Input: A set $X = \{x_1, x_2, \ldots, x_n\}$ of n available items. For every item $x \in X$ there is an associated integer value $u(x)$.

Output: A subset $S \subseteq V$, such that $u(S) = \sum_{x \in S} u(x)$ is maximum.

SORTING

Input: A list L with n numbers $x_1 \ldots x_n$.

Output: A list L' with numbers $x_1 \ldots x_n$ such that for all items x_i and x_j in L', $i \leq j$ if $x_i \leq x_j$.

SPANNING TREE

Input: A graph $G = (V, E)$.

Output: A spanning tree T of G. (Here a *spanning tree* is a connected acyclic graph that contains all vertices in V and only $|V - 1|$ edges from E.)

MINIMUM SPANNING TREE

Input: An edge-weighted graph $G = (V, E)$.

Output: A spanning tree T of G such that the sum of the weights on the edges in T is minimum.

BINARY SUBSET CHOICE

Input: A set $X = \{x_1, x_2, \ldots, x_n\}$ of n available items. For every item $x \in X$ there is an associated integer value $u(x)$ and for every pair of items (x_i, x_j) there is an associated integer value $\delta(x_i, x_j)$.

Output: A subset $S \subseteq V$, such that $u(S) = \sum_{x \in S} u(x) + \sum_{x, y \in S} \delta(x, y)$ is maximum.

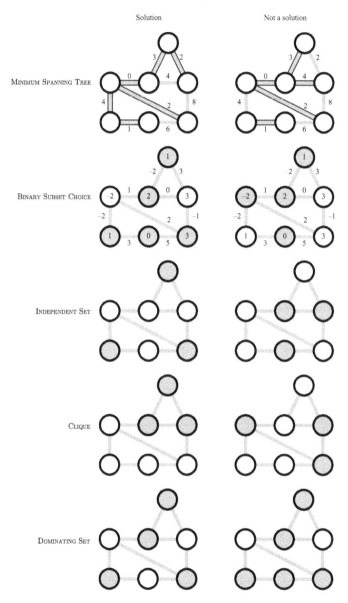

Figure 2.6 Illustration of solutions and non-solutions for several graph optimization problems.

Exercise 2.5.2 Give an algorithm for the following problems, and show that this algorithm will take exponential time (it *will*, for reasons we will discuss in Chapter 4). If your algorithm does not take exponential time, check whether it really solves the problem for all possible instances.

INDEPENDENT SET
Input: A graph $G = (V, E)$ and an integer k.
Question: Does there exist an independent set $V' \subseteq V$ such that $|V'| \geq k$? (Here a vertex set V' is called an *independent set* if there exists no two vertices $u, v \in V'$ such that $(u, v) \in E$.)

CLIQUE
Input: A graph $G = (V, E)$ and an integer k.
Question: Does there exist a clique $V' \subseteq V$ such that $|V'| \geq k$? (Here a vertex set V' is called a *clique* if for all two vertices $u, v \in V'$ there is an edge $(u, v) \in E$.)

DOMINATING SET
Input: A graph $G = (V, E)$ and an integer k.
Question: Does there exist a dominating set $V' \subseteq V$ such that $|V'| \leq k$? (Here a vertex set V' is called a *dominating set* if for every vertex $v \in V'$ we have $v \in V'$ or there is a neighbor u of v such that $u \in V'$; here a vertex u is a *neighbor* of v if $(u, v) \in E$.)

CONSTRAINT SATISFACTION
Input: A set of variables $V = \{V_1, \ldots, V_n\}$, a set $D = \{D_1, \ldots, D_n\}$ of domains of V (describing the values that each variable can take), and a set $C = \{C_1, \ldots, C_m\}$ of constraints. Each constraint c_j is a pair (V_j, R_j), where $V_j \subseteq V$ is a subset of k variables in V and R_j is a k-ary relation on the corresponding domains $D_j \subseteq D$.
Question: Is there a value assignment $t : V_i \rightarrow d \in D_i$ for each $V_i \in V$ and $D_i \in D$ such that every constraint $C_j \in C$ is satisfied?

Exercise 2.5.3 Determine the order of magnitude of the following functions.

1. The number of edges in a graph as a function of the number of vertices
2. The number of subsets of vertices as a function of the number of vertices
3. The number of maximum degree vertices in a graph as a number of vertices
4. The number of candidate tours for a set of n points (e.g., in the TRAVELING SALESPERSON PROBLEM)

Exercise 2.5.4 Give the best-case and worst-case time complexity of the following algorithms.

Algorithm 2.10 Sort an unsorted array with n values

$BogoSort(\mathbf{A}[1\ldots n])$

1: **for all** permutations of **A do**
2:    **if A** is sorted **then**
3:       **return** $\mathbf{A}[1\ldots n]$
4:    **end if**
5: **end for**

Algorithm 2.11 Sort an unsorted array with n values

$RandomBogoSort(\mathbf{A}[1\ldots n])$

1: **while A** is not sorted **do**
2:    shuffle **A**
3: **end while**
4: **return** $\mathbf{A}[1\ldots n]$

Exercise 2.5.5 In a connected graph G with weighted (non-negative) edges, a *spanning tree* is a subgraph G_T of G that leaves out as many edges as possible, while demanding that all the vertices in G are still connected. If the edges of G are *weighted* then a *minimal spanning tree* (MST) G_M is a spanning tree with the minimal total weight of all edges in G.

1. Argue that G_T by definition is a tree, i.e., a graph with no cycles. Note that a consequence thereof is that, if G has n vertices, G_T has $n-1$ edges.
2. See the weighted graph in Figure 2.7. Try to find an MST. Is this MST unique?
3. What was your approach in finding this MST? Formalize this approach in pseudo-code. Does it always give correct results?

2.6   Further Reading

Sorting is one of the key problems in computer science that attracted a lot of attention in the 1950s–1970s (Knuth, 1968). The sorting algorithms you saw in this chapter are straightforward, but not optimal: Sorting a list of n items can be done in $O(n\log(n))$. Typical sorting algorithms that are included in your favorite programming language are *mergesort* and *quicksort*. Both are based on an algorithmic technique that we call *divide and conquer*: Try to solve a problem by dividing it, recursively, into smaller chunks and combine the

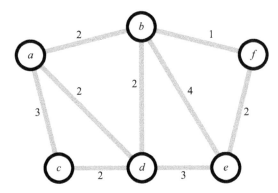

Figure 2.7   A weighted graph G. Can you find a minimal spanning tree in this graph?

chunks together. Sorting can be done quicker ($O(n)$) in special cases if we may assume particular constraints on the input (e.g., the minimum and maximum numbers and the distribution of the numbers over this range).

Another key problem is the minimal spanning tree problem which is relevant for routing problems, planning, data analysis, etc. Two famous algorithms for this problem are *Prim's algorithm* (Prim, 1957) and *Kruskal's algorithm* (Kruskal, 1956) named after Robert C. Prim and Joseph Kruskal, respectively. Their approach is an example of the so-called *greedy* algorithmic technique: Solve a problem by looking for the local optimal improvement. Prim grows a tree by starting with a single node and iteratively finding the node that connects to this tree with lowest weight until all nodes are connected. Kruskal grows multiple trees at the same time, looking at edges with the lowest weight that connect yet unconnected trees, until all trees are connected. The running time of both algorithms is $O(m \log(n))$, where m is the number of edges and n the number of nodes in the graph. The $\log(n)$ part is due to the sorting necessary to add the node with the lowest edge weight.

3   Polynomial-Time Reductions

In this chapter we introduce the notion of polynomial-time reductions. We explain how this technique can be used to transform an input for problem A to an input for problem B, mapping *yes*-instances for A to *yes*-instances for B and vice versa. If this transformation can be done in polynomial time, this implies that if B is polynomial-time computable, then so is A; also, it implies that if A has an exponential-time lower bound, then so must B. These polynomial-time reductions are thus a powerful technique to relate problems to each other. We will demonstrate several reduction strategies, namely reduction by restriction, by local replacement, and by component design. We include several exercises for practicing this technique.

3.1   Exponential-Time Lower Bounds

In Chapter 1 we explained why exponential time is typically considered intractable, making functions that take exponential time to be computed unsuitable computational-level theories of cognition. We saw in Table 2.1 that, despite many efforts, we have not yet succeeded in designing a polynomial-time algorithm for VERTEX COVER, giving rise to the suspicion that none exists. However, the best lower bound we were able to establish was $\Omega(m)$ for a graph with m edges (recall the definition of $\Omega(.)$, $\Theta(.)$, and $O(.)$ from the previous chapter).

Stop and Think

1. Have a look at the algorithm for solving the decision version of VERTEX COVER that we presented earlier (Algorithm 2.3); give an example input where it takes exponential time (in k) to solve VERTEX COVER.

2. Can you *prove* it always takes worst-case exponential time to solve VERTEX COVER?

Recall that Algorithm 2.3 tested for all choices of k distinct vertices out of all n vertices in the graph. If there is no vertex cover of size k in the graph (or if only the last vertex set of k vertices we test happens to be a vertex cover), we will not know unless we tested all $\binom{n}{k} = \frac{n!}{k!(n-k)!}$ choices of k vertices. Now, for $k = {}^{n}/{}_{2}$, this binomial grows as fast as $O(2^n/n)$ and thus takes exponential time. However, this only proves that *this particular algorithm* takes exponential time. It is far from easy to actually prove that there *cannot exist* any algorithm that requires only sub-exponential time to decide VERTEX COVER. No such proof is known, and the establishment of a (correct) proof would be a *major* breakthrough in computer science.

As it turns out, proving exponential lower bounds is *very* hard. In fact, there are only a few decision problems that *provably* take worst-case exponential time to be solved. For only a few problems has it been possible to prove that no algorithm whatsoever can solve them in polynomial time; one such problem happens to be GENERALIZED CHESS (Fraenkel and Lichtenstein, 1981):

> GENERALIZED CHESS
> **Input:** An $n \times n$ chessboard, with an arbitrary number of pieces set on them (but one king each); the normal rules of chess apply save the "50-moves-rule" (i.e., 50 subsequent moves without a pawn being moved or a piece taken does *not* automatically result in a draw).
> **Question:** Does white have a winning strategy that always checkmates black in a finite number of moves?

For this problem it is possible to prove that any algorithm that solves it, necessarily takes worst-case exponential time (in n). For many, many other interesting problems for which no polynomial-time algorithm is known (such as VERTEX COVER, CLIQUE, INDEPENDENT SET, or DOMINATING SET as you have already encountered) no such proof has been produced, despite *many* efforts by leading researchers in the field of computer science. However, even if we cannot prove that VERTEX COVER, CLIQUE, INDEPENDENT SET, or DOMINATING SET cannot be decided in polynomial time, we *can* prove the following powerful statement regarding these (and literally hundreds of thousands of comparable problems): If we find a polynomial-time algorithm for *any* of them, there exists a polynomial-time algorithm for *all* of them. Likewise, should we be able to prove exponential-time lower bounds for *one* of them, this immediately leads to exponential-time lower bounds for *all* of them. The proof of this statement will take an additional concept, namely, that of the so-called *polynomial-time reduction*.

3.2   Polynomial-Time Reductions

Observe that sometimes you may have the intuition that a problem has no polynomial-time algorithm, but that you cannot prove it, like in Exercise 2.5.2.

What you may be able to prove, however, is that if one of the problems is polynomial-time computable, then so is another. The strategy that we use is to come up with an algorithm A that *translates* every instance of a particular decision problem D_1 into a corresponding instance of another decision problem D_2, and that takes polynomial time on every instance of D_1. This algorithm may be trivial or complex, but it must be such that every time the answer to D_1 is *yes*, the answer to D_2 is *yes*, and every time the answer to D_1 is *no*, the answer to D_2 is *no*. We call such an algorithm a *reduction* as it "reduces" the burden to solve D_1 to "merely" solving D_2: we can translate every instance i_1 of D_1 to a corresponding instance i_2 of D_2, solve i_2, and then output the answer to i_2 – by construction, the answer to i_2 is the same as the answer to i_1.

We will start by giving the formal definition of a polynomial-time reduction. Then we will guide you through an easy reduction, from CLIQUE to INDEPENDENT SET, and we will ask you to show that this is indeed a polynomial-time reduction.

DEFINITION 3.1 *Let $D : I \rightarrow \{yes, no\}$ be a decision problem and let $i \in I$ be an instance for D. We say i is a yes-instance if $D(i) = yes$ and a no-instance if $D(i) = no$.*

DEFINITION 3.2 *For two decision problems D_1 and D_2 we say that D_1 reduces to D_2, if there exists an algorithm A that transforms any instance i_1 of D_1 into an instance $i_2 = A(i_1)$ of D_2 such that i_2 is a yes-instance for D_2 if and only if i_1 is a yes-instance for D_1. We furthermore say the reduction is a polynomial-time reduction if the algorithm A runs in polynomial time. The notation $D_1 \leq_m^P D_2$ means that D_1 polynomial-time reduces to D_2. The "m" in this notation can be ignored for now; we will get back to it in Section 3.3.*

Stop and Think

Imagine you are studying a decision problem D_2 and you would like to know if it is solvable in polynomial time or not. You try, possibly for a long time, to come up with a polynomial-time algorithm, but so far you have failed to find one. You now have built up the intuition that a polynomial-time algorithm does not exist for solving D_2 and, if this is indeed the case, you would like to be able to prove this. Imagine further, that there is a problem D_1 for which it has already been shown that there exists no polynomial-time algorithm. How could you use polynomial-time reduction (as defined in Definition 3.2) to prove that D_2 also has no polynomial-time algorithm?

Polynomial-time reductions are very useful in relating the time complexity of a problem of interest to other problems. Let us assume (as in Definition 3.2) that D_1 polynomial-time reduces to D_2. Now the following two statements hold:

1. If D_2 can be decided in polynomial time, then so can D_1.
2. If D_1 cannot be decided in polynomial time, then D_2 cannot either.

Let us examine both claims. Assume we have a polynomial-time algorithm for D_2. How can we use that algorithm to solve D_1 in polynomial time? Well, given that D_1 polynomial-time reduces to D_2, we can first reduce D_1 to D_2. That can be done in polynomial time by definition. Then we solve D_2. As both *yes*- and *no*-answers to D_2 map onto *yes*- and *no*-answers to D_1, respectively, the answer to D_2 equals the answer to D_1. The other claim is a direct consequence: if we have proof that D_1 cannot be solved in polynomial time, then there cannot be any polynomial-time algorithm for D_2, otherwise we would arrive at a contradiction.

Take care not to swap D_1 and D_2 in these statements! Even if D_1 can be solved in polynomial time and D_1 polynomial-time reduces to D_2, that tells us *nothing* about the complexity of D_2! That may be best understood with an analogy. Say that there are two reasons why my garden might have gotten wet: either by rain or by watering. Now, from the statement "if it rained, my garden got wet" it logically follows that "if my garden did not get wet, it didn't rain." On the other hand, from the information that my garden got wet it does *not* follow that it rained, nor that it did not rain. We simply cannot tell. We will get back to this later on when we have covered more theoretical ground.

3.2.1   Reducing CLIQUE to INDEPENDENT SET

Now that we know the consequences of reducing D_1 to D_2, how can we come up with an algorithm doing the actual reduction, and how do we show that it is indeed a valid reduction? We will illustrate that process with a reduction from CLIQUE to INDEPENDENT SET. Recall the definitions of these decision problems:

CLIQUE
Input: A graph $G = (V, E)$ and an integer k.
Question: Does there exist a clique $V' \subseteq V$ such that $|V'| \leq k$? (Here a vertex set V' is called a *clique* if for all pairs of vertices $u, v \in V'$ there is an edge $(u, v) \in E$.)

INDEPENDENT SET
Input: A graph $G = (V, E)$ and a positive integer k.
Question: Does there exist an independent set $V' \subseteq V$ such that $|V'| \leq k$? (Here a vertex set V' is called an *independent set* if there exist no two vertices $u, v \in V'$ such that $(u, v) \in E$.)

Stop and Think

Think of these two problems. What is related between them and what is different? Think of a generic transformation that we can apply to every instance of CLIQUE such that it becomes an instance of INDEPENDENT SET. Does that transformation map both *yes*-instances and *no*-instances of CLIQUE to corresponding *yes*-instances and *no*-instances of INDEPENDENT SET? Can that transformation be done in polynomial time?

From these problem definitions it follows that a vertex set is a clique if *every* pair of two vertices in the set is connected; the set is an independent set if *no* pair of two vertices in the set is connected. Now how can we transform the input of CLIQUE to match this difference in the problem? The idea is easy, once you have thought of it: we transform each input to CLIQUE to an input to INDEPENDENT SET by "negating the edges": if there is an edge in the CLIQUE instance, we'll have the absence of an edge in the INDEPENDENT SET and vice versa. See Figure 3.1 for an example. Note the duality of both graphs: for each edge in the CLIQUE instance to the left, there is the absence of an edge in the INDEPENDENT SET instance to the right; for each missing edge in the CLIQUE instance, there is an edge in the INDEPENDENT SET instance. Observe that $\{a, b, c\}$ forms a clique in the left graph *and* an independent set in the right graph.

Practice 3.2.1 Argue why the previous observation also holds in general: let G be the graph of the CLIQUE instance and G' the graph that is obtained by

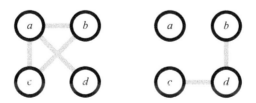

Figure 3.1   Example of transforming the input for a CLIQUE instance to the input for an INDEPENDENT SET instance.

"negating the edges" of G. Show that there is an independent set of size k in G', if and only if there is a clique of size k in G.

Practice 3.2.2   Argue that this transformation takes time polynomial in the size of G and thus is a polynomial-time reduction from CLIQUE to INDEPENDENT SET.

Practice 3.2.3   Show that the reduction is symmetrical: using the same reduction, we can prove that INDEPENDENT SET polynomial-time reduces to CLIQUE as well as CLIQUE polynomial-time reduces to INDEPENDENT SET.

In general, to show that a problem D_1 polynomial-time reduces to a problem D_2 by mathematical proof, all of the next proof steps have to be explicated:

1. Describe an algorithm A that transforms instances for D_1 into instances for D_2, possibly using an example (as we did in Figure 3.1).
2. Consider an arbitrary instance i_1 for D_1. Prove that $i_2 = A(i_1)$ is a *yes*-instance for D_2 *if and only if* i_1 is a *yes*-instance for D_1. The "if and only if" proof has two sub-steps:

   (a) Assume i_1 is a *yes*-instance for D_1. Show that then also i_2 is a *yes*-instance for D_2 (i.e., give a convincing argument).
   (b) Assume i_2 is a *yes*-instance for D_2. Show that then also i_1 is a *yes*-instance for D_1. (i.e., give a convincing argument). Or as an alternative to this sub-step: Assume i_1 is a *no*-instance for D_1. Show that then also i_2 is a *no*-instance for D_2.

3. Show that A runs in polynomial time.

Here, with *arbitrary instance* we mean that the proof must hold for *all* instances, but we consider just an unspecified one without loss of generality. It does *not* mean you can hand-craft an instance yourself and show that the proof holds *for that specific instance* (only)! Observe that we map all instances of D_1 to corresponding instances of D_2 by the transformation algorithm A. This need not necessarily be symmetrical: there may be instances of D_2 that do not map back to instances of D_1. However, if the reduction works both ways, then it is *symmetrical*, and there is indeed a mapping from all instances of D_2 to D_1, as well as the other way around. The reduction we saw earlier, from CLIQUE to INDEPENDENT SET, is indeed symmetrical; we will also encounter reductions that are not.

3.2.2 Reduction by Local Replacement

The transformation that we saw in the previous subsection used a technique that we call *local replacement*. In local replacement, we systematically transpose one aspect of the input of D_1 to a corresponding aspect of the input of D_2. For example, we transposed the graph edges in the input from "present" to "absent" and vice versa. Local replacement is one of the example techniques we will encounter in this chapter, the others being *restriction* and *component design* in the next subsections. A different example of a proof by local replacement is the following reduction from INDEPENDENT SET to VERTEX COVER. Recall the definition:

VERTEX COVER
Input: A graph $G = (V, E)$ and a positive integer k.
Question: Does there exist a vertex cover $V' \subseteq V$ such that $|V'| \le k$? (Here a vertex set V' is called a *vertex cover* if for every edge $(u, v) \in E$ we have $u \in V'$ or $v \in V'$.)

Now have a look at the INDEPENDENT SET instance at the right of Figure 3.1. Note that the nodes *outside* the independent set $\{a, b, c\}$ form a vertex cover: every edge in this graph is covered by the node $\{d\}$. This is no coincidence: if $V' \subseteq V$ is an independent set in G, then $V \setminus V'$ is a vertex cover in G. Note that a vertex set is a vertex cover if *every* edge in the graph is covered, that is, has at least one of its vertices in the set. As V' is an independent set, there are by definition no edges within V', but there may be "outgoing" edges (such as (b, d) in Figure 3.1). These edges have one of their endpoints in $V \setminus V'$. All other edges in G have both their endpoints in $V \setminus V'$. We conclude that if V' is an independent set, $V \setminus V'$ is a vertex cover. Thus if there exists an independent set of size k in G, there exists a vertex cover of size $|V| - k$ in G.

Practice 3.2.4 Present a polynomial-time reduction from INDEPENDENT SET to VERTEX COVER, following the steps mentioned earlier. Does the reduction also work as a reduction from VERTEX COVER to INDEPENDENT SET?

Practice 3.2.5 Argue why the following holds, given the reductions you have seen earlier and in the previous practice: if we have a polynomial-time algorithm for VERTEX COVER, then we have a polynomial-time algorithm for CLIQUE.

Practice 3.2.6 Present a polynomial-time reduction from CLIQUE to VERTEX COVER and vice versa.

We now have established that CLIQUE, INDEPENDENT SET, and VERTEX COVER are in some sense *equally hard*: if there exists a polynomial-time algorithm for one of them, there exists a polynomial-time algorithm for all three of these problems; likewise, if one of them is intractable, all three of them are.

The reductions discussed earlier were fairly simple. We will now show a more advanced reduction involving two variants of so-called *satisfiability* problems that, in essence, ask whether a logical formula is satisfiable, i.e., whether there exists a truth assignment to its Boolean variables such that the formula evaluates to *true*. Here, we consider formulas that are in *conjunctive normal form* (CNF), that is, that consist of a conjunction of clauses, where each clause is a disjunction of a subset of literals, where a literal is either a variable or the negation of that variable. An example of a formula in such a form is $(u_1 \vee \neg u_2) \wedge (u_2 \vee u_3) \wedge (u_3 \vee \neg u_1)$. Here, the variables are $U = \{u_1, u_2, u_3\}$ and the clauses are $C = \{(u_1 \vee \neg u_2), (u_2 \vee u_3), (u_3 \vee \neg u_1)\}$; the literals in the three clauses are respectively $\{u_1, \neg u_2\}$, $\{u_2, u_3\}$, and $\{u_3, \neg u_1\}$. We will reduce CNF-SAT to a more constrained variant 3SAT, defined as follows.

CNF-SAT
Input: A set of Boolean variables $U = \{u_1, \ldots, u_n\}$ and a set of clauses $C = \{c_1, \ldots, c_m\}$.
Question: Is there a truth assignment $t: U \to \{true, false\}$ such that all clauses C are satisfied?

3SAT
Input: A set of Boolean variables $U = \{u_1, \ldots, u_n\}$ and a set of clauses $C = \{c_1, \ldots, c_m\}$, where each clause has exactly three literals.
Question: Is there a truth assignment $t: U \to \{true, false\}$ such that all clauses C are satisfied?

We do local replacement by replacing every clause c_j in the CNF-SAT instance (which may have length $k = 1 \ldots n$) by a conjunction C_j of clauses in the 3SAT instance, introducing extra variables D where needed. In this, we distinguish four cases: $k = 1$, $k = 2$, $k = 3$, and $k \geq 4$. Let c_j denote an arbitrary clause in the CNF-SAT formula, and let $u_j^1, \ldots, u_j^k$ denote its literals.

$k = 1$ We introduce two dummy variables d_1 and d_2, and replace $c_j = (u_j^1)$ with the clauses $C_j = \{(u_j^1 \vee d_1 \vee d_2), (u_j^1 \vee d_1 \vee \neg d_2), (u_j^1 \vee \neg d_1 \vee d_2), (u_j^1 \vee \neg d_1 \vee \neg d_2)\}$. Note that a truth assignment t satisfies c_j if and only if it satisfies all clauses C_j: these clauses cannot be all simultaneously satisfied for any truth assignment to d_1 and d_2, unless u_j^1 evaluates to *true*.

$k = 2$ We introduce a single dummy variable d_1 and replace $c_j = (u_j^1 \vee u_j^2)$ with the clauses $C_j = \{(u_j^1 \vee u_j^2 \vee d_1), (u_j^1 \vee u_j^2 \vee \neg d_1)\}$. Again, c_j is satisfied by t if and only if all clauses C_j are satisfied by t: the dummy variable has no effect if either u_j^1 or u_j^2 evaluates to *true*, but it cannot satisfy both clauses in case both u_j^1 and u_j^2 evaluate to *false*.

$k = 3$ Nothing needs to be replaced here as c_j already contains exactly three literals.

$k \geq 4$ We introduce $k - 3$ dummy variables $d_1, \ldots, d_{k-3}$ and replace c_j with the clauses $C_j = \{(u_j^1 \vee u_j^2 \vee d_1), (\neg d_1 \vee u_j^3 \vee d_2), (\neg d_2 \vee u_j^4 \vee d_3), \ldots, (\neg d_{k-3} \vee u_j^{k-1} \vee u_j^k)\}$. Again, c_j is satisfied by t if and only if all clauses C_j are satisfied by t. If either of the literals $u_j^1, \ldots, u_j^k$ evaluates to *true*, we can set the dummy variables in such a way that all clauses are satisfied, but if all of these literals evaluate to *false*, no setting of the dummy variables can simultaneously satisfy all clauses.

Observe that we do only a polynomial amount of work, as every set of clauses C_j consists of a number of clauses which is polynomial in the number of literals in the original clause c_j. To be precise, the reduction can be done in $O(nm)$ as each of the m original clauses is replaced by at most $n-2$ new clauses. Let $t' : (U \cup D) \to \{true, false\}$ be a truth assignment that is constructed by augmenting t with a truth assignment to the variables in D. In every case we have that a truth assignment $t : U \to \{true, false\}$ satisfies c_j if and only if there is a truth assignment t' that simultaneously satisfies all clauses C_j. Thus, if there *exists* such a truth assignment t' for the CNF-SAT instance, there also exists a truth assignment t for the 3SAT instance. Hence, we have just shown that CNF-SAT polynomial-time reduces to 3SAT.

3.2.3 Reduction by Restriction

In the previous subsection we showed that CNF-SAT polynomial-time reduces to 3SAT. What about the other way around? It is easy to see that 3SAT is in fact a special case of CNF-SAT: each instance of 3SAT is also an instance of CNF-SAT. So, one (fairly easy) way of reducing D_1 to D_2 is by showing that D_1 is in fact a special case of D_2, or in other words, that D_2 is a more general problem that includes D_1. Sometimes, as with the reduction from 3SAT to CNF-SAT, this is immediately visible; sometimes, it may need a bit of rewriting. In this subsection we will give two problems for which it may not be immediately clear that one is a special case of the other. We start with the reduction from PARTITION to SUBSET SUM, defined as follows.

Partition
Input: A set of n elements $A = \{a_1, \ldots, a_n\}$ and a positive integer $s(a)$ associated with each $a \in A$.
Question: Is there a subset $A' \subset A$ such that $\sum_{a \in A'} s(a) = \sum_{a \in A \setminus A'} s(a)$?

Subset Sum
Input: A set of n elements $A = \{a_1, \ldots, a_n\}$, a positive integer $s(a)$ associated with each $a \in A$, and an integer k.
Question: Is there a subset $A' \subset A$ such that $\sum_{a \in A'} s(a) = k$?

Using these definitions, there is no direct relation between Partition and Subset Sum; but if we rewrite Partition a little bit, it becomes clear that Partition is in fact a special case of Subset Sum. Note that in the Partition problem we basically ask whether we can partition the set of elements in two subsets of equal weight, i.e., $\sum_{a \in A'} s(a) = \sum_{a \in A \setminus A'} s(a)$. But in that case, it also holds that $\sum_{a \in A'} s(a) = \sum_{a \in A \setminus A'} s(a) = \sum_{a \in A} s(a)/2$. So, the Partition problem is really identical to the Subset Sum problem with k fixed to $k = \sum_{a \in A} s(a)/2$!

So, you may have to do some rethinking and rewriting to cast one problem into a special case of another. A classical example is the reduction from Clique to Subgraph Isomorphism (see Figure 3.2):

Clique
Input: A graph $G = (V, E)$ and an integer k.
Question: Does there exist a clique $V' \subseteq V$ such that $|V'| \leq k$?

Subgraph Isomorphism
Input: Two graphs G and H.
Question: Is there a subgraph G' of G that is isomorphic to H? (Here two graphs G' and H are isomorphic if there is a mapping $m : V(G') \to V(H)$ such that $(u, v) \in E(G') \leftrightarrow (m(u), m(v)) \in E(H)$.)

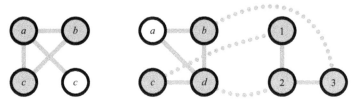

Figure 3.2   A graph with a clique of size 3 (left); an isomorphism from a subgraph G' of G to H (right).

Stop and Think

On first sight, these problems do not really resemble one other, but having a closer look at Figure 3.2 may provide a hint for how to rewrite CLIQUE in such a way as to make it a special case of SUBGRAPH ISOMORPHISM.

Now assume that H is in fact a complete graph of size k, that is, a graph with all its vertices connected. Then a subgraph of G is isomorphic to H if and only if G has a clique of size k. So, instead of the previous definition of CLIQUE, we now redefine it as follows:

CLIQUE revisited
Input: A graph G and a complete graph H with k vertices.
Question: Is there a subgraph G' of G that is isomorphic to H?

Now it is easy to see that CLIQUE is a special case of SUBGRAPH ISOMORPHISM and thus that CLIQUE polynomial-time reduces to SUBGRAPH ISOMORPHISM.

Lastly, we will show that we can reduce PARTITION to WEIGHTED MAX CUT. This reduction still uses restriction, but is somewhat more elaborate than the reduction from PARTITION to SUBSET SUM. We define WEIGHTED MAX CUT as follows:

WEIGHTED MAX CUT
Input: A weighted graph $G = (V, E)$ where a weight w_{ij} is associated with each edge $(i, j) \in E$; an integer W.
Question: Is there a cut S of G with weight W? (Here a *cut* S of a graph G is a subset $S \subseteq V$, and the weight of this cut is defined as $\sum_{i \in S, j \notin S} w(i, j)$.)

Again, it is not easy to see that PARTITION is a special case of WEIGHTED MAX CUT. We need to do some rephrasing of the input to PARTITION to let it "match" with the input to WEIGHTED MAX CUT. WEIGHTED MAX CUT deals with weighted graphs, rather than elements, so let's redefine PARTITION in terms of graphs. A has n elements that can be seen as a vertex in a graph; the integer $s(a)$ associated with each element $a \in A$ can be seen as the weight of the vertex. As WEIGHTED MAX CUT has weights defined on the *edges*, rather than on the vertices, we assume that the graph is complete, and we define the weight $c(i, j)$ of each edge (i, j) as $s(i) \cdot s(j)$. We further rephrase the problem definition slightly, to obtain the following PARTITION definition:

PARTITION revisited
Input: A complete graph $G = (V, E)$ with n nodes $V = \{v_1, \ldots, v_n\}$ and a positive integer $s(v)$ associated with each $v \in V$.
Question: Is there a subset $S \subset V$ such that $\sum_{v \in S} s(v) = \sum_{v \in V \setminus S} s(v)$?

Observe that, despite the rephrasing, nothing essential is changed in this problem definition. Now, the set S looks like a cut in the WEIGHTED MAX CUT problem.

Stop and Think

Let's pick a set $S \subset V$ and interpret it as a cut in the WEIGHTED MAX CUT problem. Given that G is a complete graph and we defined a weight $c(i, j) = s(i) \cdot s(j)$ on every edge (i, j), what would the weight of this cut be? Play with some toy examples and try to maximize the weight of the cut, selecting different subsets S.

The weight of a cut S is defined as the sum of the weight of all edges "going outside of the cut," that is, the weight of the cut S is $\sum_{i \in S, j \notin S} w(i, j) = \sum_{i \in S, j \notin S} s(i) \cdot s(j) = \sum_{i \in S} s(i) \cdot \sum_{j \notin S} s(j)$. This product is maximal if $\sum_{i \in S} s(i) = \sum_{j \notin S} s(j)$ (see Appendix A.6.2), that is, if $\sum_{i \in S} s(i) = \sum_{j \notin S} s(j) = \frac{1}{2} \sum_{i \in V} s(i)$. In fact, this weight is $(\frac{1}{2} \sum_{v \in V} s(v)) \cdot (\frac{1}{2} \sum_{v \in V} s(v)) = \frac{1}{4}(\sum_{v \in V} s(v))^2$. When can we obtain that weight? Exactly if there exists a set S such that $\sum_{v \in S} s(v) = \sum_{v \in V \setminus S} s(v)$, that is, if there exists a partition of the vertices V in two subsets with equal weight. Thus, PARTITION is a special case of WEIGHTED MAX CUT with $w_{ij} = s(i) \cdot s(j)$ and $W = \frac{1}{4}(\sum_{v \in V} s(v))^2$. This proves that PARTITION polynomial-time reduces to WEIGHTED MAX CUT.

3.2.4 Reduction by Component Design

The previous two techniques, local replacement and restriction, work in many cases. However, it may be the case that no such (relatively) straightforward reduction is possible. Then we may often rely on a powerful yet non-trivial technique called *component design*. The key idea is that we "build components" using the elements of D_2, in order to mimic the "behavior" of the instances of D_1. For example, in 3SAT, literals can be set to either *true* or *false*, literals are grouped by three in clauses, a clause is satisfied if at least one of its literals is satisfied, all clauses must be satisfiable by at least one truth assignment in a *yes* - instance, and there may be no truth assignment that simultaneously satisfies all clauses in a *no*-assignment.

We will illustrate this technique using a reduction from 3SAT to CLIQUE. Note that these two problems are quite different in nature, and local replacement does not seem to be of much help. What we will do is systematically construct a CLIQUE instance from an arbitrary 3SAT instance, that enforces the behavior of 3SAT instances described previously. Note that coming up with such a construction can be a highly creative process that more or less resembles completing a jigsaw puzzle, trying to make all pieces match.

3SAT
Input: A set of Boolean variables $U = \{u_1, \ldots, u_n\}$ and a set of clauses $C = \{c_1, \ldots, c_m\}$, where each clause has exactly three literals.
Question: Is there a truth assignment $t: U \to \{true, false\}$ such that all clauses C are satisfied?

CLIQUE
Input: A graph $G = (V, E)$ and an integer k.
Question: Does there exist a clique $V' \subseteq V$ such that $|V'| \leq k$?

We will demonstrate the construction using the example 3SAT instance (U, C), with $U = \{u_1, u_2, u_3\}$ and $C = \{(u_1 \lor u_2 \lor u_3), (\neg u_1 \lor \neg u_2 \lor u_3), (\neg u_1 \lor \neg u_2 \lor \neg u_3)\}$. You can verify that this is a *yes*-instance of 3SAT, take, e.g., the truth assignment $\{u_1 = true, u_2 = false, u_3 = false\}$. We will now construct a CLIQUE instance (G, k). For each literal u in each clause in (U, C), we have a vertex u in G. Each vertex u in G is connected to all other vertices that represent variables *in different clauses* that are not the negation of the literal associated with u. So, for example, the literal u_1 in the first clause would be connected with u_2 and u_3 in the second clause and with u_2 and u_3 in the third clause, but not with other variables. The resulting graph is depicted in Figure 3.3. Observe that there are only edges between vertices that represent literals in different clauses, and that there are no edges between vertices that are each other's negation. For example, there is no edge between u_1 and $\neg u_1$. These two properties reflect that in 3SAT we need to select one variable per clause that satisfies that clause, and that we cannot set a variable to *true* in one clause and *false* in another. Finally, we set k to the number of clauses in the 3SAT instance; in this case, $k = 3$. This enforces that *all* clauses must be satisfied. We claim that the thus-obtained graph has a k-clique if and only if (U, C) is satisfiable.

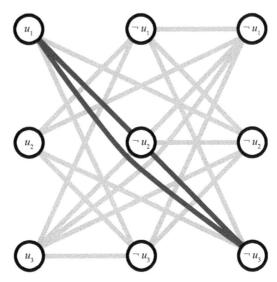

Figure 3.3   Construction used in the reduction from 3SAT to CLIQUE. Note that we
can set u_1 in the first clause to *true*, u_2 in the second clause to *false*, and
u_3 in the third clause to *false*; the corresponding nodes in the graph form
a 3-clique.

First, we show that *yes*-instances of 3SAT map onto *yes*-instances of CLIQUE.
Let (U,C) be such a *yes*-instance and let $t: U \rightarrow \{true, false\}$ be a satisfying
truth assignment to (U,C). Now, select vertices in G, one per clause, whose
corresponding literals evaluate to *true* when t is applied to that clause; for
example, for $t = \{u_1 = true, u_2 = false, u_3 = false\}$ we select u_1 from the
first clause, $\neg u_2$ from the second clause, and $\neg u_3$ from the third clause. These
vertices form a k-clique: they are from different clauses and none of them is
the negation of one of the others, so all these vertices are connected in G.

Second, we show that *yes*-instances of the thus-constructed CLIQUE problem
map onto *yes*-instances of 3SAT. Let (G,k) be such a *yes*-instance. Then, there
exists a k-clique in G and by the definition of the construction, all vertices
correspond to literals in different clauses, none of which is a negation of the
other. But that means that this k-clique represents a satisfying truth assignment
to (U,C).

Finally, we need to prove that this is indeed a polynomial-time reduction.
This is clear as we have as many vertices as literals in the clauses, and at most,
this number squared as edges in the graph. Thus, we do a polynomial amount
of work (i.e., $O(n^2)$) in the construction.

As a final reminder, we note that this reduction is not symmetrical. Obviously, there are many CLIQUE instances that are not the result of applying the reduction to a 3SAT instance. Thus, we cannot use this reduction to reduce CLIQUE to 3SAT. We have listed that reduction as an exercise in the Exercise section.

The last, and most challenging, reduction we will present here is a reduction from 3SAT to GRAPH 3-COLORABILITY. We will again use the running example 3SAT instance (U, C), with $U = \{u_1, u_2, u_3\}$ and $C = \{(u_1 \lor u_2 \lor u_3), (\neg u_1 \lor \neg u_2 \lor u_3), (\neg u_1 \lor \neg u_2 \lor \neg u_3)\}$.

3SAT
Input: A set of Boolean variables $U = \{u_1, \ldots, u_n\}$ and a set of clauses $C = \{c_1, \ldots, c_m\}$, where each clause has exactly three literals.
Question: Is there a truth assignment $t: U \to \{true, false\}$ such that all clauses C are satisfied?

GRAPH 3-COLORABILITY
Input: A graph $G = (V, E)$.
Question: Is there a three-coloring of the graph, i.e., an assignment $c : V \to \{c_1, c_2, c_3\}$ such that no vertices that share an edge have the same color?

We construct a graph G that is three-colorable if and only if the corresponding 3SAT instance is satisfiable. We need a "truth-setting-gadget" that ensures that every variable will be set to either *true* or *false*, a "clause-satisfying-gadget" that enforces that at least one of the literals in any clause satisfies that clause, and we need to enforce that all clauses are satisfied. For every variable u_i in U, we create two vertices u_i and $\neg u_i$ in G and connect them with an edge. We connect all these vertices with one of the vertices of a 3-clique. For convenience, we have labeled these vertices T, F, and C, and they connect via C. This is not a property of the reduction itself, but it helps in understanding the proof. The resulting subgraph for the example is shown in Figure 3.4.

Stop and Think

Assume that we color the vertices T, F, and C with the "colors" T, F, and C as their labels suggest. What colors can u_1 and $\neg u_1$ take? What about the other vertices?

This component effectively ensures that the vertices u_i and $\neg u_i$ can be colored as $\{T, F\}$ or $\{F, T\}$, respectively. That mimics that u_i can be set to *true* or *false*.

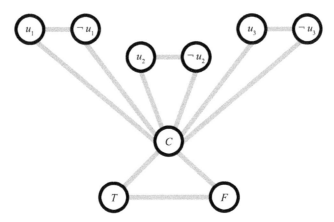

Figure 3.4   The "truth-setting-gadget" in the reduction. Note that every vertex
representing literals can be colored such that its color is the same as the
vertex labeled T or as the vertex labeled F.

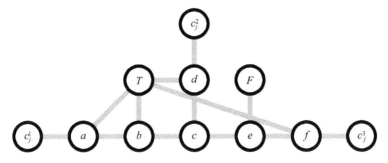

Figure 3.5   The "clause-satisfying-gadget" in the reduction. This subgraph can only
be colored with three colors if at least one of the vertices c_j^1, c_j^2, and c_j^3 is
colored with T.

Note that we could have replaced T, F, and C with any other color (like the
abstract c_1, c_2, and c_3) without changing the behavior of this subgraph: the
naming is just for our convenience.

We now add, for each clause c_j, a subgraph with six extra vertices, labeled
a to f. These vertices connect with each other, with the variable-vertices, and
with the vertices we labeled as T and F as depicted in Figure 3.5. Note that the
vertices labeled c_j^1, c_j^2, and c_j^3 refer to the first, second, and last literal occurring
in the clause. So, for example, the subgraph corresponding to the first clause in
the example would connect a to u_1, d to u_2, and f to u_3. The other subgraphs
(for the other two clauses) connect to $\neg u_1$, $\neg u_2$, and u_3; and $\neg u_1$, $\neg u_2$, and
$\neg u_3$, respectively.

We claim that at least *one* of the variables c_j^1, c_j^2, and c_j^3 must be assigned the color T for this subgraph to be validly colorable. Say, for example, c_j^1 is colored T and c_j^2 and c_j^3 are colored F. Then, to maintain a valid coloring, d and f need to be colored C, e will be colored T, and c, b, and a will be colored F, C, and F, respectively. That is a valid coloring. On the other hand, if all three variables c_j^1, c_j^2, and c_j^3 are colored F, then a, d, and f need to be colored C, b and e need to be colored F and T, respectively, and we have no color left for c. You can check for yourself that each of the remaining six colorings is valid.

So, we showed that every subgraph can be validly colored with three colors if and only if the corresponding clause has at least one of its literals evaluating to *true*. All subgraphs – and thus the entire graph – can be validly colored with three colors if and only if all clauses have one of its literals evaluating to *true*. Since literals that are the same across clauses are represented by one and the same vertex in G, we have essentially shown that G is colorable with three colors if and only if (U, C) is satisfiable. Note that we have $2n + 3$ vertices that represent the n variables, and $6m$ vertices that represent the m clauses, so we need only polynomial time in this reduction. Having seen this reduction, you might understand why these component design proofs are sometimes referred to as *the art of gadgeteering*.

Observe that we now have seen a whole chain of polynomial-time reductions: from CNF-SAT, to 3SAT, to CLIQUE, to INDEPENDENT SET, to VERTEX COVER, and also from 3SAT to GRAPH 3-COLORABILITY, from CLIQUE to SUBGRAPH ISOMORPHISM, and from PARTITION to SUBSET SUM. There exists also a known chain of reductions from 3SAT to PARTITION via 3D MATCHING: these reductions use component design and are even more complicated than the reduction from 3SAT to GRAPH 3-COLORABILITY. We also saw some of the reductions the other way around. So, it appears that all of these problems are equally hard: either all of them can be solved in polynomial time or none of them. In the next chapter we will see that there is a whole class of problems, all with no polynomial-time algorithm known (or assumed to exist) for which this property holds.

3.3   *A More Formal View on Reductions

Recall that we denoted a polynomial-time reduction from D_1 to D_2 as $D_1 \leq_m^P$ D_2. This reduction is only one specific type of a range of reductions: in particular, it is called the *many-one* reduction – hence the "m"! It is quite a restricted reduction as there is a fixed order in which the steps of the reduction take place: we take an arbitrary instance i_1 of D_1, we then do some polynomial-time computation on i_1, thus obtaining $i_2 = A(i_1)$, and then we "feed" i_2 to D_2 and it is out of our hands: we are not allowed to touch the result any more. If D_2 answers *yes*, D_1 answers *yes*, no questions asked. Polynomial-time many-one reductions are also called Karp reductions, after the computer scientist Richard Karp who first used them to relate problems such as VERTEX COVER and CLIQUE.

In contrast, a polynomial-time *Turing* reduction, named after Alan Turing and denoted as $D_1 \leq_T^P D_2$, allows polynomial-time computations which use D_2 like a subroutine, feeding it inputs multiple times and continuing calculations based on the output. In particular, in a Turing reduction we are allowed to *change* the output once we receive it from D_2. These reductions, also called Cook reductions after Stephen Cook, whom we will encounter in the next chapter, are more powerful in the sense that they can relate problems that a many-one reduction cannot. For example, have a look at the following problem:

CNF-UNSAT
Input: A set of Boolean variables $U = \{u_1, \ldots, u_n\}$ and a set of clauses $C = \{c_1, \ldots, c_m\}$.
Question: Are there no truth assignments $t: U \to \{true, false\}$ such that all clauses C are satisfied?

This is a decision problem, like the previous ones we encountered in this chapter, but it is different: instead of asking whether there is a vertex cover of size at most k, a clique of size at least k, a satisfying truth assignment, an even partition etcetera, we ask for the *non-existence* of any satisfying truth assignment. This intuitively seems like a different sort of problem, and indeed, we cannot (under the assumption that NP $\neq$ co-NP, see Section 4.4.2) reduce any of the previous problems to CNF-UNSAT using a polynomial-time many-one reduction. However, it is trivial to reduce CNF-SAT to CNF-UNSAT using a Turing reduction.

Stop and Think

Assume you have an algorithm for deciding CNF-UNSAT. How could you use this as a subroutine in an algorithm for deciding CNF-SAT? Don't be afraid of doing something trivial!

The simplest algorithm for deciding CNF-SAT would then be something like:

Algorithm 3.1 Decide whether a CNF formula is satisfiable.

CNF-Sat(U, C)

1: **if** *CNF-UnSat(U, C) = yes* **then**
2:     **return** *no*
3: **else**
4:     **return** *yes*
5: **end if**

Now note that this surely counts as a Turing reduction, but it is by no means a many-one reduction, as we change the output after feeding the input to CNF-UNSAT– even just reversing the output is not allowed in many-one reductions. In the next chapter we will briefly have another look at problems like CNF-UNSAT.

3.4   Exercises

Exercise 3.4.1   See the following problems. Present a polynomial-time reduction using *restriction*.

(a) from MAX CUT to WEIGHTED MAX CUT, and
(b) from MAX CUT to COHERENCE, and
(c) from CONSISTENT COHERENCE to COHERENCE, and
(d) from HITTING COVER to MINIMUM SET COVER, and
(e) from VERTEX COVER to HITTING COVER, and
(f) from SUBSET SUM to KNAPSACK, and
(g) from CNF-SAT to SATISFIABILITY.
(h) from SATISFIABILITY to CONSTRAINT SATISFACTION.

WEIGHTED MAX CUT
Input: A weighted graph $G = (V, E)$ where a weight w_{ij} is associated with each edge $(i, j) \in E$; an integer W.
Question: Is there a cut S of G with weight W? (Here a *cut* S of a graph G is a subset $S \subseteq V$, and the weight of this cut is defined as $\sum_{i \in S, j \notin S} w(i, j)$.)

MAX CUT

Input: An graph $G = (V, E)$ and a positive integer k.

Question: Does there exist a partition of V into sets A and B such that the number of edges in $\text{Cut}_G(A, B) \geq k$, where $\text{Cut}_G(A, B) = \{(u, v) \in E : u \in A \text{ and } v \in B\}$?

COHERENCE

Input: A network $N = (P, C)$, where $C = C^+ \cup C^-$ is a set of positive and negative constraints and $C^+ \cap C^- = \emptyset$, an integer number k.

Question: Does there exist a truth assignment $T : P \to \{\textit{true}, \textit{false}\}$ that satisfies at least k constraints in C?

CONSISTENT COHERENCE

Input: A network $N = (P, C)$, where $C = C^+ \cup C^-$ is a set of positive and negative constraints and $C^+ \cap C^- = \emptyset$.

Question: Does there exist a truth assignment $T : P \to \{\textit{true}, \textit{false}\}$ that satisfies all constraints in C? (Here a constraint $(p, q) \in C^+$ is *satisfied* if $T(p) = T(q)$ and a constraint $(p, q) \in C^-$ is *satisfied* if $T(p) \neq T(q)$.)

HITTING COVER

Input: A universe U of elements and a collection S of subsets of U; an integer k.

Question: Does U have a hitting set $H \subseteq S$ of size at most k? (Here, a hitting set is a subset of U that contains at least one element of every set in S.)

VERTEX COVER

Input: A graph $G = (V, E)$ and a positive integer k.

Question: Does there exist a vertex cover $V' \subseteq V$ such that $|V'| \leq k$? (Here a vertex set V' is called a *vertex cover* if for every edge $(u, v) \in E$ we have $u \in V'$ or $v \in V'$.)

MINIMUM SET COVER

Input: A universe U of elements and a collection S of subsets of U; an integer k.

Question: Does U have a set cover $C \subseteq S$ of size at most k? (Here, a set cover is a subset of the collection such that the union of the sets in C equals U.)

SUBSET SUM

Input: A set of n elements $A = \{a_1, \ldots, a_n\}$, a positive integer $s(a)$ associated with each $a \in A$, and an integer k.

Question: Is there a subset $A' \subset A$ such that $\sum_{a \in A'} s(a) = k$?

KNAPSACK

Input: A set of n elements $A = \{a_1, \ldots, a_n\}$, a positive integer $c(a)$ ("cost") and a positive integer $w(a)$ ("weight") associated with each $a \in A$, and integers C and W.

Question: Is there a subset $A' \subset A$ such that $\sum_{a \in A'} c(a) \geq C$, yet $\sum_{a \in A'} w(a) \leq W$?

CNF-SAT

Input: A set of Boolean variables $U = \{u_1, \ldots, u_n\}$ and a set of clauses $C = \{c_1, \ldots, c_m\}$.

Question: Is there a truth assignment $t: U \to \{true, false\}$ such that all clauses C are satisfied?

SATISFIABILITY

Input: A Boolean formula ϕ with variables $V = \{v_1, \ldots, v_n\}$.

Question: Is there a truth assignment $t: V \to \{true, false\}$ that satisfies ϕ?

CONSTRAINT SATISFACTION

Input: A set of variables $V = \{V_1, \ldots, V_n\}$, a set $D = \{D_1, \ldots, D_n\}$ of domains of V (describing the values that each variable can take), and a set $C = \{C_1, \ldots, C_m\}$ of constraints. Each constraint c_j is a pair (V_j, R_j), where $V_j \subseteq V$ is a subset of k variables in V and R_j is a k-ary relation on the corresponding domains $D_j \subseteq D$.

Question: Is there a value assignment $t: V_i \to d \in D_i$ for each $V_i \in V$ and $D_i \in D$ such that every constraint $C_j \in C$ is satisfied?

Exercise 3.4.2   See the CLUSTERING and WEIGHTED MAX CUT problems that follow. Present a polynomial-time reduction from WEIGHTED MAX CUT to CLUSTERING using *restriction*. Hint: set $k = 2$.

CLUSTERING
Input: A set X with n elements, an integer distance measure $d(x, y)$ for $x, y \in X$, and integers c and k.
Question: Is there a partition of X into k clusters $C_1, \ldots, C_k$ such that the sum of all *total cluster distances* is smaller than or equal to c? (Here, a *total cluster distance* of a cluster C_i is defined as the sum of all pairwise distances $d(x, y)$ for all $xy \in C_i$.)

WEIGHTED MAX CUT
Input: A weighted graph $G = (V, E)$, where a weight w_{ij} is associated with each edge $(i, j) \in E$; an integer W.
Question: Is there a cut S of G with weight W? (Here a *cut* S of a graph G is a subset $S \subseteq V$, and the weight of this cut is defined as $\sum_{i \in S, j \notin S} w(i, j)$.)

Exercise 3.4.3   See the problems that follow. Present a polynomial-time reduction from VERTEX COVER to DOMINATING SET using *local replacement*.

VERTEX COVER
Input: A graph $G = (V, E)$ and a positive integer k.
Question: Does there exist a vertex cover $V' \subseteq V$ such that $|V'| \leq k$? (Here a vertex set V' is called a *vertex cover* if for every edge $(u, v) \in E$ we have $u \in V'$ or $v \in V'$.)

DOMINATING SET
Input: An graph $G = (V, E)$ and a positive integer k.
Question: Does there exist a dominating set $V' \subseteq V$ such that $|V'| \leq k$? (Here a vertex set V' is called a dominating set if for every vertex $v \in V$ either $v \in V'$ or there is an edge (u, v) with $u \in V'$.)

Exercise 3.4.4   In Subsection 3.2.4 we proposed to reduce CLIQUE to 3SAT with a polynomial-time reduction using *component design*. One possible reduction uses the path from CLIQUE, to SUBGRAPH ISOMORPHISM, to CNF-SAT, to 3SAT. As we have already established that CLIQUE $\leq_m^P$ SUBGRAPH ISOMORPHISM and that CNF-SAT $\leq_m^P$ 3SAT, it remains to prove that SUBGRAPH ISOMORPHISM $\leq_m^P$ CNF-SAT.

SUBGRAPH ISOMORPHISM
Input: Two graphs G and H.
Question: Is there a subgraph G' of G that is isomorphic to H?
(Here two graphs G' and H are isomorphic if there is a mapping
$m : V(G') \rightarrow V(H)$ such that $(u,v) \in G' \leftrightarrow (m(u), m(v)) \in H$.)

CNF-SAT
Input: A set of Boolean variables $U = \{u_1, \ldots, u_n\}$ and a set of
clauses $C = \{c_1, \ldots, c_m\}$.
Question: Is there a truth assignment $t: U \rightarrow \{true, false\}$ such that
all clauses C are satisfied?

We construct a CNF formula that simulates a mapping from G' to H. That
is, the CNF formula is satisfiable, if and only if there exists a mapping m:
$V(G') \rightarrow V(H)$ satisfying the properties. Each variable in the CNF formula
corresponds to the mapping of one vertex in H to one vertex in G; we set
that variable (say $u_{h,g}$) to *true* if and only if the vertex v_h in H maps to the
vertex v_g in G.

(a) How many variables $u_{h,g}$ do we need? Check that this amount is polyno-
mial in $|G|$ and $|H|$.

Now, we need four groups of clauses, each group enforcing a particular
property of m. In particular, we need to enforce that:

- A vertex of H cannot map to more than one vertex of G. That means, $u_{h,g}$
  and $u_{h,g'}$ cannot both be set to *true*.
- A vertex of H maps to at least one vertex of G. So, for any vertex V_h,
  there exists a vertex V_g such that $u_{h,g}$ must be set to *true*.
- No two vertices of H can map to the same vertex of G. That means, $u_{h,g}$
  and $u_{h',g}$ cannot both be set to *true*.
- If $u_{h,g}$ and $u_{h',g'}$ are both set to *true*, then there must be an edge (h, h') in
  H and an edge (g, g') in G. So, if one of these edges is present in the one
  graph but not in the other, then either $u_{h,g}$ or $u_{h',g'}$ must be set to *false*.

(b) Construct, using indices and the $\forall$ operator, sets of clauses for each of
these four constraints.
(c) Show that you have added a polynomial number of clauses.
(d) Show that indeed this CNF formula evaluates to *true* for a particular truth
setting t to the variables $u_{h,g}$ if and only if m is an isomorphic mapping
from H to G.

Exercise 3.4.5   See the STEINER TREE IN GRAPHS problem that follows. We
will reduce MINIMUM SET COVER to STEINER TREE IN GRAPHS using
component design.

> STEINER TREE IN GRAPHS
> **Input:** A weighted undirected graph $G = (V, E)$, a subset $V' \subseteq V$,
> and an integer l.
> **Question:** Is there a subtree $T = (V_T, E_T)$ of G such that $V' \subseteq V_T$
> with total weight $w(E_T) < l$?

We take an instance $\{U, S, k\}$ of MINIMUM SET COVER and transform it into
a STEINER TREE IN GRAPHS instance $\{G, V', l\}$. For each element u_i in U we
add a vertex u_i in V. For each element S_j in S we add a another vertex S_j in
V; finally we add a unique vertex u_0. We add an edge (u_0, S_j) for every S_j,
and we add edges (u_i, S_j) if and only if the element u_i is contained in the
subset S_j. The weight of (u_0, S_j) equals 1 and the weight of the edges (u_i, S_j)
equals $|U| + 1$. We define $V' = \{u_0\} \bigcup_i \{u_i\}$ and $l = |U|(|U| + 1) + k$.

(a) Construct the graph that corresponds to the MINIMUM SET COVER instance
    $U = \{a, b, c, d, e\}$, $S = \{S_1, S_2, S_3, S_4\}$ where $S_1 = \{a, c, d\}$, $S_2 = \{b, e\}$,
    $S_3 = \{a, e\}$, and $S_4 = \{c\}$.
(b) Observe that $\{S_1, S_2\}$ is a minimum set cover for $\{U, S\}$. What is the
    corresponding STEINER TREE IN GRAPHS instance? Show that this is
    indeed a *yes*-instance.
(c) Show that more in general the following holds. If $\{U, S\}$ has a set cover
    S' of at most k subsets of S, then there exists a sub-tree T for the
    corresponding STEINER TREE IN GRAPHS instance of cost at most $l = |U|(|U| + 1)$.
(d) Show also the other way around: if the constructed STEINER TREE IN
    GRAPHS instance has a sub-tree T of cost at most $l = |U|(|U| + 1)$, then in
    the original MINIMUM SET COVER instance $\{U, S\}$ there exists a set cover
    S' of at most k subsets of S.
(e) Show that this reduction takes polynomial time.

3.5   Further Reading

Since the 1970s or so, there are now literally thousands of reductions known.
Using CNF-SAT as a starting point, Turing award winner Richard M. Karp
was the first to employ this technique to show that 21 well known problems,
for which no polynomial-time algorithm was known, were as least as hard as

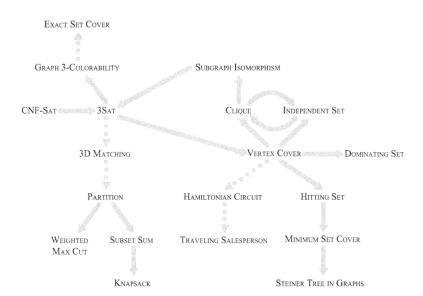

Figure 3.6   An overview of most of the reductions you have encountered so far, including their relationships. The dotted reductions have not been shown here. The reduction from 3SAT to 3D MATCHING to PARTITION and the reduction from VERTEX COVER to HAMILTONIAN CIRCUIT are covered in Garey and Johnson (1979). The reduction from HAMILTONIAN CIRCUIT to TRAVELING SALESPERSON (introduced in Chapter 4) is an example of a reduction by restriction. The reduction from GRAPH 3-COLORABILITY to EXACT SET COVER is covered in Karp's seminal paper (Karp, 1972). Note that the reduction from EXACT SET COVER to STEINER TREE IN GRAPHS in this paper happens to be incorrect; we discussed a corrected reduction from MINIMUM SET COVER in the exercises.

CNF-SAT. Many of these problems you have already encountered in this and the previous chapters. The chain of reductions depicted in Figure 3.6 relates most of these problems using reductions we have illustrated in this Chapter. A famous list of such reductions can be found in the seminal book of Garey and Johnson (1979).

4 Classical Complexity Classes

In this chapter we introduce the classical complexity classes P and NP, where P consists of decision problems that are solvable in polynomial time and NP consists of decision problems for which *yes*-instances are verifiable in polynomial time. We show that the latter problem class contains many problems for which it is conjectured that no polynomial-time algorithm exists. We introduce the formal notions of NP-hardness and NP-completeness to show that a problem is as least as hard as the hardest problems in NP, and we describe why NP-hard problems are considered to be intractable (i.e., not computable in polynomial time). We explain how one can prove that a problem is a member of either P or NP, and how one can use the technique of polynomial-time reduction, introduced and practiced in Chapter 3, to prove NP-hardness and NP-completeness.

4.1 Traveling on a Tight Budget

We start this chapter with an introduction of two decision problems that we will use as running examples in this chapter: The TRAVELING SALESPERSON (or TSP) problem (Figure 4.1) and the related BUDGET CHECK problem.

TRAVELING SALESPERSON (decision version)
Input: A set S of cities and a set C of travel costs between cities, that is, for each pair a and b of cities there is a cost associated with travel from a to b. Further, there is a budget constraint B.
Question: Does there exist an itinerary I visiting all cities – starting and ending in the same city and visiting each city exactly once – such that the total incurred cost does not exceed B?

BUDGET CHECK
Input: A set S of cities and a set C of travel costs between cities, that is, for each pair a and b of cities there is a cost associated with travel from a to b. Further, there is a budget constraint B, and a suggested itinerary I.
Question: Is the travel cost of the suggested itinerary within budget B?

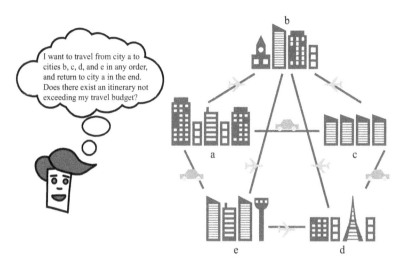

Figure 4.1   The TRAVELING SALESPERSON problem. Adapted from Scott, Stege, and van Rooij (2011).

Figure 4.2   BUDGET CHECK is easy to solve. Adapted from Scott et al. (2011).

Stop and Think

1. Observe that the two problems are related. What is the difference? Intuitively, try to think about the impact of that difference on the time complexity of these problems. Which one appears to be harder, and why?

2. Think of a possible algorithm for solving the two problems. What characterizes these algorithms?

Deciding BUDGET CHECK is rather straightforward: add the costs of the travels suggested by the itinerary I, and check whether that total cost does not exceed B (Figure 4.2). This simple strategy has a running time of $O(n)$ for n cities.

Figure 4.3   TRAVELING SALESPERSON seems harder to solve. Adapted from Scott et al. (2011).

Solving TRAVELING SALESPERSON, however, is not that straightforward. There seems to be no other way of deciding whether an itinerary I with costs not exceeding B exists, other than systematically generating candidate itineraries and checking their costs, as we did in BUDGET CHECK: in a sense, using BUDGET CHECK as a subroutine to check whether a given itinerary exceeds B (Figure 4.3).

Stop and Think

Assume there are n cities. How many possible itineraries are there that start in one of them, visit all other cities, and return?

When generating itineraries, we are essentially generating *permutations* of the cities. As it does not matter for the costs in which city we start (verify this!) we have $(n - 1) \times (n - 2) \times \ldots \times 2 \times 1 = (n - 1)$ different itineraries to check: a number which is non-polynomial in n. As each check takes $O(n)$, this algorithm takes non-polynomial time. Can we do significantly better than that, i.e., solve TRAVELING SALESPERSON in polynomial time? Honestly, we do not know – in fact, no one knows for sure – but there are very strong reasons to think that we cannot. The reason is that this problem is NP-hard. In this chapter, building on what we discussed in the previous chapter on polynomial-time reductions, we will guide you through the theory of NP-hardness. In the subsequent sections we will introduce the complexity classes P and NP, tell you what is *known* about their relationship and what is generally *assumed* about their relationship, and how we can use the reductions from the previous chapter to define when a problem is NP-hard.

4.2   The Classes P and NP

Before we can explain what "NP-hard" means we need to cover some ground first. We start by introducing the complexity classes P and NP. Recall the definition of decision problems from Chapter 2. We distinguish *yes-* and *no-*instances of these problems:

DEFINITION 4.1   *Let D: $I \rightarrow$ {yes,no} be a decision problem and let $i \in I$ be an instance of D. We say i is a yes-instance if $D(i) = yes$ and a no-instance if $D(i) = no$.*

We will sometimes partition the instances I of a decision problem D into *yes-*instances I_{yes} and *no-*instances I_{no}, and will refer to arbitrary instances in either class as $i_{yes} \in I_{yes}$, respectively $i_{no} \in I_{no}$. Using these definitions we can define P and NP as follows:

DEFINITION 4.2   P *is the class of decision problems D that are solvable in polynomial time. More formally,* P *is the class of decision problems $D: I \rightarrow$ {yes,no} for which there exists an algorithm with worst-case time complexity $O(|i|^c)$ (for a constant c) that can compute whether $D(i) = yes$ or $D(i) = no$ for every instance $i \in I$.*

DEFINITION 4.3   NP *is the class of decision problems D for which there exist a polynomial-time verifiable proof for yes-instances i_{yes}. More formally,* NP *is the class of decision problems $D: I \rightarrow$ {yes,no} for which there exists an algorithm with worst-case time complexity $O(|i_{yes}|^c)$ (for a constant c) that can verify (using a so-called* certificate *or* witness *[w] provided with the input i_{yes}) that $D(i_{yes}, w) = yes$ for every yes-instance $i_{yes} \in I_{yes}$.*

It is easy to show that BUDGET CHECK is in P: we have already seen that it takes $O(n)$ time to decide BUDGET CHECK, and thus it is solvable in polynomial time. We will show that TRAVELING SALESPERSON is in NP. Before we can do so, we need to elaborate a bit more on the concept *polynomial-time verifiable proof*.

4.2.1   Polynomial-Time Verifiable Proofs

Have a look at the following (somewhat artificial) problem:

Three Divisors
Input: A natural number n.
Question: Does n have at least three prime divisors other than 1 and n itself?

Suppose someone claims: "17,917 is a *yes*-instance of Three Divisors!" Making claims such as these is easy, but are they true? Well, you *really* don't want to check all sets of three prime numbers between 1 and 17,917 to check whether their product equals 17,917. However, your job would be considerably easier if this claim was accompanied by the three numbers 19, 23, and 41, as it is far more easy to check that $19 \times 23 \times 41 = 17,917$. Well, at least one can do it – even using paper and pencil – in time, polynomial in the number of digits of 17,917. We call $\{19, 23, 41\}$ a *certificate* or *witness* of 17,917 being a *yes*-instance of Three Divisors. Because there exists such a certificate for *every yes*-instance of Three Divisors, *yes*-instances of Three Divisors are polynomial-time verifiable.

Stop and Think

What about Traveling Salesperson? Are *yes*-instances to Traveling Salesperson polynomial-time verifiable? And if so, what could be a suitable certificate for this problem? "Verify" your answer with Figure 4.4.

Indeed, *yes*-instances to Traveling Salesperson are polynomial-time verifiable: A suitable certificate would be an itinerary It that one can check in polynomial time to cost no more than B. Thus, Traveling Salesperson is in NP. It is not obvious, however, that *no*-instances to Traveling Salesperson are polynomial-time verifiable, as Figure 4.5 suggests.

Figure 4.4   Yes-answers to the Traveling Salesperson problem can be verified in polynomial time, with the use of a suitable certificate. In this case, the certificate is an itinerary with total costs within the budget that was set. Adapted from Scott et al. (2011).

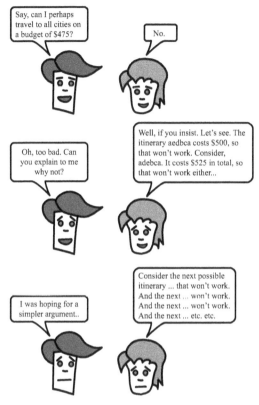

Figure 4.5   No-answers to the TRAVELING SALESPERSON problem may not have simple (i.e., polynomial-time verifiable) proofs. Adapted from Scott et al. (2011).

Stop and Think

And what about BUDGET CHECK? And in general: Is there a polynomial-time verifiable certificate for *yes*-instances of problems that are polynomial-time computable (i.e., in P)?

Yes, BUDGET CHECK has such a polynomial-time verifiable certificate. In fact, *every* certificate suffices for the simple reason that BUDGET CHECK, like any other problem in P, doesn't need to use its certificate. It can just *compute* in polynomial time whether the answer is *yes*, leading to the following trivial verification algorithm:

Algorithm 4.1 A polynomial-time verification algorithm for problems in P

$Verify(i_{yes}, w)$

  1: Throw away w
  2: $d \leftarrow D(i_{yes})$
  3: **if** $d == yes$ **then**
  4:     **return** "OK - fair enough."
  5: **else**
  6:     **return** "Hey! You don't fool around with *me!*"
  7: **end if**

Given that every problem in P has a polynomial-time verifiable certificate for *yes*-instances, every problem in P is also in NP, hence we know that P $\subseteq$ NP. We assume, but do not know for sure, that the inclusion is strict, that is, that P is really a strict subset of NP and that there are decision problems in NP that are not in P.

4.2.2   In P and/or NP, That Is the Question

Given a particular decision problem, how can one prove membership of one of these two classes P and NP? Or, maybe just as interesting, *disprove* membership? Actually, proving membership is at least conceptually easy: A decision problem is in P if there is an algorithm that can solve it in polynomial time; it is in NP if there is an algorithm that, using a certificate c that is provided together with the input i_{yes}, can verify *yes*-instances in polynomial time. So, we "only" need to come up with a polynomial-time algorithm – that will suffice to show the *existence* of such an algorithm. We call such a proof a *constructive* proof: We show that there exists an algorithm by actually constructing such an algorithm. It is more or less the formal equivalent of proving the existence of Nessie, the Loch Ness resident monster, by escorting her to the Rare and Endangered Species office. Note that it is not *necessary* to actually construct such algorithm: A non-constructive proof of existence is also sufficient (as long as it is a formal, convincing proof – as in the Nessie case, a blurred photograph will not suffice). We may thus be able to prove that a decision problem is solvable in polynomial time, *without having any clue how to actually do so.*

Disproving membership of P and NP, however, is much more complicated, as we already hinted at in Section 2.4. To show that a decision problem is not in P (or NP) one needs to give a super-polynomial lower bound for solving (or verifying) the problem at hand. As already illustrated in Section 2.4, we deeply suspect that VERTEX COVER cannot be solved in polynomial time, but the best lower bound we have is $O(m)$, which is far from super-polynomial.

Stop and Think

What if we can come up with a proof of membership in NP (i.e., a polynomial-time verifiable certificate), and a proof of non-membership in P (i.e., a super-polynomial lower bound)?

If one can show that a decision problem can be verified in polynomial time, but not solved in polynomial time, one has effectively proven that $P \neq NP$. In Section 4.2.3 we will see that this would be a *major*, and quite profitable, breakthrough in theoretical computer science.

Let's give a few examples of a proof of membership of problems in P and NP. Have a look at the following two related problems, ADDITIVE SUBSET CHOICE and BINARY SUBSET CHOICE, that we introduced in Chapter 1:

ADDITIVE SUBSET CHOICE
Input: A set $X = \{x_1, x_2, ..., x_n\}$ of n available items. For every item $x \in X$ there is an associated integer value $u(x)$. We also have an integer k.
Question: Is there a subset $S \subseteq X$, such that $u(S) = \sum_{x \in S} u(x) > k$?

BINARY SUBSET CHOICE
Input: A set $X = \{x_1, x_2, ..., x_n\}$ of n available items. For every item $x \in X$ there is an associated integer value $u(x)$ and for every pair of items (x_i, x_j) there is an associated integer value $\delta(x_i, x_j)$. We also have an integer k.
Question: Is there a subset $S \subseteq X$, such that $u(S) = \sum_{x \in S} u(x) + \sum_{x, y \in S} \delta(x, y) > k$?

Note that "integers" in these problems can be either negative or positive. For ADDITIVE SUBSET CHOICE, the problem is easy if $k < 0$: then the trivial answer is the empty set $\emptyset$. In case $k > 0$, observe that items x that have a negative value $u(x)$ can never contribute to a solution. In order to solve ADDITIVE SUBSET CHOICE, we just add items x with positive values $u(x)$ to A until either the sum $u(A) > k$ (in which case we answer *yes*) or until we run out of items with a positive value (in which case we answer *no*). We just need to consider every item once, hence, this is a polynomial-time algorithm; ADDITIVE SUBSET CHOICE is in P.

For BINARY SUBSET CHOICE it is not obvious how to decide whether there is a solution. Because of the *interaction* δ between two items, any item x with a positive value we add can indeed lower $u(A)$ overall because of a negative interaction $\delta(x, y)$ for some item y already in the set. Basically, we cannot do much better than considering each subset $A \subseteq V$ of items. One can show that there are 2^n such subsets, and a brute-force search over all subsets would take exponential time. However, once we are *given* a subset A of items (as a certificate) it is not hard to show that $\sum_{x \in A} u(x) + \sum_{x, y \in A} \delta(x, y) > k$: There are at most n elements in A and at most $n \times n$ interactions between any two elements in A, so we need to add at most $n^2 + n$ values and check whether the sum exceeds k. Hence, BINARY SUBSET CHOICE is in NP.

Practice 4.2.1 See the decision problems that follow. Are they in P? In NP? If you think they are not, can you give an argument for that intuition?

MINIMUM SPANNING TREE
Input: An edge-weighted graph $G = (V, E)$, an integer k.
Question: Is there a spanning tree T of G such that the sum of the weights on the edges in T is smaller than k?

CONSISTENT COHERENCE
Input: A network $N = (P, C)$, where $C = C^+ \cup C^-$ is a set of positive and negative constraints and $C^+ \cap C^- = \emptyset$.
Question: Does there exist a truth assignment $T: P \rightarrow \{true, false\}$ that satisfies all constraints in C? (Here a constraint $(p, q) \in C^+$ is *satisfied* if $T(p) = T(q)$ and a constraint $(p, q) \in C^-$ is *satisfied* if $T(p) \neq T(q)$.)

VERTEX COVER
Input: A graph $G = (V, E)$ and an integer k.
Question: Does there exist a vertex cover $V' \subseteq V$ such that $|V'| \leq k$? (Here a vertex set V' is called a *vertex cover* if for every edge $(u, v) \in E$ we have $u \in V'$ or $v \in V'$.)

INDEPENDENT SET
Input: A graph $G = (V, E)$ and an integer k.
Question: Does there exist an independent set $V' \subseteq V$ such that $|V'| \geq k$? (Here a vertex set V' is called an *independent set* if there exists no two vertices $u, v \in V'$ such that $(u, v) \in E$.)

CLIQUE
Input: A graph $G = (V, E)$ and an integer k.
Question: Does there exist a clique $V' \subseteq V$ such that $|V'| \geq k$? (Here a vertex set V' is called a *clique* if for all two vertices $u, v \in V'$ there is an edge $(u, v) \in E$.)

DOMINATING SET
Input: A graph $G = (V, E)$ and an integer k.
Question: Does there exist a dominating set $V' \subseteq V$ such that $|V'| \leq k$? (Here a vertex set V' is called a *dominating set* if for every vertex $v \in V'$ we have $v \in V'$ or there is a neighbor u of v such that $u \in V'$; here a vertex u is a *neighbor* of v if $(u, v) \in E$.)

COHERENCE
Input: A network $N = (P, C)$, where $C = C^+ \cup C^-$ is a set of positive and negative constraints and $C^+ \cap C^- = \emptyset$, an integer number k.
Question: Does there exist a truth assignment $T \colon P \to \{true, false\}$ that satisfies at least k constraints in C?

SATISFIABILITY
Input: A Boolean (proposition-logical) formula ϕ with n variables $x_1 \ldots x_n$.
Question: Is there a truth assignment to $x_1 \ldots x_n$ that satisfies ϕ?

UN-SATISFIABILITY
Input: A Boolean (proposition-logical) formula ϕ with n variables $x_1 \ldots x_n$.
Question: Is there *no* truth assignment to $x_1 \ldots x_n$ that satisfies ϕ?

∃∀-SATISFIABILITY
Input: A Boolean (proposition-logical) formula ϕ with n variables $x_1 \ldots x_k, x_{k+1} \ldots x_n$ (where $k < n$).
Question: Is there a truth assignment to $x_1 \ldots x_k$ such that any truth assignment to $x_{k+1} \ldots x_n$ satisfies ϕ?

4.2.3 The P ≠ NP Conjecture

In the previous section we observed that it was relatively easy to come up with a certificate for verifying that BINARY SUBSET CHOICE is in NP, but it appeared inevitable to look at every subset to solve BINARY SUBSET CHOICE. We saw earlier that P ⊆ NP but it looked like NP ⊄ P, that is, P ≠ NP. Indeed, it is strongly conjectured that P ≠ NP, both on intuitive, empirical, and formal grounds.

Intuitively, P = NP would mean that all problems whose solutions are easy to check are also easy to solve. This runs counter to (mathematical) intuition.

To illustrate, think for example of a crossword puzzle or a Sudoku – it seems that once you have found a solution it is easy to check that it is valid, but there may not always be an easy method for finding the solution. Mathematics as we know today would no longer exist in a world where $P = NP$.

Strong empirical evidence that $P \neq NP$ derives from the fact that currently tens of thousands of problems are known to be NP-hard, even problems that mathematicians worked on long before the notion of NP-hardness was introduced. Despite great efforts by many computer scientists, nobody to date has succeeded in finding a polynomial-time algorithm that computes an NP-hard problem – hence the belief that $P \neq NP$.

There is also formal evidence that speaks against $P = NP$. It would imply that various other conjectures that we currently hold would fail. For example, not only would we be able to solve SATISFIABILITY easily, but as a consequence of $P = NP$, we would also be able to solve UN-SATISFIABILITY and ∃∀-SATISFIABILITY introduced in Practice 4.2.1, problems that we currently believe not to have polynomial-time verifiable *yes*-instances.

The $P \stackrel{?}{=} NP$ question is one of the most important open problems in mathematics today. In fact, the question is so important that the Clay Mathematics Institute has offered a $1,000,000 prize to anyone who can answer it (you can look up the details of this contest at www.claymath.org/millennium-problems/p-vs-np-problem if you want to give it a try). Interestingly, the prize is paid only when it is proven that $P = NP$ or that $P \neq NP$, not when someone is able to prove that the question is formally undecidable—proving this will "only" buy you eternal fame. Why is solving this open problem so hard? Almost the sole progress in the last 40-odd years on this question is about known mathematical techniques that provably cannot separate P from NP. For example, diagonalization (the technique used to show that the set of real numbers cannot be mapped to the set of natural numbers) cannot be used to show that there is at least one problem in NP that is not in P.

Finally, an intriguing, thought-provoking question. Would we be better off in a world where $P = NP$ or in a world where $P \neq NP$? In a world where $P = NP$, there would in principle exist efficient algorithms to solve hard problems that we cannot solve right now. For example, it would be easy to solve the TRAVELING SALESPERSON problem or the SATISFIABILITY problem. It would be easy to allocate resources and maximize the number of constraints that are respected in this allocation; this has huge implications for economics, operations research, and business administration. However, note that even if we can prove that there *must exist* such efficient algorithms, that does not mean that this proof needs to be constructive. It may still be beyond our reach to find this algorithm (which would be a particularly frustrating situation). In a world where $P = NP$, there would also be no public-key cryptography; you would want to think twice before making financial transactions over the Internet! In short, there would be many implications of $P = NP$, some of which are most welcome, while others may lead to many unexpected problems. We will, for the remainder of this book, work under the relatively safe assumption that $P \neq NP$. We will, however, remind ourselves of this assumption when necessary or appropriate, to make clear that we are aware of the fact that the $P \overset{?}{=} NP$ question has not yet been settled by mathematical proof.

4.3 NP-**Hardness**

Having covered the complexity classes P and NP in this chapter, and polynomial-time reductions in the previous chapter, we can now give the definition of NP-hardness. NP-hard problems derive their name from the fact that they *are at least as hard* to compute as *any* problem in the class NP, which is formalized in the definitions that follow:

DEFINITION 4.4 *A problem A is* NP-*hard if for all decision problems $D \in$* NP *there exists a polynomial-time reduction to A.*

DEFINITION 4.5 *A decision problem D that is both* NP-*hard and in* NP *is called* NP-*complete.*

Stop and Think

Explain why the following holds: If an NP-complete problem were to be in P then $P = NP$.

An NP-complete problem D is a problem in NP such that *each and every* (other) problem D' in NP can be reduced, in polynomial time, to D. So, that gives us *in principle* a polynomial-time algorithm for all problems in NP: for every D' in NP, first reduce D' to D, then apply the polynomial-time algorithm that solves D (we know there is such an algorithm, as we assumed that D is in P). Note that we don't actually need to *have* that algorithm readily available – it suffices to prove that such an algorithm exists, and thus in principle can be applied to solve D. The challenge is, it seems, in proving that D is NP-hard Surely, we may be able to come up with a reduction from *a particular* decision problem D_1 in NP to D, but what is required is a proof that *every* decision problem D' reduces to D in polynomial time!

However, our job has been made considerably easier by Stephen Cook in 1971. He showed that *every problem in* NP can be reduced in polynomial time to CNF-SAT. Recall Figure 3.6 from the previous chapter? Ever wondered why CNF-SAT was taken as a starting point of the chain of reductions? Precisely because by that time it was already known that CNF-SAT is NP-hard! In Chapter 3 we claimed that even if we cannot directly prove that problems like VERTEX COVER, CLIQUE, INDEPENDENT SET, or TRAVELING SALESPERSON cannot be solved in polynomial time, we *can* prove that if there exists a polynomial-time algorithm for *one* of them, there exists one for *all* of them. That is because all these problems can be reduced, directly or indirectly, from CNF-SAT using a polynomial-time reduction. Because CNF-SAT is NP-hard, so is *any* problem that can be reduced (in polynomial time) from CNF-SAT. It suffices to give such a reduction from any existing NP-hard problem to D, our problem of interest, to show that D is NP-hard as well.

We will not go into details about Cook's proof as it requires much more technical detail than we can provide here. The general idea, however, is that Cook showed that the computation that leads to the acceptance of every *yes*-instance i_{yes} of an arbitrary problem D' in NP can be represented by a (huge, but polynomially sized) CNF-SAT formula ϕ, such that this computation ends with "accept" if and only if ϕ is satisfiable. That means: if we can decide that ϕ is satisfiable in polynomial time, we can confirm that i_{yes} is indeed a *yes*-instance of D', for *each and every* problem D' in NP.

4.3.1   Known NP-Hard Problems

Every problem in Figure 3.6 is NP-hard, as there is a polynomial-time reduction from CNF-SAT to that problem and CNF-SAT is NP-hard as a result of Cook's theorem. Many problems have been shown to be NP-hard, in virtually every domain of computing. Garey and Johnson (1979) provide a compendium of hundreds of problems that were then (i.e., hardly 8 years after Cook's paper that introduced NP-hardness) known to be NP-complete and can be used as a starting point of the reduction. They range from graph theory problems (such as CLIQUE and VERTEX COVER), network design (such as MAX CUT), routing (such as TRAVELING SALESPERSON), storage and retrieval (such as KNAPSACK), scheduling and packing (such as SUBSET SUM), logic, and many, *many* others.

4.3.2   Proving NP-Hardness

A common mistake when trying to prove NP-hardness is to reverse the direction of a reduction when trying to prove NP-hardness. To recap: to show that your problem A is NP-hard, you must provide a polynomial-time reduction *from* an known NP-hard problem B *to* A. It is easy to go wrong here (and it occasionally happens to all of us), so take care and try to fully understand what you are doing and why. A reduction in the wrong direction does not prove that your problem isn't NP-hard – it just doesn't prove anything.

For example, you can try to reduce 3SAT to CNF-SAT; that's easy, as 3SAT is a special case of CNF-SAT; see Section 3.2.3. However, this only shows that *if* 3SAT is NP-hard, *then* so is CNF-SAT. Now, actually this is true. We *know* that 3SAT is NP-hard (for example, because we reduced CNF-SAT to 3SAT, in Section 3.2.2), but this knowledge is not by virtue of your reduction. Likewise, it is easy to reduce 2SAT to CNF-SAT; however, 2SAT happens to be in P. The strategy that we employed to reduce CNF-SAT to 3SAT does not generalize to 2SAT: The number of clauses will explode to be exponential in the size of the formula, prohibiting that the algorithm for the reduction runs in polynomial time.

Practice 4.3.1   Assume that you have the (correct) knowledge that CLIQUE, MAX CUT, and BINARY SUBSET CHOICE are all NP-hard. Which of the following reductions prove NP-hardness, and for which problem?

1. INDEPENDENT SET polynomial-time reduces to CLIQUE
2. CLIQUE polynomial-time reduces to INDEPENDENT SET
3. VERTEX COVER polynomial-time reduces to INDEPENDENT SET
4. INDEPENDENT SET polynomial-time reduces to VERTEX COVER
5. DOMINATING SET polynomial-time reduces to VERTEX COVER
6. VERTEX COVER polynomial-time reduces to DOMINATING SET
7. MAX CUT polynomial-time reduces to COHERENCE
8. CONSISTENT COHERENCE polynomial-time reduces to COHERENCE
9. ADDITIVE SUBSET CHOICE polynomial-time reduces to BINARY SUBSET CHOICE

The strategy that we suggest to prove that your problem A is NP-hard is to first select a suitable NP-hard problem B, then to come up with a reduction from B to A, and finally to show that this reduction takes polynomial time. In principle, if A is indeed NP-hard, there exists a reduction from every problem in NP to A. But, to play on George Orwell's *Animal Farm*, "all polynomial-time reductions are equal, but some are more equal than others." A smart choice for B will make your life considerably easier. The following strategies may be helpful.

Stop and Think ————————
Can you show that there is a B that is a special case of A?

For some problems, this is trival. Take for example $B = 3\textsc{Sat}$ and $A = \textsc{Cnf-Sat}$. However, in some cases it may not be so obvious that B is in fact a special case of A. Take for example the $\textsc{Hitting Set}$ problem, defined as follows:

$\textsc{Hitting Set}$
Input: A collection C of subsets of a set S, a positive integer number k.
Question: Does C contain a hitting set S' for S such that $|S'| \leq k$?
(Here a set $S' \subseteq S$ is called a *hitting set* of S if S' contains at least one element from every subset in C.)

It may not be obvious, but there is a problem you already encountered that is in fact a special case of $\textsc{Hitting Set}$, namely $\textsc{Vertex Cover}$! Recall that a vertex set V' is a vertex cover if every edge in the graph has at least one of its endpoints in V'. Observe that we can see an edge as a subset of a set of all vertices in the graph, with size 2, and the set of all edges as a collection C of subset of V. This collection C has a hitting set V' with size $|V'| \leq k$ if and only if V has a vertex cover of size at most k. Thus, $\textsc{Vertex Cover}$ is a special case of $\textsc{Hitting Set}$ where the cardinality of every subset in C is exactly 2. Given that we know that $\textsc{Vertex Cover}$ is NP-complete, this suffices to prove that $\textsc{Hitting Set}$ is NP-complete.

Stop and Think ————————
Can you show that there is a B that is sufficiently similar to A, so that you can reduce B to A by local replacement?

The canonical example of this strategy is the reduction from $\textsc{Clique}$ to $\textsc{Independent Set}$ and vice versa, or the reduction from $\textsc{Cnf-Sat}$ to $3\textsc{Sat}$. The appendix in Garey and Johnson (1979) and Appendix B in this book may be of use to find a suitable known problem. Finally, if no such local replacement strategy seems to work, your last resort may be to try to do component design, preferably using a "general-purpose" NP-hard problem such as $3\textsc{Sat}$. The component design strategy basically means that you translate every relevant aspect (or component) of $3\textsc{Sat}$ into the language that is used to describe instances of your problem A. Relevant components are variables that can take values *true* and *false*, negations of literals, clauses that bind three variables, etc. The reductions from $3\textsc{Sat}$ to $\textsc{Clique}$ and to $\textsc{Graph 3-Colorability}$ in Chapter 3 may serve as useful examples of this strategy.

In particular with the component design strategy, it is of vital importance that you ensure that the reduction takes polynomial time, which implies that you can describe each component using only polynomial space in the language of your problem A. For example, we showed in the reduction from 3SAT to GRAPH 3-COLORABILITY that we needed only 11 nodes per clause to represent a "clause-satisfying-gadget," and two nodes per variable (and three extra nodes) to represent a "truth-setting-gadget," hence, that the number of nodes is polynomial (in this case: linear) in the number of nodes and clauses in the 3SAT instance.

4.4 *Advanced Topics

In the previous sections, and in Chapters 2 and 3, we guided you through the basics of computational complexity up to, and including, proving NP-hardness. In case you are interested, we will shortly introduce some more advanced topics from complexity theory to more-or-less complete the picture. This section is less relevant from a cognitive perspective (as we argue in "P.3 What Not to Expect" in the preface of this book) but it might satisfy your curiosity if you were wondering, for example, what would characterize a problem for which we can verify *no*-instances (rather than *yes*-instances) in polynomial time. Mind you: the field of computational complexity is huge, and one can spend a whole research career studying the formal properties of, and relations between, various complexity classes; we will only scratch the surface here to perhaps trigger your curiosity. In particular, we will look at non-determinism, at polynomially verifiable *no*-instances, at whatever is in between P and NP-complete, and we will shortly glance over the horizon to see what complexity classes exist "beyond" NP, and "within" P. In Appendix A (more in particular Sections A.1.1 and A.1.3) we give a formal definition of P and NP in terms of Turing machines.

4.4.1 *Non-Determinism

In definitions 4.2 and 4.3 we defined the classes P and NP. You might have guessed that P stands for "polynomial time," which is correct. However, despite intuition, NP does *not* abbreviate "non-polynomial time"; given that $P \subseteq NP$ that would indeed be a misleading name for this class, NP *does* stand for "non-deterministic polynomial time." In this sub-section we will explain this notion. We will start with the following theorem that "enhances" the definition for the class NP:

THEOREM 4.1 *Let D be a decision problem. The following three statements are equivalent:*

1. $D \in$ NP;
2. *There is a (deterministic) verification algorithm A such that for every yes-instance i_{yes} of D and a given certificate w $A(i_{yes}, w)$ verifies i_{yes} in polynomial time;*
3. *There is a non-deterministic algorithm N such that for every yes-instance i_{yes} of D, $N(i_{yes})$ solves i_{yes} in polynomial time.*

What does it mean for an algorithm to be deterministic, respectively non-deterministic? To explain that, think of an execution of an algorithm on a particular input i as a *computation path*: an exact description of the state of the computation with respect to i. Take for instance Algorithm 4.2 that decides whether a given integer number Z is in an array A with n elements. For each array A and integer Z, we can step through this algorithm, describing the state of the computation at every step: the value of k, of $A[k]$, of Z; the outcome of the test in line 2, etc. Whenever we run the algorithm on this particular instance $\{A[n], Z\}$, the states and the sequence of these states *will be identical*. This algorithm is deterministic, meaning from every state in the computation path of a particular instance i, there is exactly one next state: no more, no less. For example, if we feed *Find* the input $\{A[n] = \{1,2\}, Z = 2\}$, then the first test in line 2 (for $k = 1$) will fail, and the second test (for $k = 2$) will pass, and the algorithm will end with announcing "Yes: A contains Z." It will do so, whenever we run it 5, 50, or 5 million times on this input.

Algorithm 4.2 A deterministic algorithm that decides whether an array A contains an integer Z

Find$(A[n], Z)$

1: **for** $k = 1$ **to** n **do**
2:     **if** $A[k] = Z$ **then**
3:         **return** "Yes: A contains Z"
4:     **end if**
5: **end for**
6: **return** "No: A does not contain Z"

In contrast, a non-deterministic algorithm has *choice points*. Have a look at the alternative Algorithm 4.3:

Algorithm 4.3 A non-deterministic algorithm that decides whether an array A contains an integer Z

$Find'(A[n], Z)$

1: Guess a value of k in the interval $[1, \ldots, n]$;
2: **if** $A[k] = Z$ **then**
3:    **return** "Yes: A contains Z"
4: **end if**
5: **return** "No: A does not contain Z"

This algorithm may produce different results each time it is run on the input $\{A[n] = \{1, 2\}, Z = 2\}$, as there is a choice point in line 1, leading to *different* computation paths depending on whether the algorithm made the guess "$k = 1$" or the guess "$k = 2$." For $k = 1$ the algorithm will–*incorrectly!*–return "No: A does not contain Z" and for $k = 2$ the algorithm will return "Yes: A contains Z." How can this algorithm be useful at all, given that it may give a wrong answer? In practice, we will not find many non-deterministic algorithms in operation, in particular because we did not impose *any* constraints on how *Find'* makes its guesses. For all we know, *Find'* may always select $k = 1$, giving the wrong output time and again! Non-deterministic algorithms are mainly theoretical constructs. The key aspect here is the notion of *solving a decision problem*. For a regular, deterministic algorithm, when there is always the same computation path on a particular input, it is clear when it correctly "solves" an input i. For example, *Find* correctly solves $\{A[n], Z\}$ if it announces "Yes: A contains Z" if and only if A contains Z, and "No: A does not contain Z" if it does not. The notion of "solves" in a non-deterministic algorithm is different. Here "solves" means that there is *at least one computation path* that accepts i if i is a *yes*-instance, and that there is *no computation path* that accepts i if i is a *no*-instance.

─────── **Stop and Think** ───────

Test whether Algorithm 4.3 accepts the inputs $\{A[n] = \{1, 2, 3\}, Z = 2\}$, respectively $\{A[n] = \{1, 2\}, Z = 3\}$. Does Algorithm 4.3 accept the input $\{A[n] = \{1\}, Z = 1\}$?

In a way, a non-deterministic algorithm that accepts an input if it ends in an accepting state on at least one computation path is very powerful. Instead of testing each element of the array until it finds Z (what *Find* does), the non-deterministic variant *Find'* just "branches off" and *tests every element of A in parallel*. Think of it as follows: because each choice generates a different computation path, and only *one* computation path needs to accept, the

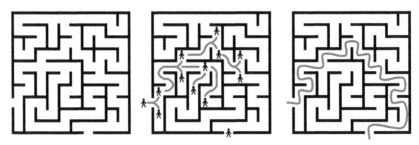

Figure 4.6   How to find your way out of this maze? By cloning yourself at every junction, or by having a road map available? Both are equally powerful, in the sense that you get to the exit equally fast. This may illustrate Theorem 4.1: the set of problems that can be verified in polynomial time and the set of problems that can be solved in polynomial time with a non-deterministic algorithm both describe the same set, namely, the class NP.

algorithm more or less clones itself at every choice point, where each clone investigates the consequences of a particular choice. Note, again, that non-deterministic algorithms are *theoretical constructs*, in contrast to deterministic algorithms. The algorithm does not really "follow" any computation path: we just show that there *exists* a computation path that leads to success.

Now, have a look at the *verification* Algorithm 4.4

Algorithm 4.4 A deterministic verification algorithm that verifies that an array A contains an integer Z

$FindV(A[n], Z, k)$

1: **if** $A[k] = Z$ **then**
2:    **return** "Yes: A contains Z"
3: **end if**
4: **return** "No: A does not contain Z"

This algorithm looks rather similar to Algorithm 4.3, but rather than *guessing* the value k, it is *given* this value as input. There is now no choice point anymore in the algorithm, making this a deterministic verification algorithm. In a sense, where non-deterministic algorithms can be characterized as "cloning" algorithms, verification algorithms can be characterized as "road-map" algorithms: When given the correct directions (which value you should take at every choice point), you can do things rather fast as you don't have to explore dead ends. This idea is illustrated in Figure 4.6.

— Stop and Think —

How much time does Algorithm 4.3 take on a input with array length n?
How much time does Algorithm 4.4 take on a input with array length n?

Each computation path in Algorithm 4.3 takes constant time: It guesses a value for k, compares $A[k]$ to Z, and decides accordingly. Also, each computation path in Algorithm 4.4 takes constant time, but now k is given. Observe that Algorithm 4.2 takes worst case $O(n)$ time, for example, if Z is not in $A[n]$. How fast can a non-deterministic algorithm be, compared with deterministic algorithms? Can it solve NP-complete problems in polynomial time?

— Stop and Think —

Recall the NP-complete 3SAT problem we encountered in Chapter 3. What would be a suitable certificate to verify a *yes*-instance? Given this certificate, can you think of a polynomial-time, non-deterministic algorithm for deciding 3SAT?

For 3SAT, a natural certificate would be a satisfying truth assignment. Given such an assignment, it is easy to verify that every clause is satisfied with this assignment and hence, that the 3SAT instance is satisfiable. If we think of each variable as a choice point where either *true* or *false* needs to be guessed, an accepting computation path will be a path that guesses a satisfying truth assignment for the formula. This is a polynomial-time, non-deterministic algorithm for deciding 3SAT. Note that the computation path branches over every variable, and thus that there are 2^n distinct computation paths, just as there are 2^n possible truth assignments to the variables. Non-determinism is thus very powerful, as we can have a non-deterministic polynomial-time algorithm for NP-complete problems.

4.4.2   *The "NP $\neq$ co-NP" Conjecture

Ouch, that was a *ridiculously* hard examination! With your fellow students you discuss it afterwards, and you're pretty sure that *no one* has passed it. The next week, your teacher enters class, and the students begin to complain that *none* of them passed the exam.

— Stop and Think —

Assume that the claim is false. How can the teacher show that the claim is false?

The only thing that the teacher needs to do in order to falsify the claim, is to produce a *single* exam with a passing grade, thus showing that at least one of the students passed the exam and thus that the claim is false. In contrast, if the students would want to argue that *none* of them passed the exam, there is no simple proof other than to go through all the exams and verify that none of them scored a passing grade.

In the previous sections we defined the class NP as the class of decision problems for which a *yes*-instance could be verified (using a suitable certificate) in polynomial time. In contrast, we can define the class co-NP as the class of problems for which a *no*-instance can be verified in polynomial time. For example, in Section 3.3 we introduced the CNF-UNSAT problem that, given a Boolean formula in CNF form, asked whether it was a contradiction (i.e., no truth assignment can possibly satisfy it). *Yes*-instances – CNF formulas that are indeed contradictions – cannot be easily verified (as far as known). *No*-instances, on the other hand, can be easily verified: One can verify that a formula is not a contradiction when provided with a satisfying truth assignment. This class co-NP is defined as follows:

DEFINITION 4.6   *co-NP is the class of decision problems D for which there exist a polynomial-time verifiable proof for no-instances $D(i_{no})$. More formally, co-NP is the class of decision problems D: $I \to \{yes, no\}$ for which there exists an algorithm with worst-case time complexity $O(|i_{no}|^c)$ (for a constant c) that can verify, given a certificate w provided with the input i_{no}, that $D(i_{no}, w) = no$ for every no-instance $i_{no} \in I_{no}$.*

To illustrate Definition 4.6, we give the following examples:

INDEPENDENT SET
Input: A graph $G = (V, E)$ and an integer k.
Question: Does there exist an independent set $V' \subseteq V$ such that $|V'| \geq k$? (Here a vertex set V' is called an *independent set* if there exists no two vertices $u, v \in V'$ such that $(u, v) \in E$.)

CO-INDEPENDENT SET
Input: A graph $G = (V, E)$ and an integer k.
Question: Does there NOT exist an independent set $V' \subseteq V$ such that $|V'| \geq k$? (Here a vertex set V' is called an *independent set* if there exists no two vertices $u, v \in V'$ such that $(u, v) \in E$.)

MINIMUM SPANNING TREE
Input: An edge-weighted graph $G = (V, E)$, and an integer w.
Question: Does there exist a spanning tree T of G such that the sum of the weights on the edges in T is at most w?

co-MINIMUM SPANNING TREE
Input: An edge-weighted graph $G = (V, E)$, and an integer w.
Question: Does every spanning tree T of G have weight exceeding w?

Alternatively, using the notion of non-determinism we discussed in Section 4.4.1, we can define co-NP as the class of problems for which *no*-instances can be solved with a polynomial-time non-deterministic algorithm. Such an algorithm for CNF-UNSAT may look like the following:

Algorithm 4.5 A non-deterministic algorithm that decides whether a CNF formula is a contradiction

---

CNF-UnSat(U, C)

1: Guess a truth assignment u of U;
2: **if** u satisfies all clauses in C **then**
3:    **return** "No: (U, C) is not a contradiction"
4: **end if**
5: **return** "Yes: (U, C) is a contradiction"

If (U, C) is *not* a contradiction, then there exists at least one computational path that correctly answers "No." If on the other hand (U, C) *is* a contradiction, then no such path exists: all paths will answer "Yes." So, where for NP-problems all computation paths on a suitable non-deterministic algorithm answer "No" on a *no*-instance and at least one such path answers "Yes" on a *yes*-instance, the results are exactly the opposite for the corresponding non-deterministic algorithm for co-NP problems. This duality is a hallmark for complement classes in general, yielding the following general definition.

DEFINITION 4.7 *Let* C *be some class of decision problems. Then co-*C *denotes the class of problems from* C *with their yes- and no-answers reversed.*

co-NP-completeness is defined similar to NP-completeness: a decision problem D is co-NP-complete if all decision problems D' in co-NP can be reduced in polynomial time to D using a (many-one) reduction. The canonical co-NP-complete problem is CNF-UNSAT.

Practice 4.4.1 Reconstruct Definition 4.6 from Definition 4.3 and Definition 4.7.

Practice 4.4.2 Observe that $P = $ co-P. Explain why this is so.

Practice 4.4.3 Given that you know INDEPENDENT SET is in NP and MINIMUM SPANNING TREE is in P, and assuming $P \neq NP$ and $NP \neq$ co-NP, prove for co-INDEPENDENT SET and co-MINIMUM SPANNING TREE whether or not these problems are in NP, co-NP, P and/or co-P.

Practice 4.4.4 In Section 3.3 we introduced Turing reductions. Show that $NP = $ co-NP under Turing reductions.

Figure 4.7 illustrates the relationship between the classes NP, co-NP, P, and co-P. The top panel is the situation how we believe the complexity classes actually are related to each other. P (=co-P) is a strict subset of NP, of co-NP, and of the intersection of NP and co-NP; there are problems in NP (co-NP) that are neither in P nor NP-complete (co-NP-complete). In the middle panel, we see the hypothetical world where $NP = $ co-NP. Note that we still have problems that are neither in P, nor NP-complete. In the bottom panel we see the hypothetical (yet possible) world where $P = NP$, and also co-$P = NP$ (because $P = $ co-P). Note that a world where NP is partitioned into problems that are in P and problems that are NP-complete is *not* possible as we will see in Section 4.4.3.

4.4.3 *NP-Intermediate

We know that there are problems in NP that are NP-complete, and that there are problems in NP that are polynomial-time decidable. If we assume that $P \neq NP$, is this then the complete picture? Is every problem in NP either NP-complete or in P? No! A famous proof by Richard Ladner from 1975 shows that if $P \neq NP$, then there are problems that are not in P, but are also not NP-complete (Ladner, 1975). The proof is constructive, in the most literal sense: Ladner actually *constructed* such a problem that by design is not solvable in polynomial time *and* is not NP-complete. The class of such problems is called NP-intermediate.

No "natural" problems are known that are known to reside in NP-intermediate, but there are a number of suitable candidates. The most prominent of these problems is the decision version of INTEGER FACTORIZATION, defined as follows:

INTEGER FACTORIZATION
Input: An integer N and an integer M such that $1 < M < N$.
Question: Does N have a prime factor p with $1 < p \leq M$?

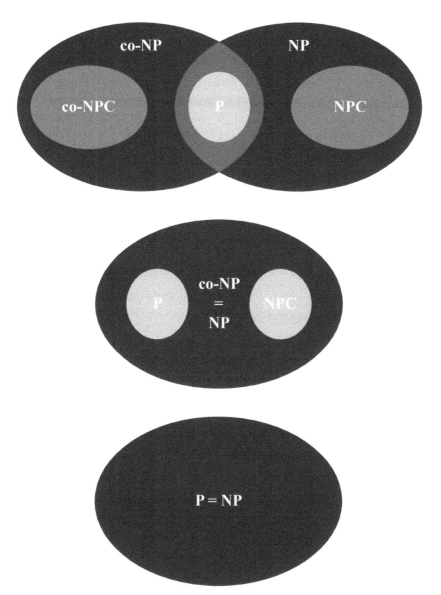

Figure 4.7 The three possible relationships between the classes P, co-P, NP, and co-NP. Top panel: the state of affairs as conjectured by most living computer scientists. P (=co-P) is a strict subset of NP, of co-NP, and of the intersection of NP and co-NP; there are problems in NP (co-NP) that are neither in P nor NP-complete (co-NP-complete). Middle panel: if any NP-complete problem were to be in co-NP, or any co-NP-complete problem were to be in NP, then we would have NP = co-NP. Bottom panel: if any NP-complete problem were to be in P, or any co-NP-complete problem were to be co-P, then we would have P = NP.

The current fastest algorithm for solving INTEGER FACTOR-IZATION runs in sub-exponential time, to be precise, in time $\exp\left(\left(\sqrt[3]{64/9} + o(1)\right)(\ln n)^{1/3}(\ln \ln n)^{2/3}\right)$, where $o(1)$ is a formal notation for a function that converges to 0. We expect that there is no polynomial-time algorithm for INTEGER FACTORIZATION. Another problem that was long believed to be a natural problem in NP-intermediate is GRAPH ISOMORPHISM, defined as follows:

GRAPH ISOMORPHISM
Input: Two graphs G and H.
Question: Is G isomorphic to H?

Note that the SUBGRAPH ISOMORPHISM problem is NP-hard (see Section 3.2.3, also for a definition of *isomorphic*), but the GRAPH ISOMORPHISM problem is most likely not NP-complete. Very recent evidence at the time of writing (early 2016) suggests that GRAPH ISOMORPHISM might be in P after all, but the jury is still out on this issue.

4.4.4   *Within P and Beyond NP

The classes P and NP are by far the most used complexity classes, where "in P" and "NP-hard" are properties of a problem that (maybe somewhat coarsely) characterize whether a problem is, respectively isn't, tractable under the P $\neq$ NP assumption. Yet, there are literally hundreds of complexity classes that all aim to capture how difficult a problem is. The *complexity zoo* (see https://complexityzoo.uwaterloo.ca/Complexity%20Zoo) shows the diversity of these complexity classes. Here we will briefly mention just a few of these complexity classes, in particular **EXP, PSPACE, L**, and the so-called polynomial hierarchy. There are many other interesting classes, dealing with probabilistic computations, quantum computations, problems that have unique solutions, etc. that we leave for the interested reader to harvest.

Recall that we argued in Chapter 3 that it is in general very hard to prove exponential lower bounds on the runtime complexity of a problem; we introduced GENERALIZED CHESS as an example of the few problems that are proven to take worst-case exponential time. In fact, GENERALIZED CHESS is EXP-complete, where the complexity class EXP is defined as follows:

DEFINITION 4.8   **EXP** *is the class of decision problems D that are solvable in exponential time. More formally,* **EXP** *is the class of decision problems* $D: I \to \{yes, no\}$ *for which there exists an algorithm with worst-case time complexity* $O(2^{|i|^c})$ *(for a constant* $c \geq 1$*) that can decide whether* $D(i) = yes$ *or* $D(i) = no$ *for every instance* $i \in I$.

Apart from *time*, another useful resource for a computation is *space*, that is, the number of memory cells (bits) needed in the computation. Obviously, one can touch only one memory cell at a time, which means that the amount of memory needed for a computation is upper bounded by the amount of time that is needed. Analogous to P we can define the class PSPACE as follows:

DEFINITION 4.9   PSPACE *is the class of decision problems D that are solvable using polynomial space. More formally,* PSPACE *is the class of decision problems* $D: I \rightarrow \{yes, no\}$ *for which there exists an algorithm that uses space complexity* $O(|i|^c)$ *(for a constant c) that can decide whether* $D(i) = yes$ *or* $D(i) = no$ *for every instance* $i \in I$.

We argued earlier that $P \subseteq PSPACE$. Moreover, we have that $NP \subseteq PSPACE$ as any computation run of the verification algorithm uses only a polynomial amount of space. Another result that can be derived is that an algorithm taking polynomial space needs at most an exponential amount of time. The argument here is somewhat more tricky. Let us assume that we have a deterministic computation that takes a polynomial amount of space, that is, $O(|i|^c)$ bits. We assume that this space is both the working memory of the program, plus the program code itself, plus any processor registers etc. that describe the program state.

Stop and Think ———————

How much time does this algorithm take at most? Can it visit any memory configuration twice?

If the program uses $O(|i|^c)$ bits, there can be at most $O(2^{|i|^c})$ distinct memory configurations (working memory plus program code plus processor state). It *cannot encounter the same state twice* as it is a deterministic algorithm: If it *would* encounter the same state twice, that effectively means that the program is in an endless loop (as it is a *deterministic* algorithm) and that it will never end. Given that it is in at most $O(2^{|i|^c})$ memory configurations and it can touch any configuration at most once, this gives an upper bound on the running time of $O(2^{|i|^c})$. That is, $PSPACE \subseteq EXP$. We can make a similar argument at the "lower end" and define the class L to describe programs that take at most a logarithmic amount of space and thus take at most a polynomial amount of time: We also have that $L \subseteq P$.

Recall the UN-SATISFIABILITY and ∃∀-SATISFIABILITY we encountered in Practice 4.2.1. Probably you established that both of them are unlikely to be in NP. Having read Section 4.4.2 you now know that UN-SATISFIABILITY is a canonical co-NP-complete problem. In fact, ∃∀-SATISFIABILITY is also a canonical complete problem: it is complete for one of the levels of the so-called *polynomial hierarchy* that includes P, NP, co-NP, and other classes that use these classes as building blocks. Let's assume you have a deterministic program that can call an algorithm for deciding an NP-hard problem as a subroutine, and let's just for the sake of the argument assume that it can call this algorithm *for free*, that is, the subroutine will return immediately with the correct answer. Such a subroutine is typically called an *oracle* in the literature on complexity theory: You ask it a difficult question and it gives you the correct answer immediately – but note that oracles are (alas!) mere theoretical constructs, like non-deterministic programs that do not exist in reality.

Stop and Think

What sort of problems could this algorithm solve in polynomial time?

This algorithm is a generalized variant of Algorithm 3.1, and it will be clear that we can solve both SATISFIABILITY and UN-SATISFIABILITY in polynomial time with this algorithm (recall, we were given access to the SATISFIABILITY oracle for free). It is thus as least as powerful as NP and co-NP. The complexity class that is associated with such algorithms is P^{NP} (pronounced as "P to the NP" or "P with an NP oracle"). If the algorithm itself is non-deterministic, the associated complexity class is NP^{NP} (or co-NP^{NP}, depending on whether *one* or *all* computation paths should accept). ∃∀-SATISFIABILITY happens to be complete for this class.

Stop and Think

See the definition of ∃∀-SATISFIABILITY in Practice 4.2.1 and think of a non-deterministic algorithm with SATISFIABILITY oracle access that can solve ∃∀-SATISFIABILITY in polynomial time.

You could just guess a truth assignment to $x_1, \ldots, x_k$, and then check whether the *negation* of ϕ (with this partial truth assignment) is satisfiable. If the negation of a formula is not satisfiable, the formula is a tautology. If there is a guessed partial truth assignment to $x_1, \ldots, x_k$ for which ϕ is a tautology, then at least one computation path will accept.

Algorithm 4.6 Decide whether an $\exists\forall$-SATISFIABILITY formula is satisfiable

$EA\text{-}Sat(\phi = x_1, \dots, x_k, x_{k+1}, \dots, x_n)$

1: Guess a (partial) truth assignment to $x_1, \dots, x_k$
2: **if** $Sat(\neg\phi) = no$ **then**
3:     **return** *yes*
4: **else**
5:     **return** *no*
6: **end if**

Complexity classes like P^{NP}, NP^{NP}, and co-NP^{NP} (but also P, NP, and co-NP) are part of the polynomial hierarchy PH. It is recursively defined as follows:

DEFINITION 4.10 *The polynomial hierarchy (PH) is defined as follows:*

1. $P \in PH$; *(the zeroth level)*
2. *if* $C \in PH$, *then* $P^C \in PH$, $NP^C \in PH$, *and co-*$NP^C \in PH$;

So, classes in the polynomial hierarchy include for example NP^{NP} (on the second level), but also co-$NP^{NP^{NP^{NP}}}$ (on the fourth level). It is increasingly difficult to visualize (or pronounce!) such complexity classes. Their computational power is assumed to grow with each level, yet, all levels use at most polynomial space. This gives us a nice hierarchy of complexity classes: $L \subseteq P \subseteq NP \subseteq PH \subseteq PSPACE \subseteq EXP$. We know that $L \subsetneq PSPACE$ and that $P \subsetneq EXP$, but complexity theorists assume that all inclusions are strict.

4.5   Exercises

Exercise 4.5.1 See the ISA-RELEVANT VARIABLE problem later (see (Kwisthout, 2012a)). Show that this problem is NP-hard by reducing it from SATISFIABILITY.

> ISA-RELEVANT VARIABLE
> **Input:** A Boolean formula ϕ with n variables, describing the characteristic function 1_ϕ: $\{false, true\}^n \rightarrow \{1, 0\}$, designated variable x_r appearing in ϕ. Here, the characteristic function 1_ϕ of a Boolean formula ϕ maps truth assignments to the variables of ϕ to $\{0, 1\}$, such that $1_\phi(x) = 1$ if and only if x denotes a satisfying truth assignment to ϕ, and 0 otherwise.
> **Question:** Is x_r a relevant variable in ϕ, that is, is $1_\phi(x_r = true) \neq 1_\phi(x_r = false)$

Exercise 4.5.2   See the MULTI-PROCESSES SCHEDULING problem that follows. Show that this problem is NP-hard by reducing it from PARTITION. Hint: use restriction.

> MULTI-PROCESSES SCHEDULING
> **Input:** A finite set A of tasks, a length $l(a)$ for each $a \in A$, a number m of processors, and a deadline D. All numbers are positive integers.
> **Question:** Is there a partition $A = A_1 \cup A_2 \cup \ldots \cup A_m$ of A into m disjoint sets such that $\max \left\{ \sum_{a \in A_i} l(a) : 1 \le i \le m \right\} \le D$?

Exercise 4.5.3   See the MAJSAT problem that follows. Show that this problem is NP-hard by reducing it from a suitable NP-hard problem. Do you think MAJSAT is in NP?

> MAJSAT
> **Input:** A Boolean formula ϕ with n variables.
> **Question:** Does the majority of truth assignments (i.e., at least $1/2 + 1/2^n$ truth assignments) satisfy ϕ?

Exercise 4.5.4   Give a full proof of NP-completeness (including membership in NP, NP-hardness by a suitable reduction, and a proof of polynomial run-time of the reduction) from CNF-SAT to VERTEX COVER and to SUBGRAPH ISOMORPHISM.

4.6   Further Reading

In 2000, Richard Kaye used the well-known game Minesweeper to illustrate the open $P \overset{?}{=} NP$ question (Kaye, 2000). Kaye's paper is honored by being listed on the Millenium prize page for the $P \overset{?}{=} NP$ problem. In 2011, Scott and colleagues wrote a follow-up paper in which they showed that actually playing the game from a player's perspective does not involve solving the NP-complete Minesweeper consistency problem that Kaye analyzed, but rather the co-NP-complete Minesweeper inference problem of Scott et al. (2011). Although for proving intractability, the difference between NP and co-NP does not matter, the exchange in these papers may serve as an entertaining illustration of the importance of making sure one has formalized the right problem at the computational-level of explanation.

In case you're curious about other complexity classes than the ones we mentioned here, have a look at the *Complexity Zoo* at https://complexity zoo.uwaterloo.ca/Complexity%20Zoo. The zoo, introduced by Scott Aaronson, is a comprehensive list of all (over 500!) complexity classes that have made it to the published literature.

The paper by Cook (1971) is one of the seminal (and most cited) theoretical computer science papers; yet it has never been published as a journal article. It was hand-typed (with written special symbols) and published in conference proceedings; recently, an effort was made by Tim Rohlfs to properly typeset the paper and fix some of the typos. This corrected manuscript is available online at http://4mhz.de/cook.html.

Also nice to know: The name NP-complete to describe the hardest problems in NP has been somewhat democratically decided on. In need of a proper name to describe that a particular problem was hard, Donald Knuth called for a vote among 30 researchers in theoretical computer science. Among the write-in votes he received were "Sisyphean" (to refer to the time-consuming task Sisyphus was given by the gods), "Ulyssean" (referring to Ulysses' persistence), the acronym PET (to stand for "probably exponential time," but to be replaced in the future by *provably* or *previously*, depending on the outcome of the $P \overset{?}{=} NP$ problem), and (very creatively) "hard-boiled" as an honor to Cook. However, the final outcome of the poll he published (Knuth, 1974) was that NP-hard and NP-complete were the most suitable words to describe the concepts of interest.

5 Fixed-Parameter Tractable Time

In this chapter, we introduce the concepts of parameterized problem and fixed-parameter tractability. Using these concepts, one can show that problems that are polynomial-time intractable in general (i.e., NP-hard) may yet be practically solvable provided only that certain input parameters are constrained in terms of their values. This conception of tractability underlies the FPT-Cognition thesis introduced in Chapter 1. We illustrate three techniques for showing that a parameterized problem is fixed-parameter tractable, namely, brute-force combinatorics, bounded search trees, and reduction to a problem kernel. We also include several exercises for practicing these techniques.

5.1 Fixed-Parameter Tractability

In the last three chapters, we have equated a problem being tractable with that problem having a polynomial-time algorithm – that is, an algorithm whose running time is upper-bounded by some polynomial function n^c of the input size n. As discussed in Section 1.2.2, under the P-cognition thesis, only polynomial-time computable problems are considered plausible computational-level theories. Any exponential-time (or, more generally, non-polynomial time) problem is rejected as computational-level theory of cognition, as they require require unrealistic amounts of time for their completion (see Table 1.1).

As you may recall from Section 1.2.2, the P-cognition thesis is argued to make a too-strict distinction between tractable and intractable. A finer-grained notion of tractability than polynomial time provides a more relevant distinction for cognitive science and is realized in parameterized complexity. Here, a (fixed-parameter) tractable problem can be solved in time that is non-polynomial only in terms of particular parameters (see Table 5.1).

To formalize fixed-parameter tractability, we first need to define a type of computational problem that allows us to specify problem parameters of interest. To this end, for any decision problem D with an input parameter set K, we denote the problem D parameterized by K as $K\text{-}D$ and call

Table 5.1 Illustration of the running times of polynomial-time versus fixed-parameter tractable versus non-polynomial time algorithms. The function $t(n)$ expresses the number of steps performed by an algorithm. For illustrative purposes, it is assumed that 100 steps can be performed per second.

n	$t(n) = n$	$t(n) = n^2$	$t(n) = 2^k n$			$t(n) = 2^n$
			$k = 5$	$k = 10$	$k = 20$	
5	50 ms	250 ms	1 sec	12 sec	14.6 hr	320 ms
10	100 ms	1 sec	3 sec	25 sec	1.2 days	10 sec
20	200 ms	4 sec	6 sec	51 sec	2.4 days	2.9 hr
30	300 ms	9 sec	9 sec	1.3 min	3.6 days	4.1 mths
40	400 ms	16 sec	12 sec	1.7 min	4.9 days	3.5 centuries
50	500 ms	25 sec	16 sec	2.1 min	6.1 days	3.6×10^3 centuries
100	1 sec	1.7 min	32 sec	4.3 min	12.1 days	4.0×10^{18} centuries
500	5 sec	41.7 min	2.7 min	21.3 min	2.0 mths	1.0×10^{139} centuries
1,000	10 sec	2.8 hr	5.3 min	42.7 min	4.0 mths	3.4×10^{289} centuries

K-D a *parameterized problem.* For example, here is a parameterized problem associated with VERTEX COVER in which the parameter is given vertex cover size limit k.

k-VERTEX COVER
Input: A graph $G = (V, E)$ and a positive integer k.
Parameter: k
Question: Is there a vertex cover of size k in G?

Stop and Think

What other parameterizations of VERTEX COVER can you think of?

It turns out that there are a very large (indeed, an infinite) number of such parameterizations. One might parameterize VERTEX COVER by any part of the input, as was the case with k in the previous example, or any quantity characterizing any such part, e.g.,

$|V|$-VERTEX COVER
Input: A graph $G = (V, E)$ and a positive integer k.
Parameter: $|V|$
Question: Is there a vertex cover of size k in G?

d-VERTEX COVER
Input: A graph $G = (V, E)$ and a positive integer k.
Parameter: d, the maximum degree of any vertex in G
Question: Is there a vertex cover of size k in G?

These quantities might themselves be the answers to other computational problems, e.g.,

l-VERTEX COVER
Input: A graph $G = (V, E)$ and a positive integer k.
Parameter: l, the length of the longest simple path in G
Question: Is there a vertex cover of size k in G?

s_{DS}-VERTEX COVER
Input: A graph $G = (V, E)$ and a positive integer k.
Parameter: s_{DS}, the size of the smallest dominating set in G
Question: Is there a vertex cover of size k in G?

Finally, we can parameterize by any combination of such individual parameters[1], e.g.,

$\{k, d\}$-VERTEX COVER
Input: A graph $G = (V, E)$ and a positive integer k.
Parameter: k, d
Question: Is there a vertex cover of size k in G?

$\{k, d, l, s_{DS}\}$-VERTEX COVER
Input: A graph $G = (V, E)$ and a positive integer k.
Parameter: k, d, l, s_{DS}
Question: Is there a vertex cover of size k in G?

Each decision problem therefore has infinitely many associated parameterized problems.

Practice 5.1.1　　Give three parameterized problems for each of the following decision problems described in Chapters 2 and 3.

(a) CLIQUE
(b) SUBGRAPH ISOMORPHISM
(c) CNF-SAT
(d) SUBSET SUM

---

[1]　Note that when we have a parameter set K consisting of more than one parameter, we enclose these parameters in parentheses in the problem name (e.g., $\{k, d\}$-VERTEX COVER); otherwise, the parentheses are omitted (e.g., k-VERTEX COVER).

Given this notion of a parameterized problem, we can now formalize the notion of fixed-parameter tractability discussed in Section 1.2.2.

DEFINITION 5.1 *Let D: I → {yes, no} be a decision problem and K = {$k_1, k_2, \ldots, k_m$} be a particular set of input parameters of D. Then D is said to be* fixed-parameter tractable *for K if there exists at least one algorithm that computes D for any input of size n in time $f(k_1, k_2, \ldots k_m)n^c$, where $f(.)$ is an arbitrary computable function and c is a constant. Such an algorithm is said to be a* fixed-parameter (fp-)tractable algorithm *and runs in* fixed-parameter tractable (fpt) time *relative to K.*

As shown in Table 5.1, fp-tractable algorithms are comparable in running time to polynomial-time algorithms and outperform non-polynomial time algorithms when parameters and inputs are small. This is just the type of tractability we would like for our real-world cognitive inputs.

5.2 Proving Fixed-Parameter Tractability

To prove the fixed-parameter tractability of a problem D relative to some input parameter set K, it suffices to produce an algorithm for D whose running time is non-polynomial only in K. In this section, we will describe several techniques for designing such algorithms – namely, brute-force combinatorics, bounded search trees, and reduction to a problem kernel.

5.2.1 Brute-Force Combinatorics

Regardless of whether a problem is an optimization, search, or decision problem, we are typically asking if there is one of a specified set of entities that satisfies one or more conditions (e.g., in the case of VERTEX COVER, if out of all possible subsets of V of size k, there is one that is a vertex cover for the given graph G). Let us call the entities in that specified set the *candidate solutions* (e.g., all possible subsets of V of size k) and any such entity that satisfies the requisite problem conditions a *viable solution* (e.g., a vertex cover for G). Note that in the case of optimization and search problems, viable solutions are solutions to problems in the sense described in Section 2.1. In the case of decision problems, the (non)existence of a viable solution translates to the solution *yes* (*no*).

This type of problem yields a particularly simple type of algorithm – namely, generate each candidate solution for a problem D and check if that candidate solution is a viable solution. Such an algorithm for VERTEX COVER would, for each subset of the vertices in a given graph G of specified size k, check if that subset is actually a vertex cover for G. We have already seen in Chapter 4 that many problems (such as VERTEX COVER) have candidate solutions that can be checked relative to the requisite conditions in time polynomial in the input size. In those cases, if the number of candidate solutions is equal to or upper-bounded by some function of a given input parameter set K of D then K-D is fixed-parameter tractable.

The key to applying this technique is thus to get upper bounds on the size of a problem's candidate-solution set. Such bounds can often be obtained by applying basic formulas from the mathematical discipline of combinatorics. Several particularly useful formulas are given in Table 5.2. Let us now see some examples of how to apply these formulas to the following parameterized problems.

$\{|V|,k\}$-VERTEX COVER
Input: A graph $G = (V, E)$ and a positive integer k.
Parameter: $|V|, k$
Question: Is there a vertex cover of size k in G?

CNF-SAT
Input: A set of Boolean variables $U = \{u_1, \ldots, u_n\}$ and a set of clauses $C = \{c_1, \ldots, c_m\}$ in conjunctive normal form.
Parameter: $|U|$
Question: Is there a truth assignment $t: U \to \{true, false\}$ such that all clauses C are satisfied?

Table 5.2 Some formulas from combinatorics that are useful in bounding the size of problem candidate-solution sets.

#	Formula		
1	The number of sequences of length k where each sequence element is drawn from a set with n elements	$=$	n^k
2	The number of orderings of a set with n elements	$\leq$	n^n
3	The number of subsets (including the empty set) of a set with n elements	$=$	2^n
4	The number of subsets of size k of a a set with n elements	$\leq$	n^k
5	The number of leaves in a rooted tree of depth d in which each non-leaf vertex has at most b children	$\leq$	b^d
6	The total number of vertices in a rooted tree of depth d in which each non-leaf vertex has at most b children	$\leq$	b^{d+1}

- $|U|$-CNF-SAT *is fixed-parameter tractable*: Each candidate solution to an input of CNF-SAT can be seen as a sequence of length $|U|$ whose sequence elements are drawn from the set {*true,false*}. Hence, by Formula 1 in Table 5.2, the number of candidate solutions for an input of CNF-SAT is $= 2^{|U|}$.

- $|U|$-CNF-SAT *is fixed-parameter tractable (Take II)*: Each candidate solution to an input of CNF-SAT can be seen as the (possibly empty) set of variables in U that are set to *true* in the truth-assignment encoded in that solution. Hence, by Formula 3 in Table 5.2, the number of candidate solutions for an instance of CNF-SAT is $= 2^{|U|}$.

- $\{|V|,k\}$-VERTEX COVER *is fixed-parameter tractable*: Each candidate solution to an instance of VERTEX COVER is a subset of size k from the set of vertices V in the given graph G. Hence, by Formula 4 in Table 5.2, the number of candidate solutions for an instance of VERTEX COVER is $\leq |V|^k$.

- $\{|V|,k\}$-VERTEX COVER *is fixed-parameter tractable (Take II)*: Consider the $k + 1$-level tree in which each vertex x has an associated set S_x containing all vertices in V that have not previously appeared as edge-labels on the path from the root of the tree to x and in which the edge to each child of x is labeled with a different element of S_x. An example of such a tree for $V = \{a,b,c,d\}$ and $k = 2$ is shown in Figure 5.1. Each candidate solution to an instance of VERTEX COVER corresponds to one or more leaves in this tree. As this tree has depth k and each non-leaf vertex has $\leq |V|$ children, by Formula 5 in Table 5.2, the number of candidate solutions for an instance of VERTEX COVER is $\leq |V|^k$.

The points just described demonstrate that one can typically derive the same result in several ways, with each way corresponding to a different encoding of the candidate solutions for a problem.

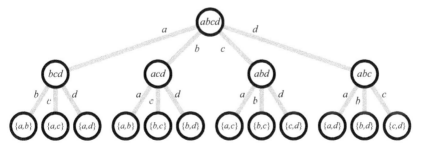

Figure 5.1   A tree whose leaves encode all candidate solutions of an instance of VERTEX COVER in which $V = \{a,b,c,d\}$ and $k = 2$.

Practice 5.2.1   Show that the following problems are fixed-parameter tractable using formulas from Table 5.2.
(a) $|V|$-GRAPH 3-COLORABILITY
(b) $|V|$-CONSISTENT COHERENCE
(c) $|A|$-SUBSET SUM

In certain situations, one need only use brute-force combinatorics to bound a subset of all candidate solutions that is guaranteed to contain a viable solution. An example of this can be found in Chapter 11 for the problem STRUCTURE-MAPPING ANALOGY DERIVATION. The problem takes two concept graphs as input, and its output is a particular (analogical) mapping between the two concept graphs, namely one with the highest possible score (systematicity value). STRUCTURE-MAPPING ANALOGY DERIVATION is fixed-parameter tractable relative to parameter o, the maximum number of objects in the two given concept graphs (see the end of Section 11.3.2). This is proved by showing that the size of the subset of all candidate solutions that is guaranteed to contain a viable solution is bounded by o: Given a mapping between a set of n objects in one concept graph to a set of n objects in the other concept graph, a maximal analogy based on that mapping can be "grown upwards" from the mapped objects in polynomial time. This allows us to skip over all non-maximal analogies based on that mapping as their scores will be less than that of the maximal analogy, and in the problem we are only interested in analogies with the highest possible score. Hence, it suffices to bound the total number of possible object mappings (which turns out to be a function of o) instead of all possible analogies between the given concept graphs.

Though results such as those discussed previously are often relatively easy to prove compared to other fixed-parameter tractability proof techniques, there is one risk of which one should be aware: With brute-force combinatorics, the input parameters involved may inadvertently bound the whole input size as well. This occurs with our fixed-parameter tractability results for $\{|V|, k\}$-VERTEX COVER (each of whose instances consist of a specified $G = (V, E)$ and k) as $|E| \leq |V|^2$ for any graph G.

Practice 5.2.2   Show that the input size of instances of CNF-SAT is bounded by a function of $|U|$.

If the input size is bounded by a function of a set K of input parameters then *any* algorithm for D (whose running time is by definition some function of the input size) has a running time which is bounded by some function of K. This renders such results useless if the goal is (as is the case here with computational-level theories of cognition) to explain how the function specified in D can be computed efficiently even for large input sizes. As long as one is aware of this, then knowing how to use combinatorics can be useful for easily deriving an algorithm that shows that the problem is fixed-parameter tractable for a given parameter set, as long as you are not inadvertently bounding the input size. Additionally, as we shall see in Section 5.2.3, the general idea of bounding the input size by a function of the parameter set turns out to play a crucial role in another technique for deriving fixed-parameter tractable algorithms called reduction to problem kernel.

5.2.2 Bounded Search Trees

Let a *search tree* for a problem be a rooted tree whose vertices encode either all or some subset of the candidate solutions (and at least one viable solution, if such a solution exists) for that problem. Such a search tree for an instance of VERTEX COVER in which $V = \{a,b,c,d\}$ and $k = 2$ is shown in Figure 5.1. The technique of bounded search trees involves constructing a search tree encoding candidate solutions of a parameterized problem K-D such that the following two conditions hold:

1. The total number of vertices in the tree is upper-bounded by $f(K)$ for some function $f(.)$.
2. Any computations done in each of the vertices of the tree (including those required to construct all of the child vertices of a vertex) run in fpt time relative to K.

Stop and Think

Why does the existence of such a bounded search tree for parameter set K for problem D imply that K-D is fixed-parameter tractable?

To see this, let us suppose that the computations done in any vertex can be done in $g(K)n^c$ time for some function $g(.)$. As there are at most $f(K)$ vertices in the tree, the total time required to construct and evaluate all candidate solutions in such a search tree for any instance of K-D is $f(K)g(K)n^c = h(K)n^c$ for some function $h(.)$, which in turn implies that K-D is fixed-parameter tractable.[2]

Many search trees satisfy these conditions relative to some combinations of parameters. For example, the search tree in Figure 5.1 for VERTEX COVER

---

[2] Observe that allowing the computations done in any vertex to be done in fpt time means that the computations done by any brute-force combinatorics algorithm can be done in the single vertex of a single-vertex search tree. Hence, the technique of proving fixed-parameter tractability by brute-force combinatorics is a special case of proving fixed-parameter tractability by bounded search trees.

relative to parameter set $\{|V|, k\}$ is bounded in the sense discussed earlier. However, such a search tree does not exploit additional structure in the problem such as the given graph G – rather, it just enumerates all subsets of size k of a vertex set V, and hence can apply to any graph based on a vertex set of the same size as V. This raises two questions: Can such additional structure be exploited to get better search trees, and if so, under what circumstances is this possible?

One such set of circumstances is when a problem can be decomposed into a set of independent subproblems such that each subproblem has a bounded number of answers and a viable solution for the problem is composed of answers to a bounded number of subproblems.[3] If this problem-decomposition property holds, one may then be able to construct a search tree whose root is any of the independent subproblems and in which (1) the children of each non-leaf vertex correspond to the answers to the subproblem encoded in that vertex and (2) the tree depth is a function of the size of a viable solution for the problem.

Let us now look at how this technique can be used to show the fixed-parameter tractability of k-VERTEX COVER.

Stop and Think

Can you show that k-VERTEX COVER is fixed-parameter tractable by (1) showing that k-VERTEX COVER has the problem-decomposition property and (2) embedding the subproblems so created in a search tree of the form described previously? (Hint: Consider a decomposition in which subproblems are individual edges in G and the answers to such a problem are the vertices in the edge associated with that subproblem.)

The problem-decomposition property is true for k-VERTEX COVER, as each edge in the given graph G must be covered (i.e., each edge in G is a subproblem), each edge in G must have at least one of its endpoints in any vertex cover for G (i.e., each edge-subproblem has two possible answers), and a vertex cover can contain at most k vertices (i.e., a viable solution for the given instance of k-VERTEX COVER is composed of answers to a bounded number of edge-subproblems).

Consider now the following search-tree algorithm based on these edge-subproblems: Select an arbitrary edge (u, v) in G to start building a vertex cover V_C for G. We then have two cases to consider:

---

[3] Algorithm design aficionados will recognize this as the hallmark of problems that are solvable by dynamic programming.

- If u is picked for V_C then all edges in G with u as an endpoint are now covered, and we only need to select future vertices for V_C to cover the remaining edges in G.
- If v is picked for V_C then all edges in G with v as an endpoint are now covered, and we only need to select future vertices for V_C to cover the remaining edges in G.

Let G' and G'' be the respective uncovered subgraphs of G remaining after these cases; both of these can be constructed in time polynomial in the size of G. Observe that if either of G' or G'' has no edges, all edges in G have been covered, and V_C is a vertex cover for G. If on the other hand neither G' nor G'' is empty, we can proceed by applying the logic mentioned previously to each of these graphs. The search tree so constructed will have depth of at most $|V|$ (as a vertex is added to V_C at each step and there are at most $|V|$ vertices in V that can be added). However, if we are only interested in vertex covers of size at most k, observe that if no vertex choice has resulted in an empty uncovered subgraph by depth k *then no vertex cover of size k exists for G* (otherwise, one would have been discovered by then). Two examples of such search trees are shown in Figure 5.2.

What is the running time of this algorithm? As the constructed search tree has depth k and each non-leaf vertex in this tree has exactly two children, by Formula 6 in Table 5.2, the size of the tree is less than 2^{k+1}, yielding a far better running time than exhaustive search trees such as the one in Figure 5.1. Moreover, unlike the brute-force algorithm based on the search tree in Figure 5.1, this algorithm establishes fixed parameter tractability for a parameter set (namely, $\{k\}$) that does *not* bound the input size. Such advantages hold for all bounded search tree-based algorithms, including those in which the number of answers to each subproblem is bounded not by a constant (e.g., two in the case of VERTEX COVER) but rather by a function of the input parameter.

Practice 5.2.3 Consider the following parameterized problem:

INDEPENDENT SET
Input: A graph $G = (V, E)$ with maximum vertex degree d and an integer k.
Parameter: k, d
Question: Does there exist an independent set $V' \subseteq V$ such that $|V'| \geq k$?

Show that this problem is fixed-parameter tractable using the bounded search tree technique. (Hint: Observe that for every vertex v in G, either v or one of its neighbors can be in the independent set and v has has at most d neighbors.)

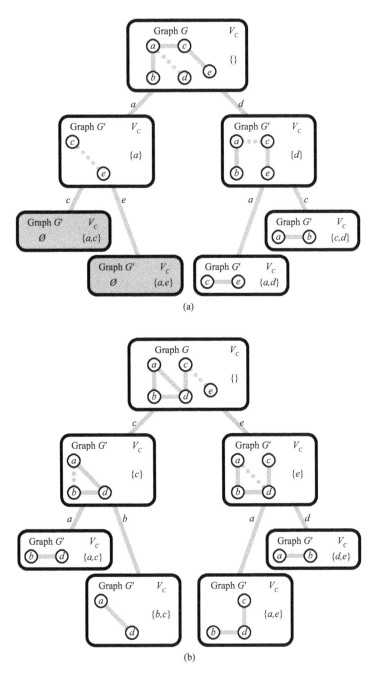

Figure 5.2 Example bounded search trees for the k-VERTEX COVER problem on two graphs of size 5 when $k = 2$. Each vertex in these trees is labeled with a subgraph G' of G remaining after the removal of the vertices in a candidate vertex cover V_C, a randomly selected edge in G' (denoted by a dotted line) that will be used to generate the child vertices of that vertex if that vertex is not already at maximum tree depth, and V_C itself. Observe that the graph in part (a) has two vertex covers of size 2 (namely, $\{A, C\}$ and $\{A, E\}$) while the graph in part (b) has none.

Additional examples of parameterized problems that are shown to be fixed-parameter tractable using the technique of bounded search trees are given in Section 11.3.2.

5.2.3   Reduction to a Problem Kernel

Recall from the end of Section 5.2.1 that if the input size of a problem D is bounded by some input parameter set K then *any* algorithm for D has a running time that is upper-bounded by a function stated purely in terms of K. This property lies at the heart of the technique of proving fixed-parameter tractability by reduction to a problem kernel. This technique involves a transformation of a given instance (i, K) of a parameterized problem K-D into a reduced instance (i', K') of K-D such that the following two conditions hold:

1. (i, K) is a *yes*-instance of K-D if and only if (i', K') is a *yes*-instance of K-D (which is why we use the term "reduction").
2. For all *yes*-instances and possibly some *no*-instances of K-D, the size of i' in the transformed instance (i', K') is upper-bounded by $f(K)$ for some function $f(.)$.

Given the small resulting input size guaranteed by Condition 2, we refer to the reduced instance (i', K') as a *problem kernel*.

Stop and Think ───────────

Why does the existence of such a transformation that runs in fpt time relative to parameter K for problem D imply that K-D is fixed-parameter tractable?

To see this, consider the algorithm A that, for an instance (i, K), applies the transformation to create (i', K') and then, if $|i'| \leq f(K)$, uses any algorithm A' for K-D to solve (i', K'). By Condition 1, such an algorithm will correctly solve K-D (as the transformation does not change the answer, all *no*-instances will be computed correctly (either by having $|i'| > f(K)$ or by the operation of A') and all *yes*-instances will be computed correctly (by the operation of A'). For any i, suppose A' runs in time $g(|i|)$ for some function $g(.)$. As any (transformed) instances passed to A' have $|i'| \leq f(K)$, A' thus runs in time $g(|i'|) - g(f(K)) = g'(K)$ for some function $g'(.)$. Moreover, as the transformation required to create (i', K') runs in fpt time, i.e., in time $f'(K)|i|^c$ for some function $f'(.)$ and constant c, algorithm A runs in time $f'(K)|i|^c + g'(K)$. This runtime has upper bound $f''(K)|i|^c$ for some function

$f''(.)$ because $f'(K)|i|^c + g'(K) \leq f'(K)|i|^c + g'(K)|i|^c = (f'(K) + g'(K))|i|^c = f''(K)|i|^c$. This means that K-D is fixed-parameter tractable.

Let us now look at how this technique can be used to show the fixed-parameter tractability of k-VERTEX COVER.

Stop and Think

Prove that k-VERTEX COVER is fixed-parameter tractable by using the technique of reduction to problem kernel. (Hint: Consider a transformation phrased as the repeated application of a set of rules, each of which reduces the size of the instance of k-VERTEX COVER in some principled way [possibly by changing the value of k as well as the structure of given graph G]).

Transformations phrased in terms of such reduction rules need not be complex. Consider the following pair of reduction rules for k-VERTEX COVER:

R_1: If there is a vertex v of degree $\geq k + 1$ in G, remove v and all edges with v as an endpoint to create G' and set $k' = k - 1$.

R_2: If there is a vertex of degree 0 in G, remove v to create G' and set $k' = k$.

These rules are used in the following algorithm: Repeatedly apply rules R_1 and R_2 to a given instance (G, k) of k-VERTEX COVER in any order until neither rule can be applied anymore, resulting in reduced instance $(G' = (V', E'), k')$. If $|V'| > k'(k' + 1)$, the answer is *no*; otherwise, the answer is that returned by the brute-force algorithm that examines each of the subsets of V' of size k' to see if it is a vertex cover for G'.

First we need to question whether this algorithm is correct, i.e., does the initial transformation in this algorithm satisfy Conditions 1 and 2? Consider each of our reduction rules.

- In the case of rule R_1, any vertex of degree $\geq k + 1$ must be in any vertex cover of size $\leq k$; otherwise, to cover all edges adjacent to that vertex, all neighbors of that vertex would have to be in the vertex cover, leading to a vertex cover of size $\geq k + 1$ and a contradiction. This means that (G', k') created by removing such a vertex and its connected edges and setting $k' = k$ has the same answer as (G, k).
- In the case of rule R_2, vertices of degree 0 have no connected edges and hence need not be in any vertex cover for G. This means that (G', k') created by removing such a vertex and setting $k' = k$ cannot change the answer to (G, k).

Hence, the application of rule R_1 or R_2 does not change the answer for (G',k') from that for (G,k), and Condition 1 is satisfied. As for Condition 2, suppose that G' has both more than $k'(k'+1)$ vertices and a vertex cover V_C of size k'. Courtesy of rule R_1, each vertex in G' has degree at most k'; hence, each vertex in V_C can cover edges to at most k' additional vertices in G'. This means that the maximum number of vertices in $V_C \cup \{N_{G'}(v'): v' \in V_C\}$ is $k' + (k' \times k') = k'(k'+1)$, where $N_G(v) = \{v': (v,v') \in E\}$. However, as $|V'| > k'(k'+1)$, this means there is at least one vertex v in G' that is not connected by an edge to any vertex in V_C but is nonetheless connected by an edge e to some other vertex in G' (because, courtesy of rule R_2, there are no singleton vertices in G'). An example of a reduced graph G' containing such an edge e is shown in Figure 5.3. As e is not covered by V_C, this is a contradiction; hence, if G' is such that $|V'| > k'(k'+1)$. G' cannot have a vertex cover of size k'. This is not to say that if $|V'| \le k'(k'+1)$, there is necessarily a vertex cover of size k' in G'; however, it does suffice to show that for all *yes*-instances and possibly some *no*-instances, $|V'|$ (and hence, as $|E'| \le |V'|^2$, $k' \le |V'|$, and $k' \le k$, the size of (G',k')) is upper bounded by some function of k. Two example runs of

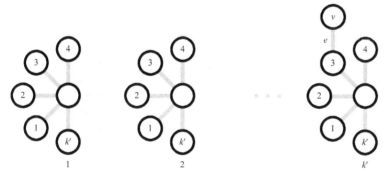

Figure 5.3   An example reduced graph for k-VERTEX COVER which violates condition 2 (adapted from Figure 4.2 in van Rooij (2003)). Graph G' consists of k' components, each of which is a star subgraph whose center is one of the vertices in a putative vertex cover V_C of G' of size k'. The first $(k'-1)$ of these stars has k' vertices connected by edges to its center, and the kth star has in addition a pendant vertex v that is connected to one of the vertices in G' not in V_C by an edge e. Observe that G' is fully reduced, as neither of the reduction rules R_1 or R_2 described in the main text can be applied to G'; moreover, $|V'| = k' + (k' \times k') + 1 = k'(k'+1)+1 > k'(k'+1)$. However, V_C is not a vertex cover of size k' for G' as edge e is not covered by any vertex in V_C. Adapted from van Rooij (2003).

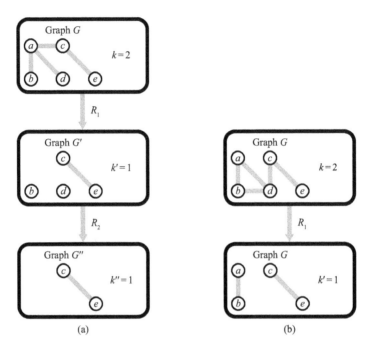

Figure 5.4   Example runs of a simple problem-kernelization algorithm for the
k-VERTEX COVER problem on two graphs of size 5 when $k = 2$. The
graphs in (a) and (b) are the graphs given in parts (a) and (b) of
Figure 5.2. This figure shows the results of applying the reduction rules
R_1 and R_2 described in the text. As the graph G'' in part (a) has
$|V''| = 2 \le k''(k'' + 1) = 1(1 + 1) = 2$, it is processed by the
brute-force algorithm (which gives the returned answer *yes*). However, as
the graph G' in part (b) has $|V'| = 4 > k'(k' + 1) = 1(1 + 1) = 2$, the
returned answer is *no*.

this algorithm relative to the graphs in parts (a) and (b) of Figure 5.2 are shown
in Figure 5.4.

Now that we know our algorithm is correct, what is its running time? The
transformation of (G, k) into (G', k') can be done in $O(|V|^c)$ time for some
constant c (as the application of each reduction rule can be done in time
polynomial in the size of the given graph, each rule removes at most one
vertex from the graph, and there are $|V|$ vertices in the original given graph
to remove). Checking if G' is such that $|V'| \ge k'(k' + 1)$ can be done by
counting the vertices in V' in time $O(|V'|) = O(|V|)$. Finally, running the
brute-force vertex cover algorithm on G' when $|V'| < k'(k' + 1)$ can be done
in time $|V'|^{k'}|E'| \le |V'|^{k'}|V'|^2 \le k'(k' + 1)^{k'}k'(k' + 1)^2$. As $k' \le k$, the

algorithm as a whole thus runs in time $O(|V|^c + |V| + k'(k'+1)^{k'}k'(k'+1)^2) = O(|V|^{c+1} + k(k+1)^k k(k+1)^2)$, which shows that k-Vertex Cover is fixed-parameter tractable.

Sometimes, a proof of fixed-parameter tractability by reduction to a problem kernel need not involve reduction rules at all. This is the case for the following parameterized problem:

Connected Max Cut

Input: A connected graph $G = (V, E)$ and a positive integer k.

Parameter: k

Question: Does there exist a partition of V into sets A and B such that the number of edges in $\text{Cut}_G(A, B) \geq k$, where $\text{Cut}_G(A, B) = \{(u, v) \in E : u \in A \text{ and } v \in B\}$?

Stop and Think

Can you prove that k-Connected Max Cut is fixed-parameter tractable by reduction to a problem kernel? (Hint: Observe that every connected graph on n vertices has a spanning tree with $n - 1$ edges.)

To see this, suppose that we have computed a spanning tree T for our given graph G. By the observation in the stop and think box, the edges in this spanning tree imply that there is a cut of size at least $n - 1$ in G. This is because, moving outwards in T from any vertex $v \in T$, the vertices encountered can be assigned in alternating fashion to the sets A or B (see part (b) of Figure 5.5). This means that all $n - 1$ edges in T will be cut by this partition. This partition may also cut additional edges in G that are not in T, but this cannot decrease the size of the cut guaranteed by the edges in T. Given this, we can construct the following fixed-parameter tractable algorithm for solving k-Connected Max Cut: First count the number n of vertices in V, which can be done in $O(|V|) = O(n)$ time. If $n > k + 1$ then the algorithm returns the answer *yes* (as there will exist a cut of size $n - 1$, which by the inequality is a cut of size greater than k). Otherwise, as $|V| \leq k$, exhaustively search for a cut, which on an instance of this size runs in time $O(2^k k^2)$. This means that the overall running time of this algorithm is $O(2^k k^2 + n)$, which is fixed-parameter tractable time relative to k.

It is important to note that this method worked because we were dealing with a *connected* graph. Things become a bit more interesting when the given graph is unconnected.

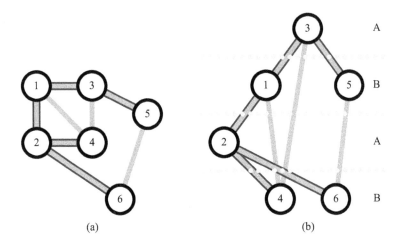

Figure 5.5   Example graph cut derived from a spanning tree. (a) An undirected graph
G on 6 vertices and one of its spanning trees T. The edges in T are
indicated in bold. (b) A partition of the vertices of G into sets $A = \{2, 3\}$
and $B = \{1, 4, 5, 6\}$ derived using T rooted at vertex 3. All edges in T are
in $\text{Cut}_G(A, B)$. Of the the remaining edges in G that are not in T, $(1, 4)$
and $(5, 6)$ are not in $\text{Cut}_G(A, B)$ (as each edge's endpoints are in B) and
$(3, 4)$ is in $\text{Cut}_G(A, B)$ (as endpoint 3 is in A and endpoint 4 is in B).

Practice 5.2.4   Consider the following parameterized problem:

MAX CUT
Input: A graph $G = (V, E)$ and a positive integer k.
Parameter: k
Question: Does there exist a partition of V into sets A and
B such that the number of edges in $\text{Cut}_G(A, B) \geq k$, where
$\text{Cut}_G(A, B) = \{(u, v) \in E : u \in A \text{ and } v \in B\}$?

Show that k-MAX CUT is fixed-parameter tractable by reduction to a
problem kernel. (Hint: In the reduction, get rid of vertices with degree 0
and 1. Observe that this ensures components have size at least 3, and each
such component on m vertices has a cut of size $\geq m$. Observe also that if
there are too many such components, then there always exists a cut of size
at least k.)

Additional examples of parameterized problems that are shown to be fixed-
parameter tractable using the technique of reduction to a problem kernel are
given in Section 10.3.2.[4]

---

[4]   Indeed, there are an infinite number of such examples. This is so because it is known that if a
problem is fixed-parameter tractable then it can be reduced to a problem kernel (Cai et al.,
1997, theorem 2.1).

5.3   Helpful Strategies for Proving Fixed-Parameter Tractability

Deriving fixed-parameter tractable algorithms from scratch can be quite challenging. Many parameterized analyses have been done over the last 25 years. Hence, it may be well worth your while to invest time to see if fixed-parameter tractable algorithms for problems similar to yours already exist. Although there are still relatively few fixed-parameter tractable algorithms known for computational-level theories, Appendix C contains a variety of parameterized complexity results that may inspire your own proofs. This search should be supplemented with index-assisted dips into other standard works on parameterized complexity (see Further Readings later in this chapter); of particular use here is the compendium of fixed-parameter tractability results given in section A.1 of Downey and Fellows (1999).

Assuming this doesn't work, you can derive fixed-parameter tractable algorithms from scratch using one of the techniques described in Section 5.2. Given your initial literature search, you may also be able to use an additional technique. As you may recall from the beginning of Section 3.2, you can prove that a problem D_1 is solvable in polynomial time by providing a polynomial-time reduction from D_1 to another problem D_2 that is known to be solvable in polynomial time. Analogously, you can prove that a parameterized problem K-D_1 is fixed-parameter tractable by providing a *parameterized reduction* from K-D_1 to a parameterized problem K'-D_2 that is known to fixed-parameter tractable. The notion of parameterized reduction required to do this is the focus of the next chapter.

5.4   Exercises

Exercise 5.4.1   The following $O(.)$ expressions represent the worst-case running times of different algorithms, where n is a measure of the input size and p, q, and r are parameters (you may assume that $p, q, r \leq n$). Which of the following running times are fixed-parameter tractable (fpt) running times? Give the smallest possible parameter set for which the running times are fpt (if one exists) and explain your answer.

(a) $O(p^q n^2)$
(b) $O(qn^p)$
(c) $O(qn^{pr})$
(d) $O(\frac{p^2}{q} 6^r n^3)$

Exercise 5.4.2   Reconsider Table 2.1 and prove that the running times listed there are fpt running times for parameter k.

Exercise 5.4.3   Prove that if a decision problem D has an algorithm then there is a parameter set K such that K-D is fixed-parameter tractable.

Exercise 5.4.4   Consider the following problem:

> LONGEST COMMON SUBSEQUENCE
> **Input:** A set of strings $S = \{s_1, s_2, \ldots, s_m\}$ of maximum length n over an alphabet Σ and a positive integer l.
> **Question:** Is there a string of length l that is a subsequence of every string in S?

A string x is a subsequence of a string y if all of the symbols of x occur (possibly non-adjacently) in the same order in y. For instance, *cab*, *aie*, and *bit* but not *abc*, *aei*, and *eta* are subsequences of *cabinet*.

(a) Show that $\{|\Sigma|, l\}$-LONGEST COMMON SUBSEQUENCE is fixed-parameter tractable by using the technique of brute-force combinatorics.

(b) Show that for some functions $f_1(.)$ and $f_2(.)$, $m \leq f_1(|\Sigma|, l)$ and $n \leq f_2(|\Sigma|, l)$ for any instance of LONGEST COMMON SUBSEQUENCE. (Hint: Show how the strings in an instance of LONGEST COMMON SUBSEQUENCE can be recoded to be of length that is upper-bounded by some function of $|\Sigma|$ and l.)

Exercise 5.4.5   Show that for some function $f(.)$, $\sum_{c \in C} |c| \leq f(|U|)$ for any instance of SATISFIABILITY.

Exercise 5.4.6   Show that $\{|H|, |G|\}$-SUBGRAPH ISOMORPHISM is fixed-parameter tractable by using the technique of brute-force combinatorics.

Exercise 5.4.7   Do the leaves of the bounded search trees constructed for an instance of k-VERTEX COVER using the algorithm described in Section 5.2.2 in which the graph G' is empty (i.e., has no vertices or edges) correspond to all possible vertex covers of size $\leq k$ for that instance? If so, give a proof. If not, give a counterexample.

Exercise 5.4.8   Show that the following parameterized problem is fixed-parameter tractable by using the technique of bounded search trees:

> l-SIMPLE PATH NUMBER
> **Input:** A graph G in which each vertex has degree 3, a pair of vertices u and v in G, and positive integers k and l.
> **Parameter:** l
> **Question:** Is the number of simple paths of length $\leq l$ between u and v in G at most k?

Exercise 5.4.9   Assume that in the algorithm for k-VERTEX COVER given in Section 5.2.3, the vertices removed by applications of reduction rule R_1 are added to each of the vertex covers of size k' for graph G' computed by the brute-force algorithm to create vertex covers of size k for graph G. For any given graph G, will this process always produce all vertex covers of size k for G? If so, give a proof. If not, give a counterexample.

Exercise 5.4.10 Show that the following parameterized problem is fixed-parameter tractable by using the technique of reduction to a problem kernel:

$\{k,d\}$-DOMINATING SET
Input: A graph $G = (V,E)$ with maximum vertex degree d and a positive integer k.
Parameter: k,d
Question: Does there exist a dominating set $V' \subseteq V$ such that $|V'| \le k$? (Here a vertex set V' is called a dominating set if for every vertex $v \in V$ either $v \in V'$ or there is an edge (u,v) with $u \in V'$.)

(Hint: Modify the proof of the fixed-parameter tractability of k-VERTEX COVER given in Section 5.2.3.)

5.5   Further Reading

The notion of fixed-parameter tractability described here was proposed by Rod Downey and Mike Fellows in the early 1990s as part of their theory of parameterized computational complexity. There are several good computer science books describing this theory (Downey and Fellows, 1999, 2013; Flum and Grohe, 2006). Given the increasing number of new techniques for and applications of parameterized complexity analysis appearing in recent years, interested readers are strongly encouraged to consult up-to-date online resources such as the Parameterized Complexity Wiki (http://fpt.wikidot.com). An accessible summary of applications of parameterized complexity analysis in cognitive science is given in van Rooij and Wareham (2008).

There are a number of techniques for proving fixed-parameter tractability in addition to those covered in this chapter. Many of these techniques invoke complex mathematical and/or algorithmic methods, e.g., iterative compression, treewidth, cuts and separators, dynamic programming, sieves, and convolutions. Readers wishing detailed and comprehensive treatments of these techniques would do well to consult Cygan et al. (2015) and Niedermeier (2006). Shorter summaries are also given in Hüffner, Niedermeier, and Wernicke (2008) and Sloper and Telle (2008).

6   Parameterized Reductions

In this chapter we introduce the notion of parameterized reductions. We explain how this technique can be used to transform an input for a parameterized problem K-A into an input or parameterized problem K-B, mapping *yes*-instances for K-A to *yes*-instances for K-B and vice versa. If this transformation can be done in fixed-parameter tractable time, this implies that if K-B is fixed-parameter tractable, then so is K-A; conversely, if K-A is not fixed-parameter tractable, then neither is K-B. Like the polynomial-time reductions introduced in Chapter 3, parameterized reductions are a powerful technique for relating problems to each other. We will demonstrate parameterized analogues of each of the reduction strategies described in Chapter 3. We also include several exercises for practicing this technique.

6.1   Fixed-Parameter Intractability: Initial Thoughts

In the previous chapter, we looked at various techniques for showing that a problem is fixed-parameter tractable relative to a particular parameter set. We also know, courtesy of Exercise 5.4.3, that every problem that has an algorithm is fixed-parameter tractable relative to *some* aspects of that problem. It is to be be expected, though, that this is not the case relative to *any* aspect. Consider the following parameterized problem associated with the problem GENERALIZED CHESS given in Section 3.1:

t-GENERALIZED CHESS
Input: An $n \times n$ checkerboard, with an arbitrary number of pieces set on them (but one king each); the normal rules of chess apply save the "50-moves rule."
Parameter: The number t of types of chess pieces.
Question: Does white have a winning strategy that always checkmates black in a finite number of moves?

This problem cannot be fixed-parameter tractable by an algorithm with running time $f(t)n^c$; otherwise, as there are $t = 6$ types of pieces in chess, such an algorithm would solve GENERALIZED CHESS in $f(6)n^c = c'n^c$ = polynomial time, which would contradict the non-polynomial time complexity of GENERALIZED CHESS.

Unfortunately, simple proofs like this one are rare.

───────────────── **Stop and Think** ─────────────────

Can you think of an fp-tractable algorithm for k-CLIQUE? If not, (a) what is the best fp-tractable algorithm you can think of in which k is part of the parameter set, and (b) can you prove that there is no fp-tractable algorithm for k-CLIQUE?

It is easy to show that $\{|V|, k\}$-CLIQUE is fixed-parameter tractable – simply generate each of the $|V|^k$ subsets of V of size k in the given graph G and for each subset, see if it is a k-clique in G (the latter can be done in polynomial time because CLIQUE is in NP [see Practice 4.2.1]). However, no one has yet either found an fp-tractable algorithm for k-CLIQUE or shown that no such algorithm exists. Indeed, this is the case for a great many parameterized problems.

How, then, do we establish fixed-parameter intractability? Recall that questions about the polynomial-time intractability of a given problem D were answered in Chapters 3 and 4 by proving a weaker but nonetheless useful statement – namely, that if D is solvable in polynomial time then so are all NP-complete problems. Parameterized intractability can be addressed in an analogous manner – namely, if K-D is fixed-parameter tractable then so are all parameterized problems that are complete for some class of parameterized problems that is either known or strongly conjectured to include the class of all parameterized problems that are fixed-parameter tractable. To do this, we will need two new concepts: (1) a reducibility between parameterized problems and (2) classes of parameterized problems whose hardest members are either known or strongly conjectured to be fixed-parameter intractable. These two concepts will be defined and explained in this chapter and the following one, respectively.

6.2 Parameterized Reductions

We define parameterized reducibility as follows.

DEFINITION 6.1 *For parameterized problems K_1-D_1 and K_2-D_2 we say that K_1-D_1 parameterized reduces to K_2-D_2,*[1] *if there exists an algorithm A*

───

[1] Note that this is also written as K_1-$D_1 \leq_m^{fpt} K_2$-D_2 in the computer science literature.

that transforms any instance (i_1, K_1) of K_1-D_1 into an instance (i_2, K_2) of K_2-D_2 such that the following conditions are met:

1. *For each parameter $k \in K_2$, we have $k \leq g(K_1)$ for some function g depending only on the elements of K_1.*
2. *(i_2, K_2) is a yes-instance for K_2-D_2 if and only if (i_1, K_1) is a yes-instance for K_1-D_1.*
3. *A runs in time $O(f(K_1)|i_1|^\alpha)$ for some function f and some constant α.*

Like the polynomial-time reductions described in this book, parameterized reductions are also many-one reductions as described at the beginning of Section 3.3. Aside from the obvious differences in running time of the underlying instance transformation algorithms, the main difference between parameterized reductions and the polynomial-time reductions defined in Chapter 3 is the requirement encoded in Condition 1 that the parameters in the two parameterized problems involved be numerically related. This ensures the following very useful observations:

Observation 6.2.1 *If K_1-D_1 parameterized reduces to K_2-D_2 and K_2-D_2 is fixed-parameter tractable then K_1-D_1 is also fixed-parameter tractable.*

Observation 6.2.2 *If K_1-D_1 parameterized reduces to K_2-D_2 and K_1-D_1 is not fixed-parameter tractable then K_2-D_2 is not fixed-parameter tractable either.*

Practice 6.2.1   Prove Observations 6.2.1 and 6.2.2.

Stop and Think

Suppose K_1-D_1 parameterized reduces to K_2-D_2. If we know that K_1-D_1 is fixed-parameter tractable, does this imply anything about K_2-D_2? Similarly, if we know that K_2-D_2 is not fixed-parameter tractable, does this imply anything about K_1-D_1?

It turns out that neither of these situations imply anything about their respective problems. As was the case with polynomial-time reductions in the introduction to Section 3.2, this is because the given results cannot be combined with the reduction to either imply that k_2-D_2 is fixed-parameter tractable (in the first case) or that k_1-D_2 is not fixed-parameter tractable (in the second case). Hence, as with polynomial-time reductions, one should be very careful with the order of the problems in parameterized reductions – only certain combinations of reduction problem order and known results for one of those problems can be used to get new information about the other problem.

In the remainder of this chapter, let's look at various ways of creating parameterized reductions, starting once again as in Section 3.2.1 with a simple reduction from CLIQUE to INDEPENDENT SET.

6.2.1   Reducing CLIQUE to INDEPENDENT SET Redux

Consider the following two parameterized problems associated with the problems CLIQUE and INDEPENDENT SET.

k-CLIQUE
Input: A graph $G = (V, E)$ and an integer k.
Parameter: k
Question: Does there exist a clique $V' \subseteq V$ such that $|V'| \geq k$? (Here a vertex set V' is called a *clique* if for all two vertices $u, v \in V'$ there is an edge $(u, v) \in E$.)

k-INDEPENDENT SET
Input: A graph $G = (V, E)$ and a positive integer k.
Parameter: k
Question: Does there exist an independent set $V' \subseteq V$ such that $|V'| \geq k$? (Here a vertex set V' is called an *independent set* if there exists no two vertices $u, v \in V'$ such that $(u, v) \in E$.)

Recall that in Section 3.2.1, we gave a polynomial-time reduction from CLIQUE to INDEPENDENT SET in which an instance $(G = (V, E), k)$ of CLIQUE was transformed into an instance $(G' = (V, E'), k)$ of INDEPENDENT SET in which E' was the set of all possible edges on the vertices in V that were *not* in G. This built on the observation that in a clique *every* pair of vertices are connected by an edge while in an independent set *no* pair of vertices are connected by an edge. A consequence of this observation is that any clique in G has a corresponding independent set in G' of exactly the same size. It is this consequence (along with the observation that any instance transformation algorithm that runs in polynomial time also runs in fixed-parameter time relative to any parameter) that proves that the polynomial-time reduction between CLIQUE and INDEPENDENT SET given in Section 3.2.1 is also a parameterized reduction between k-CLIQUE and k-INDEPENDENT SET.

Practice 6.2.2   Prove that any algorithm for a problem D that runs in polynomial time also runs in fixed-parameter time relative to any parameter of D.

In general, to formally prove that a parameterized problem K_1-D_1 parameterized reduces to a parameterized problem K_2-D_2, all of the following steps have to be followed:

1. Describe an algorithm A that transforms instances of K_1-D_1 into instances of K_2-D_2 (this description can be greatly aided by an example as was given in Figure 3.1 for the reduction from CLIQUE to INDEPENDENT SET in Section 3.2.1).

2. Verify that for *any* given instance of K_1-D_1, A constructs an instance of K_2-D_2 such that for any $k \in K_2$ we have $k \leq g(K_1)$ for some function g depending only on the elements in K_1.

3. Consider an *arbitrary* instance i_1 of K_1-D_1. Prove that i_1 is a *yes*-instance for K_1-D_1 *if and only if* $i_2 = A(i_1)$ is a *yes*-instance for K_2-D_2. The "if and only if" proof can be broken into two subproofs:

   (a) Assume that i_1 is a *yes*-instance of K_1-D_1. Show then that i_2 is also a *yes*-instance of K_2-D_2.

   (b) Assume that i_2 is a *yes*-instance of K_2-D_2. Show then that i_1 is also a *yes*-instance of K_1-D_1.

   Several ways of doing these subproofs were already discussed in Section 3.2.1.

4. Show that A runs in fixed-parameter tractable time relative to K_1.

Practice 6.2.3   Prove that the polynomial-time reduction from CLIQUE to INDEPENDENT SET given in Section 3.2.1 is also a parameterized reduction from k-CLIQUE to k-INDEPENDENT SET using the proof steps given above.

Re-using existing polynomial-time reductions to show parameterized reducibility can be a great time-saver. That being said, as we shall see later, this doesn't always work.

6.2.2   Reduction by Local Replacement

The transformation in the previous subsection was an example of the reduction technique that we call local replacement (see Section 3.2.2), as the transformation from an instance i_1 of problem D_1 to an instance i_2 of problem D_2 proceeded by local modifications of structures in i_1 to create the corresponding structures in i_2. If D_1 and D_2 involve the same type of entities, e.g., both are graph problems, such reductions can be particularly simple and elegant.

Practice 6.2.4   Reconsider the polynomial-time reduction from INDEPENDENT SET to CLIQUE that you did in Section 3.2.1. Show why this is also a parameterized reduction from k-INDEPENDENT SET to k-CLIQUE.

Given the previous discussion, it is tempting to think that polynomial-time reductions are *always* parameterized reductions as well. It turns out that this is true, but in an unexpected way.

Stop and Think

Reconsider the polynomial-time reduction from VERTEX COVER to INDEPENDENT SET and INDEPENDENT SET to VERTEX COVER that you did in Section 3.2.2. Are these also parameterized reductions from k-VERTEX COVER to k-INDEPENDENT SET and k-INDEPENDENT SET to k-VERTEX COVER? If so, why? If not, why not?

Recall from the reductions given in Section 3.2.2 that there exists an independent set of size k in G if and only if there is a vertex cover of size $|V| - k$ in G. The size of the vertex cover in G is thus a function of both the size k of the independent set and $|V|$ in the reduction from INDEPENDENT SET to VERTEX COVER. Similarly, the size of the independent set is a function of both the size k of the vertex cover and $|V|$ in the reduction from VERTEX COVER to INDEPENDENT SET. Hence, these reductions are not parameterized reductions because the parameters in k-VERTEX COVER and k-INDEPENDENT SET are not functions of each other in the manner specified in Condition 1 in Definition 6.1. This is not to say that this is not true of other parameters. For example, as the number of vertices in the graphs does not change under these reductions, the polynomial-time reductions in Section 3.2.1 between VERTEX COVER and INDEPENDENT SET are actually parameterized reductions between $|V|$-MINIMUM SET COVER and $|V|$-INDEPENDENT SET. Hence, our tempting earlier statement should perhaps be rewritten thus: Polynomial-time reductions are *always* parameterized reductions relative to *some* parameters – however, these parameters need not be the parameters for which results are wanted.

Practice 6.2.5 Show that the polynomial-time reductions between VERTEX COVER and INDEPENDENT SET that you did in Section 3.2.2 are also parameterized reductions between $\{|V|, k\}$-VERTEX COVER and $\{|V|, k\}$-INDEPENDENT SET.

Practice 6.2.6 Reconsider the polynomial-time reduction from CNF-SAT to 3SAT given in Section 3.2.2. Is this also a parameterized reduction, and if so, relative to which parameterized problems associated with CNF-SAT and 3SAT?

The previous reductions are between graph problems. However, with a bit of ingenuity, reductions by local replacement can also be constructed between problems of different types. Such reductions essentially involve different representations of the same entity. For example, consider the following reduction from k-DOMINATING SET to k-MINIMUM SET COVER:

k-DOMINATING SET

Input: An graph $G = (V, E)$ and a positive integer k.

Parameter: k

Question: Does there exist a dominating set $V' \subseteq V$ such that $|V'| \leq k$? (Here a vertex set V' is called a *dominating set* if for every vertex $v \in V$ either $v \in V'$ or there is an edge (u, v) with $u \in V'$.)

k-MINIMUM SET COVER

Input: A universe U of elements, and a collection S of subsets of U; an integer k.

Parameter: k

Question: Does U have a set cover $C \subseteq S$ of size at most k? (Here, a *set cover* is a subset of the collection such that the union of the sets in C equals U.)

Although graphs are typically encoded as sets of vertices and edges (see Figure 6.1(a)), we can also encode a graph as the set of vertex neighborhoods, where the neighborhood of vertex v in graph G consists of v itself and all vertices in G that are directly connected to v by an edge in G. Let $N[G] = \{N[v_1]_1, \ldots, N[v_{|V|}]\}$ be the encoding of graph G as a set of closed vertex neighborhood sets, one for each vertex in G. Figure 6.1(b) shows $N(G)$ for a simple graph G. Observe that the vertices dominated by a vertex v in G are precisely those vertices in the closed neighborhood of v – that is, $N[v]$. Hence, the question of whether there is a dominating set of size k in G can be rephrased as the question of whether there are k sets in $N(G)$ whose elements correspond

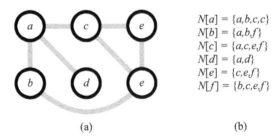

(a)   (b)

Figure 6.1   Two encodings of a simple graph. (a) A graph encoded in terms of sets of vertices and edges (shown in a diagram). (b) A graph encoded in terms of vertex neighborhoods.

to all of the vertices in G, which is the question answered in MINIMUM SET COVER.

Given this observation, our reduction is as follows: Given an instance $(G = (V, E), k)$ of k-DOMINATING SET, construct an instance (U, S, k') of k-MINIMUM SET COVER such that $U = \{u_1, \ldots, u_{|V|}\}$, $S = \{S_1, \ldots, S_{|V|}\}$ such that $S_i = \{u_i\} \cup \{u_j : (v_i, v_j) \in E\}$, and $k' = k$. As this transformation involves the creation of the $|V|$ entities in each of U and S, and the creation of each element in S involves looking at all edges in E, it can be done in polynomial time. The parameters of the two problems are related by the identity function; furthermore, it follows from the logic of the previous discussion that there is a dominating set of size k in G if and only if there is a set cover of size k' in S. Hence, we have just shown that k-DOMINATING SET parameterized reduces to k-MINIMUM SET COVER.

Practice 6.2.7 Give and prove the correctness of a parameterized reduction from k-INDEPENDENT SET to the following problem:

k-SET PACKING
Input: A finite family of sets $S = \{S_1, \ldots, S_n\}$ and a positive integer k.
Parameter: k
Question: Is there a subset $S' \subseteq S$ of size k such that for all $S_i', S_j' \in S'$, $S_i' \cap S_j' = \emptyset$?

Additional examples of reduction by local replacement can be found in Sections 10.3 and 11.3.

6.2.3   Reduction by Restriction

We now consider two examples of parameterized reductions that are reductions by restriction (see Section 3.2.3) – namely, reductions in which the transformation in the reduction exploits the fact that the problem being reduced from is either directly or courtesy of rephrasing a restricted case of the problem being reduced to.

Our first example involves the following two parameterized problems associated with CLIQUE and SUBGRAPH ISOMORPHISM.

k-CLIQUE
Input: A graph $G = (V, E)$ and an integer k.
Parameter: k
Question: Does there exist a clique $V' \subseteq V$ such that $|V'| \leq k$?

$\{|V(H)|, |E(H)|\}$-SUBGRAPH ISOMORPHISM
Input: Two graphs G and H.
Parameter: $\{|V(H)|, |E(H)|\}$
Question: Is there a subgraph G' of G that is isomorphic to H? (Here two graphs G' and H are *isomorphic* if there is a mapping $m:V(G') \to V(H)$ such that $(u,v) \in E(G') \leftrightarrow (m(u), m(v)) \in E(H)$.)

Recall that in Section 3.2.3, we have a polynomial-time reduction from CLIQUE to SUBGRAPH ISOMORPHISM in which an instance $(G = (V, E), k)$ of CLIQUE was transformed into an instance $(G = (V, E), H = K_k)$ of SUBGRAPH ISOMORPHISM where K_k is the complete graph on k vertices. This reduction demonstrated that CLIQUE is a special case of SUBGRAPH ISOMORPHISM. Moreover, as both the number of vertices and the number of edges in graph H in the constructed instances of SUBGRAPH ISOMORPHISM are functions of k in the given instance of CLIQUE (namely, $|V(H)| = k$ and $|E(H)| = k(k-1)/2$), this is also a parameterized reduction from k-CLIQUE to $\{|V(H)|, |E(H)|\}$-SUBGRAPH ISOMORPHISM.

Our second example is slightly more complex and involves the following two parameterized problems associated with SUBSET SUM and KNAPSACK.

k-SUBSET SUM
Input: A set of elements $A = \{a_1, \ldots, a_n\}$, a positive integer $s(a)$ associated with each $a \in A$, and an integer k.
Parameter: k
Question: Is there a subset $A' \subseteq A$ such that $\sum_{a \in A'} s(a) = k$?

$\{C, W\}$-KNAPSACK
Input: A set of n elements $A = \{a_1, \ldots, a_n\}$, a positive integer $c(a)$ ("cost") and a positive integer $w(a)$ ("weight") associated with each $a \in A$, and integers C and W.
Parameter: $\{C, W\}$
Question: Is there a subset $A' \subset A$ such that $\sum_{a \in A'} c(a) \geq C$, yet $\sum_{a \in A'} w(a) \leq W$?

On the surface, there seems to be a serious mismatch in the structures of these problems – namely, SUBSET SUM has only a single weight function that must sum over a group of elements to equality, and KNAPSACK has two weight functions that must sum to less than or equal to and greater than or equal to separate limits over the same set of elements. Consider, however, the following two obvious but most useful observations:

1. Two differently labeled weight functions can encode the same numerical weight function.
2. If $x \leq y$ and $x \geq y$ then $x = y$.

We can exploit these by setting $c(.) = w(.) = s(.)$ and $C = W = k$ in our constructed instance of KNAPSACK. This will not only force the sum of the costs $c(.)$ and weights $w(.)$ of any selected subset A' of A to be the same but also force this sum to be the same as the sum of $s(.)$ over A'. Moreover, if the sums of the weights and the costs are respectively $\leq W = k$ and $\geq C = k$, these sums will all be forced to have value k. Hence, we can now see that SUBSET SUM is indeed a special case of KNAPSACK. As the previous transformation only involves copying entities in a given instance of SUBSET SUM to create the constructed instance of KNAPSACK, it can be done in polynomial time. Hence, it shows that k-SUBSET SUM parameterized reduces to $\{C, W\}$-KNAPSACK.

Practice 6.2.8 Reconsider the polynomial-time reduction from PARTITION to SUBSET SUM given in Section 3.2.3. Is this also a parameterized reduction, and if so, relative to which parameterized problems associated with PARTITION and SUBSET SUM?

Practice 6.2.9 Reconsider the polynomial-time reduction from PARTITION to MAX CUT given in Section 3.2.3. Is this also a parameterized reduction, and if so, relative to which parameterized problems associated with PARTITION and MAX CUT?

Practice 6.2.10 Give and prove the correctness of a parameterized reduction from VERTEX COVER to HITTING COVER.

6.2.4   Reduction by Component Design

The final reduction technique that we will discuss here is reduction by component design (see Section 3.2.4), in which a reduction from a problem D_1 to a problem D_2 essentially constructs an instance of D_2 in terms of so-called components which encode both the given instance of D_1 as well as mechanisms for generating and checking the validity of all possible candidate solutions for that instance. Such reductions are typically employed when reductions by restriction and local replacement cannot be derived.

A nice example of a parameterized reduction by component design is that from k-DOMINATING SET to the following problem:

k-STEINER GRAPH
Input: A graph $G = (V, E)$, a subset $S \subseteq V$, and a positive integer k.
Parameter: k
Question: Is there a subset $T \subseteq V - S$ of size at most k such that the subgraph of G composed of the vertices in $S \cup T$ and all edges in G connecting these vertices is connected?

This problem differs from the STEINER TREE IN GRAPHS problem defined in Exercise 3.4.5 in that the derived subgraph here is only required to be connected instead of being a tree and can hence include cycles. Recall from Section 6.2.2 that the question of finding a dominating set of size at most k in a graph G can be rephrased in terms of finding at most k vertex neighborhoods whose union is the vertices in G. Given this, our reduction needs to create components in an instance $(G' = (V', E'), S, k')$ of STEINER GRAPH which encode the following entities and processes in an instance $(G = (V, E), k)$ of DOMINATING SET:

1. The vertex neighborhoods in G
2. Selections of at most k of these vertex neighborhoods
3. Verification that the union of the neighborhoods of such a selection from (2) is V

Let G' be an undirected graph divided into three vertex levels: (1) a topmost level consisting of a vertex v_G, (2) a middle level consisting of $|V|$ vertices $v_{N_1}, v_{N_2}, \ldots, v_{N_{|V|}}$, and (3) a bottom level consisting of $|V|$ vertices $v_{V_1}, v_{V_2}, \ldots, v_{V_{|V|}}$. There will be edges in G' between v_G and every vertex in the middle level and between every vertex v_{N_i} in the middle level and v_{V_j} in the bottom level such that v_j is in the neighborhood of v_i in G. An example of such a three-level graph is shown in Figure 6.2. Finally, set $S = \{v_G, v_{N_1}, v_{N_2}, \ldots, v_{N_{|V|}}\}$ and $k' = k$. Observe now the following:

1. The vertices in the middle level of G' encode the vertex neighborhoods in G.
2. As T can only consist of vertices in the middle level of G', T corresponds to a selection of at most k vertex neighborhoods in G.
3. The requirement that T must allow the connection of all vertices in $S \cup T$ means that any T for any such constructed instance of STEINER GRAPH must correspond to a dominating set of size at most k in G.

Note that our components are a mixture of entities in (Item 1) and constraints on solutions to (Items 2 and 3) the constructed instance of STEINER GRAPH. As there are $2|V| + 1$ vertices and at most $|V| + |V|^2$ edges in G', the

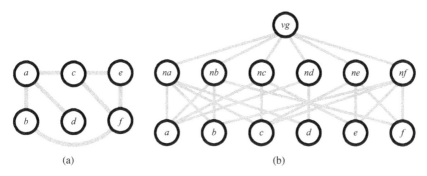

Figure 6.2   The parameterized reduction from k-Dominating Set to k-Steiner
Graph. (a) A sample graph in the given instance of k-Dominating Set.
(b) The corresponding graph in the created instance of k-Steiner Graph.

previous transformation can be done in polynomial time; furthermore, the
parameters k in the given and constructed instances of k-Dominating Set and
k-Steiner Graph are identical. Hence, this is a parameterized reduction from
k-Dominating Set to k-Steiner Graph.

Though elegant and simple, the previous reduction is unfortunately atypical.
As seen in Section 3.2.4, creating polynomial-time reductions by component
design is a complex and difficult task. One might initially think that the extra
running time allowed by parameterized reductions might make this easier.
However, it turns out to be arguably even harder to create parameterized
reductions by component design because of the complications introduced into
components and their interactions by having to preserve relations between
parameters across the transformations encoded in those reductions.

Practice 6.2.11   Reconsider the polynomial-time reduction from 3Sat to
  Clique given in Section 3.2.4. Is this also a parameterized reduction, and
  if so, relative to which parameterized problems associated with 3Sat and
  Clique?

Practice 6.2.12   Reconsider the polynomial-time reduction from 3Sat to
  Graph 3-Colorability given in Section 3.2.4. Is this also a parameterized
  reduction, and if so, relative to which parameterized problems associated
  with 3Sat and Graph 3-Colorability?

Practice 6.2.13   Reconsider the polynomial-time reduction from Minimum
  Set Cover to Steiner Tree in Graphs given in Exercise 3.4.5. Is this
  also a parameterized reduction, and if so, relative to which parameterized
  problems associated with Minimum Set Cover and Steiner Tree in
  Graphs?

Creating parameterized reductions by component design can, however, be made much simpler by the use of two standard component-design templates based on reductions from k-CLIQUE and k-DOMINATING SET which are described in more detail in Section 6.4.

6.3   Helpful Strategies for Deriving Parameterized Reductions

As was the case in Section 5.3 with respect to deriving algorithms from scratch to prove fixed-parameter tractability, deriving parameterized reductions from scratch can also be quite challenging. Many parameterized analyses have been done over the last 25 years. Hence, it may be well worth your while to invest time to see if reductions involving problems similar to yours already exist. Looking in the results in Appendix C and at the appendices in Garey and Johnson (1979) and Downey and Fellows (1999) is an excellent start. This search should also be supplemented with index-assisted dips into other standard works on parameterized complexity (see Further Readings at the end of this chapter).

Assuming this didn't work and you really do need to derive a reduction from scratch, start simple – that is, first try to create a reduction to your problem by restriction (Section 6.2.3), and if that fails, only then by local replacement (Section 6.2.2) or component design (Section 6.2.4). All of these efforts can be sped up greatly if you have found parameterized reductions for problems similar to your own during your initial literature search.

6.4   * Templates for Parameterized Reduction by Component Design

As mentioned in Section 6.2.4, creating parameterized reductions by component design is a very complex and difficult task. It has been made easier by the development of two standard templates for parameterized reductions from the following problems:

k-CLIQUE
Input: A graph $G = (V, E)$ and an integer k.
Parameter: k
Question: Does there exist a clique $V' \subseteq V$ such that $|V'| \geq k$?

k-DOMINATING SET
Input: An graph $G = (V, E)$ and a positive integer k.
Parameter: k
Question: Does there exist a dominating set $V' \subseteq V$ such that
$|V'| \leq k$? (Here a vertex set V' is called a dominating set if for every
vertex $v \in V$ either $v \in V'$ or there is an edge (u, v) with $u \in V'$.)

We will illustrate each of the following templates using reductions to
parameterized versions of the following problem:

DFA INTERSECTION
Input: A set $D = \{d_1, \ldots, d_k\}$ of deterministic finite-state automata
(DFA), each of which has a most $|Q|$ states and operates over a
common alphabet Σ, and a positive integer l.
Question: Is there a string over Σ of length l that is accepted by every
DFA in D?

A finite-state automaton (FSA) is essentially a simple machine for determining
which strings over an alphabet Σ are and are not in a specified set. A FSA
consists of a set Q of states, with one state being designated the start state (q_0)
and a subset of the states being designated as final states (Q_F). Pairs of states
are joined by transitions labeled with individual symbols; if for every $q \in Q$
and symbol $\sigma \in \Sigma$ there is at most one outgoing transition with label σ from
q, then the FSA is *deterministic*. Two example DFA accepting strings over the
alphabet $\Sigma = \{0, 1\}$ are shown in Figure 6.3. Given a string s and a FSA f, one

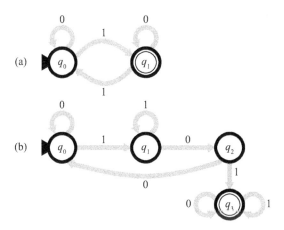

Figure 6.3   Two example DFAs that accept strings over the alphabet $\Sigma = \{0, 1\}$. (a)
A DFA that accepts all strings with an odd number of 1's. (b) A DFA that
accepts all strings containing the substring 101. Initial states are
indicated by bold arrows and final states are indicated by double circles.

starts in state q_0 and attempts to construct a sequence of transitions labeled with the successive symbols in s. If this sequence uses all of s and ends up in a final state, f *accepts* s; otherwise, f *rejects* s. For example, strings $s = 10101, 111$, and 101 are accepted by both the first and second automata, the first automaton, and the second automaton in Figure 6.3, respectively.

6.4.1   Reduction from k-CLIQUE

To reduce from an instance $(G = (V, E), k)$ of k-CLIQUE, we need to structure components to encode the following three processes:

1. **Candidate clique encoding**: Encode a subset of vertices of V.
2. **Candidate clique generation**: Select k vertices $v_1, v_2, \ldots, v_k$ from V, and ensure that no vertices in the selection are repeated, *i.e.*, for each pair of vertices v_i and v_j, $1 \leq i < j \leq k$, in the selected set, $v_i \neq v_j$.
3. **Candidate clique verification**: For each pair of selected vertices, ensure that there is an edge between them in G, i.e., for each pair of vertices v_i and v_j, $1 \leq i < j \leq k$, in the selected set, $(v_i, v_j) \in E$.

As there are $k(k-1)/2$ distinct pairs of positions in a sequence of length k, these processes are encoded by $k(k-1)/2 + k(k-1)/2$ constraints on the candidate clique, which is purely a function of k. Hence, this template is good for creating parameterized reductions from k-CLIQUE that link to parameters corresponding to the size of the candidate solution and the number of constraint-components in the problem instance constructed by the reduction.

Consider now how to use this template to create a parameterized reduction from k-CLIQUE to $\{k, l\}$-DFA INTERSECTION. Let us encode subsets of vertices from G by strings over an alphabet $\Sigma = \{v_1, \ldots, v_{|V|}\}$. The remaining two processes essentially correspond to two groups of constraints on these strings, and each of these constraints can be encoded as a group of one or more DFAs. One way of doing this is as follows:

- **Candidate clique generation**: One can ensure a string of length k using a $k + 1$ state linear DFA that allows each position in the string to be filled by any symbol in Σ (see Figure 6.4(b)). This DFA has $k|V|$ transitions. For each pair of positions i and j, $1 \leq i < j \leq k$, in the string, one can ensure that the symbols in positions i and j in the string are different by using a DFA that reads any symbols up to position i, branches based on the position at symbol i, and on each such branch, reads any symbol up to position j and accepts only if the symbol at position j is not the symbol corresponding to that branch (see Figure 6.4(c)). Note that each of these DFAs has at most

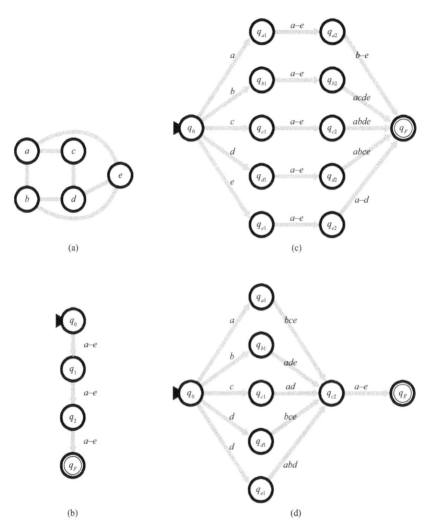

Figure 6.4 Encoding CLIQUE solution constraints using DFAs. (a) An undirected graph G. (b) A DFA encoding the constraint that we want to select subsets of $k = 3$ vertices in G. (c) A DFA encoding the constraint that the first and third vertices in the candidate-clique string are different. (d) A DFA encoding the constraint that the first and second vertices in the candidate-clique string are connected by an edge in G. DFA transitions with multi-symbol labels are shorthand for collections of arcs with one arc for each symbol in the label.

$2 + (k - 1)|V|$ states and at most $|V| + (k - 1)|V|^2$ transitions, with the maximums occuring if G is a clique and the encoded constraint is relative to the first and last vertices in the candidate-clique string.

- **Candidate clique verification**: One can ensure that for each pair of positions i and j, $1 \leq i < j \leq k$, in the string there is an edge in G between the vertices corresponding to the symbols at these positions using a variant of the second type of DFA in (1) which branches as before and accepts on reaching position j in the string only if there is an edge in G between the vertex corresponding to the branch and the vertex corresponding to the symbol at position j (see Figure 6.4(d)). Note that by the logic in the previous point, each of these DFAs has at most $2 + (k - 1)|V|$ states and at most $|V| + (k - 1)|V|^2$ transitions.

The total number of DFAs encoding the constraints mentioned earlier is $k' = 1 + k(k - 1)/2 + k(k - 1)/2 = 1 + 2k(k - 1)/2 = 1 + k(k - 1)$. AS $k \leq |V|$, given the maximum DFA sizes noted previously, the instance of DFA INTERSECTION consisting of these DFAs with $l = k$ can be constructed from a given instance of CLIQUE in polynomial time. Furthermore, by the construction of these DFAs, the given instance of CLIQUE has a clique of size k if and only if the constructed instance of DFA INTERSECTION has a string of length l over Σ that is accepted by all DFAs in D. As both k' and l are functions of k, this is thus a parameterized reduction from k-CLIQUE to $\{k,l\}$-DFA INTERSECTION.

An additional example of reduction by component design using this template is given in Section 12.3.1.

6.4.2   Reduction from k-DOMINATING SET

To reduce from an instance $(G = (V, E), k)$ of k-DOMINATING SET, we need to structure components to encode the following three processes:

1. **Candidate dominating set encoding**: Encode a subset of vertices of V.
2. **Candidate dominating set generation**: Select k vertices $v_1, v_2, \ldots, k_k$ from V.
3. **Candidate dominating set verification**: For each vertex v in V, ensure that there is at least one vertex v' selected in (1) such that either $v = v'$ or v is adjacent to v' in G, i.e., $(v, v') \in E$.

Note that as we are looking for dominating sets of size $\leq k$ (as opposed to cliques of size $\geq k$ as in Section 6.4.1), we do not need to ensure that there are no repeated elements in the set selected in item (2). As there are $|V|$ vertices in G that need to be checked against the candidate dominating set, the processes can be encoded by $|V|$ constraints on the candidate dominating set. This is unfortunately not a function of k. However, as these individual constraints are simple and can be encoded in correspondingly simple components, this template is good for creating parameterized reductions from k-DOMINATING SET that link to parameters characterizing the sizes of the components in the problem instance constructed by the reduction.

Consider now how to use this template to create a parameterized reduction from k-DOMINATING SET to $\{|Q|,l\}$-DFA INTERSECTION. Let us once again encode subsets of vertices from G by strings over an alphabet $\Sigma = \{v_1,\ldots,v_{|V|}\}$. The remaining two processes correspond to two groups of constraints on these strings, and each of these constraints can be encoded as a group of one or more DFAs. One way of doing this is as follows:

- **Candidate dominating set generation**: One can ensure a string of length k using the $k + 1$ state linear DFA given in Section 6.4.1 that allows each position in the string to be filled by any symbol in Σ (see Figure 6.4(b)).
- **Candidate dominating set verification**: One can ensure that for each vertex v in V that there is a vertex v' in the selected set such that either $v = v'$ or $(v,v') \in E$ by constructing for each v in V a two-state DFA in which the second state is the final state and the only transitions from the initial to final state are those labeled with the vertices in the neighborhood of v (see Figure 6.5(b)). Note that each of these DFAs has exactly $2|V|$ transitions.

The total number of DFAs encoding these constraints is $k' = 1 + |V|$. As $k \leq |V|$, given the DFA sizes noted previously, the instance of DFA INTERSECTION consisting of these DFAs with $l = k$ can be constructed from a given instance of DOMINATING SET in polynomial time. Furthermore, by the construction of these DFAs, the given instance of DOMINATING SET has a dominating set of size $\leq k$ if and only if the constructed instance of DFA

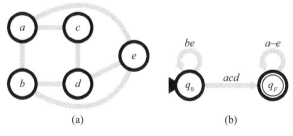

(a)   (b)

Figure 6.5   Encoding DOMINATING SET solution constraints using DFA. (a) An undirected graph $G = (V, E)$. (b) A DFA encoding the constraint that for vertex C in G, there is a vertex v' in the candidate dominating set such that either $v' = C$ or $(C,v') \in E$. DFA transitions with multi-symbol labels are shorthand for collections of arcs with one arc for each symbol in the label.

INTERSECTION has a string of length l over Σ that is accepted by all DFAs in D. As both l and $|Q|$ are functions of k, this is thus a parameterized reduction from k-DOMINATING SET to $\{|Q|, l\}$-DFA INTERSECTION.

6.5   Exercises

Exercise 6.5.1   Reconsider the following polynomial-time reductions in Exercise 3.4.1:

(a) from MAX CUT to COHERENCE
(b) from CONSISTENT COHERENCE to COHERENCE
(c) from HITTING COVER to MINIMUM SET COVER

Is each of these reductions also a parameterized reduction, and if so, relative to which parameterized problems associated with the problems involved in that reduction?

Exercise 6.5.2   Give and prove the correctness of a parameterized reduction from k-INDEPENDENT SET to the following problem:

k-KERNEL
Input: A directed graph $G = (V, A)$ and a positive integer k.
Parameter: k
Question: Does there exist a kernel in G of size k? (Here a vertex set $V' \subseteq V$ is called a *kernel* if V' is an independent set in G and for all $v \in V - V'$, there exists a $v' \in V'$ such that $(v', v) \in A$.)

Exercise 6.5.3   Give and prove the correctness of a parameterized reduction from k-MAX CUT to c-COHERENCE.

Exercise 6.5.4   Give and prove the correctness of a parameterized reduction from k-VERTEX COVER to k-DOMINATING SET.

Exercise 6.5.5   Give and prove the correctness of a parameterized reduction from k-DOMINATING SET to the following problem:

k-HITTING COVER
Input: A universe U of elements, a collection S of subsets of U, and an integer k.
Parameter: k
Question: Does U have a hitting set $H \subseteq U$ of size at most k? (Here, a hitting set is a subset of U that contains at least one element of every set in S.)

Exercise 6.5.6 Give and prove the correctness of a parameterized reduction from k-CLIQUE to the following problem:

d-CLIQUE CONFIGURATION
Input: A graph G and positive integers k, l, and d.
Parameter: d
Question: Does G contain a set C of at most k l-cliques such that each clique in C is connected by edges to at most d other l-cliques in C and each l-clique in G is either in C or connected by an edge from one of its vertices to a vertex of an l-CLIQUE in C?

6.6   Further Reading

The parameterized reducibility described in this chapter was proposed by Rod Downey and Mike Fellows in the early 1990s as part of their theory of parameterized computational complexity (Downey and Fellows, 1999, 2013; Flum and Grohe, 2006). Various print and online resources describing this theory in more detail are listed in the Further Reading section at the end of Chapter 5.

The reductions described in this chapter come from a number of sources. The reductions among CLIQUE, INDEPENDENT SET, and VERTEX COVER in sections 6.2.1 and 6.2.2 are given in section 3.1 of Garey and Johnson (1979). The reduction from INDEPENDENT SET to SET PACKING in section 6.2.2 is given on page 142 of Ausiello, D'Atri, and Protasi (1991). The reduction from DOMINATING SET to MINIMUM SET COVER in Section 6.2.2 is given on page 271 of Paz and Moran (1981). The reduction from k-DOMINATING SET to k-STEINER GRAPH in section 6.2.4 is given in an unpublished manuscript by Hans Bodlaender and Dieter Kratsch from 1994. Finally, the reductions from CLIQUE and DOMINATING SET to DFA INTERSECTION are given in section 4 of Wareham (1999).

7 Parameterized Complexity Classes

In this chapter we introduce the parameterized analogues of P and NP, namely, FPT and other complexity classes such as W[1], W[2], and XP comprising with FPT the W-hierarchy, and the formal notions of W-hardness and W-completeness. We describe why W-hard parameterized problems are considered to be fixed-parameter intractable (i.e., not computable in fixed-parameter tractable time). We explain how one can prove that a problem is a member of a class in the W-hierarchy and how one can use the technique of parameterized reduction, introduced and practiced in Chapter 6, to prove W-hardness and W-completeness.

7.1 Fixed-Parameter Intractability: Putting It All Together

Courtesy of the previous chapter, we now know how to relate pairs of parameterized problems by reductions. Over the course of that chapter and its practices and exercises, we encountered and created a number of reductions that taken together can be viewed as a web interrelating these problems (see Figure 7.1). Such reductions ultimately derive their analytic power from the observations (proven at the beginning of Section 6.2) that fixed-parameter tractability propagates backwards and fixed-parameter intractability propagates forwards along such reductions. For example, given the reduction web in Figure 7.1, if we know that k-STEINER GRAPH is fixed-parameter tractable then we know that k-DOMINATING SET is fixed-parameter tractable, which in turn implies that k-VERTEX COVER is fixed-parameter tractable. Similarly, if k-CLIQUE is fixed-parameter intractable then this immediately implies that $\{|V(H)|, |E(H)|\}$-SUBGRAPH ISOMORPHISM, $\{k, l\}$-DFA INTERSECTION, and k-INDEPENDENT SET are fixed-parameter intractable; the last of these in turn implies that k-SET PACKING and k-KERNEL are also fixed-parameter intractable.

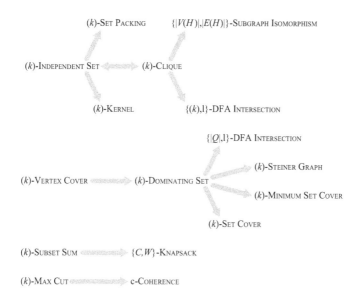

Figure 7.1   An overview of the parameterized reductions you have encountered or created in Chapter 6.

Practice 7.1.1   Suppose we know the following sets of results:
(a) k-MINIMUM SET COVER is fixed-parameter tractable.
(b) k-CLIQUE is fixed-parameter tractable and k-DOMINATING SET is fixed-parameter intractable.
(c) $\{k, l\}$-DFA INTERSECTION is fixed-parameter tractable.
(d) c-COHERENCE is fixed-parameter intractable and $\{C, W\}$-KNAPSACK is fixed-parameter tractable.

Using the parameterized reduction web in Figure 7.1, work out for each of these sets of results what is implied (if anything) about the parameterized complexity of each of the problems included in the web.

We have already seen in Chapter 5 how to prove fixed-parameter tractability of parameterized problems, and at the beginning of Chapter 6 that there are parameterized problems such as t-GENERALIZED CHESS that are provably fixed-parameter intractable. Unfortunately, the latter problems do not seem to be reducible to many problems in which we are interested such as k-CLIQUE and k-DOMINATING SET whose parameterized complexities remain open questions.

In the remainder of this chapter, we will first complete our parameterized complexity analysis framework by defining (as we did analogously in Chapter 4 for polynomial-time intractability) a set of complexity classes comprising the so-called W-hierarchy that will grant us generally usable techniques for proving fixed-parameter intractability. We will then look at how to exploit all the techniques we have developed to analyze the computational difficulty of problems under sets of one or more restrictions.

7.2　The W-Hierarchy

In this section, we shall define the various classes in the W-hierarchy, demonstrate for each class how to show that parameterized problems are contained in that class, and look at the various inclusion relationships (both proven and conjectured) among these classes.

7.2.1　The Classes FPT and XP

We know from Chapter 4 that before we can use problem classes to investigate intractability, we first need to define a class of problems that are tractable. For polynomial-time tractability, this was the class P. The following is the corresponding class relative to fixed-parameter tractability.

DEFINITION 7.2.1　FPT *is the class of parameterized problems that are fixed-parameter tractable. More formally,* FPT *is the class of parameterized problems K-D for which there exists an algorithm with worst-case running time $f(K)|i|^c$ (relative to some computable function $f(.)$ and constant c) that can decide whether $D(i)$ is yes or no for each instance (i, K) of K-D.*

We already know a number of parameterized problems such as k-VERTEX COVER and $\{k, d\}$-INDEPENDENT SET that are fixed-parameter tractable and hence in FPT.

　　We now need a class that includes FPT and contains parameterized problems that are fixed-parameter intractable. We already know a number of problems that are not known to be fixed-parameter tractable relative to their given parameter but are solvable by an algorithm whose running time has that parameter as an exponent of the input size. For example, k-CLIQUE is solvable in $O(|V|^k|V|^2) = O(|V|^{k+2})$ time. This suggests the following.

DEFINITION 7.2.2　XP *is the class of parameterized problems K-D for which there exists an algorithm with worst-case running time $f(K)|i|^{f'(K)}$ (relative to some functions $f(.)$ and $f'(.)$) that can decide whether $D(i) = yes$ or $D(i) = no$ for each instance (i, K) of K-D.*

Practice 7.2.1   Show that each of the following problems is in XP:

(a) k-INDEPENDENT SET
(b) k-SUBSET SUM
(c) $\{|V(H)|\}$-SUBGRAPH ISOMORPHISM

It has been shown that FPT is properly contained in XP, so problems that are hard or complete for XP under parameterized reduction are provably fixed-parameter intractable. However, almost no typical problems of interest like k-CLIQUE seem to have reductions from such XP-complete or hard problems. To prove these problems fixed-parameter intractable, we need to define classes between FPT and XP. This will be done next.

7.2.2   Verifying Solutions to Parameterized Problems: The W-Classes

Recall from Chapter 4 that the problem class enclosing P that is most typically used in proving polynomial-time intractability is NP, the class of decision problems whose candidate solutions can be verified in polynomial time. How might one define classes that verify candidate solutions for parameterized problems? An initial thought might be (by direct analogy with NP) to define a class based on problems whose candidate solution can be verified in fpt time. However, it turns out that a much more fine-grained set of classes can be created using a simpler model of verification – namely, Boolean circuits.

A *Boolean circuit* consists of a set of inputs, each of which can be *true* or *false*, and an output which also can be *true* or *false*. Linking the inputs and outputs are one or more layers of Boolean gates. There are three basic types of Boolean gates:

1. A NOT gate, which flips the value of its only input
2. An AND gate, whose output is *true* if *all* of its inputs are *true* and *false* otherwise
3. An OR gate, whose output is *true* if *any* of its inputs are *true* and *false* otherwise

Given a particular set of input values, the outputs of the gates are calculated layer by layer, moving upwards from the inputs, and the output of the circuit is the output of the only gate in the topmost layer. Several example Boolean circuits are shown in Figure 7.2.

Two properties will be useful in defining solution verification circuits. First, the *weft* of a circuit is the maximum number of AND or OR gates with more than two inputs encountered on any path in the circuit from an input to the

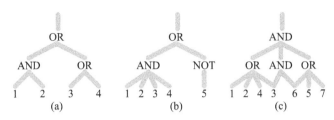

Figure 7.2 Several Boolean circuits. (a) A two-layer 4-input circuit of weft 0.
(b) A two-layer 5-input circuit of weft 1. (c) A two-layer, 7-input circuit
of weft 2.

output. For example, the three circuits in Figure 7.2 have weft 0, 1, and 2,
respectively. Second, the *weight* of a set of input values for a circuit is the
number values in that set that are *true*. For example, the weights of inputs
FFFFF, *FFTTF*, *FTTTF*, and *TTTTT* to circuit (b) in Figure 7.2 are 0, 2, 3,
and 5, respectively.

Let us now use these properties to define verification circuits for parameterized problems. Unlike a polynomial-time verification algorithm, which is the
same for each input to the problem, we shall define a separate circuit for each
input. Moreover, we shall incorporate different parameter values associated
with an input by circuit input vectors of different weights. This allows us to
define the classes of the W-hierarchy, which differ in the wefts of the circuits
required to verify candidate solutions for the problems in each class.

DEFINITION 7.2.3 *For each integer* $t \geq 1$, W[t] *is the class of all
parameterized problems K-D whose candidate solutions can be encoded in
input vectors of weight* $g(K)$ *for some function* $g(.)$ *and for which: (1) there
is a weft-t circuit C for each instance* (i, K) *of K-D such that the answer to
that instance is "yes" if and only if the appropriate circuit C relative to the
Boolean input encoding* (i, K) *outputs* true, *and (2) the depth of these circuits
for all instances of D is bounded by some constant.*

Such circuits can be built relatively easily for a problem by encoding the
constraints on solutions to that problem into the circuits. Let us look at
examples of such circuits for two familiar problems.

- k-INDEPENDENT SET: For any input $(G = (V, E), k)$ of k-INDEPENDENT SET,
  construct a circuit with $|V|$ inputs such that an input vector is evaluated *true*
  by that circuit if and only if the set $\{v_i\colon$ position i is set to *true* in the input
  vector$\}$ is an independent set in G. One such circuit has three layers: (1) $|E|$
  2-input AND gates linking each pair of inputs i and j such that $(v_i, v_j) \in E$,
  (2) a $|V|$-input OR gate linking all outputs of gates in the first layer, and (3) a

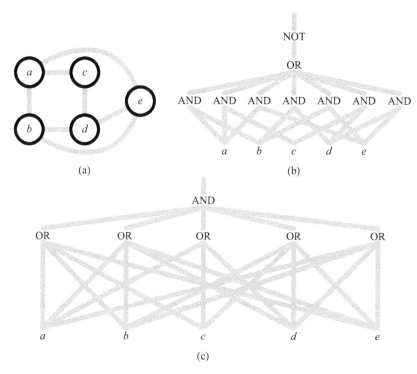

Figure 7.3   Solution verification circuits for parameterized problems. (a) An undirected graph G. (b) A circuit for verifying candidate independent sets of G. (c) A circuit for verifying candidate dominating sets of G.

NOT gate whose input is the output of the only gate in the second layer. An example of such a circuit is shown in Figure 7.3(b).

Recall that a set of vertices in G is an independent set if no pair of vertices in the set is connected by an edge. This is encoded directly in the second and third layers of this circuit. Hence, this circuit will output *true* for an input-vector of weight k if and only if the vertices corresponding to the inputs set to *true* in this vector form an independent set of size k in G.

- k-DOMINATING SET: For any input $(G = (V, E), k)$ of k-DOMINATING SET, construct a circuit with $|V|$ inputs such that an input vector s evaluated to *true* by that circuit if and only if the set $\{v_i:$ position i is set to *true* in the input vector$\}$ is a dominating set in G. One such circuit has two layers: (1) $|V|$ OR gates, one for each vertex v in G that takes as inputs every input in the input vector corresponding to a vertex v' in the neighborhood of v in G

and (2) a $|V|$-input AND gate whose inputs are the outputs of the gates in the first layer. An example of such a circuit is shown in Figure 7.3(c).

Recall that a set of vertices in G is a dominating set if, for each vertex v in G, there is at least one vertex v' in the neighborhood of v that is in the set. This is encoded directly in the first and second layers of this circuit. Hence, this circuit will only output *true* for an input-vector weight k if and only if the vertices corresponding to the inputs set to *true* in this vector form a dominating set of size k in G.

These circuits have weft 1 and 2, respectively, which demonstrates that k-INDEPENDENT SET and k-DOMINATING SET are in classes W[1] and W[2], respectively.

Practice 7.2.2   Show that k-VERTEX COVER is in W[1].

Practice 7.2.3   Show that k-MINIMUM SET COVER is in W[2].

The lowest levels of the W-hierarchy have obvious intuitive characterizations – namely, problems in W[1] are characterized by collections of local constraints between elements in candidate solutions (e.g., all pairs of vertices in a clique must be linked by an edge) and problems in W[2] are characterized by collections of non-local constraints (e.g., every vertex neighborhood in the graph must contain at least one vertex in a dominating set). Moreover, the wefts of the circuits for problems in these classes correspond to progressively deeper nestings of logical quantifiers over these constraints ("for all pairs of vertices ..." in the case of k-CLIQUE, "for all vertex neighborhoods there exists a vertex ..." in the case of k-DOMINATING SET). Such intuitive characterizations of classes higher in the W-hierarchy are harder to come by; however, these classes are also all based on candidate solution verification, albeit relative to more exotic kinds of circuits.

7.2.3   The FPT $\neq$ W[1] Conjecture

The classes of the W-hierarchy are related as follows:

$$\text{FPT} \subseteq \text{W[1]} \subseteq \text{W[2]} \subseteq \ldots \subseteq \text{XP}$$

The inclusions among the W-classes are obvious from the definitions of these classes. However, unlike the obvious inclusion of P in NP, the facts that FPT $\subseteq$ W[1] and all W-classes are contained in XP require somewhat involved technical arguments. At present, the only proper inclusion in the hierarchy is that between FPT and XP. Analogous to the P $\neq$ NP conjecture discussed in Sections 4.2.2 and 4.2.3, it is conjectured that each remaining inclusion in the W-hierarchy is also a proper inclusion, such that

$$\text{FPT} \subset W[1] \subset W[2] \subset \ldots \subset \text{XP}$$

or, to put it another way,

$$\text{FPT} \neq W[1] \neq W[2] \neq \ldots \neq \text{XP}$$

There are interesting relationships between these conjectures that come to light when we consider problems that are hard or complete relative to these classes in the sense defined in Section 4.3.

DEFINITION 7.2.4   *A parameterized decision problem K-D is* W[i]*-hard if for* every *parameterized decision problem in* W[i] *there exists a parameterized reduction to K-D.*

DEFINITION 7.2.5   *A problem K-D that is* W[i]*-hard and in* W[i] *is called* W[i]-complete.

Stop and Think

Consider two W-classes W[i] and W[j] such that $i < j$. Is it true that if a problem is W[j]-hard then it is also W[i]-hard? If so, why? If not, why not?

This is true by the definition of W[i]-class hardness given earlier. If a problem D is W[j]-hard, then every problem in W[j] parameterized reduces to D. However as W[i] is contained in W[j] by the W-hierarchy class relations given earlier, this means that every problem in W[i] parameterized reduces to D, which by definition implies that D is also W[i]-hard.

Practice 7.2.4   Consider two W-classes W[i] and W[j] such that $i < j$. If FPT $\neq$ W[i], can a W[j]-hard problem be fixed-parameter tractable? If so, why? If not, why not?

Practice 7.2.5   Consider two *W*-classes W[i] and W[j] such that $i < j$. If FPT $\neq$ W[j], must a W[i]-hard problem be fixed-parameter intractable? If so, why? If not, why not?

Given this discussion, it turns out that the key conjecture here is FPT $\neq$ W[1] – precisely when this holds, no problem that is complete or hard for any W-class can be fixed-parameter tractable. This conjecture is not nearly as well known as the P $\neq$ NP conjecture (nor is it a very handsomely-funded open problem). That being said, like its more famous cousin, the FPT $\neq$ W[1] conjecture has strong intuitive, empirical, and formal support (with the strongest of these supports being the empirical fact that no one has yet shown that any W[1]-hard problem is fixed-parameter tractable). As we will see in the next section, by working under the assumption that this conjecture is true, we will be able to prove fixed-parameter intractability by reductions from known W[1]-hard (and, in some cases, NP-hard!) problems.

7.3   Proving Fixed-Parameter Intractability

It turns out that there are several ways of proving fixed-parameter intractability using reductions and the classes defined earlier. In this section, we will look at each of these ways.

7.3.1   Fixed-Parameter Intractability Through W-Hardness

The most obvious route for proving fixed-parameter intractability is to show that a problem K-D is hard for a class W[i] above FPT by a parameterized reduction from a problem K'-D' that is known to be complete or hard for that class. Given such a reduction and our working assumption that FPT $\neq$ W[1], this suffices to demonstrate the fixed-parameter intractability of K-D.

Complete problems are known for each W-class above FPT in the W-hierarchy. These were obtained in a manner analogous to Cook's derivation of the first NP-complete problem SATISFIABILITY by generic reductions from verification-circuit problems to various versions of SATISFIABILITY parameterized by (among other things) the number of variables set to *true* in their candidate truth-assignments. More "natural" complete problems were then obtained by parameterized reductions from these versions of SATISFIABILITY.[1] Two key W[1]- and W[2]-complete problems are k-INDEPENDENT SET and k-DOMINATING SET, respectively.

Practice 7.3.1   Consider the following known results:
  (a) k-VERTEX COVER is fixed-parameter tractable.
  (b) k-MAX CUT is fixed-parameter tractable.
  (c) k-INDEPENDENT SET is W[1]-complete.
  (d) k-DOMINATING SET is W[2]-complete.
  Using the parameterized reduction web in Figure 7.1, work out what is implied (if anything) about the parameterized complexity of each of the problems included in the web.

---

[1]   An exception was the class W[1], whose circuit-verification problem reduced in a particularly direct fashion to k-INDEPENDENT SET.

Practice 7.3.1 highlights two important aspects of using reductions from W-hard problems to prove fixed-parameter intractability. First, as was already mentioned in Section 6.2, make sure that you are reducing **from** and not **to** a fixed-parameter intractable problem if you want to prove fixed-parameter intractability, as fixed-parameter intractability is only passed forward along reductions. Second, make sure that the parameterized problem you are reducing from is actually fixed-parameter intractable. Given that each problem has many possible parameters and a problem can switch (often counter-intuitively) between fixed-parameter tractability and intractability from parameter to parameter, mistakes are very easy to make. For example, though we know from Section 6.2.3 that k-Subset Sum parameterized reduces to $\{C, W\}$-Knapsack this does not imply the fixed-parameter intractability of $\{C, W\}$-Knapsack because Subset Sum is only known to be $W[1]$-hard relative to the parameter $|A'|$, the number of elements in the subset that are being summed.

It might be appropriate at this point to highlight a common difference in goals between computational complexity analyses in computer science and cognitive science. In computer science, researchers are often interested in the tightest possible characterizations of the parameterized complexity of a problem. Hence, much effort must be put into establishing both the highest W-class relative to which a problem of interest is hard and the lowest W-class that contains this problem. Here, the entire W-hierarchy is relevant. However, in cognitive science, the goal of parameterized complexity analysis is to establish whether or not a computational-level theory is fixed-parameter intractable (as explained in Section 1.2.2). For these purposes, the precise degree of intractability is typically not relevant. In these cases, we can therefore ignore issues of W-inclusion and focus purely on W-hardness, often relative to lower levels of the W-hierarchy such as $W[1]$ and $W[2]$ for which the reductions may be much simpler. It is thus a very good idea to think about what type of results you actually require and to tailor your efforts to obtain these results

7.3.2   Fixed-Parameter Intractability Through NP-Hardness

Every fixed-parameter intractability result derived in Section 7.3.1 holds relative to the conjecture $\text{FPT} \neq W[1]$. However, it is sometimes possible to get results that hold relative to conjectures with even more support such as $P \neq NP$. For example, suppose we are interested in the parameterized complexity of a problem K D and we know that D is NP-hard when K is a constant c. We have already seen several examples of this – namely, Satisfiability when the maximum length of each clause in the given formula is three (see Section 3.2.2) and Graph Colorability when the number of colors available to color the given graph is three (see Section 3.2.4). If K-D is fixed-parameter tractable, then by definition, there is an algorithm for any instance (i, K) of K-D that runs in time $f(K)|i|^{c'}$ for some function $f(.)$ and constant c'. However, this means that you can solve an NP-hard instance i of D in $f(c)|i|^{c'} = c''|i|^{c'} =$ polynomial time, which by the definition of NP-hardness would imply that $P = NP$. Hence, we have the following.

Observation 7.3.1 *Let D be a decision problem, and let K-D be one of its parameterizations. If D is NP-hard when K is fixed to a constant value, then K-$D \notin$ FPT unless $P = NP$.*

This observation is very useful, as there are many problems that are known to be NP-hard when certain parameters are constants. Two noted previously are SATISFIABILITY and GRAPH COLORABILITY. Another is DOMINATING SET, which is known to be NP-hard when the maximum degree d of any vertex in the given graph is 3 (thus proving by the observation above that d-DOMINATING SET is not fixed-parameter tractable unless $P = NP$).

Such results may at first sight seem less satisfying than those derived in the previous subsection, in that they do not give a precise measure of the degree of fixed-parameter intractability of a problem relative to a particular W-class. However, in cases such as those introduced later in this book, where one is only interested in the fact rather than the precise degree of parameterized intractability, the proofs granted by Observation 7.3.1 may be quite useful.

Practice 7.3.2   Show that k-CLUSTERING is not fixed-parameter tractable unless $P = NP$.

Practice 7.3.3   Prove the following stronger version of Observation 7.3.1: Let D be a decision problem and let K-D be one of its parameterizations. If D is NP-hard when K is fixed to a constant value, then K-$D \notin$ XP unless $P = NP$.

7.4   Parameterized Complexity Analysis

Over the last several chapters, we have looked at various techniques for deriving fixed-parameter tractability and intractability results relative to a given parameterized problem. We can now return to the more general question raised in Section 1.2.2 that motivated our discussions of these techniques in the first place – namely, how can we look at the effects of groups of one or more input restrictions on the tractability of computational-level theories of cognition? This is the realm of parameterized complexity analysis.

There are two types of parameterized complexity analyses. The first of these – in which one applies progressively more complex techniques to derive the best possible algorithm for a problem relative to one or more parameters – is typically of most interest to computer scientists, who are interested in engineering the fastest possible algorithm (see Table 2.1 for an example of such an analysis for k-VERTEX COVER). However, the second type of parameterized complexity analysis – in which one wants to characterize relative to a set of parameters for a problem those combinations of parameters for which fixed-parameter tractable algorithms are and are not possible – is of more use to cognitive scientists, who are interested in explaining how people may efficiently perform seemingly intractable computations. Indeed, such analyses are instrumental in exploring possible (psychologically plausible) constraints on the inputs of computational-level theories of cognition that can guarantee tractability in real-world situations.

Analyses of this second type are also known as *systematic parameterized complexity analyses* and their results can be displayed in tables called *intractability maps* whose entries correspond to all combinations of the given parameters. Intractability maps for DOMINATING SET relative to parameter set $\{k,d\}$ and DFA INTERSECTION relative to parameter set $\{k,l,|Q|,|\Sigma|\}$ are shown in Table 7.1; additional intractability maps are given in Sections 11.4 and 12.3.2. Intractability maps are very useful summaries of both those combinations of restrictions that do and do not allow fixed-parameter tractability in a problem and those combinations of restrictions whose fixed-parameter tractability status has not yet been determined.

Given a set of n parameters of interest, deriving a completely filled-in intractability map initially seems a daunting task as there are $2^n - 1$ parameter

Table 7.1 Intractability maps. (a) An intractability map for DOMINATING SET relative to parameter set $\{k,d\}$. (b) An intractability map for DFA INTERSECTION relative to parameter set $\{k,l,|Q|,|\Sigma|\}$. A ✓ or ✗ table entry means that relative to the parameter set consisting of the union of the parameter sets labelling the row and column of that entry, the problem is fixed-parameter tractable or intractable, respectively.

	−	d
−	NPh	✗
h	✗	✓

(a)

	−	l	$|\Sigma|$	$l,|\Sigma|$
−	NPh	✗	✗	✓
k	✗	✗	✗	✓
$|Q|$	✗	✗	✓	✓
$k,|Q|$	✓	✓	✓	✓

(b)

subsets whose parameterized complexities need to be evaluated. However, courtesy of the following, the task of constructing such maps is often much easier.

Observation 7.4.1 *Given two parameter sets K and K' for a problem D, if K'-D is fixed-parameter tractable and $K' \subset K$ then K-D is also fixed-parameter tractable.*

This holds because any fixed-parameter tractable algorithm A for a problem D relative to parameter set K' is also a fixed-parameter tractable algorithm for D for any parameter set K such that $K' \subset K$ (as $f(.)$ in the runtime-bound for A already ignores all parameters in K that are not in K'). For example, given that $\{|\Sigma|, l\}$-LONGEST COMMON SUBSEQUENCE is fixed-parameter tractable, we also know that $\{|\Sigma|, l, m\}$-LONGEST COMMON SUBSEQUENCE is fixed-parameter tractable.

Observation 7.4.2 *Given two parameter sets K and K' for a problem D, if K-D is fixed-parameter intractable and $K' \subset K$ then K'-D is also fixed-parameter intractable.*

Practice 7.4.1   Prove Observation 7.4.2.

For example, given that $\{|Q|, l\}$-DFA INTERSECTION is fixed-parameter intractable, we also know that $\{|Q|\}$-DFA INTERSECTION is fixed-parameter intractable.

By using these observations, one can often get away with deriving only a small number of "seed" results to populate all entries in an intractability map. Two good general rules for doing this are to prove fixed-parameter tractability relative to the smallest possible sets of parameters and fixed-parameter intractability relative to the largest possible sets of parameters. This process is illustrated for DFA INTERSECTION relative to the parameter set $\{k, l, |Q|, |\Sigma|\}$ in Table 7.2. Although there are $2^4 - 1 = 15$ distinct parameter combinations in this map, observe that the parameterized complexities relative to all of these combinations are implied by only six proven results. Similar savings were also made in the derivations of the intractability maps in Sections 11.4 and 12.3.2.

In the remainder of this book, we will show how parameterized complexity analyses can be used to help analyze and revise computational-level theories of cognition.

Table 7.2 Deriving an intractability map for the DFA INTERSECTION problem relative to parameter set $\{k, l, |Q|, |\Sigma|\}$. (a) After fixed-parameter tractability relative to $\{l, |\Sigma|\}$ (theorem 8(2)). (b) After fixed-parameter tractability relative to $\{k, |Q|\}$ (theorem 8(3)). (c) After fixed-parameter tractability relative to $\{|Q|, |\Sigma|\}$ (theorem 8(4)). (d) After fixed-parameter intractability relative to $\{k, l\}$ (theorem 8(5)). (e) After fixed-parameter intractability relative to $\{l, |Q|\}$ (theorem 8(6)). (f) After fixed-parameter intractability relative to $\{k, |\Sigma|\}$ (theorem 8(7)). All theorem references are to Wareham (2001). All starred (*) table entries indicate original results and all non-starred table entries are those derived from original results by the application of Observations 7.4.1 and 7.4.2.

	$-$	l	$|\Sigma|$	$l, |\Sigma|$
$-$	NPh	???	???	✓*
k	???	???	???	✓
$|Q|$	???	???	???	✓
$k, |Q|$	???	???	???	✓

(a)

	$-$	l	$|\Sigma|$	$l, |\Sigma|$
$-$	NPh	???	???	✓*
k	???	???	???	✓
$|Q|$	???	???	???	✓
$k, |Q|$	✓*	✓	✓	✓

(b)

	$-$	l	$|\Sigma|$	$l, |\Sigma|$
$-$	NPh	???	???	✓*
k	???	???	???	✓
$|Q|$	???	???	✓*	✓
$k, |Q|$	✓*	✓	✓	✓

(c)

	$-$	l	$|\Sigma|$	$l, |\Sigma|$
$-$	NPh	✗	???	✓*
k	✗	✗*	???	✓
$|Q|$	???	???	✓*	✓
$k, |Q|$	✓*	✓	✓	✓

(d)

	$-$	l	$|\Sigma|$	$l, |\Sigma|$
$-$	NPh	✗	???	✓*
k	✗	✗*	???	✓
$|Q|$	✗	✗*	✓*	✓
$k, |Q|$	✓*	✓	✓	✓

(e)

	$-$	l	$|\Sigma|$	$l, |\Sigma|$
$-$	NPh	✗	✗	✓*
k	✗	✗*	✗*	✓
$|Q|$	✗	✗*	✓*	✓
$k, |Q|$	✓*	✓	✓	✓

(f)

7.5 Exercises

Exercise 7.5.1 Show that (a) k-CLIQUE is in W[1], (b) k-SET PACKING is in W[1], and (c) k-HITTING COVER is in W[2].

Exercise 7.5.2 Suppose that it is proven that FPT $=$ W[1]. Using the parameterized reduction web in Figure 7.1 and the known results stated in Practice 7.3.1, work out what is implied (if anything) about the parameterized complexity of each of the problems included in the web.

Exercise 7.5.3 Give the intractability map for VERTEX COVER relative to the parameter set $\{k, d, |V|\}$ (where d is the maximum degree of any vertex in the given graph) relative to (1) the complexity results for VERTEX COVER given or proven in the exercises in this book, (2) any results you derive yourself, and (3) and all additional results implicit in the results in (1) and (2) by Observations 7.4.1 and 7.4.2.

Exercise 7.5.4 Given two sets K and K' of numerically-valued parameters for a problem D, we say $K \leq K'$ if for every $k \in K$, there is a function $g_k(.)$ such that $k \leq g_k(K')$. For example, in the LONGEST COMMON SUBSEQUENCE problem, $\{l\} \leq \{x\}$ where x is the length of the shortest given string because there cannot be a subsequence of all of the given strings that is longer than x.

Prove each of the following:

(a) Given two numerical-valued parameter sets K and K' for a problem D, if K-D is fixed-parameter tractable and $K \leq K'$ then K'-D is also fixed-parameter tractable.

(b) Given two numerical-valued parameter sets K and K' for a problem D, if K'-D is fixed-parameter intractable and $K \leq K'$ then K-D is also fixed-parameter intractable.

(c) $\{x, m, n\}$-LONGEST COMMON SUBSEQUENCE is fixed-parameter tractable relative to parameter x defined earlier.

7.6   Further Reading

The original classes in the W-hierarchy were defined by Downey and Fellows in the early 1990s and are described in detail (along with the proofs that FPT $\subseteq$ W[1] and FPT $\subset$ XP) in Downey and Fellows (1999). The process by which complete problems were found for these classes is a technically complex tale; a very good summary of this process (including the proofs of the W[1]- and W[2]-completeness of k-INDEPENDENT SET and k-DOMINATING SET) is given in chapter 10 of Downey and Fellows (1999). Many more classes of parameterized problems (each with their own complete problems) have been defined since; for a description of these, see Downey and Fellows (2013).

It is worth noting that parameterized complexity theory as described in Chapters 5 and 6 and this chapter is actually the third version of this theory. Although the notion of parameterized problem dates to the first version given in Fellows and Langston (1988), both this and the second version (Abrahamson et al., 1989; see also page 25 in Downey and Fellows, 1999) were based on a broader non-uniform notion of intractability in which each input to a problem was allowed its own distinct algorithm; compare this with the uniform version of fixed-parameter tractability given here in which there is a single algorithm for all inputs of a problem. Moreover, the reduction and classes used to prove fixed-parameter intractability in Abrahamson et al. (1989) are simultaneously much more complex but much less powerful than those described here. This goes to show that in computer science, as in life in general, it can sometimes take several tries to get it right.

The concepts of systematic parameterized complexity analysis and intractability maps were first defined in section 2.1 of Wareham (1999). This section also includes the first formal statements and proofs of Observations 7.4.1 and 7.4.2.

Part III

Reflections and Elaborations

8   Dealing with Intractability

In this chapter we review different "coping strategies" that cognitive scientists have been adopting for dealing with the intractability of computational-level theories and reflect on their validity and usefulness. We next turn to the question of how the concepts and techniques from Chapters 2 to 7 can be useful tools for cognitive scientists to deal with intractability of computational-level theories of cognition in a constructive and conceptually coherent way.

8.1   Recap and Setting the Stage

At this point, it may be good to refresh some of the content covered in Chapter 1. Quiz yourself with the following Practices 8.1.1, 8.1.2, and 8.1.3. If answering any of the questions is hard, then you may want to first reread Chapter 1 before proceeding in this chapter.

Practice 8.1.1   Can you explain in your own words the three levels of cognitive explanation introduced by Marr (1981) and widely used in cognitive science? What is the nature of the question asked at each level and what counts as an answer? How are the levels related and why are they to some extent independent?

Practice 8.1.2   Why do we focus in this book on computational-level theories? How is this choice of focus related to a top-down modeling methodology, and how can it be motivated?

Practice 8.1.3   Can you explain in your own words how and why intractability of computat-ional-level theories poses a theoretical challenge for cognitive scientists? What is meant by the intractability constraint on computational-level theories, and how can this constraint be formalized?

In Chapter 1, we introduced the notion of intractability. We explained why it is a problem for computational-level theories of cognition and mentioned "NP-hardness" as a formal notion of intractability. It is, however, only after having studied the technical chapters (Chapters 2–4 in particular) that you are able to prove NP-hardness of computational-level theories yourself. In fact, you might have already done so without realizing it. For instance, if you performed the practices in Chapters 2–4 then you proved some computational-level theories to be NP-hard. Those proofs involved polynomial-time reductions from (graph theoretical) NP-hard problems in computer science with no specific relevance to cognitive science. We next illustrate that it is also possible to prove computational-level theories to be NP-hard by polynomial-time reducing them to each other.

Consider the following two computational-level theories:

HARMONY MAXIMIZATION

Input: A network $G = (V,E)$, with for every edge $(v_i, v_j) \in E = V \times V$ a weight $w_{ij} \in \{-1,0,1\}$.

Output: An activation pattern a: $V \rightarrow \{-1, +1\}$ such that the harmony value $H(a) = \sum_i \sum_{j \neq i} a_i a_j w_{ij}$ is maximized.

COHERENCE

Input: A network $N = (P,C)$, where $C = C^+ \cup C^-$ is a set of positive and negative constraints and $C^+ \cap C^- = \emptyset$

Output: A truth assignment T: $P \rightarrow \{true, false\}$ that satisfies a maximum number of constraints in C.

HARMONY MAXIMIZATION describes the computational problem of determining a maximum harmony activation pattern a in a Hopfield network (i.e., a fully connected neural network). One can think of this problem as modeling the "what" of the neural network process that starts in some initial state and, by updating activations along the way, converges and settles on a maximum harmony end state. COHERENCE describes the problem of determining how to assign truth values (*true* or *false*) to the propositions in P such that the most constraints in C are satisfied. One can think of this problem as modeling the "what" of a belief fixation process that operates on some network of coherence and incoherence relations between possible beliefs that yields a maximally coherent set of beliefs (see also Chapter 10).

Now perform the next two practices.

Practice 8.1.4   Using the technique of polynomial-time reduction, prove that COHERENCE is NP-hard. Hint: You can choose any problem from Appendix B, but a straightforward reduction is known to exist from the known NP-hard problem MAX CUT (see also Exercise 3.4.1 in Chapter 3). Don't forget to first transform the optimization problems mentioned earlier into their corresponding decision problem variants.

Practice 8.1.5 Prove that HARMONY MAXIMIZATION is NP-hard by polynomial-time reduction from COHERENCE.

Stop and Think

Consider the polynomial-time reduction that you came up with in Practice 8.1.5. What do you notice?

The reduction from HARMONY MAXIMIZATION to COHERENCE has two notable properties:

(1) The reduction also works in reverse (i.e., by reversing the transformation in the reduction it is also possible to polynomial-time reduce COHERENCE to HARMONY MAXIMIZATION).
(2) The transformation involves little more than a rewriting of the problem in a new vocabulary (i.e., none of the more sophisticated reduction techniques, such as component design, were required).

The properties (1) and (2) show that the two problems are so closely related that for classical complexity-theoretic purposes one may consider them equivalent. This observation is important as COHERENCE is a computational-level theory that would be traditionally associated with the symbolic modeling tradition in cognitive science and the HARMONY MAXIMIZATION with the subsymbolic, connectionist modeling tradition. The possibility of transforming computational-level theories between generally competing frameworks for cognitive science explanations has some interesting implications, as we will see shortly.

The problem of intractability is ubiquitous in cognitive science. See Table 8.1 for an illustrative sample of computational-level theories that are known to be intractable in the sense of NP-hard. The table illustrates how the problem of intractability is not specific to any particular cognitive domain nor any specific modeling framework. For instance, the table includes domains as diverse as perception, motor planning, reasoning, learning, and language processing. Also, it includes a wide variety of modeling frameworks such as neural network, logical, probabilistic (Bayesian), symbolic, dynamical, and heuristic models (see also Appendix C).

Table 8.1 A sample of intractable computational-level theories for illustrative purposes.

Cognitive domain	Computational-level theory	References
Analogy	Structure-mapping theory	Gentner (1983); van Rooij et al. (2018)
Insight problem solving	eRCT	Wareham (2017)
Action understanding	Goal inference	Baker et al. (2009); Blokpoel et al. (2012)
Theory of mind	Dynamic epistemic logic	van de Pol et al. (2018)
Belief fixation	Most probable explanation	Abdelbar and Hedetniemi (1998)
Belief fixation	Coherence	Thagard (2000)
Belief revision	Default logic	Reiter (1980)
Belief revision	Bayesian updating	Cooper (1990)
Decision-making	Subset choice	Fishburn and LaValle (1993, 1996)
Decision-making	Adaptive toolbox theory	Otworowska et al. (2018)
Language	Grammar processing	Ristad (1990, 1993)
Language	Grammar processing	Berwick et al. (1987)
Network learning	Weight assignment	Judd (1990)
Network settling	Harmony maximization	Bruck and Goodman (1990)
Planning	STRIPS	Bylander (1994)
Cognitive control	Reactive architecture	Wareham et al. (2011b)
Similarity	Representational distortion	Hahn et al. (2003)
Vision	Bottom-up visual matching	Tsotsos (1990)

Stop and Think

Imagine you are a cognitive scientist who is invested in theory F of capacity ϕ. You really believe this theory has merit, as it seems to fit with your intuitions about the "what" of ϕ and it seems to explain a wide variety of empirical findings to date. Imagine now that a colleague tells you that F is NP-hard. You verify the proof, and see that your colleague is right. What would you do?

8.2   How (Not) to Deal with Intractability

Being confronted with an NP-hardness result for one's computational-level theory, what is a cognitive scientist to do? The opinions seem to vary. In the cognitive science literature at least four different responses can be identified. We will refer to these responses as follows (adapted from van Rooij, 2008):[1]

- **Framework rejection** Some researchers consider the finding that a computational-level theory F is NP-hard reason to reject the general framework underlying F. For example, Oaksford and Chater (1993); Oaksford and Chater (1998) argued that logicists' approaches to modeling common sense reasoning are untenable because checking whether a set of beliefs is logically consistent (i.e., the SATISFIABILITY problem) is NP-hard. Similarly, Gigerenzer, Hoffrage, and Goldstein (2008) have argued against both logicist and Bayesian models of human decision-making because classical logic and Bayesian problems can be shown to be NP-hard.
- **Devising heuristics** Other researchers consider the finding that a computational-level theory F is NP-hard no reason to reject the theoretical framework underlying F, nor to reject F itself as an intractable computational-level theory. Instead they assume that, at the algorithmic level, F is being computed by heuristics (i.e., inexact algorithms). This approach is taken, for example, by Thagard and Verbeurgt (1998) in the domain of coherence-based belief fixation (see also Thagard [2000], Falkenhainer, Forbus, and Gentner [1989], and Markman and Gentner [2000]) in the domain of analogical reasoning. It seems that these researchers recognize the constraint that tractability places upon algorithmic-level theories, but consider the constraint irrelevant at the computational level.
- **Claim approximability** There are also researchers who, like the previous group, assume tractability at the computational level is best dealt with by assuming inexact algorithms at the algorithmic level. But contrary to the former group of researchers, this latter group postulates that these inexact algorithms are not mere heuristics, but actually "good approximations." This is the approach taken, for instance, by researchers such as Chater, Tenenbaum, and Yuille (2006) and Sanborn, Griffiths, and Navarro (2010)

---

[1] Disclaimer: Our partitioning is an oversimplification, however, which we adopt for ease of presentation. In reality these groups of researchers overlap: one and the same researcher may give different responses at different times for different Fs. Also, sometimes researchers mix the different responses. It is our hope, that by clearly distinguishing them, the reader will be better able to recognize the different responses in the literature and identify their key differences.

for Bayesian models of cognition. It seems that these researchers recognize the constraint that tractability places upon algorithmic-level theories, but are furthermore committed to an approximation relation between the algorithmic and the computational level.

• **Theory revision** A last group of researchers views the theory of computational complexity as a tool for refining (not all-round rejecting) computational-level theories such that they satisfy tractability constraints. For example, Levesque (1989), like Oaksford and Chater (1993) and Oaksford and Chater (1998), recognized the inherent exponential-time complexity of general logic problems, but unlike Oaksford and Chater, he concluded that we need to adjust logic, not abandon it, in order to obtain psychologically realistic models of human reasoning. Similarly, upon finding that visual search in its general (bottom-up) form is NP-complete, Tsotsos (1990, 2001) did not abandon his model of vision, but instead adjusted it by assuming that top-down information helps constrain the visual search space.

Stop and Think

Consider each of these possible responses. Which one did you consider at the previous Stop and Think box? And which of them do you think is a valid approach?

We will now consider each of the coping strategies in more detail and assess their validity.

8.2.1   Theory Revision

Stop and Think

Why is Theory Revision a valid response to the intractability of ones computational-level theory?

An intractability result for a computational-level theory F indicates that it is not (plausibly) possible that the mind/brain computes exactly F (for anything but trivially small inputs). Yet, it may still compute something quite similar to F. If one believes this is the case, then theory revision is a natural way to go. To illustrate, recall our discussion of the following three computational-level characterizations of subset choice from Chapter 1:

GENERALIZED SUBSET CHOICE
Input: A set $X = \{x_1, x_2, ..., x_n\}$ of n available items, a value function u assigning a value to every subset $S \subseteq X$.
Output: A subset $S \subseteq X$ such that $u(S)$ is maximized over all possible $S \subseteq X$.

BINARY SUBSET CHOICE
Input: A set $X = \{x_1, x_2, ..., x_n\}$ of n available items. For every item $x \in X$ there is an associated integer value $u(x)$ and for every pair of items (x_i, x_j) there is an associated integer value $\delta(x_i, x_j)$.
Output: A subset $S \subseteq X$, such that $u(S) = \sum_{x \in S} u(x) + \sum_{x, y \in S} \delta(x, y)$ is maximum.

ADDITIVE SUBSET CHOICE
Input: A set $X = \{x_1, x_2, ..., x_n\}$ of n available items, a value function u assigning a value to every element $x \in X$.
Output: A subset $S \subseteq X$ such that $u(S) = \sum_{x \in S} u(x)$ is maximized over all possible $S \subseteq X$.

We earlier observed that GENERALIZED SUBSET CHOICE is intractable. Yet, we did not immediately reject the idea that subset choices are based on utility maximization. Instead we considered the possibility that GENERALIZED SUBSET CHOICE was an *overgeneralization* (more on this notion later on). That is, it could be that human decision-makers do not have arbitrary utility functions, but ones that can be decomposed into the utility of options (i.e., ADDITIVE SUBSET CHOICE) and/or their interactions (i.e., BINARY SUBSET CHOICE). This approach makes sense because – as you have learned in Chapter 4 – even if a more general problem is NP-hard, one or more of its special cases may be tractable. Hence, if a theory F is found to be NP-hard, a natural next step is to see if it is possible to revise it. Of course, it would be important to also assess to what extent the revision is still empirically supported. This can be done, for instance, by deriving predictions that follow from the restrictions on the input domain (e.g., a prediction of ADDITIVE SUBSET CHOICE is that the value of a subset is always equal to the value of its individual elements) and put them to an empirical test (in the case of pizza topping selection the prediction of ADDITIVE SUBSET CHOICE would probably be falsified). In other words, the traditional empirical cycle in cognitive science may be interlaced with a tractability analysis cycle (see Figure 8.1), e.g., as per the following steps:

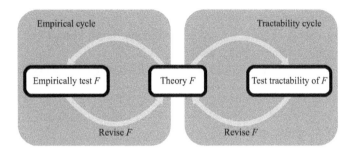

Figure 8.1   Illustration of how the empirical cycle can be interlaced with the tractability cycle.

1. Consider computational-level theory F.
2. Assess tractability of F:

   3. If F is intractable, then revise F to F' and repeat step 2 where now $F = F'$.
   4. If F is tractable, then continue with step 5 where now $F' = F$.

5. Test empirical predictions of F':

   6. If F' is falsified then revise F' to F'', and repeat step 2 where now $F = F''$.
   7. If F' is empirically supported, propose F' as new theory.

There are many different ways in which one may choose to revise a theory. For instance, one can throw F away and start anew, one can change details of the functional form of F (i.e., the nature of the mapping), one can even switch the framework altogether and replace a logic-based F by a probabilistic or neural network model F'. But as we illustrated earlier for subset choice, no such revisions may be called for or necessary. For instance, it could be that one's theory is really on the right track, but it is an overgeneralization of the to-be-explained ϕ. We will consider this option in more depth, as we build on this idea later.

Let us start by precisely defining ways in which computational-level theories relate to the capacities they intended to characterize. Recall that defining a computational-level theory F of some cognitive capacity ϕ involves defining both the input domain I and output domain O and the nature of the mapping, $F: I_F \rightarrow O_F$, between them. We will say that F is an accurate (or veridical) characterization of a cognitive capacity $\phi: I_\phi \rightarrow O_\phi$ if and only the following three conditions are met:

(1) $F(i) = \phi(i)$, for every $i \in I_\phi$
(2) $F(i) = \phi(i)$, for every $i \in I_F$
(3) $I_F = I_\phi$

It may happen that condition (1) is met without conditions (2) and (3) being met. This can happen, for instance, when $I_F \supset I_\phi$. In that case, we say that F is an *overgeneralization* of ϕ. Note that an overgeneralization describes ϕ accurately for inputs confined to $I_\phi \subset I_F$, but that I_F includes inputs in its domain that are outside the scope of the capacity ϕ. Conversely, it can also happen that condition (2) is met, without conditions (1) and (3) being met. This can happen, for instance, when $I_F \subset I_\phi$. In that case, we say that F is an *undergeneralization* of ϕ. Note that an undergeneralization describes ϕ accurately for inputs confined to $I_F \subset I_\phi$, but that I_F fails to include inputs in its domain that are within the scope of the capacity ϕ. In cases where neither condition (1) or (2) is met, we consider F to be a *mischaracterization* of ϕ.

Let us say that a computational-level theory $F\colon I_F \to O_F$ *subsumes* another $F'\colon I'_F \to O'_F$ whenever $F(i) = F'(i)$ for all $i \in I_F$ and $I_{F'} \subset I_F$. In such case, we also say F' *reduces* to F.[2] It is known that intractability is inherited along the direction of the reduction relation, and tractability is inherited in the opposite direction. Put differently, if a theory F is intractable, then so are all theories that it reduces to; and if a theory F is tractable then so are all theories that reduce to it.

In Figure 8.2 subsumption relations between theories (circles) are denoted by solid arrows, with the reduction relation running in the opposite direction. Other (less direct) forms of inter-theory reductions are depicted by dotted arrows (see footnote 2). For the sake of argument, let the filled circle (11) denote an accurate computational-level characterization F of ϕ. Note that F subsumes undergeneralizations of ϕ that belong to toy domains and is subsumed by overgeneralizations of ϕ that are intractable. Many accurate computational-level theories of relevance for cognitive science may similarly lie somewhere on a path crossing the boundary between tractable and intractable domains. This is to be expected, given that cognitive capacities require quite expressive formalisms for their accurate characterization, and expressive functions are typically intractable for unrestricted domains.

From this perspective, hitting upon an intractable characterization F does not mean that one has mischaracterized the cognitive capacity ϕ. It could

---

[2] The inverse of subsumption is a special case of the more general notion of polynomial-time (or parametrized) reduction that we covered in Chapter 3 (Chapter 6). By using reductions, it can also be shown that theories in different frameworks are of comparable (in)tractability (dotted lines, Figure 8.2). We saw, for instance, that this is the case for COHERENCE and HARMONY MAXIMIZATION in Practice 8.1.5.

simply mean that F is an overgeneralization. By exploring computational-level theories that are subsumed by F, one may identify several tractable, but still quite domain-general, candidates for an accurate computational-level characterization. Such a strategy would also help map out the border between tractable and intractable computational-level theories for cognitive capacities. This can provide cognitive science with a useful view on what are the scope and limits of domain generality of different cognitive capacities.

Note that the empirical and tractability cycles in Figure 8.1 may help the theorist to navigate the space in Figure 8.2. This navigation occurs under the influence of two forces. On the one hand, the empirical cycle pushes for the minimal generality needed to account for the empirical phenomena associated with ϕ. On the other hand, the tractability cycle pulls overgeneralized theories within the boundary of tractability. By combining these forces, a theorist may be able to hone in on an accurate computational-level theory of ϕ, which is general enough to be empirically adequate but no so general as to be intractable.

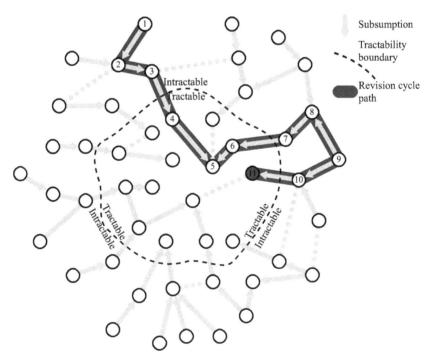

Figure 8.2   Illustration of a hypothetical space of possible computational-level theories (circles) for a given capacity ϕ. See text for details.

8.2.2   Framework Rejection

Stop and Think

The Framework Rejection response is to reject the entire framework (i.e., the class of functions to which F is believed to belong) if a computational-level theory F is found to be intractable. Why is such a rejection of an entire class not warranted?

As an illustration, consider the critique of logicist approaches to reasoning by Oaksford and Chater (1998), as they stated:

> "Consistency checking constitutes a general class of problems in complexity theory called satisfiability problems" (p. 76) and "consistency checking, like all satisfiability problems, is NP-complete" (p. 77)

Here, Oaksford and Chater (1998) based themselves on Cook's (1971) finding that SATISFIABILITY is NP-complete. They took this observation as a reason to reject the logicist framework altogether. It is as if here an intractability result for a given problem was assumed to "infect" all versions and variants of that problem. This inference is, however, not entirely correct. For instance, there exist versions of SATISFIABILITY that are in P (e.g., 2SAT; Garey and Johnson, 1979). Besides being unwarranted, such a framework rejection response is also counterproductive. Any sufficiently rich framework for modeling cognition will almost certainly give rise to some (possibly many) models that are NP-hard.

Stop and Think

The Framework rejection response seems to be applied when researchers are committed to a competing framework to which F does not belong. Why do you think this is?

It is not uncommon for cognitive scientists to try to discredit competing frameworks by pointing out that theories in those frameworks run into intractability issues. But this is no use. For instance, both connectionists and Bayesians have argued against symbolic and logic approaches, respectively, because the latter two would yield intractable theories of cognition (Haselager 1997, Oaksford, 1998). Yet, it is now well known that connectionist and Bayesian theories can also be intractable (Cooper, 1990; Judd, 1990; Kwisthout et al., 2011b; Parberry, 1997). Moreover, even heuristic and dynamical systems theories, both often lauded for being tractable, seem unable to live up to that image when forced to scale beyond toy domains (Otworowska et al., 2018; Siegelmann and Sontag, 1994; van Rooij et al., 2012)

As we illustrated in the previous section, the ubiquity of NP-hardness of computational-level theories can be understood as a natural consequence of attempting to scale one's computational-level models to general domains, without regards for tractability. A theory F being intractable is no reason to reject the framework that motivated F. If we did we would soon have no theories or frameworks left. It makes more sense to explore whether or not F can be revised (see Figure 8.1). It is only when many possible candidate theories F for ϕ are considered – and none can be shown to be tractable, or none that are tractable are empirically supported – that we are justified in believing that our theoretical framework may be entirely on the wrong track (or possibly the hypothesized capacity ϕ does not exist at all). Given that tractability analysis of computational-level theories is still in its infancy, we think this conclusion is not yet warranted for any of the major modeling frameworks pursued in cognitive science.

8.2.3   Devising Heuristics

───────────────── **Stop and Think** ─────────────────
How is the Devising Heuristics response different from the Theory Revision and Framework Rejection response?

According to structure-mapping theory of analogy (Gentner, 1983), finding analogical correspondences between two disparate domains (e.g., seeing structural resemblances between the solar system and the atom in Rutherford's model of the atom) is seen as a type of graph matching problem. Given that some graph matching problems (e.g., SUBGRAPH ISOMORPHISM) are NP-hard, Markman and Gentner (2000) argued as follows:

> Graph matching is known to be in the class of NP-hard problems, meaning that the running time needed for any algorithm that is guaranteed to find the best match increases as an exponential function of the size of the domains being compared. Thus, any psychologically plausible process for finding analogical correspondences must either restrict itself to trivial problems (an unacceptable course) or simplify the solution process (at the risk of finding sub-optimal matches). Markman and Gentner (2000, p. 507)

There are two things to note in this quote. First, like Oaksford and Chater, these authors seem to infer that intractability spreads from one problem to others in the same class (see the previous section for an explanation why this inference is unwarranted). Second, unlike Oaksford and Chater, these authors do not reject the modeling framework, nor pursue restriction of the computational-level theory to make it tractable, but rather they propose to simplify the solution process at the algorithmic level. This type of simplified process is also called a *heuristic*. Hence, we refer to this as the Devising Heuristics response.[3]

The Devising Heuristics response is one of the most common responses to NP-hardness of computational-level theories in cognitive science. Despite its popularity, it seems to be a flawed coping strategy. To see why this is so, consider the following definitions:

DEFINITION 8.2.1   *A procedure A is said to be an* algorithm *just in case A is a computational procedure with a finite description and, for any given input to process, A halts in a finite number of steps, possibly producing some output.*

DEFINITION 8.2.2   *An algorithm A is said to be an* algorithm for *a function F: I → O if and only if for any input i ∈ I the algorithm A produces as output $A(i) = F(i)$. (To emphasize that A computes* exactly *F for all inputs in its domain, we may also refer to A as an* exact algorithm*).*

DEFINITION 8.2.3   *An algorithm H is said to be a* heuristic for *a function F: I → O if and only if the following two conditions obtain: Let F_H be the function computed exactly by H, then (1) there exist some i ∈ I such that $F(i) \neq F_H(i)$ for at least some i ∈ I; and (2) some relationship – weaker than equality[4] – is believed to obtain between F and F_H.*

Note that a heuristic H for a function F can be tractable, even if F is intractable, because there is no guarantee on how F_H and F relate exactly.[5]

Stop and Think

Consider Definitions 8.2.2 and 8.2.3. Why is devising a heuristic as an algorithmic-level theory an invalid way of dealing with intractability of computational-level models? (Hint: think of the relationship between computational- and algorithmic-level theories.)

There are two fundamental problems. First, the appeal to heuristics introduces an inconsistency between the computational- and algorithmic-level explana-

---

[3] See Forbus and Oblinger (1990) for a specific heuristic proposed as algorithmic-level theory for structure-mapping theory; and see Grootswagers (2013) for a comparison of the performance of this heuristic with the exact (fixed parameter tractable) algorithm described in Chapter 11.

[4] For example, it may be conjectured that the heuristic computes $F(i)$ correctly for many inputs i, or it may be conjectured that the difference between $F(i)$ and $F_H(i)$ is small for many inputs $i \in I$.

[5] If there were a guarantee, then we would call H an approximation algorithm, instead of a heuristic. In that case refer to the Claiming Approximability response in the next section.

tions, and second, it leaves the computation of F unexplained for any and all $i \in I$ with $F(i) \neq H(i)$.

We demonstrate the inconsistency as follows: Let F denote our intractable computational-level theory, and let F_H be the function computed by heuristic H. From the definition of heuristics, it follows that there exists a nonempty set of inputs $I' \subseteq I$, such that $F(i) \neq F_H(i)$, for all $i \in I'$.[6] Suppose that a cognitive scientist maintains that $F(i)$ is a computational-level explanation of some ϕ *and* that H is its associated algorithmic-level explanation. What should she predict as the outcome of presenting a subject directly with some input $i \in I'$ as produced by the capacity of interest? According to the computational-level explanation, she should predict the output will be $F(i)$; but, according to the algorithmic-level explanation, she should predict $F_H(i)$. Since $F(i) \neq F_H(i)$. The computational-level explanation is confirmed by the data only if the algorithmic-level theory is disconfirmed, and the algorithmic-level theory is confirmed by the data only if the computational-level explanation is disconfirmed. In other words, $F(i)$ and $H(i)$ are a priori incompatible and competing theories. This is not how things should be. The different levels of explanations – computational and algorithmic – should be complementary not competing.

Besides the inconsistency between the computational- and algorithmic-level explanations that is introduced by maintaining the heuristic H as an algorithmic-level explanation for F, H also fails as an explanation of how the computation of F is achieved by cognizers. This follows from the fact that H does not compute F, but instead computes F_H, which is a distinct computational problem from F. After all, there exist (infinitely many; see Practice 8.2.2 later) $i \in I$ such that $F(i) \neq F_H(i)$, and for all those i, the heuristic H cannot explain the "how" of F.

Can a cognitive scientist resolve the aforementioned problems of inconsistency and explanatory failure? Certainly. The most obvious resolution would be to revise the computational-level explanation of ϕ to be the function F_H instead of F. This is possible if the cognitive scientist is not really committed to F, but rather believes that H is a legitimate and accurate algorithmic-level explanation of ϕ. The upshot of this revision is, however, that it turns out to be a Theory Revision response and not a Devising Heuristics response. After all, the algorithm H has now become an *exact* algorithm for the computational-level theory (viz., F_H).[7] This possible resolution illustrates that an initial Devising

---

[6] In fact, there must be infinitely many such i, otherwise F would not be intractable (Schöning [1990]; see also Practice 8.2.2)

[7] Whether or not such revision is empirically supported would need to be independently assessed of course (cf. Figure 8.1).

Heuristics response may inspire a Theory Revision response. It is just that the former is invalid and unstable as a solution in and of itself.

Stop and Think

We have explained why the Devising Heuristics response (without Theory Revision) is not valid. Why do you think that it is nevertheless such a popular strategy adopted by cognitive scientists?

Possibly, the popularity of Devising Heuristics response is due to a confusion between the reverse engineering approach of cognitive science (Dennett, 1995) and the traditional forward engineering approach of computer science (Garey and Johnson, 1979). It is conventional wisdom in computer science that, when faced with NP-hard problems, "the search for an efficient, exact algorithm should be accorded low priority [and it is] more appropriate to concentrate on other, less ambitious, approaches" (Garey and Johnson, 1979, p. 3). Many cognitive scientists seem to accept this wisdom as applying also to cognitive explanation. This reasoning overlooks, however, a crucial difference between reverse and forward engineering. Table 8.2 illustrates these differences.

In the case of forward engineering, the problem to be solved is user-defined and a software engineer is to devise and implement an algorithm for solving it. In reverse engineering, on the other hand, the input/output specification of the to-be-modeled (naturally evolved) system needs to be *discovered*. While the goal of the forward engineer is to compute as best as possible the user-specified input/output function, the reverse engineer aims at modeling as best as possible an existing cognitive capacity. Consequently, intractability should signal something very different for forward and reverse engineers: For forward engineers it may mean that they should give up the hope of general

Table 8.2 Traditional forward versus cognitive reverse engineering. Adapted from van Rooij and Wareham (2008).

Characteristic	Traditional	Cognitive
Origin of input/output function	Derived from user specifications	Hypothesized on the basis of observations and intuition
Goals of input/output function	Should meet user's needs	Should be a veridical model of cognitive capacity
Consequence of intractability	Devise heuristic methods	Revise hypothesized function

exact procedures and instead settle for weaker heuristic methods, whereas for reverse engineers it means that the hypothesized input-output mapping is computationally unrealistic, so they had better get back to the drawing board and revise it.

8.2.4   Claim Approximability

> **Stop and Think**
>
> How is the Claim Approximability response different from the Devising Heuristics response?

The Claim Approximability response resembles the Devising Heuristics response. It, too, assumes that intractability at the computational-level is best dealt with by postulating tractable but inexact algorithms at the algorithmic level. We will speak of the Claim Approximability response instead of the Devising Heuristics response, however, if in addition it is postulated that these inexact algorithms are not mere heuristics but *approximation* algorithms. The latter are inexact algorithms that – in contrast to heuristics – have well-defined performance guarantees. This idea is captured by the following definition.[8]

DEFINITION 8.2.4   *An algorithm A_{approx} is said to be an* approximation algorithm *for a function F: $I \to O$ if and only if the following two conditions obtain: Let F_{approx} be the function computed exactly by A_{approx}, then (1) there exist some $i \in I$ such that $F(i) \neq F_{approx}(i)$; and (2) some known close relationship – weaker than equality[9] – obtains between F and F_H.*

> **Stop and Think**
>
> As approximation algorithms have a well-defined "close" relationship with the functions that they approximate, they may not be susceptible to the same criticism as heuristics as algorithmic-level explanations. Why not?

A cognitive scientist may argue approximation algorithms do not face the same inconsistency and explanatory failures as heuristics when assumed as

---

[8] For clarity, we will use the notions "exact algorithm" and "approximation algorithm" as mutually exclusive in this section. For completeness, we note that in reality one can see the former as a special case of the latter, i.e., exact algorithms are just extremely good approximation algorithms. Yet, for the sake of argument, we will adopt the pragmatic meaning of "approximation algorithm" as a *non-exact* algorithm in this section.

[9] For example, it may be known that Difference $(F(i), F_{approx}(i)) \leq \epsilon$, or that there exist only ϵ inputs i such that $F(i) \neq F_{approx}(i)$, for some constant ϵ.

algorithmic-level theories. This is illustrated in Figure 8.3. An approximation algorithm A_{approx} has a well-defined relationship with a computational-level theory F that it approximates, since it approximates F in some well-defined way that guarantees that its output is "close" to that of F (and thus $F_{approx} \approx F$). For instance, if one knows the approximation algorithm's outputs will differ from the function's output only by a small margin (possibly even smaller than measurement precision) or only on a handful of inputs (such that the probability of encountering them in the set of infinitely many possible inputs would be negligible), then such minor differences between algorithmic and computational-level explanations may not be taken as theoretically problematic. After all, all theories are at best approximations of reality anyway, and we do not take this imperfection as a reason to reject all theories. On the contrary, if the fit between theory and explanandum is good enough and well-understood, we generally take this as the mark of a good (approximate) theory. Why then would one require inter-theory relations to be fully strict? Why not also allow for small margin of (non-systematic) error?

This seems a fair question. We do not disagree.

Stop and Think

Can you explain why postulating approximation algorithms as algorithmic-level explanations is still unnecessary?

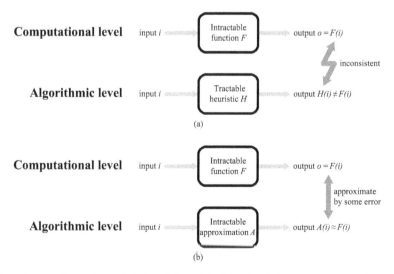

(a)

(b)

Figure 8.3   Illustrations of the invalidity of devising heuristics (or approximation algorithms) and of claiming approximability.

If one knows exactly which F_{approx} is computed by the approximation algorithm A_{approx} then one could also revise F to be F_{approx} and have the A_{approx} be the exact algorithm for the newly revised theory F_{approx}. In other words, a Theory Revision response is always open as an option, even if one hypothesizes approximation algorithms as algorithmic level theories. Be that as it may, we agree that such revision may not be strictly necessary if the approximation bounds are so good that for all intents and purposes the two theories – F at the computational level and A_{approx} at the algorithmic level – are practically indistinguishable. This raises the question, however, if intractable Fs indeed have tractable approximation algorithms that approximate them to such high degrees of closeness. This question is vital. In the literature regularly claims are made of "approximability" of intractable functions, without specifying what is meant by "approximation" and without giving a proof of the relevant form of approximation. Or proofs are given, but these show only approximation guarantees for unlimited computational resources (Sanborn et al. [2010]; see also Cooper and Peebles [2017]); hence, rendering such proofs irrelevant for the assessment of the *tractable* approximability of intractable Fs.

Stop and Think

Assume a degree of approximation that warrants a Claiming Approximability response. Do you think NP-hard problems are never/seldom/sometimes/often/always approximable to that degree in polynomial time?

Now perform the following two practices to build a more informed intuition about how likely such approximation algorithms are to exist for a given intractable function F.

Practice 8.2.1 Reconsider the computational-level theory COHERENCE. Prove that there cannot exist any polynomial-time approximation algorithm for COHERENCE that always outputs a truth assignment that differs in at most ϵ truth values from the maximally coherent truth assignment, for some constant ϵ (assuming P $\neq$ NP). (Hint: Proof by contradiction. That is, assume that such an approximation algorithm does exist. Then show that this would imply that P = NP.)

Practice 8.2.2 Reconsider the computational-level theory COHERENCE. Prove that there cannot exist any polynomial-time approximation algorithm for COHERENCE that outputs a truth assignment that differs from the maximally coherent truth assignment on only ϵ inputs, for some constant ϵ (assuming P $\neq$ NP). (Hint: Proof by contradiction. That is, assume that such

an approximation algorithm does exist. Then show that this would imply that
P = NP.)

Having performed these practices, reconsider your answer for the preceding
Stop and Think box. Did your intuition stay the same, or did it change?

The important take-home message is that not all intractable Fs are tractably
approximable. Whether or not they are will depend on the precise criterion
defined for approximation and the nature of F. In any event, the practices
demonstrate that tractable approximability cannot be assumed a priori or
assessed based on intuition. A claim of approximability should be accompanied
by a formal proof. In case where such proofs are possible and the criterion
of approximability is such that no non-negligible inconsistency between
computational- and algorithmic-level explanation is induced, then this response
seems valid. Otherwise, it is not. At present, few if any claims of approximability in the cognitive science literature have been accompanied by the required
proofs, rendering such claims vacuous at the moment.

8.3   Identifying Sources of Intractability

Up to this point in the chapter, we have implicitly adopted the P-Cognition
thesis when talking about ways of dealing with intractability. Or at least,
nothing we said so far contradicted that thesis. Yet, as we explained in
Chapter 1, there are good reasons to consider that formalization of the Tractable
Cognition thesis is too strict for computational-level theories. The reason is that
ecologically relevant inputs may have many parameters of varying sizes. Even
if the overall input size is typically large for real-world inputs, some parameters
of the inputs may be small for real-world inputs. If our intractable theory F is
fixed-parameter tractable for such small parameters then the theory can still
be tractable for real-world inputs despite its intractability for unrestricted input
domains. This is illustrated in Table 8.3.

Table 8.3 Illustration of running time for an fp-tractable algorithm running in time $O(2^k n)$ for
different input sizes (n) and values of the parameter (k).

n	$k = 2$	$k = 5$	$k = 10$	$k = 20$	$k = 50$
5	20	160	5,120	$>10^6$	$>10^{15}$
10	40	320	10,240	$>10^7$	$>10^{16}$
20	80	640	20,480	$>10^7$	$>10^{16}$
50	200	1,600	51,200	$>10^7$	$>10^{16}$
100	400	3,200	102,400	$>10^8$	$>10^{17}$

Table 8.3 illustrates the running time of an example fp-tractable lgorithm $(2^k n)$ as a function of parameter $K = \{k\}$ and input size n. The table illustrates that in such cases the impact of n is negligible compared to the impact of k. It is for this reason that we say that k is a source of intractability. In other words, the parameter k can by itself confine *all* non-polynomial time complexity inherent in the problem. This means that the problem is efficiently solvable, even for larger n, provided only that k remains small.

Stop and Think

How can parameterized complexity be used to implement a systematic version of the tractability cycle in Figure 8.1?

This perspective yields a further refinement of the intractability cycle that we introduced in Section 8.2.1. Specifically, we can refine step 3 in that cycle. There we simply wrote "If F is intractable then revise F to F', and repeat step 2." But we did not specify any systematic procedure for revising F. The parameterized complexity approach suggests one (more or less) systematic way to explore if there are tractable revisions of F, viz., ones that have input domains restricted to small parameters for which F is fixed-parameter tractable. This could be done as per the following steps:

1. Consider computational-level theory F.
2. Assess tractability of F as follows:

    2a. Consider one or more *parameters* $k_1, k_2, ..., k_m$ that may (or may not) be sources of intractability in F.

    2b. Determine if F is *fixed-parameter tractable* for parameter set $K = \{k_1, k_2, ..., k_m\}$ (i.e., the problem is computable in time $f(K) \cdot poly(n)$).

3. If No, then K is not a source of intractability, return to Step 2a (unless one runs out of parameters to consider; then reconsider the functional form of F in step 1).
4. If Yes, then K is a source of intractability in the problem; continue with step 5.
5. Assess to what extent it is plausible that the parameters in the set K are small for ecologically relevant inputs, and test empirical predictions of F with restricted parameters in set K.
6. If (F, K) is falsified then revise F to F' and/or K to K', and repeat step 2.
7. If (F, K) is empirically supported, propose (F, K) as the new theory.

In the following chapters, we will consider three example computational-level theories and analyze them for sources of intractability as per step 2a and 2b.

8.4 Exercises

Exercise 8.4.1 In this chapter we covered four ways of (not) dealing with intractability of computational-level theories. Try to identify each approach in at least one paper in the literature.

Exercise 8.4.2 In this chapter we covered four ways of (not) dealing with intractability of computational-level theories. Can you think of others that we have not covered? If so, can you find examples of them in the cognitive science literature?

Exercise 8.4.3 Reconsider Exercise 1.3.1. If you performed that exercise then you came up with one or more formalizations for a cognitive capacity of interest to you. Now try to answer the following questions for yourself: Is your formalization NP-hard or not? If it is not NP-hard, is it an undergeneralization? If it is NP-hard, apply the intractability cycle using parameterized complexity analysis to identify sources of intractability in your formalization and, where plausible, consider restrictions on your theory.

Exercise 8.4.4 Read one or more of the Application chapters (Chapters 10–12) and perform the practices therein.

8.5 Further Reading

If you have worked through this book from the start, you are now equipped with the tools to address questions and claims regarding the (in)tractability of computational-level theories of cognition. There is a whole world of further reading: All of cognitive science, but perhaps the application chapters are a nice starting point (since you have this book in front of you now). Otherwise, if you want to learn more about common objections to the methodology and how these objections hold up under close scrutiny then consider reading Chapter 9.

Two points of entry in the literature that may be of special use and interest after having read this chapter are: (1) van Rooij et al. (2018), who discuss how the intractability cycle discussed in this chapter can be integrated with the rational analysis as championed by, among others, John Anderson (1990); and (2) van Rooij and Wareham (2012), and Kwisthout and van Rooij (2013) who discuss different forms of approximation, called structure-, value- and expectation-approximation, of which we covered the first in Section 8.2.4.

9 Replies to Common Objections

This chapter discusses a set of possible objections to the tractability constraint on computational-level theories. Any of these objections may naturally arise when reading Chapter 1. It is an option to read this chapter directly after Chapter 1. Yet, we believe that the responses to the listed objections can be best appreciated after having mastered the formal concepts and techniques in Chapters 2–7 and familiarized oneself with the conceptual arguments in Chapter 8.

In Chapter 1 we explained why intractable (NP-hard) computational-level theories of human cognition cannot plausibly scale to situations of real-world complexity. It follows that such theories need to obey the tractability constraint. We referred to this as the Tractable Cognition thesis, and discussed two possible formalizations: the P-Cognition thesis and the FPT-Cognition thesis. The Tractable Cognition thesis is not without its critics or skeptics, however. In fact, a considerable number of potential objections can be raised. In this chapter we make a compilation of in total 14 possible objections. The first 11 of these were also covered in an article by van Rooij in 2008 (pp. 939–984). We repeat these objections verbatim here, but have updated the responses where relevant. We add two further objections inspired by other publications (see the Further Reading section), plus one objection not previously published but commonly raised by students.

By responding to each of these 14 objections, we hope to clarify that the concerns raised are typically based on misconceptions or uninformed intuitions, and that they dissolve upon explanation and clarification. Each of the objections that we discuss arises from a particular theoretical perspective. We distinguish between three perspectives: the perspective of (A) a researcher who subscribes to the P-Cognition thesis, but who questions the FPT-Cognition thesis; (B) a researcher who subscribes to the computational approach to cognition, but who questions the Tractable Cognition thesis; and (C) a researcher who does not subscribe to the computational approach to cognition. For clarity, we indicate for each objection the perspective from which we believe it arises.

9.1   The Empiricist Objection

Cognitive models should be evaluated on how well they explain empirical data, not on their a priori computational plausibility. (Perspective B or C)

This objection is sometimes raised by cognitive scientists who may feel that the Tractable Cognition thesis is a rationalist attempt to accept or reject computational-level theories solely on theoretical grounds, a practice that would seem to contradict the empirical nature of cognitive science. But the Tractable Cognition thesis is not intended to replace empirical evaluation of computational-level theories at all. It is well understood that, in the end, all computational-level theories must stand the test of empirical scrutiny. To optimally benefit from both tractability and empirical constraints on computational-level theories, we have argued that tractability testing and empirical testing should be interlaced (see Chapter 8). What the Tractable Cognition thesis does offer is a way of recognizing computationally unfeasible theories, or theory variants, that can be rejected even before they need to be put to an empirical test. Even if such a computationally unfeasible theory were to produce models that fit the empirical data, it would not be satisfactory as a theory, because explanation requires more than fitting data alone (Cummins, 2000). For example, the theory should be able to explain how the postulated computations can scale beyond the toy domains in the lab to situations of real-world complexity. An intractable computational-level theory cannot do this. In sum, the Tractable Cognition thesis helps constrain the vast space of possible computational-level theories one may postulate for any given cognitive capacity. This seems particularly helpful because many such theories are about unobservable, or only indirectly observable, cognitive processes, and thus they are typically vastly underconstrained by the available observational data (see also Anderson, 1987, 1990, and Chapter 1). If the objection comes from the Perspective C (non-computationalism), then this response may not yet be satisfactory. In that case, refer to the cognition-is-not-computation objection described next.

9.2   The Cognition-Is-Not-Computation Objection

Computational complexity theory has nothing to offer cognitive science because cognition is not computation. (Perspective C)

What is meant by this objection depends crucially on the meaning of the phrase "cognition is not computation."

Stop and Think ───────────

What could be meant by "cognition is not computation"?

The phrase is traditionally associated with a multitude of meanings. We distinguish four possible versions of the objection:

1. *Complexity analysis does not apply to cognition because cognition is not symbolic computation.* In cognitive science, the terms computation and computationalism have become associated with the symbolic tradition, and sometimes even with particular models in this tradition (e.g., Anderson, 1987, 1990; Fodor, 1987; Newell and Simon, 1988a,b; Pylyshyn, 1991). All that the Tractable Cognition thesis requires, however, is a commitment to a minimal computationalism (Chalmers, 2011). Many theories that are considered "non-computational" may still fall under the heading of computationalism in this broad sense. For example, despite their presumed non-computational status (e.g., Port and van Gelder, 1995; Thelen and Smith, 1994; van Gelder, 1995; van Gelder, 1998, 1999), dynamical systems models can be subjected to computational complexity analysis (Siegelmann and Sontag, 1994; van Rooij, 2012), and the same holds for neural network models as subsymbolic models of cognition (Frank et al., 2009; Šíma, 1996; see also the Further Reading section).

2. *Complexity theory does not apply to cognitive systems, because cognitive systems do not realize input/output functions.* In this book we adopt the convention that cognitive capacities can be understood (at Marr's computational level) as the computation of input/output functions. It may be, however, that the purpose of some (or all) cognitive systems is not to compute any input/output functions at all. Instead, their purpose may be to cycle through a set of states indefinitely, without ever halting and producing an output (cf. Levesque, 1989, p. 385). Such processes may seem to fall outside the scope of the Tractable Cognition thesis. However, this is not necessarily the case. Even unhalting or cyclical processes can be conceptualized as computations of input/output functions where the inputs and outputs are internal states. Consider, for example, those processes whose functionality is to maintain certain (representational) states over time or to ensure that certain system values do not grow out of bounds (e.g., homeostatic processes). Such so-called "maintenance" computations are similarly constrained by the requirement of tractability and models about them can be subjected to the same types of computational complexity analyses as standard input/output computations (see, e.g., Dunne, Laurence, and Wooldridge, 2003; Wooldridge and Dunne, 2005).

3. *Cognitive functions need not be computationally tractable because cognitive systems realize their input/output mappings via non-computational means.* Some non-computationalists may not question that cognitive capacities realize input/output mappings (i.e., they do not subscribe to Version 2 of this objection), but they may postulate that cognitive systems realize such mappings in *non-computational* ways (e.g., Horgan and Tienson, 1996; Krueger and Tsav, 1990). On this view, it seems, cognitive functions need not be computationally tractable. Be that as it may, the non-computationalist is faced with the problem that non-computationalist explanations seem to be made of mysterious stuff and lack explanatory value (see also Cherniak, 1986; Levesque, 1989). John Tsotsos (1990) put it as follows:

> Experimental scientists attempt to explain their data, not just describe it (...) There is no appeal to non-determinism or to oracles that guess the right answer or to undefined, unjustified, or "undreamed of" mechanisms that solve difficult components. Can you imagine theories that do have these characteristics passing a peer-review procedure? (p. 466)

In a similar vein, Prasse and Rittgen (1998) objected to Wegner's (1997) claim that so-called "interactive machines" would be able to exceed the computing powers of Turing machines by performing "non-algorithmic procedures." Prasse and Rittgen explained how the purported non-algorithmic aspects of interactive machines seem to be an artifact of Wegner leaving the process of interaction unmodeled, undefined, and hence unexplained. They furthermore illustrated that existing well-defined models of interactive computability are known not to supersede Turing computability (see also Cockshott and Michaelson, 2007; Wegner, 1997).

4. *Complexity theory does not apply to cognition because computation is an altogether wrong way of thinking about cognition.* This last version of the cognition-is-not-computation objection represents the non-computationalist unpersuaded by any of our reactions to Versions 1 through 3. In our opinion, even this researcher should appreciate the contribution that the Tractable Cognition thesis makes to cognitive science; namely, a non-computationalist can still recognize that tractability is a constraint on *computational* theories of cognition. Then, the Tractable Cognition thesis offers the non-computationalist a way of evaluating the success of his or her competition. If, in the long run, human cognition systematically defies tractable computational description and explanation, then this can be taken as empirical support for the idea that computation is the wrong way of thinking about cognition.

9.3   The Super-Human Objection

Humans are known to perform tasks that are computationally intractable. This goes to show that tractability is not a constraint on human computation. (Perspective B or C)

Many of our best theories of cognitive capacities that operate on the time scale of seconds or minutes postulate intractable (NP-hard) computations (see Table 8.1 in Chapter 8). Some researchers interpret this as evidence that people can efficiently realize intractable computational capacities (e.g., Siegel, 1990). In our view, the argument is flawed. There are two possibilities: Either one is a computationalist (Perspective B), or one is not (Perspective C). If one is a computationalist, then one should concede that either the capacities are incorrectly modelled (i.e., requiring a Theory Revision response as discussed in Chapter 8) or that the wrong criterion for tractability has been adopted. If one is not a computationalist, then one does not recognize that the models truly capture the nature of the capacity in the first place, and thus their classification as "intractable" is irrelevant to the conceptualization of the capacity. In that case see our response to the cognition-is-not-computation objection, discussed earlier.

9.4   The Heuristics Objection

Humans often use heuristics instead of exact algorithms. Then intractability is not an issue. (Perspective B)

In our response to this objection, we distinguish between two possible meanings of the word heuristic: one pertaining to the computational level of explanation (heuristic$_1$) and one pertaining to the algorithmic level (heuristic$_2$). We will argue either form of the objection is unfounded.

An input/output function postulated at Marr's computational level may be a heuristic$_1$ procedure for solving a real-world problem (assumed to be) faced by the cognitive system. This heuristic$_1$ does not guarantee that the problem is always solved in all situations, but it is believed to solve the problem often enough or close enough to be of practical use. It is a mistake to think that such a heuristic$_1$ is always computationally cheap or even tractable. Take, for example, the problem faced by people to decide what to believe and what not to believe. There does not seem to exist any procedure that given observations about the world produces only true (non-trivial) beliefs. Coherentists propose that a good heuristic$_1$ for coming to have many true beliefs is to maximize the coherence among one's beliefs and observations.

But note that, despite its heuristic₁ status, the computational-level theory of Paul Thagard for coherence maximization, called Coherence (see Chapter 10), is known to be computationally intractable (i.e., NP-hard; Thagard, 2000; Thagard and Verbeurgt, 1998).

One may object that a heuristic₁ being computationally intractable does nothing to affect its descriptive validity at the computational level because humans may use an algorithmic-level heuristic₂ to compute the computational-level heuristic₁ (i.e., an inexact algorithm H postulated as the algorithmic-level theory for the computational-level theory F). This approach has been extensively discussed in the previous chapter, where we already explained that this approach is explanatorily incoherent. We briefly restate the point here: The assumption that humans use inexact algorithms to compute the functions postulated in NP-hard computational-level theories introduces an inconsistency between the computational-level explanation and the algorithmic-level explanation of one and the same process. After all, if H is an inexact algorithm for computing function $F: I \rightarrow O$ then there exist inputs $I' \subset I$ such that $H(i) \neq F(i)$ for all $i \in I'$.[1] But that means that for all those $i \in I'$ the algorithm A does not explain how the function F is computed by human minds/brain because of the simple fact that the algorithm does not compute $f(i)$ for those i. Note that heuristic₂ H for F does not compute F but rather some other function F_H (which may be superficially similar to F, but still importantly different, because one can be intractable while the other is not). Therefore, it is F_H, and not F, that should be adopted as the computational-level theory if H is adopted as algorithmic-level theory. Note that H hereby ceases to be a heuristic₂ and instead becomes an exact algorithmic-level explanation of how the system computes F_H, as it should be. Now observe that if H is tractably computable, then so is F_H.

Practice 9.4.1   To help build intuition of the degree of inconsistency created by using a tractable inexact algorithm as an algorithmic-level explanation for some intractable computational-level theory F, perform the following practices:

1. Assume a computational-level theory $F: I \rightarrow O$ is intractable, and that H is a tractable heuristic (inexact algorithm) for F. Prove that there must exist infinitely many inputs $i \in I$, such that $F(i) \neq H(i)$. (Hint: Prove by contradiction and/or look back at Chapter 8)

2. Consider a known NP hard problem (e.g., VERTEX COVER, TRAVELING SALESPERSON, or any other problem you have some familiarity and

---

[1]   In fact, there must exist infinitely many such inputs, otherwise F would not be intractable (Schöning, 1990; van Rooij, Wright, and Wareham, 2012).

affinity with). Come up with a simple heuristic for this problem (e.g., a greedy search algorithm). Can you think of an instance of the problem that "fools" that heuristic (i.e., that makes it produce the wrong output)? Reflect on how hard or easy it is to come up with such an adversarial input.

9.5   The Average-Case Objection

A computation that is classified as intractable on a worst-case analysis may still be tractable in practice. An average-case measure of complexity should be used instead. (Perspective B)

In this book we have adopted a worst-case measure of complexity (see $O(.)$ notation introduced in Chapter 2). According to this measure the computational complexity of an input/output mapping is defined by the hardest input in its input domain. This measure is appropriate for assessing (in)tractability of computational-level models because for a computation to be tractable it must be tractable for all its possible inputs, including the worst-case input. One possible objection may be that the worst-case input may never happen in practice and that, therefore, the worst-case complexity measure overestimates the real complexity of the computational-level theory. This objection becomes self-contradictory, however, once we accept that the hypothesized input domain is part of the computational-level theory (as we have done throughout this book): The cognitive scientist postulating a computational-level theory $F\colon I \to O$ is, by definition, assuming that every input $i \in I$ can happen in practice.

If there were to exist any input $i \in I$ for which the cognitive theorist believed it could not or does not happen in practice, then he or she should instead postulate a different computational-level theory $F'\colon I' \to O$, where input domain $I' \subset I$ is restricted so as to exclude those inputs not assumed to occur in practice (as in what we called "Theory Revision" in Chapter 8). The new theory F' again has its own worst-case inputs. Clearly, a cognitive theorist could mistakenly be assuming that an input situation i arises in the real world when in fact it never does. Then a worst-case analysis of the computational-level theory could indeed overestimate the worst-case complexity of the computation performed by the relevant cognitive capacity in the real world. But this mismatch would be due to a mistake on the side of the theorist in hypothesizing the capacity's input domain, not a reason to object to worst-case analysis. After all, both the computational-level theory and the real-world capacity have a worst-case scenario, and the problem here is that the two worst-case scenarios do not match up, not that an average-case analysis of the computational-level theory would have been more appropriate.

This is not to say that average-case complexity is never a preferred measure of computational complexity. It may very well be for purposes other than assessing tractability, for example, when cognitive scientists are interested in comparing the time-complexity of different (tractable) algorithmic-level explanations with reaction time data obtained via experimentation. In this case, comparing mean reaction time with the algorithms' average-case complexity may be more informative than comparing it with their worst-case complexity (cf. Dry et al., 2006; Pizlo et al., 2006).

9.6   The Parallelism Objection

Cognitive computation is (to a large extent) parallel, not serial. A function that is intractable for a serial machine need not be intractable for a parallel machine. (Perspective B)

The complexity measures adopted in this article are defined with reference to computation by *serial* Turing machines. Nevertheless, the arguments put forth here for the Tractable Cognition thesis can naturally be extended to include parallel computation (see also Frixione, 2001). From a complexity perspective, the difference between serial and parallel computation may be quite insubstantial as far as tractability is concerned. To illustrate, let us first consider a parallel machine M with c processing channels, such that M computes a given serial computation by performing c steps in parallel (i.e., simultaneously). Further, let F be an input/output function with time-complexity $O(f(n))$, where $n = |i|$ is a measure of input size. Then M computes F at best in time $O(\frac{f(n)}{c})$. Note that, if c is a constant, then the speed-up due to c parallelization is by a constant factor only, and $O(\frac{f(n)}{c}) = O(f(n))$. The speed-up factor c can be taken into account in the analysis – there is nothing inherent in complexity theory that prevents one from doing so – but if $F(n)$ is a non-polynomial function, then the speed-up due to c becomes negligibly small very fast as input size n grows (see also Practice 1.1.1 in Chapter 1). This means that non-polynomial time complexity computations are unrealistic also for parallel machines for all but small inputs. The same is true if c is bounded by some polynomial function of n. If c were to grow non-polynomially as a function of n, then $O(\frac{f(n)}{c})$ may become a polynomial running time. In that case, indeed time would no longer be a limiting factor, but the space required for implementing the astronomical number of parallel processing channels would be.

In other models of parallel computation, the speed-up due to a constant c need not be constant, but may grow with n. This is the case, for example, in the parallel random access machine model, where a parallel machine M is assumed to have available c processors that can all communicate to each other in constant time (e.g., Gibbons and Rytter, 1988). Although such a parallel machine can compute certain computations faster than a serial Turing machine, the difference in speed between the two machine models is never more than a polynomial amount of time, and, hence, negligible for non-polynomial time computations (see, e.g., Jaja, 1992; van Emde Boas, 1990). The same is true for other reasonable models of parallel computation (e.g., circuits and neural nets Parberry, 1994; Siegelmann and Sontag, 1994). In general, it is believed that for any reasonable parallel machine the speed-up due to c will be by at most a polynomial amount and, hence, the Invariance thesis applies both to serial and parallel computation (Frixione, 2001; Parberry, 1994; Tsotsos, 1990). This means that if the Invariance thesis is true, then parallel machines cannot compute functions outside P in polynomial time nor compute parameterized functions outside FPT in fpt time.

9.7   The Non-Determinism Objection

Cognitive systems are not deterministic machines, and thus functions that are intractable for deterministic machines may still be tractable for cognitive systems. (Perspective B or C)

The complexity measures that we adopted in this book are defined with reference to computation by *deterministic* Turing machines. If indeed P $\neq$ NP, then we know that there exist functions that cannot be computed in polynomial time by any deterministic Turing machine, but that can be computed in polynomial time by a non-deterministic Turing machine. This shows that non-deterministic computations can be more powerful than deterministic computations, at least as far as polynomial-time computability is concerned. This observation could have been misinterpreted by some researchers as showing that probabilistic or randomized computation is more powerful than deterministic computation (see, e.g., Martignon and Hoffrage, 2002). This is an invalid inference, however, presumably based on an equivocation on the word *non-determinism*. Later we clarify the important difference between non-determinism as it is understood in computation theory and non-determinism as it applies to probabilistic models of cognition.

In computability theory, a non-deterministic Turing machine is one that can pursue an unbounded number of possible computation paths in parallel (see Appendix A). Such a non-deterministic machine M "computes" a function $F\colon I \to O$ if, for all i, at least one of the possible paths leads to an output corresponding to $F(i)$. In other words, M can be seen as a serial "oracle" that always knows ("magically") which guess to make at every fork in the road. This conceptualization makes clear why non-deterministic Turing machines are generally not considered reasonable models of resource-bounded computation. Consider a probabilistic interpretation of M, called M', which has exactly the same set of possible computation paths as M; but in contrast to M, machine M' can make random guesses about which computation paths to pursue. Such a probabilistic machine M' is said to compute a function $F\colon I \to O$ with high probability if for all i the probability that the output of M' corresponds to $F(i)$ is large (e.g., approaches 1). Now note that if M has an arbitrarily large number of possible computation paths, corresponding to an arbitrarily large number of possible outputs for M, then the probability that M' "guesses" the right output for any given input can be arbitrarily small. This means that the non-deterministic computation power of M is not automatically matched by the probabilistic computation power of M'.

This is not to say that probabilistic computational models of cognitive systems are impractical or useless. On the contrary, they may very well provide better models of certain cognitive systems than deterministic models. But one should not be fooled into thinking that probabilistic machines have the same abilities as non-deterministic machines. Even if it turns out that probabilistic machines have different abilities than deterministic machines, this does not obviate complexity analyses in cognitive psychology. Tractability is as much a requirement on probabilistic computation as it is on deterministic computation. Moreover, current theoretical investigations into the computational power of probabilistic computation are generating evidence that NP-hard input/output functions cannot be computed in polynomial time by probabilistic machines unless P = NP. This provides hope that formalizations of the Tractable Cognition thesis for deterministic cognitive computations can be generalized directly to a formalization of the thesis for probabilistic cognitive computations. To illustrate, consider, for instance, the class BPP, defined as the class of decision problems for which it is possible to guess the correct answer "yes" or "no" with a constantly bounded probability of error. In theoretical computer science it is conjectured that BPP − P. This means that if it were possible to solve NP-hard problems efficiently (in polynomial time) with a constantly bounded probability of error then this would imply BPP = NP. Given the P = BPP conjecture this would in turn contradict the P ≠ NP conjecture.

Practice 9.7.1   Assume that both the BPP $=$ P and the P $\neq$ NP conjecture are true. Prove that then no NP-hard problem can be computed in polynomial time by a constantly bounded-error probabilistic algorithm. (Hint: recall the definition of NP-hardness and prove by contradiction)

9.8   The Quantum Computing Objection

Cognitive systems may have quantum computing powers, and if they do then they can efficiently compute functions that are intractable for classical computing machines. (Perspective B)

This objection is in a sense a combination of the parallelism objection and the non-determinism objection, as a quantum computer is a (theoretical) machine that performs a probabilistic computation using a (potentially unbounded) number of parallel channels. For the formalisms underlying this non-classical model of computation, we refer the reader to Deutsch (1985), Fortnow (2003), and Arora and Barak (2009). The following informal characterization may suffice to support the reader's intuitions about the nature and computational powers of quantum computers: A quantum computer can be thought of as a non-deterministic Turing machine where each computation path exists in a different, parallel universe (or, mathematically equivalently, each path exists only in potentiality in this universe). To decide which of the potentially many paths is to be selected as the actual computation, a quantum computer can resort to a process called "quantum interference," which is a computational operation that can only expensively be simulated by a deterministic Turing machine by considering all possible computational paths explicitly (see Figure 9.1; for an explanation of the workings of quantum interference, see Arora and Barak [2009]).

Let us now analyze the quantum computing objection into its two component parts and assess their respective plausibility. First, how likely is it that cognitive systems have quantum computing powers? At present, there is no evidence that human brains can reliably utilize quantum effects for purposes of cognitive computation, and there is some evidence that they cannot (Grush and Churchland, 1995; Litt et al., 2006). For one, the physical conditions required for stable superimposed states and error-free quantum interference do not seem to be met by the physical milieus that exist in human brains (Litt et al., 2006). Also, as argued by both Litt et al. and Grush and Churchland, there are as of yet no examples of cognitive phenomena that are amenable to quantum computational modeling but not to classical computational modeling.

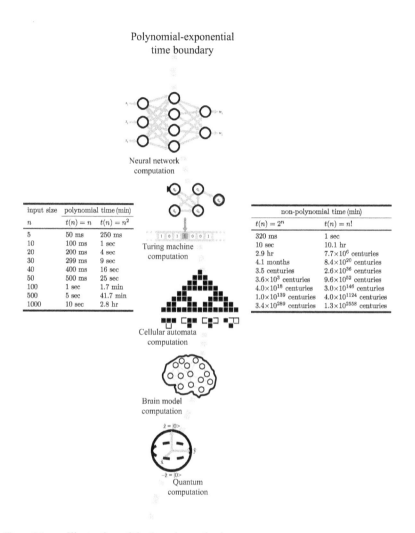

Polynomial-exponential
time boundary

Neural network
computation

input size	polynomial time (min)	
n	$t(n) = n$	$t(n) = n^2$
5	50 ms	250 ms
10	100 ms	1 sec
20	200 ms	4 sec
30	299 ms	9 sec
40	400 ms	16 sec
50	500 ms	25 sec
100	1 sec	1.7 min
500	5 sec	41.7 min
1000	10 sec	2.8 hr

Turing machine
computation

non-polynomial time (min)	
$t(n) = 2^n$	$t(n) = n!$
320 ms	1 sec
10 sec	10.1 hr
2.9 hr	7.7×10^6 centuries
4.1 months	8.4×10^{20} centuries
3.5 centuries	2.6×10^{36} centuries
3.6×10^3 centuries	9.6×10^{52} centuries
4.0×10^{18} centuries	3.0×10^{146} centuries
1.0×10^{139} centuries	4.0×10^{1124} centuries
3.4×10^{289} centuries	1.3×10^{2558} centuries

Cellular automata
computation

Brain model
computation

$\hat{z} = |0\rangle$

$\hat{y}$

$-\hat{z} = |0\rangle$

Quantum
computation

Figure 9.1 Illustration of the Invariance thesis.

For example, arguments made by Penrose (1994, 1997) that Gödel's first incompleteness theorem would imply that human mathematical understanding requires non-computable (and presumably quantum type) processes in the brain turn out to be fallacious (Grush and Churchland, 1995). Be that as it may, we cannot completely rule out the possibility of quantum computing powers in human brains. So, we may ask, if we grant Part 1 of the objection, to what extent is there substance to Part 2: That is, can quantum computers really compute intractable functions?

As the informal characterization given previously may make clear, a quantum computer can potentially draw upon an exponential number of computation channels while using, at most, a polynomial amount of space (in any given universe). In other words, quantum computation can lead to an super-polynomial speed-up, without being subject to the same criticism as classical parallel machines (see our response to the parallelism objection). This ability has been misread by some researchers as implying that quantum computers can compute NP-hard problems in polynomial time (Kak, 2000; Narayanan, 1999). This overlooks the computational limits of quantum interference. It is true that there can exist functions outside P that quantum computers may be able to compute in polynomial time. The so-called Integer Factorization problem (Shor, 1997) provides an example: No polynomial-time algorithm is known (nor believed) to exist for Integer Factorization, yet the problem is efficiently computable by a quantum computer. Contrary to claims made by Narayanan (1999), however, Integer Factorization is not (known to be) NP-hard. There are an infinite number of complexity classes in between P and NP (Garey and Johnson, 1979; of course, unless P = NP), and the Integer Factorization problem belongs to one such class, known as BQP, where it is known that $P \subset BQP$ and conjectured that $NP \not\subset BQP$ (informally, BQP is the class of polynomial-time quantum computations). There is no NP-hard problem known to be polynomial-time quantum computable, and assuming $NP \not\subset BQP$ no such NP-hard problem can exist. Moreover, there are few problems outside P known to be amenable to polynomial-time quantum computation. In sum, even if BQP were used as a formalization of the Tractable Cognition thesis (yielding a BQP-Cognition thesis), it would instantiate a much more restricted relaxation of the P-Cognition thesis than the FPT-Cognition thesis. After all, many NP-hard problems are known to be fixed-parameter tractable for one or more parameters.

Practice 9.8.1   There is a lot of information to unpack in that last paragraph. If you have trouble unpacking it, perform the following practices:

1. Assume that the conjecture $NP \not\subset BQP$ is true. Prove that then no NP-hard problem can be computable in polynomial time by a quantum computer. (Hint: Recall the definition of NP-hardness and prove by contradiction.)
2. Would more or fewer computational-level theories meet the tractability constraint if we were to adopt the BQP-Cognition thesis instead of the FPT-Cognition thesis? Explain your answer.

9.9   The Small-Inputs Objection

For some cognitive capacities, the size of the input is small in practice. In those cases, intractability is not an issue. (Perspective B)

Although the statement is true, it should not be considered an objection to the Tractable Cognition thesis. For example, the statement is perfectly in line with the FPT-Cognition thesis because all input/output functions are in FPT when parameterized by their input size. Thus, if the input size is small then, on the FPT-Cognition thesis, the problem is classified as tractable. It should be noted that also no one who subscribes to the P-Cognition thesis would claim that tractability is an issue if input size is small. The problem is, of course, that for many cognitive capacities the size of the input as a whole is not small (see, e.g., Thagard and Verbeurgt, 1998, p. 8: "Each person has thousands or millions of beliefs"). It is then that the P-Cognition thesis and the FPT-Cognition thesis diverge. To illustrate, recall this quote from Gigerenzer and colleagues in Chapter 1:

> The computations postulated by a model of cognition need to be tractable in the real world in which people live, not only in the small world of an experiment with only a few cues. This eliminates NP-hard models that lead to computational explosion (...). (Gigerenzer, Hoffrage, and Goldstein, 2008, p. 236)

This quote expresses the important point that even though inputs may seem small when considering toy domains in lab settings, they cannot be assumed small in the real world.[2]

Practice 9.9.1   To further develop your own intuitions about this objection and the response, perform the following two practices.

- Consider a cognitive capacity (e.g., from the domain of decision making, belief revision, problem solving, language processing) and think about *all* aspects that need to be part of the input for a computational-level theory of that capacity. Which of those aspects is small (say, size 10 or smaller), which intermediate (say, between 10 and 100), and which large (say, on the order of hundreds or thousands, or more). Consider both a typical lab

---

[2] A common concern about lab experiments is that they need to ensure ecological validity. An experiment is considered ecologically invalid, for instance, if the conditions in the lab fail to tap into the cognitive processes as they naturally occur in the real world. Note that the concern that intractable theories do not scale beyond the lab is an orthogonal concern. That is, even if one's lab experiment is ecologically valid, and a model derived from an intractable theory fits the data obtained in that experiment, the problem that an intractable computational-level theory cannot scale to account for real-world cognition remains.

setting in which a cognitive scientist may study the chosen capacity and situations of real-world richness and complexity.

- In answering the previous question you may have unintentionally limited the size of input parameters because you (implicitly) presupposed that only "relevant" aspects of the input needed to be considered. But now think about how a cognizer can know what is "relevant" a priori. It seems that knowing what is relevant and what not is itself a to-be-explained cognitive capacity. What would that capacity look like at the computational level, and do you think it would itself be tractable?

9.10   The Nothing-New Objection

The requirement that a computational-level theory be in FPT *for some 'small' input parameters is not essentially different from the requirement that the theory is in* P *for a restricted input domain.* (Perspective A)

The objection reflects a misunderstanding about the relationship between P and FPT.

> ——————— **Stop and Think** ———————
>
> What could the nature of the misunderstanding be?

Parameterization is not the same as input restriction: It just determines how we analyze and express the complexity of an input/output function. Recall that parameterized complexity theory expresses a computation's time complexity as a function of both input size $|i|$ and a specified parameter k. If a computational-level theory F, with input parameter k, can be computed by an algorithm that runs in time $O(f(k)n^c)$, with $n = |i|$ and constant c, then the parameterized function k-F is said to belong to the class FPT. It is important to realize that in this analysis the value of k is not fixed to be constant – it remains a variable just like $|i|$ (In that sense, the expression "fixed-parameter tractability" may be a misnomer.) It is true that if we were to fix k to be constant, then $O(f(k)n^c)$ would be $O(n^c)$ and thus polynomial time, but the same is true for $O(n^k)$, which is *not* fixed-parameter tractable time (even though it is polynomial time if k is a constant). This means that the requirement that a computational-level theory be in FPT for some small parameter k is more stringent than the requirement that a computational-level theory is in P for constant k. At the same time, the requirement that the computational-level theory be in FPT for some small parameter k is more lenient than the requirement that the computational-level theory be in P. The FPT-Cognition thesis is thus really a new and importantly different formalization of the Tractable Cognition thesis.

9.11   The Too-Liberal Objection

Polynomial-time computability is already a too liberal constraint on computational-level theories. Thus, the FPT-Cognition thesis only makes matters worse. (Perspective A)

Some researchers subscribe to the idea that most, if not all, (higher order) cognitive functions are of extremely low complexity (e.g., Gigerenzer and Goldstein, 1996; Gigerenzer, Todd, and ABC Research Group, 2000; Martignon and Hoffrage, 2002; Martignon and Schmitt, 1999; Todd and Gigerenzer, 2000). For example, cognitive computations "requiring more than a quadratically growing number of computation steps already appear to be excessively complicated" to Martignon and Schmitt (p. 566). To such researchers, the proposal that cognitive systems perform non-polynomial fpt-time computations may seem outrageous: If the P-Cognition thesis is already too liberal, then its relaxation in the form of the FPT-Cognition thesis may seem to only make matters worse. Two responses to this too-liberal objection can be made. First, for purposes of constraining the space of feasible cognitive theories, it is better to use a (slightly) more liberal criterion for formalization than a too strict formalization because the latter will risk excluding veridical theories from consideration. It is for this reason that one may propose to replace the P-Cognition thesis by the relaxation in the form of the FPT-Cognition thesis. Second, it is not true that fpt computation is necessarily of higher complexity than a polynomial-time computation – it all depends on the size of the parameters and the function describing the algorithm's running time. Figure 9.2 illustrates, for example, how an algorithm that runs in non-polynomial fpt time can be much faster than an algorithm that runs in polynomial time, provided only that the parameter k is small.

9.12   The Turing-Machine Objection

The brain is not a Turing machine. Hence, Turing machine-based complexity analyses do not apply to the cognitive capacities of the human brain. (Perspective B)

The objection reflects a misunderstanding about the relationship between brains, computational-level theories and Turing machines.

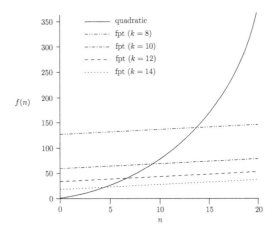

Figure 9.2   The figure compares quadratic polynomial time $O(n^2)$ with fixed-parameter tractable (fpt) time $O(\sqrt{2}^k + n)$ for parameter $k = 8, 10, 12, 14$. Note: Increasing the value of k causes the curve for fpt-time to translate upwards. Adapted from van Rooij (2008)

Stop and Think ───

What could the nature of the misunderstanding be?

In this book we have adopted the Church-Turing thesis. This thesis states that all functions (or problems) that can be computed, in principle, are computable by a Turing machine. This means that the set of computable functions is the same as the set of Turing computable functions (see Figure 1.4 in Chapter 1). We furthermore adopted a computationalist perspective on cognition: i.e., we take cognitive capacities to be computational capacities (if one rejects computationalism, then refer to the cognition-is-not-computation objection). This does not mean that we adopt the view that the brain is a Turing machine. On the contrary, we think brains are *not* Turing machines. For one, brains are physical entities, whereas Turing machines are mathematical entities. Hence, the two cannot be the same in any ontological sense. That as an aside, we also think that Turing machines are unlikely to be useful as mathematical descriptions of a brain's computational processes.

   Our concern in this book is with computational-level theories and their, in principle, computability and tractability. In computational-level analyses we abstract away from algorithmic- and implementational-level assumptions, other than that such explanations must be ultimately possible (see Section 1.2 in Chapter 1). From this it follows that cognitive capacities – i.e., functions

F: $I \rightarrow O$ that transform inputs $i \in I$ to outputs $F(i) \in O$ – must be computable and tractable. At present all formalizations of computation – including any candidates of models of brain computation, such as spiking neural networks – have computational power directly equivalent to Turing machines (i.e., they are so-called Turing-equivalent). Hence, the set of cognitive capacities computable by brains is equal to the set of functions computable by a Turing machine (unless the Church-Turing thesis is false; see Practice 9.12.1 later). As for tractability, here the Invariance thesis plays a crucial role (see also the non-determinism objection).

The Invariance thesis states that, given a "reasonable encoding" of the input and two "reasonable machines" M_1 and M_2, the complexity of a given computation F for M_1 and M_2 will differ by at most a polynomial amount (see, e.g., Frixione, 2001; Garey and Johnson, 1979) – that is, if M_1 is computable in time $O(t(|i|))$, then M_2 is computable in time $O(t(|i|)^c)$ where c is a constant. Here, with "reasonable encoding" is meant an encoding that does not contain irrelevant information and in which numbers are represented in b-ary with $b > 1$ (e.g., binary, or decimal, or any fixed base other than 1). Further, with "reasonable machine" is meant any type of Turing machine (with possible extensions as described in Appendix A) or any other realistic computing machine under a different formalization (including, e.g., neural networks, cellular automata). Note, however, that a machine capable of performing arbitrarily many computations in parallel (cf. non-deterministic Turing machine or quantum computer) is not considered a "reasonable" machine (Arora and Barak, 2009; Garey and Johnson, 1979).

Like the Church-Turing thesis, the Invariance thesis is widely accepted among computer scientists and cognitive scientists. The Invariance thesis, if true, implies that we can analyze the worst-case complexity of problems, independent of the machine model, up to a polynomial amount of precision. In other words, if a problem is of polynomial-time complexity under one model it will be of polynomial-time complexity (or fp-tractable) under any other reasonable model. Similarly, if a problem is of non-polynomial time complexity (or fp-intractable) under one model it will be of non-polynomial complexity (or fp-intractable) under any other reasonable model.[3]

---

[3] Frixione (2001) used the term *Invariance thesis* to express both the Invariance thesis itself and what we call the Tractable Cognition thesis. Because we distinguish two alternative formalizations of tractability in this book (viz., classical and fixed-parameter tractability), whereas Frixione (2001) only considered one option (classical tractability), while it is assumed that the Invariance thesis applies to both, we purposely divorce the Invariance thesis from the Tractable Cognition thesis.

Practice 9.12.1 The response to the Turing-machine objection assumes that both the Church-Turing thesis and the Invariance thesis are true. To develop an intuition about how likely they are to be true, perform the following two practices.

- Why do most computer scientists believe that the Church-Turing thesis is true? What would it take to show it is false?
- Why is the Invariance thesis a reasonable working assumption given what we currently know? What would be the ramifications if the Invariance thesis would turn out to be false? (Hint: See Chapter 4.)

9.13 The Approximation Objection

The brain does not use exact algorithms but approximation algorithms. Brains can tractably approximate functions that are intractable to compute exactly. (Perspective B)

Like the heuristic objection, this objection was also touched upon in the previous chapter (Chapter 8). We reiterate the main observations made there and add broader context.

The objection seems to assume that NP-hard computations are only intractable to compute exactly, but can otherwise be approximated tractably. Whether or not this is the case is dependent, however, on what is meant exactly by "approximated" as well as the nature of the NP-hard problem under study. Substantiating the objection, then, entails explicating the precise notion of approximation that is intended and proving that the NP-hard computation under consideration can be tractably so approximated. One should be warned, though, that many NP-hard problems cannot be tractably approximated for several different definitions of "approximation," especially if the degree of approximation is to be reasonably high (a condition which seems desirable in the context of scientific explanation).

To illustrate, let us first consider a very loose sense of approximation.

Practice 9.13.1 Consider the NP-hard problem COHERENCE.

> COHERENCE
> **Input:** A network $N = (P, C)$, where $C = C^+ \cup C^-$ is a set of positive and negative constraints and $C^+ \cap C^- = \emptyset$.
> **Output:** A truth assignment $T: P \rightarrow \{true, false\}$ that satisfies a maximum number of constraints in C. (Here a positive constraint $(p, q) \in C^+$ is satisfied iff $T(p) = T(q)$, and a negative constraint $(p, q) \in C^-$ is satisfied iff $T(p) \neq T(q)$.

Prove that there exists an approximation algorithm that, for any instance of COHERENCE, outputs a truth assignment that differs in at most $0.5 \times |P|$ truth values from the optimal truth assignment (Here $|P|$ is the number of propositions that are to be assigned a value). (Hint: Start by considering an algorithm that would randomly assign truth values to propositions in P.)

You are unlikely to be convinced that the approximation algorithm that you came up with in Practice 9.13.1 is a suitable algorithmic-level theory. After all, it makes the wrong prediction for about half the propositions in P. Given that COHERENCE is hypothesized to operate on a scale of thousands of more beliefs (see Thagard and Verbeurgt, 1998, p. 8), an algorithmic-level theory that predicts about half of all beliefs incorrectly is probably not considered a very good algorithmic-level theory.

Things would look better, if you would be able to come up with an algorithm that makes a very small number of errors. If you could guarantee that this number of error remains very small regardless of the size of the input, then one would have a strong case that the outputs produced by the approximation algorithm are for practical intents and purposes indistinguishable from the computational-level function. Yet, as we saw in Chapter 8 (Practice 8.2.1), no such approximation algorithm exists for COHERENCE (unless $P = NP$).

This is just an illustration. The point is not specific to COHERENCE. In fact, inapproximability results for computational-level theories abound in cognitive science. For instance, most probabilistic (Bayesian) models of cognition are as hard to approximate as they are to compute exactly (Kwisthout et al., 2011b). Computing probability distributions exactly is NP-hard (Cooper, 1990) and it is no less hard to approximate these distributions (Dagum and Luby, 1993). Likewise, inferring explanations that have maximum posterior probability given the evidence is NP-hard (Shimony, 1994) and it is as hard to compute an explanation that approximates the maximum posterior probability or whose inner structure either resembles the optimal solution or is just guaranteed to have a non-zero probability (Abdelbar and Hedetniemi, 1998; Kwisthout, 2011a; Kwisthout and van Rooij, 2013).

Neural network models face inapproximability as well (Judd, 1990; Yao, 1992). For instance, Judd (1990) showed the following problem to be NP-complete: "Given a neural network and a set of training examples, does there exist a set of edge weights for the network so that the network produces the correct output for all the training examples?" But he also showed that "the problem remains NP-complete even if it is only required a network produce the correct output for two-thirds of the training examples, which implies that even approximately training a neural network is intrinsically difficult in the worst case." (Blum and Rivest, 1992, p. 495).

The idea that approximation is tractable can also be shown to be false, more generally. For example, most NP-hard functions cannot be tractably value-approximable unless P = NP (Arora, 1998), efficient expectation-approximation of any NP-hard function is impossible unless BPP $\neq$ P (Kwisthout and van Rooij, 2013; see also the non-determinism objection), and the efficient value- or structure-approximation of an NP-hard function is ruled out if that function is self-paddable (van Rooij and Wareham, 2012) – a property apparently holding for most problems in NP.[4]

In sum, it is very well possible that the brain computes by various approximation algorithms. But this means that the computational-level theories that we postulate should be tractably approximable. At present few computational-level theories that are intractable are tractably approximable. It seems thus that the tractability constraint applies even if one posits approximation algorithms for computational-level theories. By definition, tractable functions are tractably approximable. Hence, adopting the Tractable Cognition thesis will ensure the existence of tractable approximation algorithms for computational-level theories.

9.14   The As-If Objection

It does not matter if computational-level theories postulate intractable functions, because the claim is not that cognizers compute those functions. The claim is merely that they act "as if" they do. (Perspective B)

This objection is traditionally inspired by economic theories of human decision making and rationality. It may be best illustrated by a few quotes:

> (...) if we adopt the view that we have been advocating, that rational explanation should be understood in terms of 'rational description' rather than 'rational calculation,' then these concerns about computational complexity disappear. (Chater et al., 2003, p. 70)

> An analogy may be useful: The wings of a bird may approximate the results of a rational calculation of optimal aerodynamic design. Moreover, this observation helps explain why the wing has the structure that it does; but there is, of course, no presumption that the bird conducts any calculations in designing its wing. (Chater et al., 2003, p. 67)

---

[4] A function F is self-paddable if and only if a set of instances $i_1, i_2, ..., i_m$ of F can be embedded in a single instance i_E of F such that $F(i_1), F(i_2), ..., F(i_m)$ can be derived from $F(i_E)$. For instance, Coherence and many other problems in NP are self-paddable. For more details, see definition 6 in van Rooij and Wareham (2012).

There is, moreover, a recognition in economics that applying rational theories, such as probability theory, expected utility theory, and game theory will only provide an approximation model of people's behavior. Economists allow that (...) faced with complexity, individuals resort to rules of thumb, to 'back of the envelope' calculations, to satisficing behavior. (...) Economists thus recognize that behavior only approximates to rationality (...) For our purposes, the important point is that most economists interpret their theories as about rational description, but not rational calculation (at best, people act 'as if' they made rational calculations; but they do not actually perform such calculations). (Chater et al., 2003, p. 67)

In sum, the view seems to be that the computational-level theory is a merely descriptive tool without any commitment to how the functions that it postulates are realized by people. When confronted with the intractability of the functions, the claim seems to be that the functions need not be tractably computable for people for the theories to be descriptive of people's behavior, because people do not need to compute ("calculate") the functions, but only behave "as if" they do.

As with many of the other objections, the force of the objection comes down to semantics: what is meant exactly by "as if"? Van Rooij et al.(2018) analyzed the relevant literature (the previous as well as other quotes), and distilled five candidate meanings:

(1) Noncomputationalism
(2) Implicit or subsymbolic computation
(3) Heuristic computation
(4) Approximate computation
(5) Offline computation

Of these, (1) and (2) have been covered under the heading of the noncomputationalism objection, and (3) and (4) have been covered under the headings of the heuristic and approximation objection, respectively. For those possible meanings of "as if" refer to the responses to those objections. This leaves still the "offline computation" as a candidate interpretation of "as if" to respond to. This particular interpretation of "as if" may be illustrated by the following quote:

Economists do not assume that people make complex game-theoretic or macro-economic calculations; zoologists do not assume that animals calculate how to forage optimally; and, in psychology, rational analyses of, for example, memory, do not assume that the cognitive system calculates the optimal forgetting function with respect to the costs of retrieval and storage. Such behavior may be built in by evolution or be acquired via a long process of learning, but it need not require on-line computation of the optimal solution. (Chater and Oaksford, 2000, p. 110)

Stop and Think

What could be meant by 'not require online computation'?

It is unclear what proponents of the 'as if' objection envision is computed offline, and how such offline computation would yield tractability. For instance, one possibility is that the nature of F is determined offline, e.g., by evolutionary processes. This interpretation would be consistent with the claim that intractable optimal functions explain why birds' wings have the structure that they do without there being any presumption that birds conduct any calculations in *designing* their wings. (Here, wing design by evolution is presumably analogous with the design of some cognitive capacity ϕ by evolution, where ϕ is characterized by F.) Yet, the problem of intractability as we consider in this book is not about the design of $F: I \rightarrow O$, but about the resource requirements of an algorithm that can compute $F(i)$ for all $i \in I$.

A second interpretation then could be that what is assumed to be pre-computed offline (by evolution) is the $F(i)$ for each and every $i \in I$, such that agents would need to only recall (or trigger by some direct, non-inferential process) $F(i)$ whenever receiving input i (as in reading off a list of pre-computed answers per i). But that would be clearly unrealistic for most human cognitive capacities. Even for a clearly evolved capacity such as vision this would not work as we can perceive and interpret many visual objects and scenes that our ancestors never could have encountered. Hence, those perceptions cannot have been precomputed by evolution. By analogy, action selection cannot operate by such pre-computed functions either, since we can flexibly adapt our actions and choices to novel situations and environments.

Note that even if pre-computation by evolution were possible, the lists of direct (non-inferential) input-output mappings would need to be infinite to account for the productivity of human cognition. If this would yield tractable computation with respect to the resource "time," we would need an unrealistic amount of space to store such an infinite list in memory (unless one would compress the list somehow, but then inferential processes would be needed again to decode it to know what output corresponds to a given i). All in all, offline computation does not seem to produce a plausible story about how intractable functions may be realized by resource-bounded agents. Possibly one of the other interpretations (1)–(4) of "as if" has more merit, but as said, also those fail to disprove the Tractable Cognition thesis as per our responses to the earlier objections.

Stop and Think

Is there perhaps an interpretation of "as if" that may have been overlooked?

We close by noting that van Rooij et al. (2018) did propose a possible meaning of "as if" that can work (albeit never pursued by proponents of the "as if" objection so far). They explain the idea intuitively, by reconsidering the bird analogy of Marr (1981) and Chater and Oaksford (2000).

> Flight may be intractable for birds if the conditions under which they were expected to fly would be outside the normal ranges in which they can effectively fly (e.g., in a storm with exceptional speeds of wind that move in arbitrarily complex ways). Under such exceptional conditions birds would fail to fly successfully; their mechanism for flight cannot effectively deal with such extreme circumstances. Nevertheless, under normal conditions – in which air and body parameters remain within normal ranges – birds can effectively fly. Their ability to effectively fly under normal circumstances, despite the intractability of flight under arbitrary circumstances, is thus not only to be understood in terms of the internal mechanisms that support flight, but also in terms of the parameters that define 'normal' circumstances.

Note that this perspective is consistent with the notion of fixed-parameter tractability and yields a notion of "as if" that is unproblematic. That is, having discovered a pair consisting of intractable function F and tractable restricted-domain function F', one may contend that it is "as if" cognitive agents compute F in the sense that they compute F' and in the normal range of inputs the functions F' and F are indistinguishable.[5] The identification of parameter ranges that are "normal" and yield tractability is exactly what is prescribed by the FPT-Cognition thesis and the tractability cycle that we described in Chapter 8. Hence, this reading of "as if" resonates with, rather than opposes, the Tractable Cognition thesis.

---

[5] Importantly though, this indistinguishability is mere appearance, for if one were to present the cognitive agents with inputs outside the normal range then the behavior of the cognitive agents would no longer be guaranteed to look anything like F. Indeed, such behavior would necessarily differ from F on infinitely many inputs outside the normal range (otherwise F would not be intractable).

9.15   Exercises

As a reviewer once pointed out: one never knows when one has covered all possible objections. We realize that the list may be endless, especially if new objections can be variants or rewordings of the ones considered in this chapter. We nevertheless hope that the objections and responses considered so far provide a solid basis for evaluating novel objections one may encounter. To further test and train ones conceptual abilities, perform the following exercises:

Exercise 9.15.1   Consider the following objection to the Tractable Cognition thesis:

> Human brains compute in parallel and subsymbolic ways comparable to biologically inspired neural networks. Hence, tractability of human cognition is guaranteed.

Write a response to this objection based on what you learned in this chapter.

Exercise 9.15.2   Herbert Simon (1955) proposed that human decision makers do not optimize, but instead satisfice: That is, humans search alternatives and accept the first option that is satisfactory (regardless of whether or not it has optimal (expected) utility). The notion remains influential today in the work of Gigerenzer et al., 2008). From this perspective one may formulate an objection as follows:

> Human beings do not optimize but satisfice. Whereas intractability is an issue for optimizers, it isn't for satisficers.

Present an argument against this objection based on what you have learned about the formal relationship between decision problems, search problems and optimization problems in Chapters 2 and 3. Consider both the claim that optimization is intractable and that satisficing is tractable.

Exercise 9.15.3   From the perspective of two influential theories in cognitive science, known as the Adaptive Toolbox theory (Gigerenzer and Todd, 1999; Todd and Gigerenzer, 2012) and Massive Modularity theory (Carruthers, 2005; Cosmides and Tooby, 1994; Sperber and Wilson, 2002), the following objection to the Tractable Cognition thesis may be formulated:

> The human brain is an evolved system that solves complex problems by a divide and conquer strategy: it has specialized processes for solving parts of the complex problem, effective partitioning a complex problem into simple subproblems. This way the brain overcomes the problem of intractability.

Present an argument for why this proposed method of divide and conquer cannot work for intractable computational problems (see also van Rooij et al., 2012, p. 481, and Haselager, van Dijk, and van Rooij, 2008, p. 280).

Exercise 9.15.4 Can you think of an objection for which you believe no straightforward rebuttal exists? If so, try to formulate it as precisely as possible, and invite someone to debate you on this objection.[6]

9.16 Further Reading

For some of the objections in this chapter we could only scratch the surface. In particular, we refer the interested reader to the following sources for more in-depth treatments of the following objections:

- The heuristic objection (van Rooij et al., 2012)
- The approximation objection (Kwisthout et al., 2011b; van Rooij and Wareham, 2012)
- The as-if objection (van Rooij et al., 2018)

The regularity with which we encounter the Turing-machine objection may reflect strong intuitions among cognitive scientists about the nature of human brain computation. Neural network (both spiking or not) and probabilistic (sampling) algorithms seem to be among the most popular candidate algorithmic level explanations in contemporary cognitive science. There is a rich field of computational complexity analysis of neural networks, including deep learning as is currently very popular in Artificial Intelligence. See for example the reviews by Orponen (1994) and Šíma and Orponen (2003), and the classical complexity results by Judd (1990), Bruck and Goodman (1990), and Blum and Rivest (1993). No notable parameterized complexity results are known for neural networks. We believe that (deep) neural network models will provide fertile ground for parameterized complexity analysis in the future. For state of the art of parameterized complexity of probabilistic computations, see the work by Kwisthout (2018) and Montoya and Müller (2013). This latter line of complexity theoretic work is currently also being extended to the analysis of predictive processing theory, an influential theory of cognitive brain functioning in cognitive neuroscience.

---

[6] If you think you have identified an important new objection that needs addressing, also feel free to write us!

Part IV

Applications

10 Coherence as Constraint Satisfaction

In this chapter, we consider a computational-level theory of coherence as constraint satisfaction. We illustrate the use of classical and parameterized complexity analysis to assess the theory's (in)tractability and identify some of its sources of intractability.

10.1 Introduction

In 1998, computational philosopher Paul Thagard, in collaboration with computer scientist Karsten Verbeurgt, proposed a computational-level characterization of coherence as a type of constraint satisfaction problem. Prior to 1998 the theory existed as a class of algorithmic-level explanations (e.g., the algorithm called ECHO) and as an intuitive computational-level theory (i.e., that function that is computed by algorithms like ECHO). Coherence as constraint satisfaction is intended as a theory of all kinds of cognitive cognitive capacities, all of which include processes that seem to maximize coherence. These capacities include, for instance, perception, reasoning, belief, judgment, proof, explanation, analogy, etc. (see Table 1 in Thagard and Verbeurgt [1998]). An overview of applications of the theory can also be found in Thagard's 2000 book entitled *Coherence in Thought and Action*.

Thagard and several other researchers have developed a generalization of his algorithmic-level connectionist theory of coherence to include the role of emotional processes. This has resulted in an algorithm-level model called HOTCO. In his 2006 book entitled *Hot Thought: Mechanisms and Applications of Emotional Coherence*, Thagard reviews a host of applications of his HOTCO model, including jury decision-making, religious judgment, and the motivational and reasoning processes of scientists. Thagard himself has not yet proposed a computational-level theory associated with the HOTCO model.

Analyzing the function computed by HOTCO, van Rooij (2007) did propose a formalization of emotional coherence at the computational level, and proved it to be equivalent to COHERENCE.

10.2   Formalizing the Theory

What is coherence? The problem can be intuitively expressed as follows:

> Given a large number of elements (propositions, concepts, or whatever) that are coherent or incoherent with each other in various ways, how can we accept some of these elements and reject others in a way that maximizes coherence? (Thagard and Verbeurgt, 1998, p. 1)

In this chapter, we will use the application of the theory to belief fixation as a running example. In belief fixation, one is given a set of propositions. For each proposition you can either believe it to be true or false. Further, there are coherence and incoherence relations between propositions. Some propositions cohere or "fit together" (e.g., the belief "it snows" and the belief "it is freezing" cohere), whereas others may incohere or "resist fitting together" (e.g., the belief "Bob had the murder weapon in his closet" and the belief "Bob is innocent" incohere). The theory of Coherence assumes that when we settle on what we believe, we (our brains) compute what is most coherent to believe against the background of all such coherence and incoherence relations in our minds.

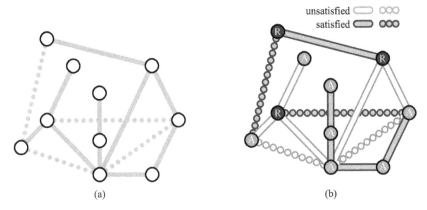

(a)   (b)

Figure 10.1   An illustration of a COHERENCE instance. (a) the instance itself, and (b) the instance with a possible truth assignment. Note that some constraints are satisfied by this assignment and others are not.

How to formalize the intuitive idea of coherence? Thagard and Verbeugt proposed that we can think of the set of propositions (P) as nodes in a network N (see Figure 10.1 for an illustration). Both the coherence and incoherence relations are connections in the network, and are conceived of as constraints (C). Hence, the network can be denoted using graph notation: $N = (P, C)$. Yet, it is important to distinguish between the two distinct types of constraints:

- **Coherence** relations are modeled by so-called *positive* constraints C^+. These are constraints that are satisfied if the propositions that they connect both are assigned the value *true* or both are assigned the value *false* (in other words, a constraint $(p, q) \in C^+$ is satisfied if and only if $T(p) = T(q)$). This definition aims to capture the intuition that if two propositions cohere then it is most coherent to either believe them both to be true, or believe them both to be false.
- **Incoherence** relations are modeled by so-called *negative* constraints C^+. These are constraints that are satisfied if one of the two propositions that they connect is assigned the value *true* and the other is assigned the value *false* (in other words, a constraint $(p, q) \in C^+$ is satisfied if and only if $T(p) \neq T(q)$). This definition aims to capture the intuition that if two propositions incohere then it is most coherent to believe one of them true and the other false.

Next you will find a formalization of Coherence based on these ideas.

COHERENCE

Input: A network $N = (P, C)$, where $C = C^+ \cup C^-$ is a set of positive and negative constraints and $C^+ \cap C^- = \emptyset$. (Note: The Coherence theory assumes that any two propositions can only cohere or incohere. Therefore the possibility is excluded that two propositions could be connected by both a positive and negative constraint.)

Output: A truth assignment $T: P \rightarrow \{true, false\}$ that satisfies a maximum number of constraints in C. (Here a positive constraint $(p, q) \in C^+$ is satisfied if and only if $T(p) = T(q)$, and a negative constraint $(p, q) \in C^-$ is satisfied if and only if $T(p) \neq T(q)$.)

We have also encountered this formalization in several practices and exercises in the book. In the paper by Thagard and Verbeurgt (1998) the theory actually took a more generalized form, where coherence and incoherence relations could be differentially weighted (expressing the intuition that propositions can cohere and incohere to different degrees):

WEIGHTED COHERENCE

Input: A belief network $N = (P,C)$ where P denotes a set of propositions, and $C = C^- \cup C^+ \subseteq P \times P$ denotes a set of positive and negative constraints, with $C^+ \cap C^- = \emptyset$. Each constraint $(p,q) \in C$ has a weight $w(p,q) \geq 0$.

Output: A truth assignment $T: P \to \{true, false\}$, such that $COH(T) = \sum_{(p,q)\in C^+, T(p)=T(q)} w(p,q) + \sum_{(p,q)\in C^-, T(p)\neq T(q)} w(p,q)$ is maximized.

Further careful reading of the work of Thagard and Verbeurgt (1998) reveals that not all of their intuitions are captured by the WEIGHTED COHERENCE formalization yet. Consider, for example, the following quote, in which the authors distinguish three versions of the coherence problem (p. 16):

> A *pure* coherence problem is one that does not favor the acceptance of any particular set of elements. A *foundational* coherence problem selects a set of favored elements for acceptance as self-justified. A *discriminating* coherence problem favors a set of elements but their acceptance still depends on their coherence with all the other elements.

The introduction of elements (in our case, propositions) that are self-justified derives from the idea that propositions that describe observations have an acceptability of their own prior to coherence or incoherence with other beliefs. Thagard (2000) referred to this as the *data priority principle*. The quote illustrates that this principle can be formalized in two ways: In foundational coherence, observations are taken to be undoubtable "facts" (e.g., if you see it snowing then you believe it is snowing), whereas in discriminating coherence observations will tend to believed unless, in the context of one's total web of beliefs, it is most coherent to disbelieve them (e.g., imagine it is summer, you feel it is warm, and you are on a movie set. If you then see it snowing (observation), you may not believe it is really snowing, but rather believe that the white fluffy stuff you see falling from the sky is "fake snow" made by a machine behind the scenes).

These intuitions are captured in the following two problem variants:

FOUNDATIONAL COHERENCE

Input: A set of observations (or data) D, a set of hypotheses H and a set of constraints $C = C^- \cup C^+ \subseteq (D \cup H) \times (D \cup H)$, with $C^- \cap C^+ = \emptyset$. Each $(p,q) \in C$ has a weight $w(p,q) > 0$.

Output: A truth assignment $T: H \cup D \to \{true, false\}$, with $T(d) = true$ for all $d \in D$, such that $COH(T) = \sum_{(p,q)\in C^+, T(p)=T(q)} w(p,q) + \sum_{(p,q)\in C^-, T(p)\neq T(q)} w(p,q)$ is maximized.

DISCRIMINATING COHERENCE

Input: A set of observations (or data) D, a set of hypotheses H and a set of constraints $C = C^- \cup C^+ \subseteq (D \cup H) \times (D \cup H)$, with $C^- \cap C^+ = \emptyset$. Each $d \in D$ has a weight $w_D(d) \geq 0$ and each $(p,q) \in C$ has a weight $w(p,q) > 0$.

Output: A truth assignment $T: H \cup D \to \{true, false\}$ such that
$$COH(T) = \sum_{(p,q) \in C^+, T(p)=T(q)} w(p,q) + \sum_{(p,q) \in C^-, T(p) \neq T(q)} w(p,q) + \sum_{d \in D, T(d)=true} w_D(d) \text{ is maximized.}$$

10.3 Complexity Analyses

10.3.1 Classical Complexity Results

In Exercise 3.4.1 and Practice 8.1.4, you have proven that there exists a polynomial-time reduction from MAX CUT to COHERENCE. Given that MAX CUT is known to be NP-hard, this proves that COHERENCE is NP-hard as well. Now perform the following Practice 10.3.1.

Practice 10.3.1 Prove that WEIGHTED COHERENCE $\notin$ P (unless P = NP). Important: Don't forget to rewrite the search variant of the problem into a decision version of the problem, before performing the polynomial-time reduction.

Does the fact that WEIGHTED COHERENCE is NP-hard automatically imply that (decision versions of) DISCRIMINATING COHERENCE and FOUNDATIONAL COHERENCE are NP-hard as well? Yes! Each of these problems subsumes WEIGHTED COHERENCE as a special case. Namely, WEIGHTED COHERENCE is equivalent to DISCRIMINATING COHERENCE and FOUNDATIONAL COHERENCE on inputs with $D = \emptyset$. In other words, DISCRIMINATING COHERENCE and FOUNDATIONAL COHERENCE are generalizations of WEIGHTED COHERENCE. The latter is in turn a generalization of COHERENCE (if all weights are set to "1" the problem is identical to COHERENCE). Hence, COHERENCE reduces to all these more general problems, and thus DISCRIMINATING COHERENCE and FOUNDATIONAL COHERENCE are also NP-hard.

So far, we have established that COHERENCE and its generalizations are all NP-hard. Does this mean that all coherence problems are intractable? Surely not. This difference between "a general problem being NP-hard" and "a problem being generally NP-hard" is sometimes confused (see also Chapter 8). Consider, for example, the following synopsis by (Thagard, 2000, p. 15):

Coherence problems are inherently computational intractable, in the sense that, (...) [assuming $P \neq NP$], there are no efficient (polynomial-time) procedures for solving them.

Here, the words "coherence problems" seem to refer to a general class of coherence problems. Hence, the statement suggests that coherence problems are of non-polynomial time complexity *across the board*. However, this conclusion is not warranted: NP-hardness is not automatically inherited by every special case, or variant, of an NP-hard problem. For instance, there can be special cases of COHERENCE that are polynomial-time computable.

To illustrate, consider the network depicted in Figure 10.2. Note that this network has the special property that all its constraints can be satisfied simultaneously. In general, let us call a network $N = (P, C)$ *consistent* if it is possible to satisfy all constraints in N; in other words, N is consistent if there exists a truth assignment T such that $COH(T) = \sum_{(p,q) \in C} w(p,q)$.

COHERENCE ON CONSISTENT NETWORKS
Input: A *consistent* belief network $N = (P, C)$ where P denotes a set of propositions, and $C = C^- \cup C^+ \subseteq P \times P$ denotes a set of positive and negative constraints, with $C^+ \cap C^- = \emptyset$. Each constraint $(p,q) \in C$ has a weight $w(p,q) \geq 0$.
Output: A truth assignment $T: P \rightarrow \{true, false\}$, such that $COH(T) = \sum_{(p,q) \in C^+, T(p) = T(q)} w(p,q) + \sum_{(p,q) \in C^-, T(p) \neq T(q)} w(p,q)$ is maximized.

To see that the previous optimization problem is polynomial-time solvable, consider the following decision problem and note that it is in P.

CONSISTENT COHERENCE
Input: A network $N = (P, C)$, where $C = C^+ \cup C^-$ is a set of positive and negative constraints and $C^+ \cap C^- = \emptyset$.
Question: Does there exist a truth assignment $T: P \rightarrow \{true, false\}$ that satisfies all constraints in C? (Here a constraint $(p,q) \in C^+$ is *satisfied* if $T(p) = T(q)$ and a constraint $(p,q) \in C^-$ is *satisfied* if $T(p) \neq T(q)$.)

Stop and Think

Can you think of an algorithm that proves that CONSISTENT COHER-ENCE is in P? Does the same algorithm solve the search problem COHERENCE ON CONSISTENT NETWORKS in polynomial-time computable as well?

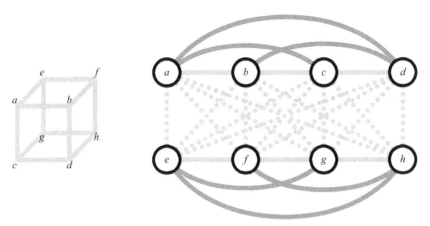

Figure 10.2   Example of a CONSISTENT COHERENCE problem. The Necker cube (left) can be interpreted in two qualitatively different ways: Either the face with vertices a, b, c and d is in the front (in which case the face with vertices e, f, g and h is in the back) or the face with vertices e, f, g and h is in the front (in which case the face with vertices a, b, c and d is in the back). The task of disambiguating between the two possible interpretations can be modeled as a coherence problem (right): Every vertex $p \in \{a,b,c,d,e,f,g,h\}$ of the Necker cube is modeled by an element $p \in P$. If two vertices p and q in P are part of the same interpretation of the Necker cube then $p,q \in C^+$ (solid lines), else $p,q \in C^-$ (dotted lines). Now a partition of P of maximum coherence into vertices that are "in the front" (set to *true*), and vertices that are "in the back," (set to *false*), will correspond to one of the two possible interpretations of the Necker cube. Adapted from van Rooij (2003).

Observe that if one is dealing with a consistent network then one knows that there always exists a truth assignment that satisfies *all* constraints. Imagine the following search procedure: Start at any proposition p in P. It does not matter where you start, because every proposition will have to be assigned a truth value in the end. Furthermore, you can safely set the truth value of this first proposition to true (or false, regardless), because there always exist two maximum truth assignments T and its complement T' where every proposition assigned true in T is assigned false in T' and vice versa.[1] Next, consider any other proposition q connected to p, and set the truth value of q such that the constraint (p,q) is satisfied. Repeat this procedure for new propositions

---

[1] As an aside, we note that it is for this reason that COHERENCE may be limited as a theory of belief, and FOUNDATIONAL COHERENCE and DISCRIMINATING COHERENCE, which do not have this symmetry property, may be more realistic models.

connected to propositions that have already been assigned. This procedure must guarantee that the final truth assignment satisfies all constraints.

Practice 10.3.2   Give pseudo-code for the procedure described previously. Prove correctness of the algorithm and prove that it runs in polynomial time.

We saw that some of the perceptual problems modeled by the COHERENCE problem (e.g., the Necker cube or other ambiguous figures) are of the special type that their inputs can be modeled by consistent networks. If the theory is applied to those perceptual phenomena, then it does not seem to face any problem of intractability (since COHERENCE ON CONSISTENT NETWORKS is polynomial-time computable). This observation may motivate a theory revision response: Perhaps we can restrict the input domain of the Coherence theory to consistent networks, thereby ensuring tractability of the theory. But remember, any theory revision response needs to be assessed on its empirical merits.

Stop and Think —————

How psychologically plausible is the assumption that *all* networks relevant for coherence computations by humans are consistent networks?

Not so plausible, we think. Take, for instance, again the application of belief fixation. It is quite unlikely that all our thousands of beliefs about the world are fully consistent. More plausibly, our belief networks are more or less consistent but not perfectly so (cf. the well-known phenomenon of cognitive dissonance, where apparently there is no way to assign truth values to a triple of propositions that are fully consistent). The classical complexity result for COHERENCE ON CONSISTENT NETWORKS does not yet tell us if perhaps computing maximally coherent truth assignments is tractable for networks that are *close* to being consistent. To address that question, we need parameterized complexity theory, which can assess to what extent the parameter u (the number of constraints that cannot be satisfied by any maximum coherent truth assignment) is a source of intractability. We turn now to these types of parameterized complexity analyses.

10.3.2   Parameterized Complexity Results

We will consider the parameterized complexity of COHERENCE for several different parameters (for parameterized complexity analyses of its generalizations

Table 10.1 Overview of parameters that may be sources of intractability in COHERENCE.

Name	Definition
$|C^+|$	The number of positive constraints
$|C^-|$	The number of negative constraints
s	Lower bound on the number of constraints to be satisfied
u	Upper bound on the number of constraints that can be unsatisfied

we refer the reader to the Exercise section). Table 10.1 shows an overview of the parameters that we will consider. This set is by no means exhaustive, but it serves for illustrative purposes.

We start by considering the following parameterization of COHERENCE.

$|C^+|$-COHERENCE
Input: A network $N = (P,C)$, where $C = C^+ \cup C^-$ is a set of positive and negative constraints and $C^+ \cap C^- = \emptyset$, and a positive integer s.
Parameter: $|C^+|$
Question: Does there exist a truth assignment $T: P \rightarrow \{true, false\}$ that satisfies at least s constraints in C?

Stop and Think

Recall the polynomial-time reduction from MAX CUT to COHERENCE in Practice 3.4.1. How did the instance of COHERENCE in this reduction look? Did it have any positive constraints?

The polynomial-time reduction from MAX CUT to COHERENCE produces instances for COHERENCE with only negative constraints. Using this observation, perform Practice 10.3.3.

Practice 10.3.3 Prove that $|C^+|$-COHERENCE $\notin$ FPT (assuming P $\neq$ NP).

Practice 10.3.3 demonstrates that the parameter $|C^+|$ is not a source of intractability in COHERENCE. We next show that the other three parameters from Table 10.1 are sources of intractability in COHERENCE. We start by considering the parameter $|C^-|$.

$|C^-|$-COHERENCE
Input: A network $N = (P,C)$, where $C = C^+ \cup C^-$ is a set of positive and negative constraints and $C^+ \cap C^- = \emptyset$, and a positive integer s.
Parameter: $|C^-|$
Question: Does there exist a truth assignment $T: P \to \{true, false\}$ that satisfies at least s constraints in C?

Consider the following two problems that we will use to prove that $|C^-|$-COHERENCE is fixed-parameter tractable.

ANNOTATED COHERENCE
Input: A belief network $N = (P,C)$ where P denotes a set of propositions and $C = C^- \cup C^+ \subseteq P \times P$ denotes a set of positive and negative constraints, with $C^+ \cap C^- = \emptyset$. Each constraint $(p,q) \in C$ has a weight $w(p,q) \geq 0$. For some $p \in P' \subseteq P$ the truth value has already been predetermined, as specified by a function $A: P' \to \{true, false\}$.
Output: A truth assignment $T: P \to \{true, false\}$ such that $A(p) = T(p)$ for all $p \in P'$ and $COH(T) = \sum_{(p,q) \in C^+, T(p)=T(q)} w(p,q) + \sum_{(p,q) \in C^-, T(p) \neq T(q)} w(p,q)$ is maximized.

One way to think of ANNOTATED COHERENCE is as the problem that arises when one is in the middle of the process of solving COHERENCE; i.e., some elements in P have already been assigned (the ones in P'), but other elements in P still remain to be assigned (the ones in $P \backslash P'$).

MIN CUT
Input: An edge-weighted graph $G = (V,E)$ with for each edge $(u,v) \in E$, there is an associated positive integer weight $w(u,v)$ and a positive integer k. Further, there are two special vertices, called source $s \in V$ and sink $t \in V$.
Output: A partition of V into sets A and B, with $s \in A$ and $t \in B$, such that the total weight of the edges in $\text{Cut}_G(A,B)$ is minimum.

It is known that MIN CUT is solvable in time $O(|V|^3)$ (see, e.g., Cormen et al., 2009)

Observe that one can transform any instance of (WEIGHTED) COHERENCE into one or more instances of ANNOTATED COHERENCE by considering different possible truth assignments for some of the propositions in the COHERENCE instance. This way one can build a search tree. For instance, we can make a search tree where we consider all the possible truth assignments to propositions connected to at least one negative constraint. Since there are at most $2 \times |C^-|$ such propositions, the number of possible truth assignments for these subsets of propositions is upper bounded by a function depending only on $|C^-|$ (viz., $2^{2|C^-|}$ possible truth assignments). The creation of all these subsets can thus be done in fp-tractable time relative to parameter $|C^-|$.

Note that each of the newly created instances of ANNOTATED COHERENCE can be further transformed into instances that have only positive constraints (since for each of the negative constraints both its end points will have a set truth assignment, so we can delete those constraints from the network if we keep track of whether or not they were satisfied). The resulting instances of ANNOTATED COHERENCE can be furthermore transformed into instances of MIN CUT by merging all the positive constraints connected to the propositions with the value set to *true* (and adding their weights), on the one hand, and merging all the positive constraints connected to the propositions with their value set to *false* (and adding their weights).

Have a look at the ideas expressed in Figure 10.3 and perform the following practice.

Practice 10.3.4 Using the knowledge that MIN CUT $\in$ P, prove that $|C^-|$-WEIGHTED COHERENCE $\in$ FPT. (Hint: Use the ideas described earlier. If you get stuck, full formal details of the proof argument can be found in (van Rooij, 2003).)

Next, consider the following two parameterized decision problems, and perform Practices 10.3.5, 10.3.6, and 10.3.7.

s-COHERENCE
Input: A network $N = (P,C)$, where $C = C^+ \cup C^-$ is a set of positive and negative constraints and $C^+ \cap C^- = \emptyset$, and a positive integer s.
Parameter: s
Question: Does there exist a truth assignment $T: P \rightarrow \{true, false\}$ that satisfies at least s constraints in C?

s-CONNECTED COHERENCE
Input: A connected network $N = (P,C)$, where $C = C^+ \cup C^-$ is a set of positive and negative constraints and $C^+ \cap C^- = \emptyset$, and a positive integer s.
Parameter: s
Question: Does there exist a truth assignment $T: P \rightarrow \{true, false\}$ that satisfies at least s constraints in C?

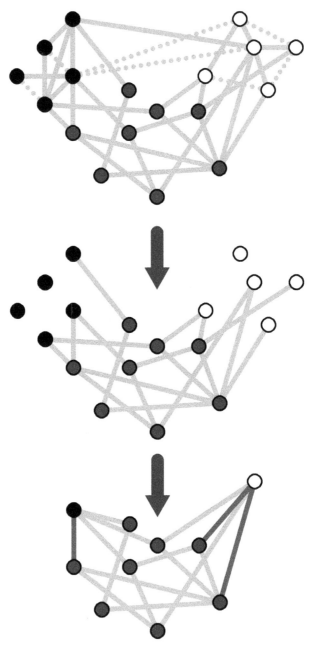

Figure 10.3   Illustration of how COHERENCE can be solved by first branching into instances of ANNOTATED COHERENCE and then transforming those into instances of the MIN CUT problem. Adapted from van Rooij (2003).

Practice 10.3.5 Prove that s-CONNECTED COHERENCE $\in$ FPT. (Hint: Use the technique of reduction to problem kernel: Observe that if the connected network is too large then the answer is always Yes.)

Practice 10.3.6 Prove that s-COHERENCE $\in$ FPT. (Hint: Use the technique of reduction to problem kernel: Get rid of degree 0 and 1 vertices, and then observe that if there are too many components then the answer is always Yes.)

Practice 10.3.7 Prove that s-WEIGHTED COHERENCE $\in$ FPT.

Consider the following two parameterized decision problems and perform Practice 10.3.8.

u-COHERENCE
Input: A network $N = (P, C)$, where $C = C^+ \cup C^-$ is a set of positive and negative constraints and $C^+ \cap C^- = \emptyset$, and a positive integer u.
Parameter: s
Question: Does there exist a truth assignment $T: P \rightarrow \{true, false\}$ that leaves at most u constraints in C unsatisfied?

k-EDGE BIPARTIZATION
Input: A graph $G = (V, E)$ and a positive integer k.
Parameter: k
Question: Does there exist a partition of V into sets A and B such that the number of edges in Bipartization$_G(A, B) \leq k$? (Here Bipartization$_G(A, B) = \{(u, v) \in E : u, v \in A \text{ or } u, v \in B\}$).

Observe that k-EDGE BIPARTIZATION is the so-called *parametric dual* of k-MAX CUT (like k-VERTEX COVER is the parameteric dual of k-INDEPENDENT SET). Namely, a graph has a cut of size k if and only if the same graph has a bipartization of size $|E| - k$ (cf. a graph has a vertex cover of size k if and only if the same graph has an independent set of size $|V| - k$). It is known that k-EDGE BIPARTIZATION $\in$ FPT.

Practice 10.3.8 Using the knowledge that k-EDGE BIPARTIZATION $\in$ FPT, prove that u-COHERENCE $\in$ FPT. (Hint: Use the technique of parameterized reduction.)

Practice 10.3.9 Prove that u-WEIGHTED COHERENCE $\in$ FPT. (Hint: Present a parameterized reduction from u-WEIGHTED COHERENCE to u-COHERENCE by first getting rid of edges with weight higher than u and then getting rid of weighted edges.)

10.4   Discussion

Tables 10.2 and 10.3 present an overview of the complexity results you proved in this application chapter.

Stop and Think ───────

What do these results mean or imply for possible ways in which COHERENCE may be revised to satisfy the tractability constraint?

We had already considered the option of constraining the input domain to consistent networks, but ruled that option out as psychologically implausible (see end of Section 10.3.1). However, we found subsequently that COHERENCE is fixed-parameter tractable for the parameter s. This means that as long

Table 10.2 Overview of classical complexity results for COHERENCE and some of its variants.

Problem	Classical complexity
COHERENCE	$\notin$ P
WEIGHTED COHERENCE	$\notin$ P
DISCRIMINATING COHERENCE	$\notin$ P
FOUNDATIONAL COHERENCE	$\notin$ P
CONSISTENT COHERENCE	$\in$ P

Table 10.3 Overview of parameterized complexity results for COHERENCE and some of its variants.

Problem	Parameter	Parameterized complexity
COHERENCE	$|C^+|$	$\notin$ FPT
COHERENCE	$|C^-|$	$\in$ FPT
CONNECTED COHERENCE	s	$\in$ FPT
COHERENCE	s	$\in$ FPT
WEIGHTED COHERENCE	s	$\in$ FPT
COHERENCE	u	$\in$ FPT
WEIGHTED COHERENCE	u	$\in$ FPT

as human belief networks are mostly consistent, even if not perfectly so, COHERENCE is tractable to compute for those networks. An alternative domain restriction, namely that belief networks would be mostly inconsistent (i.e., s would be small) yields tractability but seems to lack the plausibility of the previous restriction (after all, if human belief networks would be mostly inconsistent – in the sense that one could never satisfy more than a handful of constraints – then why would maximizing coherence lead to any useful belief fixation at all?). The last option is to assume that human belief networks have relatively few negative constraints (or equivalently, mostly positive constraints). This too would guarantee tractability of the Coherence theory, as we have shown that COHERENCE is fixed-parameter tractable for $|C^-|$. It is the latter restriction that Thagard and Findlay (2011) find supported in their research on modeling beliefs about climate change.

10.5   Exercises

Exercise 10.5.1   Consider the following parameterized decision problem:

> $\{w_{max}, |C^+|\}$-WEIGHTED COHERENCE
> **Input:** A belief network $N = (P, C)$ where P denotes a set of propositions, and $C = C^- \cup C^+ \subseteq P \times P$ denotes a set of positive and negative constraints, with $C^+ \cap C^- = \emptyset$. Each $(p, q) \in C$ has a weight $w(p, q)$, such that $0 \leq w(p, q) \leq w_{max}$, and positive integers w_{max} and s.
> **Parameter:** w_{max} and $|C^+|$
> **Question:** Does there exist a truth assignment $T: P \rightarrow \{true, false\}$, such that $COH(T) = \sum_{(p,q) \in C^+, T(p)=T(q)} w(p, q) + \sum_{(p,q) \in C^-, T(p) \neq T(q)} w(p, q) \geq s$?

Prove that $\{w_{max}, |C^+|\}$-WEIGHTED COHERENCE $\notin$ FPT (unless P = NP). (Hint: Use Observation 7.3.1 from Chapter 7.)

Exercise 10.5.2   Prove that w_{max}-WEIGHTED COHERENCE $\notin$ FPT (unless P = NP). (Hint: Use Observation 7.4.1 or 7.4.2 from Chapter 7.)

Exercise 10.5.3   Prove that $|C^+|$-WEIGHTED COHERENCE $\notin$ FPT (unless P = NP). (Hint: Use Observation 7.4.1 or 7.4.2 from Chapter 7.)

Exercise 10.5.4   Consider the following parameterized decision problem:

$\{w_{max}, |C^+|, |D|\}$-FOUNDATIONAL COHERENCE
Input: A set of observations (or data) D, a set of hypotheses H, and a set of constraints $C = C^- \cup C^+ \subseteq (D \cup H) \times (D \cup H)$, with $C^- \cap C^+ = \emptyset$. Each $(p, q) \in C$ has a weight $w(p, q)$, such that $0 \leq w(p, q) \leq w_{max}$, and positive integers w_{max} and s.
Parameter: w_{max}, $|C^+|$, and $|D|$
Question: Does there exist a truth assignment $T: H \cup D \rightarrow \{true, false\}$, with $T(d) = true$ for all $d \in D$, such that $COH(T) = \sum_{(p,q) \in C^+, T(p)=T(q)} w(p, q) + \sum_{(p,q) \in C^-, T(p) \neq T(q)} w(p, q) \geq s$?

Prove that $\{w_{max}, |C^+|, |D|\}$-DISCRIMINATING COHERENCE $\notin$ FPT (unless P = NP).

Exercise 10.5.5   Consider the following parameterized decision problem:

$\{w_{max}, |C^+|, |D|\}$-DISCRIMINATING COHERENCE
Input: A set of observations (or data) D, a set of hypotheses H, and a set of constraints $C = C^- \cup C^+ \subseteq (D \cup H) \times (D \cup H)$, with $C^- \cap C^+ = \emptyset$. Each $(p, q) \in C$ has a weight $w(p, q)$, such that $0 \leq w(p, q) \leq w_{max}$, and positive integers w_{max} and s.
Parameter: w_{max}, $|C^+|$, and $|D|$
Question: Does there exist a truth assignment $T: H \cup D \rightarrow \{true, false\}$ such that $COH(T) = \sum_{(p,q) \in C^+, T(p)=T(q)} w(p, q) + \sum_{(p,q) \in C^-, T(p) \neq T(q)} w(p, q) + \sum_{d \in D, T(d)=true} w_D(d) \geq s$?

Prove that $\{w_{max}, |C^+|, |D|\}$-FOUNDATIONAL COHERENCE $\notin$ FPT (unless P = NP).

Exercise 10.5.6   Are there other parameters that you think are interesting to consider for COHERENCE and/or its variants? State which parameters those are, why they are relevant or interesting to consider, and do you think they are sources of intractability for COHERENCE and/or its variants.

10.6   Further Reading

Most of the results in Tables 10.2 and 10.3 also appeared in (van Rooij, 2003), where you can also find more fine-grained parameterized analyses and formally worked out proofs for some of the practices in this chapter.

If you are interested in reading more about the theoretical foundations and applications of the theory of coherence as put forth by Paul Thagard, both his 2000 book *Coherence in Thought and Action* and his 2006 book *Hot Thought: Mechanisms and Applications of Emotional Coherence* are a good place to start. These books compile a large number of papers that Thagard has co-authored with others on the topic of coherence. The compiled papers illustrate how the theory can be applied to a vast array of domains, spanning legal judgment, social judgement, mathematical reasoning, action planning, analogy, and even religious beliefs. A critical commentary of Thagard's formalization of coherence as COHERENCE was written by the philosopher Elijah Millgram (2000), to which Paul Thagard responded (Thagard, 2012). In a paper where he argues that his theory can provide an explanation for jury decision making (see Thagard, 2003), he pitches his coherentist account against a Bayesian explanation. Last, it is noteworthy that Thagard has even used his coherentist theory of human belief fixation to explain why computer scientists believe that $P \neq NP$ (Thagard, 1993).

11 Analogy as Structure Mapping

In this chapter, we consider a computational-level theory of analogy derivation as structure mapping. We again illustrate the use of classical complexity analysis to assess the theory's intractability. In addition, we show how parameterized complexity analysis can be used to formally assess intuitive conjectures about possible sources of this intractability. This illustration demonstrates that such intuitions can often be wrong, underscoring the importance of formal analyses.

11.1   Introduction

An analogy is at its heart a relationship between two things that at first sight may seem very different but are, on examination, similar in interesting and useful ways. For example, when we say "falling in love is like going to school," though these are very different things on the surface, the analogy between them highlights the surprising number of features and relations they have in common (e.g., initial nervousness, learning new things over time, meeting new people). We are good at both making and judging the goodness of analogies; for example, the analogy just described is much more satisfying than "an orange is like an elephant." Analogies seem to be part of our everyday lives, from judgments of similarity to implicitly communicating information ("my girlfriend's cat is like the devil incarnate") to helping us cope with new situations based on past experience (how to dine at a Japanese restaurant given we have eaten at the local takeaway). Indeed, some even believe that analogy is a core part of how we as humans think (Gentner, 2003).

It is thus not surprising that how people derive analogies and evaluate how good these analogies are has long been a subject for psychological research. One of the most popular frameworks for investigating analogy is the *Structure Mapping Theory (SMT)* (Gentner, 1983). Since its inception, the evolution of SMT has been driven by the results of both psychological experiments and simulations done using various AI software systems that implement analogy-based processes. This evolution has in turn raised several issues:

- Given the horrendous runtimes of the AI system implementing an exact algorithm for SMT (Falkenhainer, Forbus, and Gentner, 1989) a faster heuristic-based AI implementation was developed (Forbus and Oblinger, 1990). Based on several simulations, this heuristic was conjectured to be a good approximation to SMT (Forbus and Oblinger, 1990). However, more recent and systematic simulations have revealed that this heuristic does not reliably approximate SMT (Grootswagers, 2013). Besides, even if SMT is intractable, we have learned in this book that fixed-parameter tractable algorithms may yet exist for computing it exactly.
- Based on psychological experiments (Gentner et al., 2009; Halford, Wilson, and Phillips, 1998), several conjectures can be made about what restrictions of the analogy derivation process do and do not make analogy derivation tractable in practice. However, none of these conjectures have been formally proven.

In this chapter, we will apply the techniques described earlier in this book to investigate both of these issues.

11.2   Formalizing the Theory

As we have seen previously in Chapter 10, the correct formalization of a cognitive theory is a critical prelude to computational complexity analysis of that theory, Hence this section, we review first the Structure Mapping Theory of analogy derivation as proposed by Gentner and then the formalization of this theory given in van Rooij et al. (2008).

11.2.1   Intuitive Basis of the Theory

An analogy is essentially a mapping between two conceptual structures. In SMT, conceptual structures are modelled by predicate structures. A *predicate structure* is a set of objects corresponding to individual entities (SUN, PLANET) and a set of predicates specifying various relationships both among objects (ATTRACTS(SUN, PLANET)) and among predicates (CAUSE(GRAVITY(MASS(SUN)), ATTRACTS(SUN, PLANET))). If the order of the entities in a relationship matters, the predicate is *ordered*; otherwise, the predicate is *unordered*. For example, BITES(x,y) is an ordered predicate because BITES(DOG,MAN) means something very different from BITES(MAN,DOG) and AND(X,Y) is an unordered predicate because AND(ISGREEN(GRASS),ISYELLOW(SUN)) means the same thing as AND(ISYELLOW(SUN), ISGREEN(GRASS)). Multi-layer predicate structures can represent very complex concepts. Figure 11.1 shows predicate structures representing the solar system (part (a)), a simple model of an atom (part (b)), and a musical performance and a military battle (part (d)).

Given predicate structures B and T referred to as the *base* and *target*, respectively, an *analogy "T is (like) a B"* is a mapping from a portion of B to a portion of T that satisfies the following three conditions:

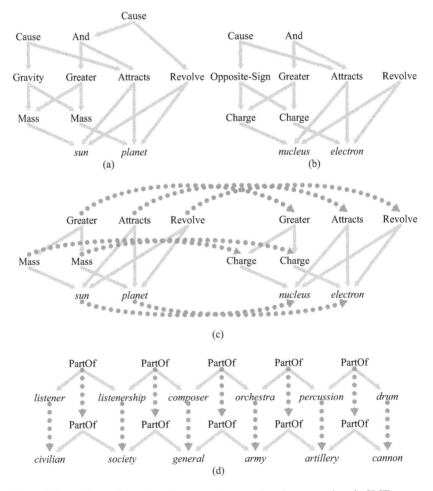

Figure 11.1 Illustrations of predicate structures and analogy mappings in SMT. Adapted from van Rooij et al. (2008).

1. The mapping is *structurally consistent*, i.e., it satisfies the following two conditions:

   (a) *Parallel connectivity*: Matching relations must have matching arguments.
   (b) *One-to-one correspondence*: Any element in one predicate structure matches at most element in the other predicate structure.

2. *Relational focus*: The mapping must involve common predicates but need not involve common objects, i.e., matched predicates must have the same name, argument, number and order but matched objects need not have the same name. For example ATTRACTS(SUN, PLANET) can match ATTRACTS(NUCLEUS, ELECTRON) but would not match SHINESON(SUN, PLANET).

3. *Systematicity*: The mapping tends to match interconnected predicate sub-structures, which are deeply nested and involve high-order predicates wherever possible. This is preferable because (in Gentner's own words) "a matching set of relations interconnected by higher-order constraining relations makes a better analogical match than an equal number of matching relations that are unconnected to each other."

Courtesy of parallel connectivity, the mapping of B onto T extends all the way down to objects that are descendants of matched predicates – hence, all analogy matchings must be grounded in object matches as well as predicate matches and cannot consist purely of matching predicates. As part of its first AI software implementations, SMT was modified to distinguish a subcategory of predicates called *functions* which return numerical or enumerated values for some attribute of the lone argument-entity, e.g, TEMPERATURE(SUN), CHARGE(ELECTRON). Unlike regular predicates, they need not match by name, e.g., MASS(SUN) can match CHARGE(NUCLEUS) (see Figure 11.1(c)).

We can now define analogy derivation under SMT as follows:

STRUCTURE-MAPPING ANALOGY DERIVATION (Informal)
Input: Predicate structures B and T.
Output: A most systematic analogy between B and T.

11.2.2 The Formalization

To do the computational complexity analysis that we want to do to investigate the issues raised in Section 11.1, we need to be much clearer about what we mean by a predicate structure, an analogy mapping, and systematicity.

The mathematical structures required to completely and accurately formalize these concepts are somewhat daunting. Readers interested in these details are encouraged to follow up on the references given in the Further Readings at the end of this chapter. For our purposes here, the following abbreviated descriptions will suffice.

Let's start with predicate structures. As predicate structures have a natural direction, with objects at the bottom and layers of predicates built upwards from these objects, it is appropriate to model predicate structures as directed graphs $G = (V, A)$ based on sets V of vertices and A of arcs. Moreover, as we do not want circular relations between predicates, we model predicate structures using directed acyclic graphs (DAGs). In our DAG models of predicate structures, we need to:

- Distinguish predicates and objects (as they behave differently in analogy mappings).
- Distinguish unordered and ordered predicates (as they also behave differently in analogy mappings).
- Ensure that whatever we use to model predicates behaves like and has the same properties and restrictions as real predicates.

All these conditions are met by specifying appropriate labels on the vertices and edges of the DAGs to create what we call concept-graphs, which are essentially the graphs shown in Parts (a), (b), and (d) of Figure 11.1.

Consider now how to formalize analogy mappings between predicate structures. Such an analogy mapping is essentially a type of subgraph isomorphism between our given concept-graphs. This analogy isomorphism differs in three ways from that in the SUBGRAPH ISOMORPHISM problem that we have seen previously:

1. Analogy isomorphisms are between vertex- and edge-labeled DAGs rather than undirected graphs.
2. An analogy isomorphism maps a subgraph of B onto a subgraph of T of equal size rather than mapping all of B onto a subgraph of T or vice versa.
3. The vertex mappings in an analogy isomorphism must be based not only the existence of matching edges but also on appropriate vertex and arc labels such that the first two of Gentner's conditions, structural consistency and relational focus, are met.

We call analogy isomorphisms analogy morphisms for short, and they are essentially the mappings between subgraphs of concept-graphs shown in Parts (c) and (d) of Figure 11.1.

We formalize the systematicity of an analogy as a function *syst*() defined on the subgraph $A(B,T)$ common to B and T that is isolated by an analogy morphism. We adopt the same systematicity function that is used in AI implementations of SMT, which works as follows: A standard matching score is given to each of the vertices in the topmost layer of $A(B,T)$. The scoring progresses downwards layer by layer, with each vertex v getting a score equal to the sum of the scores of all vertices v' in higher layers such that there is an arc from v' to v. Once every vertex has been scored, these scores are summed to give the score for $A(B,T)$ itself. Courtesy of the "snowballing" of scores from top to bottom in $A(B,T)$ (an effect that increases dramatically with graph height and interconnectivity), this function will be of highest value for analogy morphisms that are both deeply nested and highly interconnected.

This description gives the following formal version of SMAD:

STRUCTURE-MAPPING ANALOGY DERIVATION (SMAD)
Input: Concept-graphs B and T.
Output: An analogy morphism $A(B,T)$ between B and T with the highest possible $syst(A(B,T))$ value.

Our analysis in turn will focus on the associated decision problem:

STRUCTURE-MAPPING ANALOGY DERIVATION (SMAD)
Input: Concept-graphs B and T and a positive integer k.
Question: Is there an analogy morphism $A(B,T)$ between B and T such that $syst(A(B,T)) \geq k$?

11.3   Complexity Analysis

11.3.1   Classical Complexity Results

The analogy matching in SMT looks like the subgraph matching in the SUBGRAPH ISOMORPHISM problem, which we know from Section 3.2.3 to be NP-hard. On the basis of this similarity, SMT has been claimed to be polynomial-time intractable as well. As noted in the previous section, the relation between these two types of graph isomorphism is not at all straightforward. However, it turns out that with a bit of ingenuity, the intuition just discussed does in fact yield a useful reduction.

The key to this reduction is to realize how an undirected graph can be mapped into a concept-graph. This comes from the following obvious local replacement: An edge is an unordered relation between two vertices! Let

$C(G)$ be the concept-graph created from a graph G by making each vertex in G an object and adding an unordered edge-relation of type e between every pair of objects corresponding to vertices linked by an edge in G. An example undirected graph G and its associated concept-graph $C(G)$ are shown in Figure 11.2(b).

The reduction itself is as follows: Given an instance (G, H) of SUBGRAPH ISOMORPHISM construct an instance (B, T, k) of SMAD such that $B = C(G)$, $T = C(H)$, and $k = syst(C(H))$. This instance of SMAD can be constructed in polynomial time. To prove the correctness of this reduction, observe that courtesy of the assigned value of k, the only acceptable analogy morphisms in the constructed instance of SMAD require that all of T match some subgraph of B. However, by the construction of T and B, this can only happen if all of H matches some subgraph of G. Hence, the given instance of SUBGRAPH ISOMORPHISM is a *yes*-instance if and only if the constructed instance of SMAD is a *yes*-instance.

The previous reduction suffices to show that SMAD is NP-hard and hence polynomial-time intractable if all predicates in the given concept-graphs are unordered. A valid complaint is that in practice, the majority of predicates in concept-graphs are ordered, so this result says nothing about the computational difficulty of everyday analogy making. This, however, can be addressed in an easy fashion – namely, replace every occurrence of the transformation $C(G)$ with the transformation $C'(G)$, in which an edge in G is replaced by two directed predicates, one going each way, between the corresponding vertex-objects. This builds on the well-known equivalence between an undirected edge between a pair of vertices and a pair of opposite-direction arcs between those vertices.

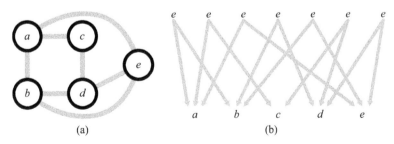

(a)   (b)

Figure 11.2   Transforming undirected graphs into concept-graphs. (a) An undirected graph G. (b) The concept-graph $C(G)$ associated with undirected graph G by the transformation described in the main text. Adapted from van Rooij et al. (2008).

Practice 11.3.1 Give a complete formal proof that SMAD operating on concept-graphs consisting purely of ordered predicates is NP-hard.

11.3.2 Parameterized Complexity Results

There are several claims (either based on or made in the scientific literature) that certain restrictions make SMAD tractable in practice even if it is polynomial-time intractable in general; a smaller number of claims state that certain restrictions make no difference at all. Two of the former type of claim are:

1. Restrict the maximum number of arguments to any predicate (Halford et al., 1998).
2. Restrict the maximum size of the derived analogy (Gentner et al., 2009).

The first of these claims was motivated by research into how children and adults make analogies and the second by research into memory retrieval. An example of the latter type of claim (motivated by AI implementations of SMT Falkenhainer et al., 1989) is that restricting the maximum number of objects in either given concept-graph does not make analogy derivation easier. Problem parameters encoding all three of these restrictions are listed in Table 11.1.

Let's attempt to prove some of these claims formally by considering the parameterized complexity of SMAD relative to these parameters. It turns out that we already know the answer to the first two claims – namely, that they are false. In the case of a, this is because in both of the reductions in the previous subsection, $a = 2$ in the concept-graphs in our constructed instances of SMAD. Hence, by Observation 7.3.1, $\{a\}$-SMAD is not fixed-parameter tractable unless $\mathsf{P} = \mathsf{NP}$. In the case of m, we already know from Section 3.2.3 that CLIQUE is a restricted case of SUBGRAPH ISOMORPHISM. Hence we can rephrase our reductions in the previous subsection such that for a given instance $(G = (V, E), k)$ of CLIQUE we construct instances $(B = C(G), T = C(K_k), k' = syst(C(T)))$ and $(B = C'(G), T = C'(K_k), k' = syst(C'(T)))$

Table 11.1 Overview of parameters that may be sources of intractability in SMAD.

Name	Definition
a	Maximum number of arguments per predicate in B and T
m	Minimum size of B and T, i.e., maximum size of derived analogy
o	Maximum number of objects in B and T

of unordered and ordered concept-graph SMAD, respectively, where K_k is the undirected complete graph on k vertices. Note that the smallest graphs in both instances are $C(K_k)$ and $C'(K_k)$, which have sizes $k + k(k-1)/2$ and $k + 2k(k-1)/2 = k + k(k-1)$, respectively. Hence, we have reductions from k-CLIQUE to both unordered and ordered concept-graph $\{a,m\}$-SMAD, which means that both of these problems are W[1]-hard and hence fixed-parameter intractable unless FPT = W[1].

The answer to the third claim is also surprisingly easy. Observe that given any mappings between sets of objects of the same size in B and T in a given instance of SMAD, one can "grow" the largest possible analogy based on those object sets upwards from the objects by incorporating relations between objects and relations occurring in both B and T that are grounded in entities that have already been matched lower down. This growth can be done in polynomial time for any object mapping. Consider that the brute-force algorithm that generates all possible object mappings between B and T generates the best analogy for each mapping by the growth process sketched earlier, and it outputs the analogy with the largest systematicity score. The number of possible object mappings is the sum, over all possible object-set sizes, of the number of ways you can select two object sets of that size from each of B and T and the number of ways you can order the objects in each set to create a mapping. This is $=$

$$\sum_{i=2}^{o} \binom{o}{i}\binom{o}{i} o! \leq \sum_{i=2}^{o} o^i o^i o^o \leq \sum_{i=2}^{o} o^o o^o o^o = (o-1)o^{3o}, \text{ which}$$

is a function purely of o. Hence, by this algorithm, unordered and ordered concept-graph o-SMAD are both fixed-parameter tractable.

11.4   Discussion

A summary of the classical and parameterized complexity results derived in Section 11.3 is given in Table 11.2.

Stop and Think   ———

What do these results imply for the specific issues raised for SMT in Section 11.1?

Our NP-hardness results for unordered and ordered concept-graph SMAD in Section 11.3.1 do indeed verify the intuition that deriving analogies under SMT in general is intractable. Our parameterized results in Section 11.3.2 in turn point out that of the three conjectures considered concerning what

Table 11.2 Complexity results for SMAD

	–	o
–	NP-hard	✓
a	✗	✓
m	✗	✓
a, m	✗	✓

restrictions do and do not make analogy derivation under SMT tractable, *none* are correct. Moreover, in the case of the conjectured restrictions on a and m, even restricting *both* of them simultaneously does not yield tractability. The main take-home lesson is that it is vital to use computational complexity analyses for verifying intuitions about sources of intractability.

Another important lesson for SMT is that the decision to use a heuristic as algorithmic-level theory may have been unnecessary. After all, we have shown that SMT is fixed-parameter tractable for, for instance, the parameter o.[1] Results such as these illustrate that an intractable computational-level theory, like SMT, may be tractable for the right kinds of input restrictions.

11.5   Exercises

Exercise 11.5.1   A function $f(.)$ is increasing if for any inputs x and y, $|x| < |y|$ if and only if $f(x) < f(y)$. Prove that all intractability results in Section 11.3 hold if the systematicity-score function $syst()$ is an arbitrary increasing function.

Exercise 11.5.2   It has been conjectured that given predicate structures that are "flat," i.e., of very small depth, are responsible for the intractability in SMAD (Falkenhainer et al., 1989; Veale and Keane, 1997). Though all reductions in Section 11.3 created instances of SMAD in which the height of the created concept-graphs is one, this does not answer this conjecture because we need a parameter whose value is small when the given predicate structures are flat and large otherwise. One such parameter is n/h, which is the larger for B and T of dividing the total size of the predicate structure by its height.

---

[1] Simulation studies have furthermore revealed that the fp-tractable algorithm based on this result outperforms the heuristic implementation of SMT both in speed and accuracy for small o (Grootswagers, 2013)

Prove that unordered and ordered concept-graph $\{n/h\}$-SMAD are fixed-parameter intractable (Hint: Don't be afraid of doing something that is simple or silly [but not explicitly forbidden] in your reduction.)

Exercise 11.5.3   Consider the following version of SMAD that explicitly limits the size of the produced analogy:

STRUCTURE-MAPPING ANALOGY DERIVATION II (SMAD-II)
Input: Concept-graphs B and T and positive integers k and s.
Question: Is there an analogy morphism $A(B,T)$ between B and T such that (1) $syst(A(B,T)) \geq k$ and (2) the analogy associated with $A(B,T)$ is of size $\leq s$, i.e., the total number of objects and predicates in the analogy is $\leq s$?

(a) Prove that unordered SMAD-II $\notin$ P unless P = NP.
(b) Prove that unordered s-SMAD-II $\notin$ FPT unless FPT = W[1].

Exercise 11.5.4   A linear concept-graph is a concept-graph in which each object is the argument of at most two predicates and no two predicates can have more than one argument in common. For example, both concept-graphs in part (d) of Figure 11.1 are linear concept-graphs. Consider the following restricted versions of SMAD:

STRUCTURE-MAPPING ANALOGY DERIVATION III(a)
(SMAD-III(a))
Input: Two concept-graphs B and T, where each concept-graph is a set of one or more linear concept-graphs and a positive integer k.
Question: Is there an analogy morphism $A(B,T)$ between B and T such that $syst(A(B,T)) \geq k$?

STRUCTURE-MAPPING ANALOGY DERIVATION III(b)
(SMAD-III(b))
Input: Two concept-graphs B and T, where B is a single linear concept-graph and T is a set of two or more linear concept-graphs, and a positive integer k.
Question: Is there an analogy morphism $A(B,T)$ between B and T such that $syst(A(B,T)) \geq k$?

STRUCTURE-MAPPING ANALOGY DERIVATION III(c)
(SMAD-III(c))
Input: Two concept-graphs B and T in which both B and T are single linear concept-graphs and a positive integer k.
Question: Is there an analogy morphism $A(B,T)$ between B and T such that $syst(A(B,T)) \geq k$?

STRUCTURE-MAPPING ANALOGY DERIVATION III(d)
(SMAD-III(d))
Input: Two concept-graphs B and T in which both B and T are
single linear concept-graphs and a positive integer k.
Question: Is there an analogy morphism $A(B,T)$ between B and T
such that (1) $syst(A(B,T)) \geq k$ and (2) the analogy associated with
$A(B,T)$ is a single linear concept-graph?

(a) Prove that unordered SMAD-III(a) $\notin$ P unless P $=$ NP. (Hint: You
may find the reduction in chapter 4 of Garey and Johnson (1979) from
3-PARTITION to SUBGRAPH ISOMORPHISM useful.)
(b) Prove that unordered SMAD-III(b) $\notin$ P unless P $=$ NP.
(c) Prove that unordered SMAD-III(c) $\notin$ P unless P $=$ NP.
(d) Prove that unordered SMAD-III(d) is in P.

11.6   Further Reading

A comprehensive survey of computational models of analogy is given in
Gentner and Forbus (2011). Notable AI systems implementing aspects of
SMT include the Structure Mapping Engine (analogy derivation; Falkenhainer
et al., 1989), MAC/FAC (memory retrieval; Forbus, Gentner, and Law, 1994),
SEQL (categorization and abstraction; Kuehne et al., 2000), and Compan-
ions (general-purpose reasoning; Forbus and Hinrichs, 2006). The extensive
literature on both psychological and AI investigations of SMT can be readily
accessed through the publications listed on the home pages of Dedre Gentner
and Ken Forbus.

The first proof of the NP-hardness of analogy derivation under SMT
was given in Veale and Keane (1997). As this was a conference paper of
restricted length, details therein are somewhat sketchy. The first complete
proof of NP-hardness (consisting of both a detailed formalization of SMT and
complete proof details) was given in van Rooij et al. (2008) and its associated
online supplementary materials. This paper also gave the first parameterized
analysis of analogy derivation under SMT. The formalization of SMT and
all complexity proofs given in this chapter are from that paper. This work
has subsequently been extended to look at the computational difficulty of
various analogy based processes under SMT (Hamilton and Wareham, 2012;
Wareham, Evans, and van Rooij, 2011a; Wareham, Robere, and van Rooij,
2012; Wareham and van Rooij, 2011).

12 Communication as Bayesian Inference

In this chapter, we consider a computational-level theory of communication as Bayesian inference. We again illustrate the use of classical complexity analysis to assess the theory's intractability. In addition, we show that parameterized complexity analysis can converge with theoretically-informed intuitions about possible sources of this intractability, in this case based on the Gricean Maxims in pragmatic theories of communication.

12.1 Introduction

Humans have the ability to understand the intentions underlying communicative actions of others. This is a remarkable ability given that intention recognition involves reasoning from effects (observed actions) to their likely causes (hypothesized intentions) and is therefore best seen as a form of "inference to the best explanation," also known as *abduction* (see, e.g., Baker, Saxe, and Tenenbaum, 2009; Levinson, 2006; Sperber and Wilson, 1996). Computational models of abduction are notorious for their computational intractability (Abdelbar and Hedetniemi, 1998; Thagard and Verbeurgt, 1998; Bylander et al., 1991; Nordh and Zanuttini, 2008). It has been suggested that the computational demands of intention recognition in human communication could be alleviated when a communicator does recipient design (Clark, 1996; Grice, 1989; Sperber and Wilson, 1996). For example, Sperber and Wilson (1996, p.67) write that "...comprehension is almost instantaneous, and is achieved with the active help of the information source ...." However, this idea raises a so-far neglected question: If recipient design is assumed to make intention recognition tractable for addressees, does it not simply move the computational load from the addressee to the agent generating the communicative action? To investigate these tractability claims, we will first take a closer look at intention recognition and recipient design.

12.1.1 Basis of the Theory

Let's look at Bob and Mary (Figure 12.1) to understand the nature of intention recognition and recipient design. Bob and Mary are chatting, while suddenly Bob's favorite composition by Bach plays faintly in the background. At this point, Bob wants to communicate three things to Mary:

1. Please be quiet.
2. Listen to the music.
3. I am listening to the music.

Now suppose that Bob knows that Mary knows they both enjoy Bach very much. To communicate (1), (2), and (3) to her he might simply just put his finger in front of his mouth (Figure 12.1, left). By taking into account his beliefs about Mary, Bob designs his communicative signal specifically for Mary in this situation. Mary has to recognize these intentions from Bob's signal.

When he has different beliefs Bob might communicate differently. If he knows Ann likes to keep talking and that she is not interested in music, he might put his finger in front of his mouth to signal Ann to be quiet (1), but he would also close his eyes to tell her he is listening (3) (Figure 12.1, middle). To emphasize that he is listening (3) even more, Bob then tilts his head slightly and puts his finger up in the air, signaling Ann to pay attention and listen to the music (2) (Figure 12.1, right).

We can informally define the problem of intention recognition as follows:

INTENTION RECOGNITION (informal)
Input: The observed states S and actions A of the communicator and knowledge about how these states and actions might relate to possible communicative goals G_C and non-communicative goals G_I.
Output: The best value assignment to the possible communicative goals G_C given S, A, and the knowledge.

Figure 12.1 Example communicative interaction. Bob is communicating three intentions to Ann: Please be quiet, listen to the music, and I am listening to the music. Adapted from van Rooij et al. (2011) and illustrations by Bas Maes.

A communicator performs recipient design by taking into account their beliefs about how their recipient will recognize their intentions. Recipient design can now be informally defined as follows:

RECIPIENT DESIGN (informal)
Input: Knowledge about how possible states S, actions A, and communicative goals G_C and non-communicative goals G_I relate, and a value assignment to all goals $G_C \cup G_I$.
Output: The best value assignment to the actions A (and associated states S) such that INTENTION RECOGNITION(S,A) = G_C and the actions are the best with respect to achieving the instrumental goals G_I.

12.2   Formalizing the Theory

As before, to perform complexity analysis we need to have formal versions of the informal problem definitions. Unfortunately, there were none available in the communication literature. Taking inspiration from Bayesian models of action understanding (Baker et al., 2009) and teaching (Shafto and Goodman, 2008) we can formally define INTENTION RECOGNITION and RECIPIENT DESIGN as Bayesian inference problems. For a primer on probabilities, conditional dependence and Bayesian inference see Appendix A.5.

We define the following variables which we will use to formalize the input–output mappings for RECIPIENT DESIGN and INTENTION RECOGNITION. In the Bayesian formalism capital letters denote variables, whereas small letters denote values; bold letters denote sets of variables or values, whereas non-bold letters denote singletons.

1. $\mathbf{S} = \{S_1, \dots, S_T\}$, a sequence of T state variables that can encode values of state sequences $\mathbf{s}$.
2. $\mathbf{A} = \{A_1, \dots, A_{T-1}\}$, a sequence of $T - 1$ action variables that can encode values of action sequences $\mathbf{a}$.
3. $\mathbf{G_I} = \{G_{I1}, \dots, G_{Ij}\}$, a set of instrumental goal variables that can encode the values of the communicator's instrumental goals $\mathbf{g_I}$.
4. $\mathbf{G_C} = \{G_{C1}, \dots, G_{Ck}\}$, a set of communicative goal variables that can encode the values of the communicator's communicative goals $\mathbf{g_C}$.

RECIPIENT DESIGN (formal)
Input: A Bayesian network $\mathcal{B} = (G_{\mathcal{B}} = (V_{\mathcal{B}}, A_{\mathcal{B}}), \text{Pr}_{\mathcal{B}})$, a value assignment $\mathbf{g_I}$ for $\mathbf{G_I}$ and a value assignment $\mathbf{g_C}$ for $\mathbf{G_C}$ encoding the communicator's goals. Here, $\mathbf{S, A, G_I, G_C} \subseteq V_{\mathcal{B}}$. The structure of $\mathcal{B}$ is illustrated in Figure 12.2, and $\text{Pr}_{\mathcal{B}}$ is an arbitrary conditional probability distribution over $G_{\mathcal{B}}$.
Output: A value assignment $\mathbf{a}$ to $\mathbf{A}$, such that $\mathbf{a} = \text{argmax}_{\mathbf{a}} \text{Pr}(\mathbf{A} = \mathbf{a} \mid \mathbf{G_I} = \mathbf{g_I})$ and Intention Recognition$(\mathcal{B}, \mathbf{a}, \mathbf{s}) = \mathbf{g_C}$, or $\varnothing$ if no such sequence of actions $\mathbf{a}$ exists. Here $\mathbf{s} = \text{argmax}_{\mathbf{s}} \text{Pr}(\mathbf{S} = \mathbf{s} \mid \mathbf{A} = \mathbf{a})$, i.e., the most likely states $\mathbf{s}$ to follow from the actions.

INTENTION RECOGNITION (formal)
Input: A Bayesian network $\mathcal{B} = (G_{\mathcal{B}} = (V_{\mathcal{B}}, A_{\mathcal{B}}), \text{Pr}_{\mathcal{B}})$, just as in the RECIPIENT DESIGN network, a value assignment $\mathbf{a}$ for $\mathbf{A}$ and a value assignment $\mathbf{s}$ for $\mathbf{S}$ encoding the observed actions and states.
Output: The most probable value assignment $\mathbf{g_C}$ to the communicative goals $\mathbf{G_C}$, i.e., $\text{argmax}_{\mathbf{g}} \text{Pr}(\mathbf{G_C} = \mathbf{g_C} \mid \mathbf{S} = \mathbf{s}, \mathbf{A} = \mathbf{a})$, or $\varnothing$ if $\text{Pr}(\mathbf{G_C} = \mathbf{g_C} \mid \mathbf{S} = \mathbf{s}, \mathbf{A} = \mathbf{a}) = 0$ for all possible values for $\mathbf{G_C}$.

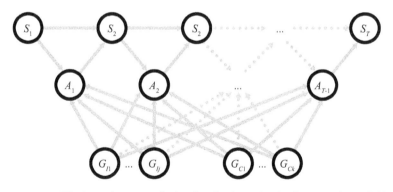

Figure 12.2 The Bayesian network showing the dependencies between the variables in the RECIPIENT DESIGN and INTENTION RECOGNITION models. Arrows denote dependencies, e.g., if Bob has his eyes open (S_t = "Bob eyes open"), then closes his eyes (A_t = "close eyes"), then S_{t+1} has a high probability of Bob having his eyes closed ($\text{Pr}(S_{t+1}$ = "Bob eyes closed" $\mid S_t$ = "Bob eyes open", A_t = "close eyes") = 0.9). Adapted from van Rooij et al. (2011)

12.3   Complexity Analysis

12.3.1   Classical Complexity Results

Although Bayesian inference problems can be depicted using directed graphs, they do not resemble any of the problems covered so far. This makes finding a suitable reduction strategy for proving NP-hardness difficult. In this section you will learn how to build a reduction by component design (see Section 3.2.4) from CLIQUE to INTENTION RECOGNITION and RECIPIENT DESIGN. Given that CLIQUE is NP-hard, this reduction will prove that INTENTION RECOGNITION and RECIPIENT DESIGN are also NP-hard.

Consider the decision problem version of CLIQUE and general Bayesian inference problem (MOST PROBABLE EXPLANATION, MPE):

CLIQUE
Input: A graph $G = (V, E)$ and an integer k.
Question: Does there exist a clique $V' \subseteq V$ such that $|V'| \leq k$?

MOST PROBABLE EXPLANATION(MPE)
Input: A Bayesian network $\mathcal{B} = (G_{\mathcal{B}} = (V_{\mathcal{B}}, A_{\mathcal{B}}), \Pr_{\mathcal{B}})$, where $V_{\mathcal{B}}$ is partitioned into a set of evidence nodes $\mathbf{E}$ and an explanation set $\mathbf{M}$, such that $\mathbf{E} \cup \mathbf{M} = V_{\mathcal{B}}$. Further, a joint value assignment $\mathbf{e}$ and $0 \leq q < 1$.
Question: Does there exist a joint value assignment $\mathbf{m}$ to the nodes in $\mathbf{M}$ given evidence $\mathbf{e}$ such that $\Pr(\mathbf{m}, \mathbf{e}) > q$?

CLIQUE can be polynomial-time reduced to MOST PROBABLE EXPLANATION. To build this reduction we will have to build components in MOST PROBABLE EXPLANATION instances such that these instances "mimic" the behavior of CLIQUE instances. Any CLIQUE instance that is a *yes*-instance will contain a subset of vertices $V' \subseteq V$ with the following properties:

1. $|V'| = k$.
2. All vertices in V' are unique, because V' is a set.
3. There exists an edge for each pair of vertices in V'.

The polynomial-time reduction will have to include a transformation for CLIQUE instances into MPE instances. This transformation will build an MPE instance that essentially "checks" if a selection of vertices has properties 1 to 3.

Stop and Think

There are multiple ways to design these components. Can you design some of the components? You might find it helpful to use the CLIQUE instance from Figure 12.3 assuming $k = 3$.

The components in the MPE instance will select k vertices (Component 1) and check if these vertices are unique (Component 2) and if there exists an edge for each pair of vertices (Component 3). Component 1 is relatively simple, we create k variables $V_1, \ldots, V_k \in \mathbf{V}_\mathcal{B}$. The domain of each of these variables is set to the vertices from the CLIQUE instance, see Figure 12.4.

If we set the prior distributions of each variable to be uniform, then any value assignment to V_1, V_2, and V_3 will have equal probability, and hence without further restrictions in place would be equally valid outputs of MOST PROBABLE EXPLANATION. This means that although Component 1 will select k vertices, they are not guaranteed to be unique. We need Component 2 to force that any non-unique value assignment will have a probability of zero. We assume an arbitrary order on the vertices in V such that $v_1 < v_2 < \cdots < v_{|V|}$. For each consecutive pair of Component 1 variables, we create an additional variable called $<_i$ which is conditionally dependent on the pair, see Figure 12.5. Each

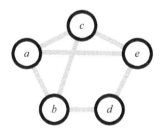

Figure 12.3   An example instance for CLIQUE.

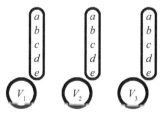

Figure 12.4   Component 1 selects k vertices based on a uniform distribution, i.e., each vertex has the same prior probability of being selected. Adapted from van Rooij et al. (2011).

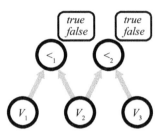

Figure 12.5   Component 2 forces that each vertex selected by V_1, V_2, and V_3 is unique. Adapted from van Rooij et al. (2011).

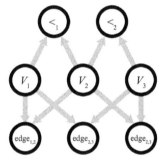

Figure 12.6   Component 3 forces that the vertices encoded by each pair of vertices selected by V_1, V_2, and V_3 contain an edge in the CLIQUE instance. Adapted from van Rooij et al. (2011).

$<_i$ variable is part of the evidence set E, can be *true* or *false* and is observed to be *true*. The conditional probability of each $<_i$ variable being *true* is 1 if and only if $V_i = a < V_{i+1} = b$ for some a, b such that $a < b$:

$$\Pr(<_i = true \mid V_i, V_{i+1}) = \begin{cases} 1 & \text{if } V_i < V_{i+1} \\ 0 & \text{otherwise} \end{cases}$$

Finally, Component 3 will force that the vertex subset corresponding to the value assignment of Component 1 is also a clique. We create another set of $k(k-1)/2$ Boolean evidence variables, each called $edge_{i,j}$. The variable $edge_{i,j}$ are conditionally dependent on each pair of Component 1 variables V_i, V_j. $edge_{i,j}$ is *true* if and only if there exists an edge in E between the two vertices selected by V_i and V_j, see Figure 12.6. All $edge_{i,j}$ variables are observed to be *true*

Practice 12.3.1 Using the components defined previously, give a complete polynomial-time reduction from CLIQUE to MOST PROBABLE EXPLANATION.

In the definition of INTENTION RECOGNITION, we have included the possibility that both communicative and non-communicative goals can underlie communicative behavior. We assume that the recipient does not explicitly infer the non-communicative goals. INTENTION RECOGNITION is thus a special case of the problem PARTIAL MAXIMUM A-POSTERIORI PROBABILITY.

PARTIAL MAXIMUM A-POSTERIORI PROBABILITY
Input: A Bayesian network $\mathcal{B} = (G_\mathcal{B} = (V_\mathcal{B}, A_\mathcal{B}), \text{Pr}_\mathcal{B})$, where $V_\mathcal{B}$ is partitioned into a set of evidence nodes **E**, a set of intermediate nodes $\mathbf{I} \neq \varnothing$ and an explanation set **M**, such that $\mathbf{E} \cup \mathbf{I} \cup \mathbf{M} = \mathbf{V}$. Additionally, a joint value assignment **e** and $0 \leq q < 1$.
Question: Does there exist a joint value assignment **m** to the nodes in **M** given evidence **e** with $\text{Pr}(\mathbf{m}, \mathbf{e}) > q$?

Practice 12.3.2 Explain how the reduction from the previous practice can be used to make a reduction from CLIQUE to PARTIAL MAXIMUM A-POSTERIORI PROBABILITY.

Because INTENTION RECOGNITION is a special case of PARTIAL MAXIMUM A-POSTERIORI PROBABILITY, a reduction from PARTIAL MAXIMUM A-POSTERIORI PROBABILITY to INTENTION RECOGNITION is not possible. However, it is possible to use the component design for reducing CLIQUE to PARTIAL MAXIMUM A-POSTERIORI PROBABILITY to make a reduction from CLIQUE directly to INTENTION RECOGNITION.

Practice 12.3.3 Prove that INTENTION RECOGNITION is NP-hard by giving a polynomial-time reduction from CLIQUE to INTENTION RECOGNITION. Note that INTENTION RECOGNITION is defined as an optimization problem, whereas PARTIAL MAXIMUM A-POSTERIORI PROBABILITY is defined as a decision problem. To make this reduction you first need to specify the decision version of INTENTION RECOGNITION. You may need to use the following two observations:

1. The conditional probability $\text{Pr}(a \mid b) > q$ when the marginal probability $\text{Pr}(a, b) > q$ if $q = 0$. You can use this observation to define a decision version of INTENTION RECOGNITION based on marginalization. The observation can be proved as follows: By definition $\text{Pr}(a \mid b) = \text{Pr}(a, b) \text{Pr}(b)$. So if $\text{Pr}(a \mid b) > q$ then $\text{Pr}(a, b) \text{Pr}(b) > q$ and $\text{Pr}(a, b) > \text{Pr}(b)q$. When $q = 0$ this implies that $\text{Pr}(a, b) > 0$ and $\text{Pr}(a \mid b) > 0$.

2. You may assume that dependencies between variables can be effectively nullified (removed) and you will need one or two additional components to deal with the restricted structure of INTENTION RECOGNITION (e.g., a logical conjunction component might prove to be useful).

Practice 12.3.4 Given that INTENTION RECOGNITION is a subproblem of RECIPIENT DESIGN, what does its NP-hardness say about the (in)tractability of RECIPIENT DESIGN?

Practice 12.3.5 Component 1, which selects k vertices, assumes that the number of values a variable can take can scale arbitrarily. This poses problems when identifying sources of intractability, because it may hide computational complexity. To prevent this, we can make a (common) assumption in Bayesian inference, namely that the number of values a variable can take has to be constant. Given this constraint design a replacement for Component 1 that uses only a polynomial number of binary variables and show that the reductions can be updated using your replacement for Component 1. Hint: Consider that binary encoding of n items can be done using only $\lceil \log_2 n \rceil$ bits.

12.3.2 Parameterized Complexity Results

The intractability results for INTENTION RECOGNITION and RECIPIENT DESIGN show that even if recipient design makes intention recognition tractable by some means, the intractability is shifted to recipient design.

Stop and Think

What do the classical results mean for explaining communication (i.e., intention recognition and recipient design) as a whole?

The NP-hardness of INTENTION RECOGNITION and RECIPIENT DESIGN implies that the computations postulated by the models require an unrealistic amount of time for their completion. Intractability of intention recognition was already believed to be the case. Recall that the claim was that by performing recipient design, communicators alleviate this computational burden. However, even if intention recognition can be made tractable by recipient design, the fact that RECIPIENT DESIGN is NP-hard implies that the computational intractability has only shifted from one computational explanation to another. Hence, without understanding under what conditions INTENTION RECOGNITION and RECIPIENT DESIGN can be tractable, we are no closer to computationally explaining the speed of everyday communication.

In this section we show under what conditions the computations postulated by INTENTION RECOGNITION and RECIPIENT DESIGN are tractable or not. No claims were present in the literature, because it was assumed that recipient design solved the intractability issues. Table 12.1 shows an overview of the parameters we will consider. This set is by no means exhaustive, but it can already lead to some useful insights. Parameterized complexity results for INTENTION RECOGNITION and RECIPIENT DESIGN can be found in Tables 12.2 and 12.3.

Table 12.1 Overview of parameters that may be sources of intractability in INTENTION RECOGNITION and RECIPIENT DESIGN.

Name	Definition
$|G_C|$	The number of communicative goals
$|G_I|$	The number of instrumental goals
$|A|$	The number of observed or planned actions

Table 12.2 Complexity results for INTENTION RECOGNITION. As in Table 7.1, a ✓ or ✗ table entry means that relative to the parameter set consisting of the union of the parameter sets labeling the row and column of that entry, the problem is fixed-parameter tractable or intractable, respectively.

INTENTION RECOGNITION	−	$|A|$
−	NP-hard	✗
$|G_C|$	✗	✗
$|G_I|$	✗	✗
$|G_C|, |G_I|$	✓	✓

Table 12.3 Complexity results for RECIPIENT DESIGN.

RECIPIENT DESIGN	−	$|A|$
−	NP-hard	✗
$|G_C|$	✗	✗
$|G_I|$	✗	✗
$|G_C|, |G_I|$	✗	✓

12.4   Discussion

The complexity results of INTENTION RECOGNITION and RECIPIENT DESIGN show that tractability is not easily explained. Even if the claim in the literature holds, namely that recipient design makes intention recognition tractable, one still needs to explain how recipient design can be tractable. This is no trivial task. With respect to the parameters considered in this chapter, the only tractability result for RECIPIENT DESIGN is for parameter set $\{|G_C|, |G_I|, |A|\}$.

Practice 12.4.1 $\{|G_C|, |G_I|, |A|\}$-RECIPIENT DESIGN is fixed-parameter tractable, but why is this result not informative about sources of complexity for RECIPIENT DESIGN?

Practice 12.4.2   RECIPIENT DESIGN is fixed-parameter intractable for parameter set $\{|G_C|, |G_I|\}$, whereas INTENTION RECOGNITION is fixed-parameter tractable for that set. What does this tell us about the relative complexity between RECIPIENT DESIGN and INTENTION RECOGNITION?

The tractability results converge with several intuitions of classic pragmatic theories such as the Gricean Maxims (Grice, 1989). This convergence suggests that INTENTION RECOGNITION and RECIPIENT DESIGN capture at least some fundamental aspects of communication. Take the following two maxims:

1. Maxim of Quantity: People should not make their contribution more informative than is required.
2. Maxim of Relation: People should make their contribution be relevant to the current discourse.

Informativeness can be operationalized as the number of communicative goals a communicator tries to convey. Relevance can be operationalized as the inverse of the number of instrumental goals that a communicator has.

Practice 12.4.3   How are the Maxim of Quantity and the Maxim of Relation related to the fixed-parameter tractability result of $\{|G_C|, |G_I|\}$-INTENTION RECOGNITION?

Although it is an empirical question whether or not the parameters in the fixed-parameter tractability results are plausibly small in reality, the convergence with the Gricean Maxims suggests that such an investigation may yield positive results.

12.5   Exercises

Exercise 12.5.1   We know that k-Clique is W[1]-hard. Prove that $\{|\mathbf{G_I}|, |\mathbf{A}|\}$-Intention Recognition is W[1]-hard by giving a parameterized reduction from k-Clique to $\{|\mathbf{G_I}|, |\mathbf{A}|\}$-Intention Recognition. You can reuse the classical polynomial-time reduction from Clique to Intention Recognition you made earlier.

Exercise 12.5.2   What does the fixed-parameter intractability of $\{|\mathbf{G_I}|, |\mathbf{A}|\}$-Intention Recognition say about the computational complexity of $\{|\mathbf{G_I}|, |\mathbf{A}|\}$-Recipient Design?

12.6   Further Reading

The idea of communication as (abductive) inference has been extensively discussed by (amongst others) Levinson (2006) and Sperber and Wilson (1996). If you are interested in reading more about why abductive inference is computationally intractable, consider reading Abdelbar and Hedetniemi (1998), Thagard and Verbeurgt (1998), Bylander et al. (1991), and Nordh and Zanuttini (2008). Claims surrounding the role of recipient design in communication have been put forward by Sperber and Wilson (1996), Grice (1989), and Clark (1996). For more details on the origins of the computational models presented in this chapter, have a look at Baker et al. (2009) for the original Bayesian model of action understanding, or our own work (Blokpoel et al., 2012; van Rooij et al., 2011).

Appendix A Mathematical Background

A.1   Turing's Model of Computation

Informally, when we say a system computes a function or solves a problem
$F: I \rightarrow O$, we mean to say that the system reliably transforms every $i \in I$ into
$F(i) \in O$ in a way that can be described by an algorithm. An algorithm (e.g.,
Algorithm 2.1 that solves VERTEX DEGREE) is a step-by-step finite procedure
that can be performed, by a human or machine, without the need for any insight,
just by following the steps as specified by the algorithm. The notion of an
algorithm, so described, is an intuitive notion. Mathematicians and computer
scientists have pursued several formalizations (e.g., Church, 1936; Kleene,
1936; Post, 1936). Probably the best-known formalization, in particular among
cognitive scientists and psychologists, is the one by Alan Turing (1936). One of
the strengths of Turing's formalization is its intuitive appeal and its simplicity.

Turing motivated his formalization by considering a paradigmatic example
of computation: the situation in which a human sets out to compute a number
using pen and paper (see Turing, 1936, pp. 249–252). Turing argued that a
human computer can be in at most a finite number of different "states of mind,"
because if "we admitted an infinity of states of mind, some of them will be
'arbitrarily close' and will be confused" (p. 250). Similarly, Turing argued a
human computer can read and write only a finite number of different symbols,
because if "we were to allow an infinity of symbols, then there would be
symbols different to an arbitrarily small extent" (p. 249). On the other hand,
Turing allowed for a potentially infinite paper resource. He assumed that the
paper is divided into squares (like an arithmetic notebook) and that symbols
are written in these squares. With respect to the reading of symbols Turing
wrote: "We may suppose that there is a bound B on the number of symbols
or squares that the computer can observe at one moment. If [s/he] wishes to
observe more [s/he] must use successive operations" (p. 250). This restriction
was motivated by the observation that for long lists of symbols we cannot tell

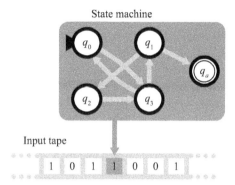

State machine

Input tape

Figure A.1 A graphical depiction of a Turing machine with an input tape, read/write head, and state machine.

them apart in "one look." Compare, for example, the numbers 96785959943 and 96785959943. Are they the same or different?

According to Turing, the behavior of a human computer at any moment in time is completely determined by his/her state of mind and the symbol(s) he or she is observing. The computer's behavior can be understood as a sequence of operations, with each operation "so elementary that it is not easy to imagine [it] further divided" (p. 250). Turing distinguished the following two elementary operations:

1. A possible change of a symbol on an observed square.
2. A possible change in observed square.

Each operation is followed by a possible change in state of mind. With this characterization of computation, Turing could define a machine to do the work of a human computer.

A.1.1   Formal Definition of a Turing Machine

After the motivation in the previous subsection, we will now give a formal definition of a Turing machine.

A Turing machine $\mathcal{M}$ is a machine that at any moment in time is in one of a finite number of machine states (analogue to "states of mind"). The set of possible machine states is denoted by $Q = \{q_0, q_1, q_2, \ldots, q_n\}$. One machine state, q_0, is designated the initial state; this is the state that $\mathcal{M}$ is in at the beginning of the computation. There is also a non-empty set, $H \subset Q$, of halting states; whenever the machine goes into a state, $q_i \in H$, then the machine halts and the computation is terminated. The machine has a read/write head that gives it access to an external memory, represented by a one-dimensional tape (analogue to the paper). The tape is divided in discrete regions called tape squares. Each tape square may contain, at most, one symbol. The machine can move the read/write head from one square to a different square, always moving the read/write head to the right or left, at most, one square at a time. The read/write head is always positioned on exactly one square, which it is said to scan. If a square is scanned, then the machine can read a symbol from or write a symbol to that square. At most one symbol can be read or written at a time. The set of possible symbols is denoted by S, and is called the alphabet of $\mathcal{M}$. S is a finite set. Often it is assumed that $S = \{0, 1, B\}$, where B is called the blank symbol. Time is discrete for $\mathcal{M}$, and time instants are ordered $0, 1, 2, \ldots$. At time 0, the machine is in its initial state, q_0, the read/write head is in a starting square, and all squares contain Bs except for a finite sequence of adjacent squares, each containing either 1 or 0. The sequence of 1s and 0s on the tape at time 0 is a called the input i.

The Turing machine can perform two types of basic operations:

1. It can write an element from S in the square it scans.
2. It can shift the head one square left (L) or right (R).

After performing an operation of either type, the machine takes on a state in Q. At any one time, which operation is performed and which state is entered is completely determined by the present state of the machine and the symbol presently scanned. In other words, the behavior of a Turing machine can be understood as being governed by a function T that maps a subset of $Q \times S$ into $A \times Q$, where $A = \{0, 1, B, L, R\}$ denotes the set of possible operations. We call T the transition function of $\mathcal{M}$. A transition $T(q, s) = (a, q)$ is interpreted as follows: If $q \in Q$ is the current state and $s \in S$ is the current scanned symbol, then the machine performs operation $a \in A$ and the machine enters the state $q \in Q$. For example, $T(q_a, 0) = (1, q_b)$ means that if $\mathcal{M}$ is in state q_a and reads symbol 0, then $\mathcal{M}$ is to write symbol 1 and go into state q_b; $T(q_a, 1) = (L, q_b)$ means that if $\mathcal{M}$ is in state q_a and reads symbol 1, then $\mathcal{M}$ is to move its read/write head one square to the left and go into state q_b. Note that Q, S, and A are finite sets. Thus we can also represent the transition function T as a finite list of transitions. Such a list is often called the machine table, and transitions are then called machine instructions.

Under the governance of T, the machine $\mathcal{M}$ performs a uniquely determined sequence of operations, which may terminate in a finite number of steps. If the machine does halt then the sequence of symbols on the tape is called its output. A Turing machine is said to compute a function $\psi : I \to O$ if for every possible input $i \in I$ it outputs $\psi(i)$. A function is called computable (or Turing-computable) if there exists a Turing machine that computes it. Turing (1936) proved that there exist (infinitely many) problems that are not computable. For example, he showed that the Halting problem is not computable. This decision problem is formulated as follows:

Halting problem
Input: A Turing machine $\mathcal{M}$ and an input i for $\mathcal{M}$.
Question: Does $\mathcal{M}$ halt on i?

A.1.2   Extensions of the Turing-Machine Concept

The reader may wonder to what extent the particular limitations placed by Turing on his machine are crucial for the limitations on computability. Therefore, a few notes should be made on the computational power of the Turing machine with certain extensions. It has been shown that several seemingly powerful adjustments to Turing's machine do not increase its computational power (see, e.g., Lewis and Papadimitriou, 1997, for an overview).

For example, the set of functions computable by the Turing machine described earlier is the same as the set of functions computable by Turing machines with one or more of the following extensions:

1. Turing machines with multiple tapes and multiple read/write heads.
2. Turing machines with any finite alphabets (i.e., not necessarily $A = \{0, 1, B\}$).
3. Turing machines with random access: These are Turing machines that can access any square on the tape in a single step.
4. Non-deterministic Turing machines: These are Turing machines that, instead of being governed by a transition function, are governed by a transition relation, mapping some elements in $Q \times S$ to possibly more than one element in $A \times Q$. Such a non-deterministic machine is said to "compute" a function ψ if for every input i there exist one possible sequence of operations that, when performed, would lead to output $\psi(i)$.

It should be noted that machines of type (4) are not considered to really compute in the sense that Turing meant to capture with his formalism; namely, in non-deterministic machines, not every step of the computation is uniquely determined, and thus, a human wishing to follow the set of instructions defined by the machine table would not be able to unambiguously determine how to proceed at each step. Even though non-deterministic machines are purely theoretical constructs, they do serve a special purpose in theories of computational intractability; see the next subsection. The extensions (1)–(3), on the other hand, are considered reasonable extensions. Throughout this article, the term Turing machine can be taken to refer to Turing machines both with and without such extensions.

A.1.3   A Formal Definition of P and NP Using Turing Machines

In Chapter 4 we gave formal definitions of the classes P (Definition 4.2) and NP (Definition 4.3), but we left the notion "algorithm" and "instance" a bit open. Now we can give a formal definition of these classes using Turing machines.

The complexity class P (short for *polynomial time*) is the class of all decision problems that are decidable on a deterministic Turing machine in a time which is polynomial in the length of the input string x. In contrast, the class NP (*non-deterministic polynomial time*) is the class of all problems that are decidable on a *non*-deterministic Turing machine in a time which is polynomial in the length of the input string x. Alternatively NP can be defined as the class of all problems that can be *verified* in polynomial time, measured in the size of the input x, on a deterministic Turing machine: For any decision problem $D \in$ NP, there exists a Turing machine $\mathcal{M}$ that, when provided with a tuple (x, w) on its input tape, can verify in polynomial time whether w is a "proof" of the fact that $x \in D$. In particular, there exists a w for which $\mathcal{M}$ accepts (x, w) in a time polynomial in the size of x if and only if $x \in D$. We will call w a *certificate* or *witness* of membership of $x \in D$. Note that certificates are restricted to be of polynomially bounded size with respect to the length of the input. This follows from the fact that the runtime should be polynomial in the input size as we have seen previously.

A.2   Set Notation

Many problems in this book are based on *sets*. A set S is basically a collection of distinct elements, where the elements (or members of the set) can be atomic or collections themselves (i.e., a set of sets). A set can be described explicitly as a list of elements inside parentheses, such as the set $S = \{a, b, c, d\}$. Order is irrelevant for sets: $\{a, b, c, d\} = \{b, a, d, c\}$. The number of elements of a set S is non-negative and possibly infinite: We use $|S|$ to denote this number (also called the cardinality of the set S). When a set contains zero elements we call this the empty set, with special designated symbol $\varnothing$. Examples of infinite sets are the set of natural numbers $\mathbb{N} = \{0, 1, 2, \dots\}$. A set can also be defined implicitly, such as the set of rational numbers $\mathbb{Q} = \{p/q : p, q \in \mathbb{N}, q \neq 0\}$ and the set $S = \{x : \exists n \in \mathbb{N} \text{ such that } x = 2n\}$ of even numbers.

Note that a set can contain sets. That means that $\{a,b,c,d\} \neq \{\{a,b,c,d\}\}$, as the former is the set containing a, b, c, and d, and the letter is the set containing a single element, namely $\{a,b,c,d\}$. In particular, the set $\{\varnothing\}$ is the set that contains the empty set as element. Sets can have *subsets*: all subsets of $\{1,2\}$ are $\varnothing$, $\{1\}$, $\{2\}$, and $\{1,2\}$. More generally, A is a subset of B (notation $A \subseteq B$) if all members of A are members of B as well: From this definition it follows that the empty set $\varnothing$ is a subset of every other set (including itself). If $A \subseteq B$ then we call B a *superset* of A. A subset or superset is *proper* or *strict* if the sets are not identical, that is, $A \subset B$ if $A \subseteq B$ but not $A = B$. The *power set* of a set S, notation $\mathcal{P}(S)$, is the set consisting of all subsets of S. For example, the power set of $\{1,2\}$ is $\{\varnothing, \{1\}, \{2\}, \{1,2\}\}$. A *universe* U is a special set that contains all elements that we are considering in a particular context; for example, when reasoning about dice throw outcomes, we may define $U = \{1,2,3,4,5,6\}$. The *complement* S^C of a set S is always relative to a universe: if $S = \{2,4,6\}$ and $U = \{1,2,3,4,5,6\}$, then $S^C = \{1,3,5\}$.

Typical operations on a combinations of two sets are intersection, union, difference, and symmetric difference:

$$A \cap B = \{x : x \in A \wedge x \in B\} \quad \text{Ex.: } \{1,2,3\} \cap \{2,3,4\} = \{2,3\} \quad \text{(intersection)}$$
$$A \cup B = \{x : x \in A \vee x \in B\} \quad \text{Ex.: } \{1,2,3\} \cup \{2,3,4\}$$
$$= \{1,2,3,4\} \quad \text{(union)}$$
$$A \setminus B = \{x : x \subset A \wedge x \notin B\} \quad \text{Ex.: } \{1,2,3\} \setminus \{2,3,4\} = \{1\} \quad \text{(difference)}$$
$$A \Delta B = (A \setminus B) \vee (B \setminus A) \quad \text{Ex.: } \{1,2,3\} \Delta \{2,3,4\} = \{1,4\} \quad \text{(symmetric difference)}$$

Note that $A^C = U \setminus A$. A *partition* of a set S is a collection of subsets which are pairwise disjoint (i.e., their intersections are empty) and whose union is the set S. For example, a partition of $S = \{1,2,3,4\}$ is $S_1 = \{1,2,3\}$ and $S_2 = \{4\}$ as $S = S_1 \cup S_2$ and $S_1 \cap S_2 = \varnothing$. The *Cartesian product* $A \times B$ of A and B is the set $A \times B = \{(a,b) : a \in A \wedge b \in B\}$. For example, the Cartesian product of $\{1,2\}$ and $\{a,b\}$ is $\{(1,a),(1,b),(2,a),(2,b)\}$.

The following identities with respect to set operations can be useful in computations:

$$A \cap \varnothing = \varnothing, A \cup \varnothing = A \qquad \text{(empty set axioms)}$$

$$A \cap A = A, A \cup A = A \qquad \text{(idempotency axioms)}$$

$$A \cap B = B \cap A, A \cup B = B \cup A \qquad \text{(commutation)}$$
$$A \cap (B \cap C) = (A \cap B) \cap C, A \cup (B \cup C) = (A \cup B) \cup C \qquad \text{(association)}$$

Figure A.2   Intersection, union, difference, and symmetric difference of A and B.

$$A \cup (B \cap C) = (A \cup B) \cap (A \cup C),$$
$$A \cap (B \cup C) = (A \cap B) \cup (A \cap C) \quad \text{(distribution)}$$

A convenient way of depicting the result of the operation of two sets uses so-called *Venn diagrams*, a set of partially overlapping figures (typically circles or rectangles) representing A and B, where the color or absence of color of parts of the areas in the resulting figure visually shows the result of a particular operation. Example Venn diagrams are given in Figure A.2 for the typical operations shown earlier.

A.3   Graph Theory

Many problems considered in this book are (or can be formulated as) graph problems. Here we present a basic introduction to graphs and define the graph theoretic notation and terminology used throughout this book. For more information on graphs and graph theory see, e.g., Foulds (1994), Gould (1988), and Gross and Yellen (1990).

A graph $G = (V, E)$ is a pair of sets, V and E. The set V is called the vertex set of G and its elements are called vertices. The set E is called the edge set and is a subset of the Cartesian product $V \times V$ (we also write $E \subseteq V^2$, where V^2 denotes the two-fold product of V). The elements of E are called edges. A graph can be thought of as a network consisting of nodes (vertices) and lines connecting some pairs of nodes (edges). Figure A.3 gives an illustration of a graph $G = (V, E)$. The nodes in the figure represent the vertices in V and the lines connecting nodes represent edges in E. In other words, the graph in Figure A.3 has vertex set $V = \{a, b, c, \ldots, z\}$ and edge set $E \subseteq V \times V$, with $E = \{(a, b), (a, d), (a, e), (b, h), \ldots, (z, y)\}$.

Note that, for the graph in Figure A.3, the number of nodes $n = |V| = 26$ and the number of edges $m = |E| = 30$.

Note that in the graph in Figure A.3 there are no connections from any vertex to itself (called a self-loop) and each pair of vertices is connected by at most one edge (i.e., there are no multi-edges). Graphs without self-loops and without

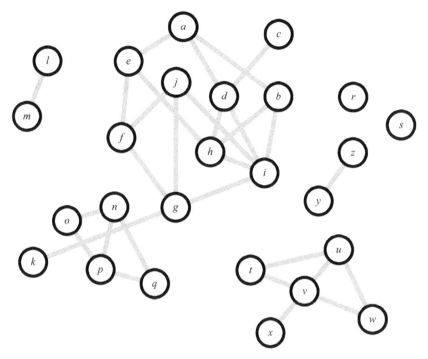

Figure A.3   An illustration of a graph.

multi-edges are called simple graphs. All graphs considered in this book are simple unless otherwise noted. Further, note that there is no particular order associated with the vertices in an edge, i.e., for all u, v, $(u, v) = (v, u)$. Graphs of this type are called undirected. If there *is* an order associated with the vertices in all edges, i.e., for all u, v, $(u, v) \neq (v, u)$, then the graph is called directed. A directed edge is also referred to as an *arc*, and the notation $G = (V, A)$ is sometimes used to emphasize that the graph is directed. If G contains both directed and undirected edges we call G a *chain graph*.

We define additional terminology for graphs. Let $G = (V, E)$ be a graph. We say a vertex $v_1 \in V$ is incident to edge (u, v) and, conversely, (u, v) is incident to v_1, if $(u, v) \in E$ and $v_1 = u$ or $v_1 = v$. If an edge $(v_1, v_2) \in E$ we also call v_1 and v_2 the end points of the edge (v_1, v_2), and if $(v_1, v_2) \in E$ we say that v_1 and v_2 are neighbors in G. For example, in Figure A.3, edge (e, f) is incident to vertex e, and e is an endpoint of (e, f). Further, e and f are neighbors, while, for example, m and f are not.

The set of vertices that are neighbors of vertex v in graph G is called the (open) neighborhood of v, denoted by $N_G(v) = \{v \in V : v$ is a neighbor of $v\}$.

Note that v itself is not a member of $N_G(v)$. We call $N_G[v] = N_G(v) \cup \{v\}$ the closed neighborhood of v. For example, in Figure A.3, vertex d has neighbors a, c, h and i. Thus we have $N_G(d) = \{a, c, h, i\}$ and $N_G[d] = \{a, c, d, h, i\}$. The number of edges incident to a vertex v is called the degree of v and is denoted by $deg_G(v)$. For example, in Figure A.3, vertex d has degree $deg_G(d) = 4$. Note that, for any vertex v in a graph G, we have $deg_G(v) = |N_G(v)|$. If a vertex v has degree k, we also say that v is a k-degree vertex. We call degree-0 vertices isolated vertices, and we call degree-1 vertices pendant vertices. For example, in Figure A.3, vertices r and s are isolated vertices, and vertices c, k, l, m, x, y and z are all pendant vertices.

Let $G = (V, E)$ be a graph and let $V' \subseteq V$ be a subset of vertices. Then $N_G(V') = \bigcup v \in V N_G(v)$ is called the (open) neighborhood of V' and $N_G[V'] = \bigcup v \in V N_G[v]$ is called the closed neighborhood of set V'. In other words, $N_G[V'] = N_G(V') \cup V'$. For example, in Figure A.3, $N_G(\{a, l\}) = \{b, d, e, m\}$ and $N_G[\{a, l\}] = \{a, b, d, e, l, m\}$. Further, $E_G(V') = \{(u, v) \in E : u \in V' \text{ and } v \in V'\}$ denotes the set of edges that have both endpoints in V', and $R_G(V') = \{(u, v) \in E : u \in V' \text{ or } v \in V'\}$ denotes the set of edges that have at least one of their endpoints in V'. For example, in the graph given in Figure A.3, we have $E_G(\{b, d, h, i, l, m\}) = \{(b, h), (b, i), (d, i), (d, h), (h, i), (l, m)\}$ and $R_G(\{e, f, l\}) = \{(a, e), (e, f), (e, h), (f, j), (f, g), (l, m)\}$.

Whenever we delete a vertex from a graph we also have to remove its incident edges (otherwise the remaining vertex and edge sets would not form a graph anymore). Hence, the set $R_G(V')$ is the set of edges that gets removed from G when we delete the vertices in V' from V. That is, if we remove V' from V the resulting graph $G^* = (V^*, E^*)$ will have vertex set $V^* = V \setminus V'$ and edge set $E^* = E \setminus R_G(V')$. We call G^* a subgraph of G.

A sequence $\langle v_1, v_2, \ldots, v_k \rangle$ of pairwise distinct vertices such that $(v_1, v_2), (v_2, v_3), \ldots, (v_{k-1}, v_k) \in E$ is called a path in G. If the path $\langle v_1, v_2, \ldots, v_k \rangle$ (with $k \geq 4$) is augmented with (v_k, v_1) then $\langle v_1, v_2, \ldots, v_k, v_1 \rangle$ is called a cycle in G. For example, in Figure A.3, $\langle k, g, i, b, h \rangle$ is a path, while $\langle g, i, b, h, i \rangle$ is not. Further, in the graph in Figure A.3, $\langle a, b, i, h, e, a \rangle$ is a cycle. We may also denote a path and a cycle by its edges instead of its vertices, as follows: $\langle (v_1, v_2), (v_2, v_3), \ldots, (v_{k-1}, v_k) \rangle$. For example, we may denote the path $\langle k, g, i, b, h \rangle$ in Figure A.3 by $\langle (k, g), (g, i), (i, b), (b, h) \rangle$ instead. The length of a path is the number of edges visited when traversing the path. Thus, path $\langle k, g, i, b, h \rangle$ in Figure A.3 has length 4. A directed graph is a-cyclic if there is no *directed* cycle in the graph. Such a graph is often called a DAG (short for "directed acyclic graph"). In particular, the graph structure of a Bayesian network is a DAG.

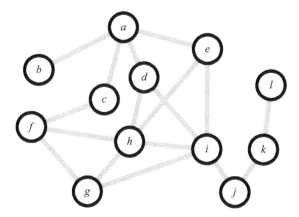

Figure A.4   An illustration of a connected graph.

A graph is connected if for every pair of vertices $u, v \in V$ there is a path in G from u to v. Note that the graph in Figure A.3 is not connected (e.g., there is no path from t to g). However the graph in Figure A.4 is connected.

Let $G' = (V, E')$ be a subgraph of G. We say G' is a component of G if (1) G' is connected, and (2) there does not exist a subgraph G^* of G, $G^* \neq G'$, such that G^* is connected and G' is a subgraph of G^*. For example, the graph in Figure A.3 consist of six components: viz., the components induced by vertex sets $\{l, m\}$, $\{a, c, b, d, e, f, g, h, i, j, k, n, o, p, q\}$, $\{t, u, v, w, x\}$, $\{y, z\}$, $\{r\}$, and $\{s\}$. Note that, for example, the subgraph of G induced by $\{t, u, v, x\}$ is not a component of G. To see why this is so, consider the subgraph $G' = (V, E')$ of G induced by $\{t, u, v, x\}$ and the subgraph $G^* = (V^*, E^*)$ of G induced by $\{t, u, v, w, x\}$. Note that G^* is connected and G' is a subgraph of G^*. We conclude that G' is not a component of G. Also note that since the graph in Figure A.4 is connected it has only one component.

A graph without any cycles is called a forest, and a connected forest is called a tree. Figure A.5 shows a graph that is a forest, and Figure A.6 shows a graph that is a tree. A rooted tree is a tree with a designated vertex called the root. Let $\mathbf{T} = (V_{\mathbf{T}}, E_{\mathbf{T}})$ be a rooted tree, with root $r \in V_{\mathbf{T}}$. A pendant vertex in a tree is called a leaf. For two vertices $u, v \in V_{\mathbf{T}}$ with $(u, v) \in E_{\mathbf{T}}$, we say u is parent of v, and v is child of u, if $\langle r, \ldots, u, v \rangle$ is a path in $\mathbf{T}$. The depth of $\mathbf{T}$ is the length of the longest path from root r to a leaf in $\mathbf{T}$. For example, for the tree $\mathbf{T} = (V_{\mathbf{T}}, E_{\mathbf{T}})$ in Figure A.6 we may call vertex A the root of $\mathbf{T}$. Then vertices b, d, h, f, i, k are leaves in $\mathbf{T}$. For example, e is a child of a, and e is parent of g. Furthermore, $\mathbf{T}$ in Figure A.6 has depth 4.

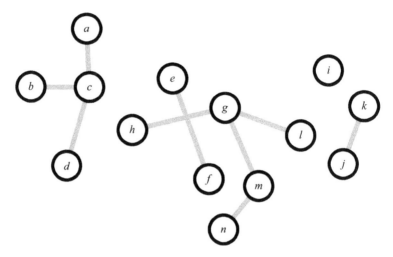

Figure A.5   An illustration of a forest.

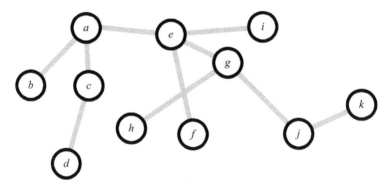

Figure A.6   An illustration of a tree.

Two convenient ways of encoding a graph are (1) using an adjacency matrix and (2) using an adjacency list. Both datastructures have pros and cons, depending on what sort of operations you wish to perform on the graph. An *adjacency matrix* is an $n \times n$ matrix M that has a 1 for each cell $M_{i,j}$ such that there is an edge from vertex i to vertex j, and a 0 if there isn't such an edge. If G is undirected, then M is symmetrical in the main diagonal (an edge (i,j) implies an edge (j,i)) but if G is directed then M typically is not. For sparse graphs (with few edges) this is a fairly inefficient encoding.

An *adjacency list* is a collection of (unordered) lists, one per vertex, that includes the neighbors of that list. It is an efficient encoding for sparse graphs (we don't encode edges that aren't there) but it is not so trivial to check whether a particular edge exists in the graph as it is when using an adjacency matrix.

A.4   Propositional Logic

If it rains, then you don't go to the beach. It rains. So, you don't go to the beach: This seems a straightforward and irrefutable conclusion. Facts and rules like these can be expressed in logic and be subject to formal rules and axioms that allow for drawing conclusions that—given that the facts on which they are based (the so-called *premises*) are correct—are logically valid. The most straightforward form of logic is *propositional logic*. Here, a proposition is a formula on so-called *variables* or atomic statements (basic building blocks, like "it rains") and logical connectives or *operators* (like "if ... then"). In the context of this book we use lower case italic letters to represent variables, for example r for "it rains" and b for "you go to the beach." We use the $\neg$ symbol to represent negation, so $\neg b$ can be interpreted as "you don't go to the beach." We use the $\rightarrow$ symbol (called *material implication*) to represent an "if ... then" construct. For example, $r \rightarrow \neg b$ can be interpreted as "if it rains, then you don't go to the beach."

But be careful—nothing is to be concluded from this statement if it does *not* rain. Whether you then go to the beach or not is all just fine, inasmuch as the material implication is concerned. This is often in contrast to natural language. The sentences "if it is my birthday I throw a party" and "if we marry we'll order a wedding cake" look similar but have a different logical interpretation. In the first sentence one can throw a party also when its not one's birthday (e.g., graduation, driver's licence, etc.) but one does not typically order a wedding cake unless one is getting married. In the first sentence we use the *material implication* and in the second the *equivalence* interpretation of the *if ... then* structure.

A bottom line of this might be that it is not straightforward to translate natural language in formal logic, nor to intuitively grasp the truth conditions of a proposition. A truth table concisely and precisely captures when a proposition is true and when it is not. Using basic truth tables (for all the connectives) one can derive for a complex proposition when (i.e., for which truth setting of its variables) this proposition is true and when it is not. For example, a truth table for negation looks like this:

x	$\neg x$
1	0
0	1

Next, we list the truth tables for the conjunction $\wedge$, the disjunction $\vee$, the material implication $\rightarrow$, the equivalence $\leftrightarrow$, and the exclusive or $\oplus$ as follows.

x	y	$x \wedge y$	$x \vee y$	$x \rightarrow y$	$x \leftrightarrow y$	$x \oplus y$
1	1	1	1	1	1	0
1	0	0	1	0	0	1
0	1	0	1	1	0	1
0	0	0	0	1	1	0

Now, you can infer the validity of any proposition. Let's take the sentence "At a road divergence, one goes either to the right or the left" (formalized as $d \leftrightarrow (n \oplus l)$) as an example.

d	r	l	$r \oplus l$	$d \leftrightarrow (r \oplus l)$
1	1	1	0	0
1	1	0	1	1
1	0	1	1	1
1	0	0	0	0
0	1	1	0	1
0	1	0	1	0
0	0	1	1	0
0	0	0	0	1

Stop and Think

When is this formula true? Why is that the case? Can you think of a way of describing the *desired* truth function?

Note that the formula is true if you are at a divergence and either go right or left, but not both, which is as intended. It is also true if you are not at a divergence, and neither go right nor left, which is also good. However, the formula is true as well if you are not at a divergence and go right and left simultaneously! A straightforward, but possibly inefficient way to circumvent these unwanted side effects is to explicitly list the *desired* clauses as a disjunction of conjunctions. We want that either of the following clauses is true, but nothing else: (divergence AND right AND NOT left) OR (divergenve AND NOT right AND left) OR (not divergence AND NOT right AND NOT left). This is accomplished by construction the following formula: $(d \wedge r \wedge \neg l) \vee (d \wedge \neg r \wedge l) \vee (\neg d \wedge \neg r \wedge \neg l)$.

Stop and Think

Make a truth table for this formula and check that it is true in the desired cases and not true in the undesired cases. (1) Can you think of a shorter formula that accomplishes the same? (2) For a given formula, is there a truth setting that makes it true?

These questions lie at the heart of computational complexity theory. The first problem is known as the circuit minimization problem (MINIMUM CIRCUIT) and the second problem as the satisfiability problem (SATISFIABILITY).

Special variants of this satisfiability problem ask whether a formula is always true or always false, independent of the truth setting to the variables. A simple formula that is always true is $x \vee \neg x$, one that is always false is $x \wedge \neg x$. The former is called a *tautology* and denoted by $\top$, the latter a *contradiction* and denoted by $\bot$. Deciding whether a formula is a tautology (or deciding whether it is a contradiction) is, like SATISFIABILITY, an important problem in computational complexity theory.

One way of determining upon the truth of a particular instantiation, or deciding whether there is a satisfying instance, is by constructing a truth table. Another powerful method is by *inference*. For example, from "it rains" and "if it rains, I don't go to the beach" you can infer "I don't go to the beach." This inference rule was already known in Ancient Greece as the *Modus Podens* rule, formally denoted as $r, r \rightarrow \neg b \vdash \neg b$, where $\vdash$ means "proves" or "can be derived from." It basically says that one can derive the right hand side of $\vdash$ from the left hand side. There are other inference rules, like the following:

$r, q \vdash (r \wedge q)$	(conjunction introduction)
$r \vdash (r \vee q)$	(disjunction introduction)
$r \rightarrow q, q \rightarrow r \vdash (r \leftrightarrow q)$	(biconditional introduction)
$\neg\neg r \vdash r$	(double negation)
$p \rightarrow q \vdash \neg q \rightarrow \neg p$	(transposition)
$p \rightarrow q \vdash p \vee \neg q$	(material implication)
$p \rightarrow q, q \rightarrow r \vdash p \rightarrow r$	(hypothetical syllogism)

A minimal set of inference rules, from which we can derive others, is called an *axiom system*. Such axiom systems can be used to infer the consequences that can be derived from a knowledge base.

A.5 Probabilities

Bayesian networks are seen by some as the most significant contribution to AI in the last 20 years. An example to motivate this claim is the Turing award (the computer science equivalent of the Nobel Prize) that was awarded in 2011 to Judea Pearl who is widely recognized as the "father" of Bayesian networks. Practical applications of Bayesian networks are in, for example, spam filtering, speech recognition, robotics, forensics, decision support systems, and many others. In recent years, however, these networks have also become very popular as computational models of various cognitive capacities (such as intention recognition, visual perception, recipient design, theory of mind, and many others). Lastly, Bayesian networks found an application as computational-level theories of information processing in the brain (e.g., in the predictive processing account).

In this part of the Appendix we will introduce some basic concepts and definitions from probability theory and Bayesian networks. We will cover the following topics:

1. Interpretation of probabilities (frequentist or subjective)
2. Priors, posteriors, joint distribution, marginal distribution, conditional distribution
3. Conditional independence
4. Bayesian networks

More background can be found in Pearl (1988), in Jensen and Nielsen (2007), or in the relevant chapters of AI textbooks like *AI: A Modern Approach* by Russell and Norvig or *Artificial Intelligence* by Poole and Mackworth.

A.5.1 Interpretation of Probabilities

What does it mean to say that: "The probability $\Pr(A = true)$ is 0.4"? How should we interpret this probability? There are two views on that: the frequentist and the subjective or Bayesian view. In the *frequentist* approach the semantics of $\Pr(A = true) = 0.4$ are as follows: "If the process that generates A is repeated very often, the outcome *true* would appear approximately 4 out of every 10 times." This is synonymous with "The relative frequency of $A = true$ is 0.4." Note that this is a constrained view on probabilities: It is limited to processes that can be repeated in principle infinitely often. The *Bayesian* or *subjective* approach includes the frequentist view, but it is broader. The semantics of $\Pr(A = true) = 0.4$ are: "The subjective degree of belief that one has in the event that A is true, based on all the available information (including, but not limited to, knowledge about relative frequencies) is 0.4."

Note that "subjective" in this definition is not synonymous to "arbitrary" or "ungrounded!" All of the following events have a meaning in the Bayesian interpretation:

1. Throwing heads with a fair coin
2. Throwing heads with a coin which is not known to be fair
3. Throwing heads with a coin which is known not to be fair
4. Reverend Green killed Dr. Black with the dagger.
5. The sun will rise tomorrow.
6. It will rain next weekend.

Note that only the probability of the first example can be expressed in the frequentist approach as we have ample experience with throwing fair coins and thus we know by experience the relative frequency of throwing heads. The second and third example cannot be expressed in probability distributions as we cannot currently assign a probability to the event due to our ignorance. We can do so in the Bayesian reading as we have no reason in either case to favor heads over tails, making the subjective probability of the event 0.5. The last three examples refer to events that have no interpretation in terms of repeatable events (there will be only one murder on Dr. Black and only one tomorrow).

An intuitive notion of "subjective" makes it analogous to "within-subject": According to the information available to the *subject*, rather than objective frequencies in the world. For example, a die may fall with one of the six sides on top. When you observe a partially occluded die your probability distribution over which side is up may be different from mine, if I see the unobstructed die from a different angle.

A.5.2 Priors, Posteriors, Joint/Marginal/Conditional Distributions

The prior and posterior probability of a random variable (e.g., the outcome of a die) only make sense when these notions are used *relative to an event*. For example, the prior probability of the outcome is $\Pr(\text{outcome} = x) = 1/6$ for $1 \leq x \leq 6$. The posterior probability of this random variable after observing the partially occluded die may be $\Pr(\text{outcome} = x) = 1/3$ for $x = 4, 5, 6$ (see Figure A.7).

A *joint probability distribution* describes the probability distribution over the Cartesian product of multiple random variables. One can envision this as a Venn diagram (see Section A.2). In Figure A.8 the light gray area refers to the probability that B is *true*. The middle gray area refers to the probability that A

Figure A.7   Prior and posterior probability of a die throw.

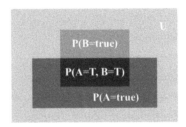

Figure A.8   In this example, we assume that $Pr(A = true) = 0.3$,
$Pr(B = true) = 0.16$, and $Pr(A = true, B = true) = 0.08$; these
distributions are visualized in a Venn diagram.

is *true*; the intersection of both (the dark gray area) is where both A and B are *true*.

Stop and Think

How would you visualize $Pr(A = false)$, $Pr(B = false)$, $Pr(A = true, B = false)$, $Pr(A = false, B = true)$, and $Pr(A = false, B = false)$ in the previous Venn diagram? Note that probability distributions always add up to 1.

A *conditional probability distribution* describes the distribution of a random variable, *given* a particular state of another (set of) variable(s). For example, $Pr(A = true \mid B = true)$ describes the probability that $Pr(A = true)$ given that we know that $Pr(B = true)$. It can be visualized using the Venn diagram above by "shrinking" the universe to the area where B is *true*. Mathematically, it can be computed using the definition $Pr(A \mid B) = \frac{Pr(A, B)}{Pr(B)}$, in this case, $Pr(A = true \mid B = true) = \frac{Pr(A=true, B=true)}{Pr(B=true)} = 0.08/0.16 = 1/2$. Note that conditional probability distributions also add up to one, and keep in mind that in this case the distribution is defined *over* A, such that $Pr(A = true \mid B = true) + Pr(A = false \mid B = true) = 1$. Note that $\{Pr(A = true \mid B = true), Pr(A = true \mid B = false)\}$ does *not* define a proba-

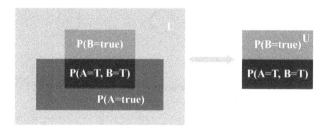

Figure A.9   Conditioning on $B = true$ by shrinking the universe to the area where B is *true*.

bility distribution and thus the sum $\Pr(A = true \mid B = true) + \Pr(A = true \mid B = false)$ can be larger than 1.

> ────────── **Stop and Think** ──────────
>
> Try to visualize $\Pr(A = true \mid B = false)$ in the earlier Venn diagram and estimate this conditional probability.

A.5.3   Conditional Independence

Two variables A and B are independent (notation $A \perp\!\!\!\perp B$) if knowing the outcome of B does not give you any information on the outcome of A and vice versa. For example, when first throwing a coin (random variable A) and then a die (random variable B) we may assume that the outcomes are independent of each other. When $A \perp\!\!\!\perp B$ all of the following holds: $\Pr(A, B) = \Pr(A) \times \Pr(B)$, $\Pr(A \mid B) = \Pr(A)$, and $\Pr(B \mid A) = \Pr(B)$. If you need to compute whether $A \perp\!\!\!\perp B$ or not ($A \not\!\perp\!\!\!\perp B$) you can use either of these equations and check whether they hold *for all values of A and B*.

> ────────── **Stop and Think** ──────────
>
> Assume that we need to throw five coins, and that the coin flips are independent. How can we use this information to efficiently represent the joint probability distribution over the outcomes?

From these equations it holds that $\Pr(C_1, \ldots C_5) = \Pr(C_1) \times \ldots \times \Pr(C_5)$ and more in general that $\Pr(C_1, \ldots, C_n) = \prod_{i=1\ldots n} \Pr(C_i)$. This allows you to represent the joint probability concisely, rather than using 2^n probabilities.

However, this independence condition is often too strong as an assumption. A usually more appropriate assumption is *conditional independence*. Two variables A and B are conditionally independent given a third variable C

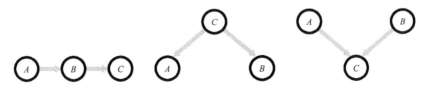

Figure A.10   Causal chain, common cause, and common effect.

(notation $A \perp\!\!\!\perp B|C$) if knowing C already tells me everything about A and information about B does not influence A any more (or A and B reversed in the previous sentence as independence is symmetrical). When $A \perp\!\!\!\perp B|C$ all of the following holds: $\Pr(A, B \mid C) = \Pr(A \mid C) \times \Pr(B \mid C)$, $\Pr(A \mid B, C) = \Pr(A \mid C)$, and $\Pr(B \mid A, C) = \Pr(B \mid C)$. There are two typical situations where A and B are conditionally independent given C: if A, C, and B are in a "causal chain" (B depends on C and C depends on A) and when C is a "common cause" of both A and B (both are dependent on C). Interestingly, if A and B have C as a common effect (i.e., C depends on both) then A and B are independent ($A \perp\!\!\!\perp B$), but they are conditionally dependent on C ($A \not\perp\!\!\!\perp B|C$).

A.5.4   Bayesian Networks

A Bayesian network $\mathcal{B} = (G_{\mathcal{B}}, \Pr_{\mathcal{B}})$ is a graphical structure that models a set of stochastic variables, the conditional independences among these variables, and a joint probability distribution over these variables. $\mathcal{B}$ includes a directed acyclic graph $G_{\mathcal{B}} = (V, A)$, modeling the variables and conditional independences in the network, and a set of conditional probability tables (CPTs) $\Pr_{\mathcal{B}}$ capturing the stochastic dependences between the variables. The network models a joint probability distribution $\Pr(V) = \prod_{i=1}^{n} \Pr(V_i \mid \pi(V_i))$ over its variables, where $\pi(V_i)$ denotes the parents of V_i in $G_{\mathcal{B}}$. By convention, we use upper case letters to denote individual nodes in the network, upper case bold letters to denote sets of nodes, lower case letters to denote value assignments to nodes, and lower case bold letters to denote joint value assignments to sets of nodes. We use the notation $\Omega(V_i)$ to denote the set of values that V_i can take. Likewise, $\Omega(V)$ denotes the set of joint value assignments to the set of variables V. A simple example of a Bayesian network, consisting of a graph and associated probabilities, is given in Figure A.11. This network, adapted from Pearl (1988) and Cooper (1984), captures some fictitious and incomplete medical knowledge related to metastatic cancer. The presence of metastatic cancer (modelled by the node MC) typically induces the development of a brain tumor (B), and an increased level of serum calcium (ISC). The latter can

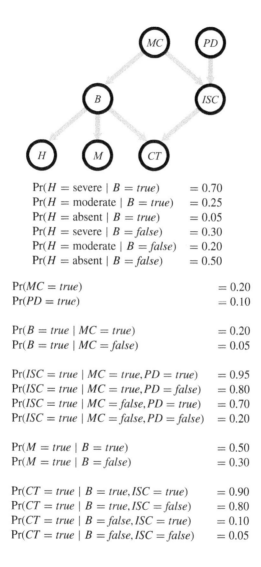

$$\Pr(H = \text{severe} \mid B = \text{true}) \quad = 0.70$$
$$\Pr(H = \text{moderate} \mid B = \text{true}) \quad = 0.25$$
$$\Pr(H = \text{absent} \mid B = \text{true}) \quad = 0.05$$
$$\Pr(H = \text{severe} \mid B = \text{false}) \quad = 0.30$$
$$\Pr(H = \text{moderate} \mid B = \text{false}) \quad = 0.20$$
$$\Pr(H = \text{absent} \mid B = \text{false}) \quad = 0.50$$

$$\Pr(MC = \text{true}) \quad = 0.20$$
$$\Pr(PD = \text{true}) \quad = 0.10$$

$$\Pr(B = \text{true} \mid MC = \text{true}) \quad = 0.20$$
$$\Pr(B = \text{true} \mid MC = \text{false}) \quad = 0.05$$

$$\Pr(ISC = \text{true} \mid MC = \text{true}, PD = \text{true}) \quad = 0.95$$
$$\Pr(ISC = \text{true} \mid MC = \text{true}, PD = \text{false}) \quad = 0.80$$
$$\Pr(ISC = \text{true} \mid MC = \text{false}, PD = \text{true}) \quad = 0.70$$
$$\Pr(ISC = \text{true} \mid MC = \text{false}, PD = \text{false}) \quad = 0.20$$

$$\Pr(M = \text{true} \mid B = \text{true}) \quad = 0.50$$
$$\Pr(M = \text{true} \mid B = \text{false}) \quad = 0.30$$

$$\Pr(CT = \text{true} \mid B = \text{true}, ISC = \text{true}) \quad = 0.90$$
$$\Pr(CT = \text{true} \mid B = \text{true}, ISC = \text{false}) \quad = 0.80$$
$$\Pr(CT = \text{true} \mid B = \text{false}, ISC = \text{true}) \quad = 0.10$$
$$\Pr(CT = \text{true} \mid B = \text{false}, ISC = \text{false}) \quad = 0.05$$

Figure A.11   The *Brain Tumor* network with its conditional probability distributions. Reprinted from Kwisthout (2011a).

also be caused by Paget's disease (*PD*). A brain tumor is likely to increase the severity of headaches (*H*). Long-term memory (*M*) is probably also impaired. Furthermore, it is likely that a CT-scan (*CT*) of the head will reveal a tumor if it is present.

A.6   Miscellaneous Topics

In this final section we provide for some useful mathematical notations and definitions that are relevant for computer science, for example, in computing or bounding running times in algorithms or proof constructs. The canonical reference here is the first volume of Knuth's *The Art of Computer Programming* (1968) where you can find anything you ever wanted to know, and more, on this topic.

A.6.1   Floors and Ceilings

Floors and ceilings are useful constructs for computing (exact) bounds on running times, relative to an input of size n. For any real number x, we define $\lfloor x \rfloor$ to be the *largest* whole number that is *smaller* than or equal to x. Likewise, we define $\lceil x \rceil$ to be the *smallest* whole number that is *larger* than or equal to x. We have that $x - 1 < \lfloor x \rfloor \le x \le \lceil x \rceil < x + 1$. If n is an even number, then we have that $\lceil n/2 \rceil = \lfloor n/2 \rfloor = n/2$; for odd n, we have that $\lceil n/2 \rceil = {}^{n+1}/2$ but $\lfloor n/2 \rfloor = {}^{n-1}/2$. For *any* integer number n we thus have that $\lceil n/2 \rceil + \lfloor n/2 \rfloor = n$. Another useful property of floors and ceilings, when dealing with logarithms, is that $\lceil \log_2(n + 1) \rceil = \lfloor \log_2 n \rfloor + 1$.

A.6.2   Factorials and Permutations

How many different itineraries can we find between five cities? We start at any one out of five places, than we have four options left to go to, then three options, two, and finally there is only one unvisited place left. For the product $5 \times 4 \times 3 \times 2 \times 1$ we introduce the shorthand notation 5! (pronounced as "five factorial") and we set $0! = 1!$ by definition, such that $n!$ is defined over all of the natural numbers. Since $n! < n^n$ we have that $n! = O(n^n)$.

Let us assume we can choose not only the order of the cities we visit, but also the cities themselves. How many different itineraries of five cities out of ten candidates are there? We have ten options for the first city, nine for the second, eight for the third, seven for the fourth and six for the final city; or, in general, $n(n - 1)(n - 2) \cdots (n - k + 1) = \frac{n!}{(n-k)!}$ options. Note that for every set of k cities there are $k!$ different itineraries (see previous), which means that the number of ways we can choose k cities from n candidates (ignoring the order) is $\frac{n!}{k!(n-k)!}$. This is an important formula that describes the *number of k-permutations* from a set of n elements. This is often noted as $\binom{n}{k}$ and the numbers thus generated for n and k are known as the *binomial coefficients*.

Stop and Think

Check that $\binom{n}{k} = \binom{n}{n-k}$. What does this mean in practice?

There are just as many ways to pick k elements from a set of n as there are ways to "not pick" k elements from a set of n. The binomial coefficients are maximal for $k = \lceil n/2 \rceil$.

A.6.3   Series

How much time would it take to add up all the integers from 1 to 100? Quite some time if you do so by hand; a German headmaster in the eighteenth century thought it was a good way of keeping his pupils busy for some while. And so it might have been, were it not for the presence of the then 8-year old Carl Gauss who found the answer 5,050 within seconds, by quickly reordering the series to $1 + 100 + 2 + 99 + \cdots + 50 + 51$ which equals $50 \times (100 + 1) = 5050$. Or at least so the story goes, as Gauss is attributed with the formula for computing the summation of the first n natural numbers.

We here list several of these so-called *series* that are useful for computing effective running time of algorithms with iterative constructs such as **while** and **for** loops. We use the notation $\sum_{i=1}^{n} a_i$ as a shorthand for $a_1 + a_2 + \ldots a_n$, where $\sum_{i=1}^{n} a_i = 0$ by definition for $n = 0$.

$$\sum_{i=1}^{n} i \qquad\qquad = 1/2 n(n+1) \qquad\qquad\qquad\qquad\qquad \text{(arithmetic series)}$$

$$\sum_{i=1}^{n} i^2 \qquad\qquad = \frac{n(n+1)(2n+1)}{6} = 1/3 n^3 + 1/2 n^2 + 1/6 n \quad \text{(sums of squares)}$$

$$\sum_{i=1}^{n} 2^i \qquad\qquad = 2^{n+1} - 1 \qquad\qquad\qquad\qquad\qquad\quad \text{(exponential series)}$$

$$\sum_{i=1}^{n} a_i - a_{i-1} \quad = a_n - a_0 \qquad\qquad\qquad\qquad\qquad\quad\ \ \text{(telescoping series)}$$

Appendix B List of Computational Problems

In this appendix, we will give a list in alphabetical order by problem name of all decision and solution problems cited in the main text; this includes decision problems associated with parameterized problems cited in the main text.

3SAT
Input: A set of Boolean variables $U = \{u_1, \ldots, u_n\}$ and a set of clauses $C = \{c_1, \ldots, c_m\}$, where each clause has exactly three literals.
Question: Is there a truth assignment $t: U \rightarrow \{true, false\}$ such that all clauses C are satisfied?

3D MATCHING
Input: Three disjoint sets X, Y, and Z; set T of triples (x, y, z) such that $x \in X$, $y \in Y$, and $z \in Z$, natural number k.
Question: Is there a k-sized three-dimensional matching M of the elements of X, Y, and Z? (Here, a three-dimensional matching is a subset $M \subseteq T$ such that for every two elements $(x_1, y_1, z_1), (x_2, y_2, z_2) \in M$ we have that $x_1 \neq x_2$, $y_1 \neq y_2$, and $z_1 \neq z_2$).

∃∀-SATISFIABILITY
Input: A Boolean (proposition-logical) formula ϕ with n variables $x_1 \ldots x_k, x_{k+1} \ldots x_n$ (where $k < n$).
Question: Is there a truth assignment to $x_1 \ldots x_k$ such that any truth assignment to $x_{k+1} \ldots x_n$ satisfies ϕ?

ADDITIVE SUBSET CHOICE
Input: A set $V = \{x_1, x_2, \ldots, x_n\}$ of n available items. For every item $x \in V$ there is an associated integer value $u(x)$.
Output: A subset $A \subseteq V$, such that $u(A) = \sum_{x \in A} u(x)$ is maximum.

ANNOTATED COHERENCE

Input: A belief network $N = (P,C)$ where P denotes a set of propositions, and $C = C^- \cup C^+ \subseteq P \times P$ denotes a set of positive and negative constraints, with $C^+ \cap C^- = \emptyset$. Each constraint $(p,q) \in C$ has a weight $w(p,q) \geq 0$. For some $p \in P' \subseteq P$ the truth value has already been predetermined, as specified by a function $A: P' \to \{true, false\}$.

Output: A truth assignment $T: P \to \{true, false\}$ such that $A(p) = T(p)$ for all $p \in P'$ and $COH(T) = \sum_{(p,q)\in C^+, T(p)=T(q)} w(p,q) + \sum_{(p,q)\in C^-, T(p)\neq T(q)} w(p,q)$ is maximized.

BINARY SUBSET CHOICE

Input: A set $V = \{x_1, x_2, \ldots, x_n\}$ of n available items. For every item $x \in V$ there is an associated integer value $u(x)$ and for every pair of items (x_i, x_j) there is an associated integer value $\delta(x_i, x_j)$.

Output: A subset $A \subseteq V$, such that $u(A) = \sum_{x\in A} u(x) + \sum_{x,y\in A} \delta(x,y)$ is maximum.

BUDGET SUBSET CHOICE

Input: A set $V = \{x_1, x_2, \ldots, x_n\}$ of n available items and an integer m. For every item $x \in V$ there is an associated integer value $c(x)$ that defines the cost of x.

Output: A subset $S \subseteq V$ of size $|S| \geq m$, such that $c(S) = \sum_{x\in S} c(x)$ is minimum.

BUDGET CHECK

Input: A set of cities. For each pair of cities, a and b, there is a cost associated with travel from a to b. Further, there is a budget constraint B, and a suggested itinerary It.

Question: Is the travel cost of the suggested itinerary within budget B?

CLIQUE

Input: A graph $G = (V, E)$ and an integer k.

Question: Does there exist a clique $V' \subset V$ such that $|V'| > k$? (Here a vertex set V' is called a *clique* if for all two vertices $u, v \in V'$ there is an edge $(u, v) \in E$).

CLIQUE CONFIGURATION
Input: A graph G and positive integers k, l, and d.
Question: Does G contain a set C of at most k l-cliques such that each clique in C is connected by edges to at most d other l-cliques in C and each l-clique in G is either in C or connected by an edge from one of its vertices to a vertex of an l-CLIQUE in C?

CLUSTERING
Input: A set X with n elements, an integer distance measure $d(x, y)$ for $x, y \in X$, and integers c and k.
Question: Is there a partition of X into k clusters $C_1, \ldots, C_k$ such that the sum of all *total cluster distances* is smaller than or equal to c? (Here, a *total cluster distance* of a cluster C_i is defined as the sum of all pairwise distances $d(x, y)$ for all $x, y \in C_i$).

CNF-SAT
Input: A set of Boolean variables $U = \{u_1, \ldots, u_n\}$ and a set of clauses $C = \{c_1, \ldots, c_m\}$.
Question: Is there a truth assignment $t: U \rightarrow \{true, false\}$ such that all clauses C are satisfied?

CNF-UNSAT
Input: A set of Boolean variables $U = \{u_1, \ldots, u_n\}$ and a set of clauses $C = \{c_1, \ldots, c_m\}$.
Question: Are there no truth assignments $t: U \rightarrow \{true, false\}$ such that all clauses C are satisfied?

CO-INDEPENDENT SET
Input: A graph $G = (V, E)$ and an integer k.
Question: Does there NOT exist an independent set $V' \subseteq V$ such that $|V'| \geq k$? (Here a vertex set V' is called an *independent set* if there exists no two vertices $u, v \in V'$ such that $(u, v) \in E$).

CO-MINIMUM SPANNING TREE
Input: An edge-weighted graph $G = (V, E)$ and an integer w.
Question: Does every spanning tree T of G have weight exceeding w?

COHERENCE
Input: A network $N = (P, C)$, where $C = C^+ \cup C^-$ is a set of positive and negative constraints and $C^+ \cap C^- = \emptyset$
Output: A truth assignment $T: P \rightarrow \{true, false\}$ that satisfies a maximum number of constraints in C.

COHERENCE ON CONSISTENT NETWORKS
Input: A *consistent* belief network $N = (P, C)$ where P denotes a set of propositions and $C = C^- \cup C^+ \subseteq P \times P$ denotes a set of positive and negative constraints, with $C^+ \cap C^- = \emptyset$. Each constraint $(p, q) \in C$ has a weight $w(p, q) \geq 0$.
Output: A truth assignment $T: P \rightarrow \{true, false\}$, such that $COH(T) = \sum_{(p,q) \in C^+, T(p) = T(q)} w(p, q) + \sum_{(p,q) \in C^-, T(p) \neq T(q)} w(p, q)$ is maximized.

CONNECTED COHERENCE
Input: A connected network $N = (P, C)$, where $C = C^+ \cup C^-$ is a set of positive and negative constraints and $C^+ \cap C^- = \emptyset$, and a positive integer s.
Question: Does there exist a truth assignment $T: P \rightarrow \{true, false\}$ that satisfies at least s constraints in C?

CONNECTED MAX CUT
Input: A connected graph $G = (V, E)$ and a positive integer k.
Question: Does there exist a partition of V into sets A and B such that the number of edges in $Cut_G(A, B) \geq k$, where $Cut_G(A, B) = \{(u, v) \in E : u \in A \text{ and } v \in B\}$?

CONSISTENT COHERENCE
Input: A network $N = (P, C)$, where $C = C^+ \cup C^-$ is a set of positive and negative constraints and $C^+ \cap C^- = \emptyset$.
Question: Does there exist a truth assignment $T: P \rightarrow \{true, false\}$ that satisfies all constraints in C? (Here a constraint $(p, q) \in C^+$ is *satisfied* if $T(p) = T(q)$ and a constraint $(p, q) \in C^-$ is *satisfied* if $T(p) \neq T(q)$).

CONSTRAINT SATISFACTION
Input: A set of variables $V = \{V_1, \ldots, V_n\}$, a set $D = \{D_1, \ldots, D_n\}$ of domains of V (describing the values that each variable can take), and a set $C = \{C_1, \ldots, C_m\}$ of constraints. Each constraint c_j is a pair (V_j, R_j), where $V_j \subseteq V$ is a subset of k variables in V and R_j is a k-ary relation on the corresponding domains $D_j \subseteq D$.
Question: Is there a value assignment $t : V_i \to d \in D_i$ for each $V_i \in V$ and $D_i \in D$ such that every constraint $C_j \in C$ is satisfied?

DFA INTERSECTION
Input: A set $D = \{d_1, \ldots, d_k\}$ of deterministic finite-state automata (DFA), each of which has a most $|Q|$ states and operates over a common alphabet Σ, and a positive integer l.
Question: Is there a string over Σ of length l that is accepted by every DFA in D?

DISCRIMINATING COHERENCE
Input: A set of observations (or data) D, a set of hypotheses H and a set of constraints $C = C^- \cup C^+ \subseteq (D \cup H) \times (D \cup H)$, with $C^- \cap C^+ = \emptyset$. Each $d \in D$ has a weight $w_D(d) \geq 0$ and each $(p, q) \in C$ has a weight $w(p, q) > 0$.
Output: A truth assignment $T : H \cup D \to \{true, false\}$ such that $COH(T) = \sum_{(p,q) \in C^+, T(p) = T(q)} w(p, q) + \sum_{(p,q) \in C^-, T(p) \neq T(q)} w(p, q) + \sum_{d \in D, T(d) = true} w_D(d)$ is maximized.

DOMINATING SET
Input: A graph $G = (V, E)$ and an integer k.
Question: Does there exist a dominating set $V' \subseteq V$ such that $|V'| \leq k$? (Here a vertex set V' is called a *dominating set* if for every vertex $v \in V'$ we have $v \in V'$ or there is a neighbor u of v such that $u \in V'$; here a vertex u is a *neighbor* of v if $(u, v) \in E$).

EDGE BIPARTIZATION
Input: An graph $G = (V, E)$ and a positive integer k.
Question: Does there exist a partition of V into sets A and B such that the number of edges in $\text{Bipartization}_G(A, B) \leq k$? (Here $\text{Bipartization}_G(A, B) = \{(u, v) \in E : u, v \in A \text{ or } u, v \in B\}$).

FOUNDATIONAL COHERENCE
Input: A set of observations (or data) D, a set of hypotheses H, and a set of constraints $C = C^- \cup C^+ \subseteq (D \cup H) \times (D \cup H)$, with $C^- \cap C^+ = \emptyset$. Each $(p,q) \in C$ has a weight $w(p,q)$, such that $0 \leq w(p,q) \leq w_{max}$, and positive integers w_{max} and s.
Question: Does there exist a truth assignment $T : H \cup D \to \{true, false\}$, with $T(d) = true$ for all $d \in D$, such that $COH(T) = \sum_{(p,q) \in C^+, T(p)=T(q)} w(p,q) + \sum_{(p,q) \in C^-, T(p) \neq T(q)} w(p,q) \geq s$?

FP ANTI-UNIFICATION
Input: Two terms f and g and a positive integer l, m, and p.
Question: Is there an anti-unifier h containing at least l 0-ary variables and at least m higher arity variables and two substitutions σ and τ using only renamings, fixations, and at most p permutations such that $h \overset{\sigma}{\to} f$ and $h \overset{\tau}{\to} g$?

GENERALIZED CHESS
Input: An $n \times n$ chess board, with an arbitrary number of pieces set on them (but one king each); the normal rules of chess apply save the "50-moves rule."
Question: Does white have a winning strategy that always checkmates black in a finite number of moves?

GRAPH 3-COLORABILITY
Input: A graph $G = (V, E)$.
Question: Is there a 3-coloring of the graph, i.e., an assignment $c : V \to \{c_1, c_2, c_3\}$ such that no vertices that share an edge have the same color?

GRAPH COLORABILITY
Input: A graph $G = (V, E)$, integer k.
Question: Is there a k-coloring of the graph, i.e., an assignment $V \to \{c_1, \ldots, c_k\}$ such that no vertices that share an edge have the same color? See Figure 2.4 for an illustration.

GRAPH ISOMORPHISM
Input: Two graphs G and H.
Question: Is G isomorphic with H?

HAMILTONIAN CIRCUIT
Input: A graph G and a starting node $V \in G$.
Question: Is there a cycle in G, starting and ending in V and visiting every node in G exactly once?

HARMONY MAXIMIZATION
Input: A Hopfield network $G = (V, E, w)$.
Question: An activation pattern $a : V \rightarrow [-1, +1]$ such that $H(a) = \sum_i \sum_{j \neq i} a_i a_j w_{ij}$ is maximized.

HITTING SET
Input: A collection C of subsets of a set S, a positive integer number k.
Question: Does C contain a hitting set S' for S such that $|S'| \leq k$? (Here a set $S' \subseteq S$ is called a *hitting set* of S if S' contains at least one element from every subset in C).

HITTING COVER
Input: A universe U of elements and a collection S of subsets of U; an integer k.
Question: Does U have a hitting set $H \subseteq S$ of size at most k? (Here, a hitting set is a subset of U that contains at least one element of every set in S).

HYPERGRAPH SUBSET CHOICE
Input: A weighted hypergraph $H = (V, E)$, with $E \subseteq \bigcup_{2 \leq h \leq |V|} V^h$. For every $x \in V$ there is a weight $u(x) \in \mathbb{Z}$ and a positive integer p.
Question: Does there exist a subset $A \subseteq V$ such that $u(A) = \sum_{x \in A} u(x) + \sum_{e \in E_H(A)} \Delta(e) \geq p$?

INDEPENDENT SET
Input: A graph $G = (V, E)$ and an integer k.
Question: Does there exist an independent set $V' \subseteq V$ such that $|V'| \geq k$? (Here a vertex set V' is called an *independent set* if there exists no two vertices $u, v \in V'$ such that $(u, v) \in E$).

INTENTION RECOGNITION
Input: A Bayesian network $\mathcal{B} = (G_\mathcal{B} = (V_\mathcal{B}, A_\mathcal{B}), \text{Pr}_\mathcal{B})$, similar as in the RECIPIENT DESIGN network, a value assignment **a** for **A**, and a value assignment **s** for **S** encoding the observed actions and states.
Output: The most probable value assignment $\mathbf{g}_C$ to the communicative goals $\mathbf{G}_C$, i.e., $\text{argmax}_{\mathbf{g}} \text{Pr}(\mathbf{G}_C = \mathbf{g}_C \mid \mathbf{S} = \mathbf{s}, \mathbf{A} = \mathbf{a})$, or $\varnothing$ if $\text{Pr}(\mathbf{G}_C = \mathbf{g}_C \mid \mathbf{S} = \mathbf{s}, \mathbf{A} = \mathbf{a}) = 0$ for all possible values for $\mathbf{G}_C$.

INTEGER FACTORIZATION
Input: An integer N and an integer M such that $1 < M < N$.
Question: Does N have a factor d with $1 < d \le M$?

ISA-RELEVANT VARIABLE
Input: A Boolean formula ϕ with n variables, describing the characteristic function $\mathbf{1}_\phi : \{false, true\}^n \to \{1, 0\}$, designated variable $x_r \in \phi$. (Here, the characteristic function $\mathbf{1}_\phi$ of a Boolean formula ϕ maps truth assignments to ϕ to $\{0, 1\}$, such that $\mathbf{1}_\phi(x) = 1$ if and only if x denotes a satisfying truth assignment to ϕ, and 0 otherwise).
Question: Is x_r a relevant variable in ϕ; that is, is $\mathbf{1}_\phi(x_r = true) \ne \mathbf{1}_\phi(x_r = false)$?

KERNEL
Input: A directed graph $G = (V, A)$ and a positive integer k.
Question: Does there exist a kernel in G of size k? (Here a vertex set $V' \subseteq V$ is called a *kernel* if V' is an independent set in G and for all $v \in V - V'$, there exists a $v' \in V'$ such that $(v', v) \in A$).

KNAPSACK
Input: A set of n elements $A = \{a_1, \dots, a_n\}$, a positive integer $c(a)$ ("cost") and a positive integer $w(a)$ ("weight") associated with each $a \in A$, and integers C and W.
Question: Is there a subset $A' \subset A$ such that $\sum_{a \in A'} c(a) \ge C$, yet $\sum_{a \in A'} w(a) \le W$?

LONGEST COMMON SUBSEQUENCE
Input: A set of strings $S = \{s_1, s_2, \dots, m\}$ of maximum length n over an alphabet Σ and a a positive integer l.
Question: Is there a string of length l that is a subsequence of every string in S?

MAJSAT
Input: A Boolean formula ϕ with n variables.
Question: Does the majority of truth assignments (i.e., at least $1/2 + 1/2^n$ truth assignments) satisfy ϕ?

MAX CUT
Input: A weighted graph $G = (V, E)$ where a weight w_{ij} is associated with each edge $(i, j) \in E$; an integer W.
Question: Is there a cut S of G with weight W? (Here a *cut* S of a graph G is a subset $S \subseteq V$, and the weight of this cut is defined as $\sum_{i \in S, j \notin S} w(i, j)$).

MIN CUT
Input: An edge-weighted graph $G = (V, E)$, with for each edge $(u, v) \in E$ there is an associated positive integer weight $w(u, v)$, and a positive integer k. Further, there are two special vertices, called source $s \in V$ and sink $t \in V$.
Output: A partition of V into sets A and B, with $s \in A$ and $t \in B$, such that the total weight of the edges in $\mathrm{Cut}_G(A, B)$ is minimum.

MINIMUM SET COVER
Input: A universe U of elements and a collection S of subsets of U; an integer k.
Question: Does U have a set cover $C \subseteq S$ of size at most k? (Here, a set cover is a subset of the collection such that the union of the sets in C equals U).

MINIMUM SPANNING TREE
Input: An edge-weighted graph $G = (V, E)$.
Output: A spanning tree T of G such that the sum of the weights on the edges in T is minimum.

MOST PROBABLE EXPLANATION (MPE)
Input: A Bayesian network $\mathcal{B} = (G_{\mathcal{B}} = (V_{\mathcal{B}}, A_{\mathcal{B}}), \Pr_{\mathcal{B}})$, where $V_{\mathcal{B}}$ is partitioned into a set of evidence nodes $\mathbf{E}$ and an explanation set $\mathbf{M}$, such that $\mathbf{E} \cup \mathbf{M} = V_{\mathcal{B}}$. Further, a joint value assignment $\mathbf{e}$ and $0 \leq q < 1$.
Question: Does there exist a joint value assignment $\mathbf{m}$ to the nodes in $\mathbf{M}$ given evidence $\mathbf{e}$ such that $\Pr(\mathbf{m}, \mathbf{e}) > q$?

MULTI-PROCESSES SCHEDULING
Input: A finite set A of tasks, a length $l(a)$ for each $a \in A$, a number m of processors, and a deadline D. All numbers are positive integers.
Question: Is there a partition $A = A_1 \cup A_2 \cup \ldots \cup A_m$ of A into m disjoint sets such that $\max \left\{ \sum_{a \in A_i} l(a) : 1 \leq i \leq m \right\} \leq D$?

PARTIAL MAXIMUM A-POSTERIORI PROBABILITY
Input: A Bayesian network $\mathcal{B} = (G_\mathcal{B} = (V_\mathcal{B}, A_\mathcal{B}), \Pr_\mathcal{B})$, where $V_\mathcal{B}$ is partitioned into a set of evidence nodes **E**, a set of intermediate nodes $\mathbf{I} \neq \varnothing$, and an explanation set **M**, such that $\mathbf{E} \cup \mathbf{I} \cup \mathbf{M} = \mathbf{V}$. Additionally, a joint value assignment **e** and $0 \leq q < 1$.
Question: Does there exist a joint value assignment **m** to the nodes in **M** given evidence **e** with $\Pr(\mathbf{m}, \mathbf{e}) > q$?

PARTITION
Input: A set of n elements $A = \{a_1, \ldots, a_n\}$ and a positive integer $s(a)$ associated with each $a \in A$.
Question: Is there a subset $A' \subset A$ such that $\sum_{a \in A'} s(a) = \sum_{a \in A \setminus A'} s(a)$?

RECIPIENT DESIGN
Input: A Bayesian network $\mathcal{B} = (G_\mathcal{B} = (V_\mathcal{B}, A_\mathcal{B}), \Pr_\mathcal{B})$, a value assignment $\mathbf{g_I}$ for $\mathbf{G_I}$, and a value assignment $\mathbf{g_C}$ for $\mathbf{G_C}$ encoding the communicator's goals. Where $\mathbf{S}, \mathbf{A}, \mathbf{G_I}, \mathbf{G_C} \in G_\mathcal{B}$; the probabilistic dependencies in N are illustrated in Figure 12.2; and $\Pr_\mathcal{B}$ is an arbitrary conditional probability distribution over $G_\mathcal{B}$.
Output: A value assignment **a** to **A**, such that $\mathbf{a} = \text{argmax}_\mathbf{a} \Pr(\mathbf{A} = \mathbf{a} \mid \mathbf{G_I} = \mathbf{g_I})$ and Intention Recognition$(\mathcal{B}, \mathbf{a}, \mathbf{s}) = \mathbf{g_C}$, or $\varnothing$ if no sequence of actions **a** is possible. (Here $\mathbf{s} = \text{argmax}_\mathbf{s} \Pr(\mathbf{S} = \mathbf{s} \mid \mathbf{A} = \mathbf{a})$; i.e., the most likely states **s** to follow from the actions).

SATISFIABILITY
Input: A Boolean (proposition-logical) formula ϕ with n variables $x_1 \ldots x_n$.
Question: Is there a truth assignment to $x_1 \ldots x_n$ that satisfies ϕ?

SET PACKING
Input: A finite family of sets $S = \{S_1, \ldots, S_n\}$ and a positive integer k.
Question: Is there a subset $S' \subseteq S$ of size k such that for all $S'_i, S'_j \in S'$, $S'_i \cap S'_j = \varnothing$?

l-SIMPLE PATH NUMBER
Input: A graph G in which each vertex has degree 3, a pair of vertices u and v in G, and positive integers k and l.
Parameter: l
Question: Is the number of simple paths of length $\leq l$ between u and v in G at most k?

SORTING
Input: A list L of numbers.
Output: An ordering of the numbers in L from small to large.

SPANNING TREE
Input: A graph $G = (V, E)$.
Output: A spanning tree T of G. (Here a *spanning tree* is a connected acyclic graph that contains all vertices in V and only edges from E).

STEINER GRAPH
Input: A graph $G = (V, E)$, a subset $S \subseteq V$, and a positive integer k.
Question: Is there a subset $T \subseteq V - S$ of size k such that the subgraph of G composed of the vertices in $S \cup T$ and all edges in G connecting these vertices is connected?

STEINER TREE IN GRAPHS
Input: A weighted undirected graph $G = (V, E)$, a subset $V' \subseteq V$, and an integer l.
Question: Is there a subtree $T = (V_T, E_T)$ of G such that $V' \subseteq V_T$ with total weight $w(E_T) < l$?

STRUCTURE-MAPPING ANALOGY DERIVATION (SMAD)
Input: Concept graphs B and T and a positive integer k.
Question: Is there an analogy morphism $A(B, T)$ between B and T such that $syst(A(B, T)) \geq k$?

SUBGRAPH ISOMORPHISM
Input: Two graphs G and H.
Question: Is there a subgraph G' of G that is isomorphic with H? (Here two graphs G' and H are isomorphic if there is a mapping $m : V(G') \rightarrow V(H)$ such that $(u, v) \in E(G') \leftrightarrow (m(u), m(v)) \in E(H)$).

SUBSET SUM
Input: A set of n elements $A = \{a_1, \ldots, a_n\}$, a positive integer $s(a)$ associated with each $a \in A$, and an integer k.
Question: Is there a subset $A' \subset A$ such that $\sum_{a \in A'} s(a) = k$?

THREE DIVISORS
Input: A natural number n.
Question: Does n have at least three divisors other than 1 and n itself?

TRAVELING SALESPERSON
Input: A set of n cities $C = \{c_1, c_2, \ldots, c_n\}$ with pairwise cost associated with travel between $c_i, c_j \in C$ and a budget B.
Question: Does there exist a tour that visits every city such that the total cost is at most B?

UN-SATISFIABILITY
Input: A Boolean (proposition-logical) formula ϕ with n variables $x_1 \ldots x_n$.
Question: Is there *no* truth assignment to $x_1 \ldots x_n$ that satisfies ϕ?

VERTEX COVER
Input: A graph $G = (V, E)$ and a positive integer k.
Question: Does there exist a vertex cover $V' \subseteq V$ such that $|V'| \le k$? (Here a vertex set V' is called a *vertex cover* if for every edge $(u, v) \in E$ we have $u \in V'$ or $v \in V'$).

VERTEX DEGREE (decision)
Input: A graph $G = (V, E)$ and an integer k.
Question: Does there exist a vertex $v \in V$ such that the degree of v is at least k?

WEIGHTED COHERENCE
Input: A graph $N = (P, C)$, with $C = C^- \cup C^+$ and $C^- \cap C^+ = \emptyset$, a positive weight $w(p, q) > 0$ for each $(p, q) \in C$, and positive integers c.
Question: Is there a partition of P into accepted A and rejected R vertices such that the total weight of satisfied constraints $\sum_{(p,q) \in S(p,q)} w(p,q) \ge c$ and the total weight of unsatisfied constraints $\sum_{(p,q) \in (C^+ \cup C^-) - S(p,q)} w(p,q) \le i$? (Here the set of satisfied constraints is defined by $S(p,q) = \{(p,q) \in C^+ | p, q \in A \text{ or } p, q \in R\} \cup \{(p,q) \in C^- | p \in A \text{ and } q \in R\}$).

WEIGHTED MAX CUT

Input: A weighted graph $G = (V, E)$ where a weight w_{ij} is associated with each edge $(i, j) \in E$; an integer W.

Question: Is there a *cut* S of G with weight W? (Here a *cut* S of a graph G is a subset $S \subseteq V$, and the weight of this cut is defined as $\sum_{i \in S, j \notin S} w(i, j)$).

MAX CUT

Input: An graph $G = (V, E)$ and a positive integer k.

Parameter: k

Question: Does there exist a partition of V into sets A and B such that the number of edges in $\text{Cut}_G(A, B) \geq k$, where $\text{Cut}_G(A, B) = \{(u, v) \in E : u \in A \text{ and } v \in B\}$?

Appendix C Compendium of Complexity Results

In this appendix we present a compendium of existing complexity results for computational-level theories in the cognitive science literature. The computational-level theories that we consider together span all the major modeling frameworks in cognitive science, including symbolic, neural network, probabilistic (Bayesian), dynamical, logic, robotic, and heuristic models of cognition. The purpose of this compendium is to give the reader a quick overview of the variety of computational-level theories for which computational complexity analyses have already been performed so far. It may also serve to highlight relationships between computational-level theories–in terms of the mathematical component structures and complexity results–in otherwise disparate cognitive domains.

C.1   How to Use This Compendium

Following Garey and Johnson (1979), this compendium should be treated not as an encyclopedia containing all known complexity results but rather as an annotated structured bibliography providing an entry into the literature. We provide three classification schemes to facilitate navigation of the compendium: We label each computational problem by (1) the mathematical constructs used in the formalism, (2) one or more cognitive subdomains for which the problem is relevant, and (3) one or more cognitive science modeling frameworks in which the problem may be situated. We provide the first classification to support the creative process of coming up with reduction proofs. For instance, if you are trying to prove that your Bayesian theory is NP-hard, you may find inspiration by looking up existing proofs for other Bayesian theories and observe that they can be reduced from graph problems (say CLIQUE) or logic problems (say 3SAT). This may give you ideas on how to construct an analogous reduction for your own theory from a problem in those mathematical domains. We provide the second classification for researchers interested in particular cognitive domains and the third classification for those researchers specifically interested in particular modeling frameworks. Importantly, our classification into cognitive domains and modeling frameworks should not be taken as strict. We realize that there is no consensus in cognitive science on how to "carve up" cognition and clearly formal modeling frameworks are not mutually exclusive. We have merely chosen classifications in a way that we think may be helpful for readers to situate the listed computational-level problems in the broader field of cognitive science.

Table C.1 presents an overview of the computational problems included in this compendium and their information relative to the three classifications. Following the table, you will find a complete list of computational problems in alphabetical order. For each entry, we include the following information: problem names and definitions, remarks if applicable, classifications, classical complexity results, and parameterized complexity results if applicable. You can also find an overview of the reductions that prove NP-hardness for the computational problems in this compendium in Figure C.1.

Table C.1: Overview of the computational-level theories in this compendium with relevant classifications.

Computational-level theory	Math domains	Cognitive domains	Modeling frameworks
ABDUCTION IN PROPOSITIONAL LOGIC	Proposition formulas Set	Reasoning	Logic Symbolic
BAYESIAN INFERENCE	Graph Value function Function optimization	Domain general	Bayesian
BAYESIAN INVERSE PLANNING (MULTIPLE GOALS)	Graph Value function Function optimization	Social cognition	Bayesian
BAYESIAN STRUCTURE LEARNING	Graph Probabilities Function optimization	Learning Domain general	Bayesian Symbolic

Computational-level theory	Math domains	Cognitive domains	Modeling framework
BOTTOM-UP VISUAL MATCHING	Matrix Value function Function optimization	Perception Vision	n/a
DYNAMIC BELIEF UPDATE	Proposition formulas Modal logic formulas Dynamic epistemic logic formulas	Reasoning Social cognition	Symbolic Logic
EXEMPLAR RETRIEVAL	Graph Value function Structure matching	Memory Analogy Problem solving	Symbolic Structure-Mapping Theory (SMT)
FP ANTI-UNIFICATION	Proposition formulas Anti-unification	Analogy Learning	Symbolic Logic
GENERALIZATION CREATION	Graph Value function Structure matching	Analogy Learning	Symbolic SMT
GENERALIZATION MODIFICATION	Graph Value function Structure matching	Analogy Learning	Symbolic SMT
HARMONY MAXIMIZATION	Graph Value function Function optimization	Domain general	Connectionist Dynamical
HYPERGRAPH SUBSET CHOICE	Set Value function Function optimization	Decision-making	n/a

Computational-level theory	Math domains	Cognitive domains	Modeling framework
LEXICAL DECODING (T)	Sequence Automaton Grammar Other	Language	Symbolic
LEXICAL ENCODING (T)	Sequence Automaton Grammar Other	Language	Symbolic
MINIMUM LEXICOGRAPHIC INCOMPATABILITY	Set Value function Other	Decision-making Learning	Symbolic Heuristic
MULTI-DIMENSIONAL GENERALIZED MOVER	Euclidean space Polyhedron Sequence	Planning Motor control	Symbolic Robotic
NEURAL NETWORK LOADING	Graph Value function Function optimization	Learning Domain general	Connectionist Dynamical
OBJECT CATEGORIZATION	Set Value function Function optimization	Categorization Perception	n/a
PARTIAL MAXIMUM A-POSTERIORI PROBABILITY	Graph Probabilities Function optimization	Domain general	Bayesian Symbolic
PREDICTIVE PROCESSING ACTIVE INFERENCE	Graph Probabilities Function optimization	Action Domain general	Bayesian Symbolic
PREDICTIVE PROCESSING BELIEF REVISION	Graph Probabilities Function optimization	Inference Domain general	Bayesian Symbolic

Computational-level theory	Math domains	Cognitive domains	Modeling framework
PREDICTIVE PROCESSING BELIEF UPDATING	Graph Probabilities Function optimization	Inference Domain general	Bayesian Symbolic
PREDICTIVE PROCESSING PREDICTION	Graph Probabilities Function optimization	Domain general	Bayesian Symbolic
PROBLEM SOLVING UNDER EXTENDED REPRESENTATION CHANGE THEORY (ERCT)	Graph Value function Other	Problem solving Insight	Symbolic
PROJECTION DERIVATION	Graph Structure matching	Analogy Reasoning	Symbolic SMT
REACTIVE CONTROL ADAPTATION	Automaton Other	Control Learning	Robotic
RECIPIENT DESIGN and INTENTION RECOGNITION	Graph Value function Function optimization	Social cognition	Bayesian
REPRESENTATIONAL DISTORTION	Sequence Boolean circuits	Similarity	Symbolic
STRIPS PLANNING	Rule Other	Planning Problem solving	Symbolic Robotic
STRUCTURE-MAPPING ANALOGY DERIVATION	Graph Value function Structure matching	Analogy	Symbolic SMT
TOOLBOX ADAPTATION	Matrix Value function Function optimization	Decision-making Learning	Symbolic Heuristic

Computational-level theory	Math domains	Cognitive domains	Modeling framework
TOOLBOX RE-ADAPTATION	Matrix Value function Function optimization	Decision-making Learning	Symbolic Heuristic
WEIGHTED COHERENCE	Graph Proposition formulas Value function Function optimization	Perception Reasoning Judgment Analogy	Symbolic Connectionist

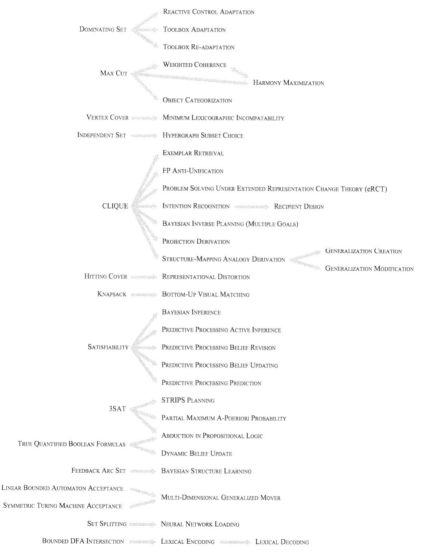

Figure C.1   Overview of the polynomial-time reductions for computational problems in the compendium. These reductions prove NP-hardness for the computational problems they reduce to.

C.2   List of Computational-Level Theories with Complexity Results

ABDUCTION IN PROPOSITIONAL LOGIC
Input: An abduction instance $\mathcal{P} = \langle V, H, M, T \rangle$ consisting of a set V of variables, a set $H \subseteq V$ of hypotheses, a set $M \subseteq V$ of manifestations, and a theory T that is a propositional formula of type $\mathcal{C}$.
Question: Is there a solution $S \subseteq H$ for $\mathcal{P}$, i.e., a set $S \subseteq H$ such that $T \cup S$ is consistent and $T \cup S \models M$?

Math domains: Propositional formulas, Set
Cognitive domains: Reasoning
Modeling framework: Symbolic, Logic

Classical complexity: NP-hard by reduction from a restricted variant of TRUE QUANTIFIED BOOLEAN FORMULAS (Eiter and Gottlob, 1995). Is NP-hard when $\mathcal{C}$ is restricted to Horn formulae, by reduction from PATH WITH FORBIDDEN PAIRS (Selman and Levesque, 1990) or 3SAT (de Haan, 2016). Is NP-hard when $\mathcal{C}$ is restricted to Krom formulae (Nordh and Zanuttini, 2008). (See the introduction of Fellows et al. [2012] and references for more details.)

Parameterized complexity: Fixed-parameter tractability and intractability results are known for a number of parameter sets when $\mathcal{C}$ is restricted to Horn, definite Horn, and Krom formulae; see Fellows et al. (2012) for details.

BAYESIAN INFERENCE
Input: A Bayesian network $\mathcal{B} = (G_\mathcal{B}, \text{Pr}_\mathcal{B})$ with directed acyclic graph $G_\mathcal{B} = (V, A)$ and set of conditional probability tables $\text{Pr}_\mathcal{B}$; a set of query variables $H \subset V$ and a non-overlapping set of evidence variables $E \subset V$, joint value assignment h to the variables in H, joint value assignment e to the variables in E, rational number q.
Question: Is $\text{Pr}(H = h \mid E = e) > q$?

Math domains: Graph, Value function, Function optimization
Cognitive domains: Domain general
Modeling framework: Bayesian

Remarks: In this formulation BAYESIAN INFERENCE is not known, or expected, to be in NP. The problem variant where q is not part of the input but fixed to 0 is NP-complete. Approximating BAYESIAN INFERENCE by an arbitrary fixed additive or relative number is NP-hard as well (Cooper, 1990).

Classical complexity: The original NP-hardness result (Cooper, 1990) uses a reduction from 3SAT to obtain specific non-approximability results; other results can be obtained by reducing from SATISFIABILITY (Kwisthout, 2009, 2011b).

Parameterized complexity: The following parameters have been considered:

- The number of hypothesis variables ($|H|$)
- The number of evidence variables ($|E|$)
- The number of intermediate variables ($|I| = |V| - |E| - |H|$)
- The maximal indegree of the variables (i)
- The cardinality (maximum number of values) of the variables (c)
- The treewidth of (the moralized graph of) $G_\mathcal{B}$ (tw)
- The threshold probability (q)

BAYESIAN INFERENCE is fixed-parameter intractable relative to parameter set $\{c, i, |H|, |E|, q\}$ (Kwisthout, 2011b) and fixed-parameter tractable relative to parameter sets $\{|H|, c, tw\}$ (Lauritzen and Spiegelhalter, 1988) and $\{|H|, c, |I|\}$ (Pearl, 1988).

BAYESIAN INVERSE PLANNING (MULTIPLE GOALS)

Input: A Bayesian network $\mathcal{B} = (G_\mathcal{B} = (V_\mathcal{B}, A_\mathcal{B}), \text{Pr}_\mathcal{B})$, a value assignment **a** for **A**, a value assignment **s** for **S** encoding the observed actions and states, and $0 \leq q < 1$. Here, $\mathbf{S}, \mathbf{A}, \mathbf{G} \subseteq V_\mathcal{B}$ and the structure of $\mathcal{B}$ is based on a Markov Decision Process.

Question: Does there exist a joint value assignment **g** to all goal variables in **G** given $\mathbf{s} \cup \mathbf{a}$, such that $\text{Pr}(\mathbf{g}, \mathbf{s}, \mathbf{a}) > q$?

Math domains: Graph, Value function, Function optimization
Cognitive domains: Social cognition
Modeling framework: Bayesian

Remarks: The structure of the Bayesian network $\mathcal{B}$ is similar to the structure of the network in RECIPIENT DESIGN and INTENTION RECOGNITION. The main difference between these two networks is that RECIPIENT DESIGN and INTENTION RECOGNITION networks have goals that are not inferred (the instrumental goals), whereas BAYESIAN INVERSE PLANNING (MULTIPLE GOALS) only has one type of goal (viz., action goals) that are all inferred. See Chapter 12 for more details on RECIPIENT DESIGN and INTENTION RECOGNITION and see Blokpoel et al. (2013) for the full definition of BAYESIAN INVERSE PLANNING (MULTIPLE GOALS).

Classical complexity: NP-hardness by reduction from CLIQUE (Blokpoel et al., 2013).

Parameterized complexity: The following parameters have been considered:

- The number of goals ($|\mathbf{G}|$)
- The number of observed or planned actions ($|\mathbf{A}|$)
- One minus the probability of the most likely joint value assignment to **G** ($1 - p$)
- The maximum cardinality of any goal variable (g)

It was shown that BAYESIAN INVERSE PLANNING (MULTIPLE GOALS) is fixed-parameter tractable relative to the following two parameter sets: $\{g, |\mathbf{G}|\}$ and $\{g, 1 - p\}$. It was also shown that BAYESIAN INVERSE PLANNING (MULTIPLE GOALS) is fixed-parameter intractable relative to parameter sets $\{g, |\mathbf{A}|\}$, $\{|\mathbf{G}|, |\mathbf{A}|\}$ by reduction from k-CLIQUE (Blokpoel et al., 2013).

BAYESIAN STRUCTURE LEARNING
Input: A local score function $f(v \in V, A = V \setminus \{v\})$ defined on a set V of variables, rational number q.
Question: Is there a directed acyclic graph D such that $\sum_{v \in V} f(v, P_D(v)) > q$? Here, $P_D(v)$ denotes the parents of v in D.

Math domains: Graph, Probabilities, Function optimization
Cognitive domains: Learning, Domain general
Modeling framework: Bayesian, Symbolic

Remarks: f can be in principle any function that scores a specific Bayesian network, which is an elementary operation in structure learning, including common scoring functions like BIC or AIC.

Classical complexity: NP-hardness by a reduction from FEEDBACK ARC SET (Chickering, 1996).

Parameterized complexity: The following parameter has been considered: the treewidth of the super-structure $G'(V, E_f)$ of f *(tw)*. Here a super-structure is the graph with nodes V containing an edge between any two nodes u and v if and only if u is a candidate parent of v considered by f.

BAYESIAN STRUCTURE LEARNING is fixed-parameter tractable for parameter *tw* (Ordyniak and Szeider, 2012).

BOTTOM-UP VISUAL MATCHING
Input: An image I, a target T, and positive integers θ and ϕ. Each pixel $p \in I$ has associated values diff(p) and corr(p) (values have fixed precision ϵ)
Question: Does there exist a subset of pixels $I' \subseteq I$ such that $\sum_{p \in I'}$diff(p) $\leq \theta$ and $\sum_{p \in I'}$corr(p) $\geq \phi$, where the functions diff(p) and corr(p) are defined as

$$\text{diff}(p) = \sum_{p \in I'} \left(\sum_{j \in M_i} |t_{x,y,j} - i_{x,y,j}| \right) \tag{C.1}$$

and

$$\text{corr}(p) = \sum_{p \in I'} \left(\sum_{j \in M_t} |t_{x,y,j} \times i_{x,y,j}| \right), \tag{C.2}$$

M_i and M_t denote the sets of measurement types in the image and target, respectively (e.g., color, brightness, motion, depth), $i_{x,y,j}$ denotes the value of pixel $p \in I$ with coordinates x and y for measurement type $j \in M_i$, and $t_{x,y,j}$ denotes the value of pixel $p \in T$ for measurement type $j \in M_t$.

Math domains: Set, Value function, Function optimization
Cognitive domains: Vision, Perception
Modeling framework: n/a

Classical complexity: NP-hard by reduction from KNAPSACK (Tsotsos, 1989, 1990).

Parameterized complexity: Parameterized analyses were performed by van Rooij (2003) relative to parameters θ and λ, where λ is the smallest integer such that $i_{x,y,j} \leq \lambda$. Using an algorithm proposed in Kube (1991), it was shown that this problem is fixed-parameter tractable relative to parameter sets $\{\theta\}$ and $\{\lambda\}$.

DYNAMIC BELIEF UPDATE

Input: A set P of propositional formulas, a set A of agents, an initial situation $(\mathcal{M}_0, W_d)$ where $\mathcal{M}_0 = (W, V, R)$ is an epistemic model, an applicable sequence $(\mathcal{E}_1, E_1), \ldots, (\mathcal{E}_u, E_u)$ of events where $\mathcal{E}_j = (E, Q, pre, post)$ is an event model, and a formula $\varphi \in \mathcal{L}_B$.

Question: Is φ true in the final updated model, i.e., does $(\mathcal{M}_0, W_d) \otimes (\mathcal{E}_1, E_1) \otimes \cdots \otimes (\mathcal{E}_u, E_u) \models \varphi$?

Math domains: Propositional formulas, Modal logic formulas, Dynamic epistemic logic formulas

Cognitive domains: Reasoning, Social cognition

Modeling framework: Symbolic, Logic

Remarks: This problem is a special case of DEL MODEL CHECKING. Aucher and Schwarzentruber (2013) and van Eijck and Schwarzentruber (2014) showed PSPACE-completeness for DEL MODEL CHECKING in the unrestricted case. Bolander, Jensen, and Schwarzentruber (2015) show PSPACE-completeness for a special case that is similar to DYNAMIC BELIEF UPDATE. van de Pol, van Rooij, and Szymanik (2018) show PSPACE-completeness for the special case of DYNAMIC BELIEF UPDATE restricted to single-pointed S5 models.

Classical complexity: PSPACE-hard by reduction from TRUE QUANTIFIED BOOLEAN FORMULAS (van de Pol et al., 2018).

Parameterized complexity: The following parameters have been considered:

- The number of agents
- The maximum size of the preconditions
- The maximum number of events in the event models
- The size of the formula
- The model depth of the formula
- The number of propositional variables in P
- The number of event models, i.e., the number of updates

A number of fixed-parameter intractability and tractability results were derived relative to subsets of these parameters; see section 4.4 and figure 24 of van de Pol et al. (2018) for details.

EXEMPLAR RETRIEVAL

Input: A library L of concept-graphs, a probe concept-graph P, and integers b and k.

Question: If L' is the largest possible subset of L of size $\leq b$ such that each member of L' has an optimal analogy-morphism with P of value that is the largest possible over the values of all optimal analogy-morphisms between P and members of L, is L' of size $\leq k$?

Math domains: Graph, Value function, Structure matching
Cognitive domains: Memory, Analogy, Problem solving
Modeling framework: Symbolic, SMT

Remarks: This problem is a formalization of the memory retrieval problem solved in a heuristic fashion by the MAC/FAC system Forbus, Gentner, and Law (1994). As such, it is the first stage of the model of analogical problem solving given in Wareham, Evans, and van Rooij (2011a).

Classical complexity: NP-hard by reduction from CLIQUE (Wareham et al., 2011a).

Parameterized complexity: The following parameters have been considered:

- The size of largest solved exemplar in L ($|B|$)
- The size of P ($|T|$)
- The maximum number of predicates in L and P (p)
- The maximum number of objects in L and P (0)
- The maximum order of predicates in L and P (h)
- The maximum number of arguments per predicate in L and P (a)
- The maximum frequency of a given predicate in L and P (f)
- The maximum number of predicate-types in L and P (t)
- The number of solved exemplars in library L ($|L|$)
- The maximum number of returned solved exemplars (b)

It was shown that EXEMPLAR RETRIEVAL is fixed-parameter intractable relative to the parameter sets $\{|B|, h, a, t, |L|, b\}$, $\{|T|, h, a, t, |L|, b\}$, and $\{h, a, f, b\}$ and fixed-parameter tractable relative to the parameter sets $\{o\}$, $\{p\}$, $\{f, t\}$, $\{|B|, f\}$, and $\{|T|, f\}$.

FP ANTI-UNIFICATION

Input: Two terms f and g and a positive integers l, m, and p.

Question: Is there an anti-unifier h containing at least l 0-ary variables and at least m higher arity variables and two substitutions σ and τ using only renamings, fixations, and at most p permutations such that $h \xrightarrow{\sigma} f$ and $h \xrightarrow{\tau} g$?

Math domains: Propositional formulas, Anti-unification
Cognitive domains: Analogy, Learning
Modeling framework: Symbolic, Logic

Remarks: This problem is one of the subcomputations postulated in Heuristic-Driven Theory Projection (HDTP) Schwering et al. (2009). HDTP is a logic-based theory of analogy derivation which focuses on the role of analogies as generalizations of given pairs of concepts.

Classical complexity: NP-hard by reduction from CLIQUE (Robere and Besold, 2012).

Parameterized complexity: The following parameters have been considered:

- The maximum size of the anti-unifier h ($|h|$)
- The maximum number of permutations (p)
- The maximum arity (r)
- The maximum number of subterms of the input term (s)

It was shown that FP ANTI-UNIFICATION is fixed-parameter intractable relative to parameter set $\{|h|, p\}$ and fixed-parameter tractable relative to parameter set $\{s, p, r\}$. Results are also known for related anti-unification problems as well as problems encoding other processes within HDTP; see Robere and Besold (2012) for details.

GENERALIZATION CREATION

Input: A set E of predicate-structures, a number $q \in [0,1]$, and numbers $s, n,$ and v.

Question: A (q,s,n,v)-generalization system (G,S) for E, if such a generalization system exists, and special symbol $\perp$ otherwise, where a (q,s,n,v)-generalization system (G,S) for E is a pair of sets G and S of predicate-structures such that:

1. for each $g \in G$, $v \leq syst(g,g)$,
2. for each $g \in G$, $size(g) \leq n$, and $|G| + |S| \leq s$,
3. for all $x, y \in G \cup S$ such that $x \neq y$, $syst(x,y)/\min$ $(syst(x,x), syst(y,y)) < q$,
4. for all $e \in E$, either $e \in S$ or there is at least one $g \in G$ such that $syst(g,e)/$ $\min(syst(x,x), syst(y,y)) \geq q$.

Math domains: Graph, Value function, Structure matching
Cognitive domains: Analogy, Learning
Modeling framework: Symbolic, SMT

Remarks: This problem (given in Wareham and van Rooij, 2011) is a formalization of the analogy-based generalization-set induction problem solved in a heuristic manner by the SEQL system Kuehne et al. (2000).

Classical complexity: NP-hard by reduction from STRUCTURE-MAPPING ANALOGY DERIVATION (Wareham and van Rooij, 2011).

Parameterized complexity: The following parameters have been considered:

- The maximum number of objects in any $e \in E$ (o)
- The maximum frequency of any predicate in any $e \in E$ (f)
- The maximum number of predicate-types in any $e \in E$ (t)
- The maximum size of any $g \in G$ (n)

It was shown that GENERALIZATION CREATION is fixed-parameter intractable relative to parameter set $\{o, f, t, n\}$.

GENERALIZATION MODIFICATION

Input: A (q,s,n,v)-generalization system $GS = (G,S)$ and a predicate-structure $e \notin G \cup S$.

Question: A (q,s,n,v)-generalization system (G',S') for $E = G \cup S \cup \{e\}$, if such a generalization system exists, and special symbol $\perp$ otherwise.

Math domains: Graph, Value function, Structure matching
Cognitive domains: Analogy, Learning
Modeling framework: Symbolic, SMT

Remarks: This problem (given in Wareham and van Rooij, 2011) is a variant of GENERALIZATION CREATION in which a given generalization-set is modified in response to the addition of a new concept (rather than the generalization-set being induced in one go from a given set of concepts as in GENERALIZATION CREATION).

Classical complexity: NP-hard by reduction from STRUCTURE-MAPPING ANALOGY DERIVATION (Wareham and van Rooij, 2011).

Parameterized complexity: The following parameters have been considered:

- The maximum frequency of any predicate in any $x \in G \cup S$ (f)
- The maximum number of predicate-types in any $x \in G \cup S$ (t)
- The maximum size of any $g \in G$ (n)

It was shown that this problem fixed-parameter intractable relative to parameter sets $\{t,n\}$ and $\{f\}$.

HARMONY MAXIMIZATION
Input: A Hopfield network $G = (V, E, w)$.
Question: An activation pattern $a \colon V \rightarrow [-1, +1]$ such that $H(a) = \sum_i \sum_{j \neq i} a_i a_j w_{ij}$ is maximized.

Math domains: Graph, Value function, Structure matching
Cognitive domains: Domain general
Modeling framework: Connectionist, Dynamical

Remarks: The problem was also studied by Bruck and Goodman (1990) who showed that even if the networks' convergence is allowed to take exponential rather than polynomial time, the networks cannot approximate the solution to the optimization version of HARMONY MAXIMIZATION (unless NP = co-NP).

Classical complexity: NP-hard by reduction from MAX CUT (Thagard and Verbeurgt, 1998) and WEIGHTED COHERENCE (van Rooij and Wareham, 2012). The version of this problem that allows for asymmetric Hopfield networks was shown NP-hard by reduction from INDEPENDENT SET (Xu, Hu, and Kwong, 1996).

HYPERGRAPH SUBSET CHOICE
Input: A weighted hypergraph $H = (V, E)$, with $E \subseteq \bigcup_{2 \leq h \leq |V|} V^h$. For every $x \in V$ there is a weight $u(x) \in \mathcal{Z}$ and a positive integer p.
Question: Does there exist a subset $A \subseteq V$ such that $u(A) = \sum_{x \in A} u(x) + \sum_{e \in E_H(A)} \Delta(e) \geq p$?

Math domains: Set, Value function, Function optimization
Cognitive domains: Decision-making
Modeling framework: n/a

Remarks: The binary case we have referred to as Binary Subset Choice throughout this book, but corresponds to what (van Rooij, Stege, and Kadlec, 2005) call Graph Subset Choice (i.e., the $h = 2$ case of Hypergraph Subset Choice).

Classical complexity: NP-hard by reduction from INDEPENDENT SET, both for the general h-ary and the binary special case.

Parameterized complexity: The following parameters have been considered:

- The threshold value of the chosen set (p)
- The threshold value of the rejected set ($q = u(S) - u(V)$)
- The maximum utility of an item (u_{max})
- The minimum utility of an item (u_{min})
- The maximum interaction value (Δ_{max})
- The maximum interaction value (Δ_{min})

The problem is known to be W[1]-hard for parameter p. Fixed-parameter tractability and intractability results are known for a number of parameter sets of the parameters listed previously, but only for special cases of the general problem. See section 4.3.1 of van Rooij (2003) for an overview and van Rooij, Stege, and Kadlec (2005) for details.

LEXICAL DECODING (T)
Input: Surface form s, lexicon D, lexical-surface form relation mechanism M of type T.
Question: Set of lexical forms U generated by D from which M can create s.

Math domains: Sequence, Automaton, Grammar, Other
Cognitive domains: Language
Modeling framework: Symbolic

Remarks: This problem (first given in this manner in Ristad, 1990) is a formalization of underlying lexical word-representation inference from a surface form relative to a grammar of type T, i.e., word comprehension under T.

Classical complexity: This problem is NP-hard relative to a variety of grammar-types T, namely, simplified segmental grammars by a reduction from LEXICAL ENCODING (SSG) (Ristad, 1992) and finite-state-transducer based rule systems, two-level morphological systems, constraint-based Declarative Phonology systems, and constraint-based Optimality Theory systems by reductions from LEXICAL ENCODING (FST), LEXICAL ENCODING (2LM), LEXICAL ENCODING (DP), and LEXICAL ENCODING (OT), respectively (Wareham, 1999).

Parameterized complexity: Parameterized analyses have been done relative to a number of parameters characterizing the length and composition of the mental lexical and perceived surface forms as well as the form-transformation systems for all of these problems; see Wareham (1999) for details.

LEXICAL ENCODING (T)
Input: Lexical form u and a lexical-surface form relation mechanism M of type T.
Question: The surface form s created by applying M to u.

Math domains: Sequence, Automaton, Grammar, Other
Cognitive domains: Language
Modeling framework: Symbolic

Remarks: This problem (first given in this manner in Ristad, 1990) is a formalization of surface word-form generation from an underlying lexical representation relative to a grammar of type T, i.e., word generation under T.

Classical complexity: This problem is NP-hard relative to a variety of grammar-types T, namely, simplified segmental grammars (SSG) by a reduction from NON-DETERMINISTIC TURING MACHINE ACCEPTANCE (Ristad, 1992), finite-state-transducer based rule (FST) systems by a reduction from BOUNDED DFA INTERSECTION (Wareham, 1999), two-level morphological (2LM) systems by a reduction from CNF-SAT (Berwick, Barton, and Ristad, 1987), constraint-based Declarative Phonology (DP) systems by a reduction from BOUNDED DFA INTERSECTION (Wareham, 1999), and constraint-based Optimality Theory (OT) systems by reductions from HAMILTONIAN PATH and BOUNDED DFA INTERSECTION, respectively (Eisner, 1997; Wareham, 1999).

Parameterized complexity: Parameterized analyses have been done relative to a number of parameters characterizing the length and composition of the mental lexical and perceived surface forms as well as the form-transformation systems for all of these problems; see Wareham (1999) for details.

MINIMUM LEXICOGRAPHIC INCOMPATABILITY
Input: A set of objects $A = \{a_1, a_2, \ldots a_m\}$ and a set of features $F = \{f_1, f_2, \ldots f_n\}$ such that each object $a \in A$ has associated value $b_i(a) \in \{0, 1\}$ for feature f_i, a complete order $S(A)$ on the objects in A, and a positive integer k.
Question: Is there a permutation $\Pi(F)$ of the features in F such that the LEX algorithm run relative A, F, and $\Pi(F)$ makes at most k incompatible ordering decisions relative to $S(A)$ when run on all pairs of objects in A?

Math domains: Set, Value function, Other
Cognitive domains: Decision-making, Learning
Modeling framework: Symbolic, Heuristic

Remarks: The formulation and notation used in this problem is from van Rooij (2003). Although Martignon and Schmitt (1999) gave a proof sketch of the NP-hardness reduction, van Rooij (2003) presented a worked-out version of the proof. Schmitt and Martignon (2006) adopt a different notation and also present a full proof.

Classical complexity: NP-hard by reduction from VERTEX COVER (Martignon and Schmitt, 1999; Schmitt and Martignon, 2006; van Rooij, 2003).

Parameterized complexity: Parameterized analyses were carried out in van Rooij (2003), where it was shown that this problem is fixed-parameter tractable relative to parameter set $m = |A|$.

MULTI-DIMENSIONAL GENERALIZED MOVER

Input: A set O of obstacle polyhedra, a set P of convex polyhedra which are freely linked together at a set of linkage vertices V such that P has k degrees of freedom of movement, and initial and final positions p_I and p_F of P in d-dimensional Euclidean space.

Question: Is there a legal movement of P from p_I to p_F, i.e., is there a continuous sequence of translation and rotations of the polyhedra in P such that at each point in time, no polyhedron in P intersects any polyhedron in O and the polyhedra in P intersect themselves only at the linkage vertices in V?

Math domains: Eclidean space, Polyhedron, Sequence
Cognitive domains: Planning, Motor control
Modeling framework: Symbolic, Robotic

Remarks: This problem a is a formalization of path planning for a robot P in a d-dimensional environment containing obstacle-set O.

Classical complexity: Polynomial-time solvable when $d \in \{2, 3\}$ *and P is a single rigid polyhedron* (Reif, 1987) but **PSPACE**-hard in general when $d = 2$ by reduction from LINEAR BOUNDED AUTOMATON ACCEPTANCE (Joseph and Plantings, 1985) and $d = 3$ by reduction from SYMMETRIC TURING MACHINE ACCEPTANCE (Reif, 1987).

Parameterized complexity: Parameterized analyses were carried out in Cesati and Wareham (1995) when $d = 3$ relative to the following parameters:

- The number of polyhedra comprising P (p)
- The maximum number of surfaces, lines, or curves needed to define any polyhedron in P (s^P) or the total number of such entities needed to define P (s^t)
- The maximum number of linkage vertices on any polyhedron in P (v^P) or the total number of such vertices in P (v^t)
- The maximum number of degrees of freedom of motion of any polyhedron in P (k^P) or the total number of such degrees for P (k^t)

It was shown that MULTI-DIMENSIONAL GENERALIZED MOVER is fixed-parameter intractable for parameter set $\{p, s^P, s^t, v^P, v^t, k^P, k^t\}$. As $s^P = 1$ in the **NP**-hardness proof in Joseph and Plantings (1985), by Observation 7.3.1, MULTI-DIMENSIONAL GENERALIZED MOVER is fixed-parameter intractable for parameter set $\{s^P\}$.

NEURAL NETWORK LOADING

Input: A set T of training examples on n inputs and positive non-zero integers l and s.

Question: Is there an l-layer neural network N with at most s nodes and an assignment of activation functions to these nodes such that N gives the correct output for each training example in T?

Math domains: Graph, Value function, Function optimization
Cognitive domains: Learning, Domain general
Modeling framework: Connectionist, Dynamical

Classical complexity: NP-hard for arbitrary-size networks with linear threshold activation functions (Judd, 1987), for two-level, three-node networks with linear threshold activation functions by a reduction from SET SPLITTING (Blum and Rivest, 1989), and for two-level, three-node networks with sigmoidal activation functions by a reduction from SET SPLITTING (Šíma, 1996). As sigmoidal activation functions are used in the back propogation neural network training algorithm, the last of these results also implies that loading neural networks using the back propogation algorithm is NP-hard. NEURAL NETWORK LOADING is also NP-hard for various other restricted cases relating to the network topology; see Judd (1988), Šíma (1994), and Šíma and Orponen (2003) for details.

Parameterized complexity: Given that NP-hardness holds when $l = 2$ and $s = 3$ (Blum and Rivest, 1989), by Observation 7.3.1, this implies that NEURAL NETWORK LOADING is fixed-parameter intractable relative to parameter set $\{l, s\}$ when either linear threshold or sigmoidal activation functions are used unless P = NP.

OBJECT CATEGORIZATION

Input: A set of objects A, with for each pair of objects $a, b \in A \times A$ an associated similarity weight $s(a, b)$ and dissimilarity weight $d(a, b)$.

Question: A partition of A into disjoint sets $A_1, A_2, \ldots, A_m$ such that $\sum_{a, b \in A_i} s(a, b) + \sum_{a \in A_i, b \in A_j, i \neq j} d(a, b)$, with $i, j \in \{1, 2, \ldots, m\}$, is maximized.

Math domains: Set, Value function, Function optimization
Cognitive domains: Categorization, Perception
Modeling framework: n/a

Remarks: This problem is a formalization of the psychological hypothesis that basic-level categories are formed so as to maximimize within-category similarity and between-category dissimilarity (Rosch, 1973).

Classical complexity: NP-hard by reduction from MAX CUT (van Rooij and Wareham, 2008).

Parameterized complexity: Given that the NP-hardness reduction works for $m = 2$ (van Rooij and Wareham, 2008), by Observation 7.3.1, this implies that OBJECT CATEGORIZATION is fixed-parameter intractable relative to parameter set $\{m\}$ unless $\mathsf{P} = \mathsf{NP}$.

PARTIAL MAXIMUM A-POSTERIORI PROBABILITY
Input: A Bayesian network $\mathcal{B} = (G_{\mathcal{B}}, \Pr_{\mathcal{B}})$ with directed acyclic graph $G_{\mathcal{B}} = (V, A)$ and set of conditional probability tables $\Pr_{\mathcal{B}}$; a set of query variables $H \subset V$ and a non-overlapping set of evidence variables $E \subset V$, joint value assignment e to the variables in E, rational number q.
Question: Is there a joint value assignment h to the variables in H such that $\Pr(H = h, E = e) > q$?

Math domains: Graph, Probabilities, Function optimization
Cognitive domains: Domain general
Modeling framework: Bayesian, Symbolic

Remarks: The special case of this problem where $H \cup E = V$ is known as MOST PROBABLE EXPLANATION. While MOST PROBABLE EXPLANATION is NP-complete, PARTIAL MAXIMUM A-POSTERIORI PROBABILITY is not known, or expected, to be in NP. Approximating MOST PROBABLE EXPLANATION (and thus also the general problem PARTIAL MAXIMUM A-POSTERIORI PROBABILITY) is NP-hard for each of the following "notions of approximation":

- A joint value assignment h' where either $\Pr(H = h, E = e) - \Pr(H = h', E = e)$ or $\frac{\Pr(H=h, E=e)}{\Pr(H=h', E=e)}$ is bounded by a constant (Abdelbar and Hedetniemi, 1998)
- A joint value assignment h' that differs from h in at most k variables for any $k \geq 1$ (Kwisthout, 2012b)
- A joint value assignment h' that is one of the k most probable explanations for any constant k (Kwisthout, 2015)

Classical complexity: For MOST PROBABLE EXPLANATION, NP-hardness was proven by reduction from 3SAT (Dagum and Luby, 1993). While NP-hardness of PARTIAL MAXIMUM A-POSTERIORI PROBABILITY follows (reduction-by-restriction), Park and Darwiche (2004) show that the problem is significantly harder than MOST PROBABLE EXPLANATION (unless P = NP). The problem of finding the k-th MOST PROBABLE EXPLANATION or k-th PARTIAL MAXIMUM A-POSTERIORI PROBABILITY for a given $k > 1$ is also significantly harder than for $k = 1$ unless P = NP (Kwisthout, Bodlaender, and van der Gaag, 2011a).

Parameterized complexity: The following parameters have been considered:

- The number of hypothesis nodes ($|H|$)
- The number of evidence nodes ($|E|$)
- The number of intermediate variables ($|V| - |E| - |H|$)
- The maximal indegree of the variables (i)
- The cardinality (maximum number of values) of the variables (c)
- The treewidth of (the moralized graph of) G_B (tw)
- The threshold probability (q)
- The total probability of the alternative joint value assignments ($1 - p$)
- The rank of the explanation (k)

Most Probable Explanation is fixed-parameter intractable relative to parameter set $\{c, i, |H|, q\}$ (Kwisthout, 2011b) and fixed-parameter tractable relative to parameter sets $\{c, tw\}$ (Sy, 1992) and $\{c, 1 - p\}$ (Bodlaender, van den Eijkhof, and van der Gaag, 2002). Partial Maximum A-Posteriori Probability is fixed-parameter intractable relative to parameter set $\{c, i, |H|, |E|, q\}$ and fixed-parameter tractable relative to parameter sets $\{c, tw, |I|\}$ and $\{c, 1 - p, |I|\}$ (Kwisthout, 2011b).

PREDICTIVE PROCESSING ACTIVE INFERENCE

Input: A causal Bayesian network $\mathcal{B}$ with designated variable subsets Pred and Hyp, a designated joint value assignment h to Hyp, a probability distribution $\mathrm{Pr}_{(\mathrm{Pred})}$ over Pred, a prediction error $\delta_{(\mathrm{Obs},\mathrm{Pred})}$, and a rational number q. Let A denote the set of intervenable variables in $\mathcal{B}$, depicting the available action repertoire.

Question: Is there a joint value assignment a to A such that the prediction error $\delta_{(\mathrm{Obs},\mathrm{Pred}')} < q$?

Math domains: Graph, Probabilities, Function optimization
Cognitive domains: Action, Domain general
Modeling framework: Bayesian, Symbolic

Remarks: This is the sub-process of decreasing a prediction error by active inference in the Predictive Processing account in neuroscience.

Classical complexity: NP-hardness by a reduction from SATISFIABILITY (Kwisthout and van Rooij, 2018).

Parameterized complexity: The following parameters have been considered:

- The number of hypothesis nodes ($|\mathrm{Hyp}|$)
- The number of prediction nodes ($|\mathrm{Pred}|$)
- The number of intervenable variables ($|A|$)
- The number of intermediate variables ($|\mathrm{Int}| = |V| - |\mathrm{Hyp}| - |\mathrm{Pred}|$)
- The maximal indegree of the variables (i)
- The cardinality (maximum number of values) of the variables (c)
- The treewidth of (the moralized graph of) $G_{\mathcal{B}}$ (tw)

PREDICTIVE PROCESSING BELIEF REVISION is fixed-parameter intractable for parameter set $\{|\mathrm{Hyp}|, |\mathrm{Pred}|, i, c, |A|\}$ and fixed-parameter tractable for parameter sets $\{|\mathrm{Pred}|, tw, c, |A|\}$ and $\{|\mathrm{Pred}|, \mathrm{Int}, c, |A|\}$ (Kwisthout and van Rooij, 2018).

PREDICTIVE PROCESSING BELIEF REVISION

Input: A causal Bayesian network $\mathcal{B}$ with designated variable subsets Pred and Hyp, a designated joint value assignment h to Hyp, a probability distribution $\text{Pr}_{(\text{Pred})}$ over Pred, a prediction error $\delta_{(\text{Obs},\text{Pred})}$, and a rational number q.

Question: Is there a (revised) prior probability distribution $\text{Pr}_{(\text{Hyp})'}$ over Hyp such that the prediction error $\delta_{(\text{Obs},\text{Pred}')} < q$?

Math domains: Graph, Probabilities, Function optimization
Cognitive domains: Inference, Domain general
Modeling framework: Bayesian, Symbolic

Remarks: This is the sub-process of decreasing a prediction error by updating hypothesized causes of observations in the Predictive Processing account in neuroscience.

Classical complexity: NP-hardness by a reduction from SATISFIABILITY (Kwisthout and van Rooij, 2018).

Parameterized complexity: The following parameters have been considered:

- The number of hypothesis nodes ($|\text{Hyp}|$)
- The number of prediction nodes ($|\text{Pred}|$)
- The number of intermediate variables ($|\text{Int}| = |V| - |\text{Hyp}| - |\text{Pred}|$)
- The maximal indegree of the variables (i)
- The cardinality (maximum number of values) of the variables (c)
- The treewidth of (the moralized graph of) $G_{\mathcal{B}}$ (tw)
- The prediction error (pe)

PREDICTIVE PROCESSING BELIEF REVISION is fixed-parameter intractable for parameter set $\{|\text{Hyp}|, |\text{Pred}|, i, c, pe\}$ and fixed-parameter tractable for parameter sets $\{|\text{Pred}|, tw, c\}$ and $\{|\text{Pred}|, \text{Int}, c\}$ (Kwisthout and van Rooij, 2018).

PREDICTIVE PROCESSING BELIEF UPDATING
Input: A causal Bayesian network $\mathcal{B}$ with designated variable subsets Pred and Hyp, a designated joint value assignment h to Hyp, a probability distribution $\text{Pr}_{(\text{Pred})}$ over Pred, a prediction error $\delta_{(\text{Obs}, \text{Pred})}$, and a rational number q.
Question: Is $\sum_p \text{Pr}(\text{Hyp} = h \mid \text{Pred} = p) \times \text{Pr}_{\text{Obs}}(\text{Pred} = p) > q$?

Math domains: Graph, Probabilities, Function optimization
Cognitive domains: Inference, Domain general
Modeling framework: Bayesian, Symbolic

Remarks: This is the sub-process of explaining away a prediction error by belief updating in the Predictive Processing account in neuroscience.

Classical complexity: NP-hardness by a reduction from SATISFIABILITY (Kwisthout and van Rooij, 2018).

Parameterized complexity: The following parameters have been considered:

- The number of hypothesis nodes ($|\text{Hyp}|$)
- The number of prediction nodes ($|\text{Pred}|$)
- The number of intermediate variables ($|\text{Int}| = |V| - |\text{Hyp}| - |\text{Pred}|$)
- The maximal indegree of the variables (i)
- The cardinality (maximum number of values) of the variables (c)
- The treewidth of (the moralized graph of) $G_{\mathcal{B}}$ (tw)

PREDICTIVE PROCESSING BELIEF UPDATING is fixed-parameter intractable for parameter set $\{|\text{Hyp}|, |\text{Pred}|, i, c\}$ and fixed-parameter tractable for parameter sets $\{|\text{Pred}|, tw, c\}$ and $\{|\text{Pred}|, \text{Int}, c\}$ (Kwisthout and van Rooij, 2018).

PREDICTIVE PROCESSING PREDICTION

Input: A causal Bayesian network $\mathcal{B}$ with designated variable subsets Pred and Hyp, current distribution Pr(Hyp) over Hyp, joint value assignment p to Pred; rational number q.

Question: Is Pr(Pred $= p$) $= \sum_{\mathbf{h}}$ Pr(Pred $= p$ | Hyp $= h$) $\times$ Pr(Hyp $= h$) $> q$?

Math domains: Graph, Probabilities, Function optimization
Cognitive domains: Domain general
Modeling framework: Bayesian, Symbolic

Remarks: This is the sub-process of making a prediction in the Predictive Processing account in neuroscience.

Classical complexity: NP-hardness by a reduction from SATISFIABILITY (Kwisthout and van Rooij, 2018).

Parameterized complexity: The following parameters have been considered:

- The number of hypothesis nodes (|Hyp|)
- The number of prediction nodes (|Pred|)
- The number of intermediate variables (|Int| $= |V| - $|Hyp| $- $|Pred|)
- The maximal indegree of the variables (i)
- The cardinality (maximum number of values) of the variables (c)
- The treewidth of (the moralized graph of) $G_{\mathcal{B}}$ (tw)

PREDICTIVE PROCESSING PREDICTION is fixed-parameter intractable for parameter set $\{$|Hyp|, |Pred|$, i, c\}$ and fixed-parameter tractable for parameter sets $\{$|Pred|$, tw, c\}$ and $\{$|Pred|, Int$, c\}$ (Kwisthout and van Rooij, 2018).

PROBLEM SOLVING UNDER EXTENDED REPRESENTATION CHANGE THEORY (ERCT)

Input: Chunk-type set T, search-operator set O, problem representation p with chunk-structure D, constraint-set $C = (C_G, C_O)$, and integers k_C, k_D, and k_S.

Question: Is there a sequence s consisting of the application of $\leq k_C$ constraint relaxation and $\leq k_D$ chunk decomposition operators followed by the application of $\leq k_S$ search operators from O that transforms p into a goal state consistent with C_G?

Math domains: Graph, Value function, Other
Cognitive domains: Problem solving, Insight
Modeling framework: Symbolic

Remarks: This problem (given in Wareham [2017]) is an ideal-case formalization of the Extended Representation Change theory of insight-based problem solving proposed by Öllinger, Jones, and Knoblich (2014).

Classical complexity: NP-hard by reduction from CLIQUE (Wareham, 2017).

Parameterized complexity: The following parameters have been considered:

• The total number of objects and predicates in p ($|p|$)
• The number of chunks in D ($|D|$)
• The total number of constraints in C_G and C_O ($|C|$)
• The number of available search operators ($|O|$)
• The maximum number of Constraint Relaxation restructurings ($|k_C|$)
• The maximum number of Chunk Decomposition restructurings ($|k_D|$)
• The maximum number of search-operator applications ($|k_S|$)
• The maximum number of search-operator application opportunities ($|O_A|$)
• The maximum number of active chunks in a chunk-structure

It was shown that this problem is fixed-parameter intractable relative to parameter sets $\{|C|, |O|, k_C, k_D, k_S\}$ when $k_C = k_D = 0$, $\{|p|, |D|, |C|, k_C, k_D, k_S, |D_A|\}$ when $k_C = k_D = 0$, and $\{|C|, |O|, k_C, k_D, k_S, |O_A|\}$ when $k_C = 0$, and fixed-parameter tractable relative to parameter sets $\{|p|, |D|, |C|, |O|, k_S\}$, $\{|C|, k_D, k_S, |O_A|, |D_A|\}$, and $\{|C|, |O|, k_D, k_S, |D_A|\}$ (Wareham, 2017).

PROJECTION DERIVATION
Input: Two predicate-structures B and T, a subset S of the predicates in B, and positive integers k and d.
Question: Is there a maximal analogy A between B and T and a projection P relative to A and B such that A and P include at least k predicates from S and each such predicate has distance at most d from the common structure of A in B?

Math domains: Graph, Structure mapping
Cognitive domains: Analogy, Reasoning
Modeling framework: Symbolic, SMT

Remarks: This problem (given in Wareham, Evans, and van Rooij, 2011a) formalizes the derivation of the best-possible inferences that can be transferred from a concept B to concept T relative to an analogy between B and T and inference-evaluation criteria described in Forbus et al. (1997).

Classical complexity: NP-hard by reduction from CLIQUE (Wareham, Evans, and van Rooij, 2011a).

Parameterized complexity: The following parameters have been considered:

- Size of B ($|B|$)
- Size of T ($|T|$)
- Maximum number of predicates in B and T (p)
- Maximum number of objects in B and T (o)
- Maximum order of predicates in B and T (h)
- Maximum number of arguments per predicate in B and T (a)
- Maximum frequency of a given predicate in B and T (f)
- Maximum number of predicate-types in B and T (t)
- Size of predicate-set S ($|S|$)
- Minimum number of members of S in the analogy and the projection (k)
- Maximum distance of predicates/objects from the base analogy in the projection (d)

It was shown that this problem is fixed-parameter intractable relative to parameter sets $\{|B|, h, a, t, |S|, k, d\}$, $\{|T|, h, a, t, k, d\}$, and $\{h, a, f, d\}$ and fixed-parameter tractable relative to parameter sets $\{o\}$, $\{p\}$, $\{f, t\}$, $\{|B|, f\}$, and $\{|T|, f\}$.

REACTIVE CONTROL ADAPTATION
Input: A world W, a reactive subsumption architecture A that can only partially perform a task T in W, a library M of layers, and integers s and l.
Question: Is there a reactive subsumption architecture A' derived from A by the addition of at most l layers from M and the addition or deletion of at most s subsumption-links that can perform T in W?

Math domains: Automaton, Other
Cognitive domains: Control, Learning
Modeling framework: Robotic

Classical complexity: NP-hard for point-to-point navigation tasks by a reduction from DOMINATING SET (Wareham et al., 2011b).

Parameterized complexity: The following parameters have been considered:

- The number of distinguishable square-types in world ($|E|$)
- The number of layers in the derived architecture A' ($|L|$)
- The maximum length of layer trigger-formulas (f)
- The maximum number of subsumption-link changes (s)
- The number of layers added to A (l)
- The number of layers in provided library ($|M|$)

For point-to-point navigation tasks, it was shown in Wareham et al. (2011b) that REACTIVE CONTROL ADAPTATION is fixed-parameter intractable relative to parameter sets $\{s, f, l, |M|\}$ and $\{s, f, l, |L|\}$ and fixed-parameter tractable relative to parameter sets $\{|L|, |M|\}$ and $\{|E|\}$.

RECIPIENT DESIGN

Input: A Bayesian network $\mathcal{B} = (G_{\mathcal{B}} = (V_{\mathcal{B}}, A_{\mathcal{B}}), \text{Pr}_{\mathcal{B}})$, a value assignment g_I for G_I and a value assignment g_C for G_C encoding the communicator's goals. Here, $S, A, G_I, G_C \subseteq V_{\mathcal{B}}$. The structure of $\mathcal{B}$ is illustrated in Figure 12.2, and $\text{Pr}_{\mathcal{B}}$ is an arbitrary conditional probability distribution over $G_{\mathcal{B}}$.

Output: A value assignment $\mathbf{a}$ to A, such that $\mathbf{a} = \text{argmax}_{\mathbf{a}} \text{Pr}(A = \mathbf{a} \mid G_I = g_I)$ and Intention Recognition$(\mathcal{B}, \mathbf{a}, \mathbf{s}) = g_C$, or $\varnothing$ if no such sequence of actions $\mathbf{a}$ exists. Here $\mathbf{s} = \text{argmax}_{\mathbf{s}} \text{Pr}(S = \mathbf{s} \mid A = \mathbf{a})$; i.e., the most likely states $\mathbf{s}$ to follow from the actions.

INTENTION RECOGNITION

Input: A Bayesian network $\mathcal{B} = (G_{\mathcal{B}} = (V_{\mathcal{B}}, A_{\mathcal{B}}), \text{Pr}_{\mathcal{B}})$, just as in the RECIPIENT DESIGN network, a value assignment $\mathbf{a}$ for A and a value assignment $\mathbf{s}$ for S encoding the observed actions and states.

Output: The most probable value assignment g_C to the communicative goals G_C, i.e. $\text{argmax}_{\mathbf{g}} \text{Pr}(G_C = g_C \mid S = \mathbf{s}, A = \mathbf{a})$, or $\varnothing$ if $\text{Pr}(G_C = g_C \mid S = \mathbf{s}, A = \mathbf{a}) = 0$ for all possible values for G_C.

Math domains: Graph, Value function, Function optimization
Cognitive domains: Social cognition
Modeling framework: Bayesian

Remarks: For simplicity, the computational-level theories here are specified as optimization problems. The complexity analyses were done relative to the decision versions of these problems, but note that RECIPIENT DESIGN contains the optimization version of INTENTION RECOGNITION as a sub-problem. For more details on this relationship see Chapter 12 (specifically Exercise 12.3.4).

Classical complexity: NP-hardness by a reduction from CLIQUE (van Rooij et al., 2011; Blokpoel et al., 2012).

Parameterized complexity: The following parameters have been considered:

• The number of communicative goals ($|G_C|$)
• The number of instrumental goals ($|G_I|$)
• The number of observed or planned actions ($|A|$)

It was shown that INTENTION RECOGNITION is fixed-parameter tractable relative to parameter set $\{|\mathbf{G_C}|, |\mathbf{G_I}|\}$. It was also shown that INTENTION RECOGNITION is fixed-parameter intractable, relative to parameter sets $\{|\mathbf{G_C}|, |\mathbf{A}|\}$, $\{|\mathbf{G_I}|, |\mathbf{A}|\}$ and the individual parameters by reduction from k-CLIQUE (Blokpoel et al., 2012; van Rooij et al., 2011).

It was shown that RECIPIENT DESIGN is fixed-parameter tractable relative only to parameter set $\{|\mathbf{G_C}|, |\mathbf{G_I}|, |\mathbf{A}|\}$. Note that this parameter set constrains the input size (Blokpoel et al., 2012; van Rooij et al., 2011).

REPRESENTATIONAL DISTORTION

Input: Two representations a and b, a set of basic transformations T, and a positive integer k.

Question: Is the length of a shortest sequence of basic transformations from T transforming a to $b \leq k$?

Math domains: Sequence, Boolean circuits
Cognitive domains: Similarity
Modeling framework: Symbolic

Remarks: This problem is a formalization of the representational-distortion theory of similarity described in Hahn et al. (2003). This problem was formalized in Müller, van Rooij, and Wareham (2009) in terms of Boolean sequences for representations and Boolean circuits for transformations. Several extended formalizations were also given incorporating a contextualized notion of similarity.

Classical complexity: All formalized versions are NP-hard by reduction from HITTING COVER.

Parameterized complexity: Parameterized analyses were carried out relative to the parameters $k, |T|$, $\max(|a|, |b|)$ and $max(|a|, |b|, |i|)$, where $|i|$ is the length of the longest intermediate representation created in transforming a into b. It was shown that REPRESENTATIONAL DISTORTION is fixed-parameter intractable relative to parameter sets $\{|T|, \max(|a|, |b|)\}$ and $\{k, \max(|a|, |b|)\}$ and fixed-parameter tractable relative to parameter sets $\{k, |T|\}$ and $\{\max(|a|, |b|, |i|)\}$. Parameterized analyses were also carried out for contextualized versions of this problem, which incorporated additional parameters encoding aspects of the context. See Müller, van Rooij, and Wareham (2009) for details.

STRIPS PLANNING

Input: A positive integer n, an initial state vector $s \in \{0, 1\}^n$, a goal vector $g \in \{0, 1, *\}^n$, a collection $O = \{o_1, \ldots, o_m\}$ of operators of the form $o_o = (P, Q)$, $P, Q \in \{0, 1, *\}^n$, and a positive integer k.

Question: Is there a sequence of operators of length at most k that, when applied in order to s, produce g?

Math domains: Rule, Other
Cognitive domains: Planning, Problems solving
Modeling framework: Symbolic, Robotic

Remarks: STRIPS stands for "Stanford Research Institute Problem Solver." This problem also formalizes state-space search problem solving encoded in the General Problem Solver (GPS) system (Newell and Simon, 1961).

Classical complexity: Polynomial-time solvable under various restrictions but NP-hard in general by reduction from 3SAT (Bylander, 1994).

Parameterized complexity: The following parameters have been considered:

- The maximum number of preconditions in any operator ($|pre|$)
- The maximum number of postconditions in any operator ($|post|$)
- The length of the operator sequence (k)
- The number of operators (m)

It was shown that STRIPS PLANNING is fixed-parameter intractable for parameter set $\{|pre|, |post|, k\}$ (Downey, Fellows, and Stege, 1999) and fixed-parameter tractable for parameter set $\{k, m\}$ (van Rooij and Wareham, 2008).

STRUCTURE-MAPPING ANALOGY DERIVATION
Input: Predicate-structures B and T and a positive integer k.
Question: Is there an analogy $A(B,T)$ between B and T such that the systematicity of this analogy is $\geq k$?

Math domains: Graph, Value function, Structure mapping
Cognitive domains: Analogy
Modeling framework: Symbolic, SMT

Remarks: This problem formalizes the derivation of analogies under Structure-Mapping Theory (SMT) (Gentner, 1983). A sketched formalization and NP-hardness proof for this problem was first given in Veale and Keane (1997); a full formalization (in terms of concept-graphs for predicate-structures and analogy morphisms for analogies) and NP-hardness proof were subsequently given in van Rooij et al. (2008).

Classical complexity: NP-hard by reduction from CLIQUE.

Parameterized complexity: The following parameters have been considered:

- The maximum size of B or T (n_1)
- The minimum size of B or T (n_2)
- The maximum order of B or T (h)
- The maximum "flatness" of B or T (n/h)
- The maximum number of predicates in B or T (p)
- The maximum number of root predicates in B or T (r)
- The maximum number of non-root predicates in B or T (s)
- The maximum number of objects in B or T (o)
- The maximum frequency of any predicate in B or T (f)
- The maximum number of arguments of any predicate in B or T (a)

It was shown that STRUCTURE-MAPPING ANALOGY DERIVATION is fixed-parameter intractable relative to parameter sets $\{h,a,f,s\}$, $\{n/h\}$ and $\{n_2,r,h,a,p\}$ and fixed-parameter tractable relative to parameter sets $\{n_1\}$ and $\{o\}$. It was subsequently shown (Wareham et al., 2011a) that this problem is also fixed-parameter tractable relative to parameter set $\{p\}$, $\{f,t\}$, $\{n_1,f\}$, and $\{n_2,f\}$, where t is the number of types of predicates in B and T.

TOOLBOX ADAPTATION

Input: An environment $E = (S, A)$, the positive integers $\#h$, $|h|$, and nc denoting the maximum number of heuristics, the maximum size of a heuristic and the maximum number of negative cues in the entire toolbox respectively, and the minimal ecological rationality $er_{min} \in [0, 1]$.

Question: Is there an adaptive toolbox T with at most nc negative cues, with at most $\#h$ heuristics each at most of size $|h|$ and with an ecological rationality $er > er_{min}$ for environment E?

Math domains: Matrix, Value function, Function optimization
Cognitive domains: Decision-making, Learning
Modeling framework: Symbolic, Heuristic

Remarks: This problem was first formalized and analyzed in an MSc thesis (Sweers, 2015). The classical complexity result formed the basis of Otworowska et al. (2018). At the time of printing of this book, the parameterized complexity results had not yet appeared in print other than in Sweers (2015).

Classical complexity: NP-hard by reduction from DOMINATING SET (Otworowska et al., 2018; Sweers, 2015).

Parameterized complexity: The following parameters have been considered:

- The number of heuristics in a toolbox ($\#h$)
- The length of a heuristic counted in the number of cues ($|h|$)
- The number of negative cues in a toolbox (nc)
- The number of positive cues in a toolbox (pc)
- The minimal ecological rationality a toolbox should have (er_{min})
- The number of information pieces in an environment ($|I|$)
- The number of actions ($|A|$)
- The number of satisfactory actions per situation (a_{max})
- The number of groups of fully correlated information pieces ($corr$)

It was shown that TOOLBOX ADAPTATION is fixed-parameter intractable relative to parameter set $\{\#h, |h|, nc, pc, er_{min}\}$ and fixed-parameter tractable relative to parameter sets $\{|A|, |A|\}$, $\{corr, |A|\}$, $\{|A|, a_{max}\}$, and $\{corr, a_{max}\}$.

TOOLBOX RE-ADAPTATION

Input: An environment $E = (S, A)$, the positive integers $\#h$, $|h|$ and nc denoting the maximum number of heuristics, the maximum size of a heuristic and the maximum number of negative cues in the entire toolbox, respectively, the minimal ecological rationality $er_{min} \in [0, 1]$, an adaptive toolbox T which has at most $\#h$ heuristics where each heuristic is at most size $|h|$, with at most nc negative cues and ecological rationality $er > er_{min}$, a new s-a pair e and a set of changes which can be made $C = \{$delete a cue-action pair, add a cue-action pair, change a cue, change an action$\}$.

Question: Is there an adaptive toolbox T' reconfigured with changes from C which has at most $\#h$ heuristics where each heuristic is at most size $|h|$, with ecological rationality $er > er_{min}$ in the new environment $E' = E \cup e$?

Math domains: Matrix, Value function, Function optimization
Cognitive domains: Decision-making, Learning
Modeling framework: Symbolic, Heuristic

Remarks: See the remarks for TOOLBOX ADAPTATION.

Classical complexity: NP-hard by reduction from DOMINATING SET (Sweers, 2015).

Parameterized complexity: Parameterized analysis was carried out relative to the same parameters as for TOOLBOX ADAPTATION. It was shown that TOOLBOX RE-ADAPTATION is fixed-parameter intractable relative to parameter set $\{\#h, |h|, nc, pc, er_{min}, a_{max}, |A|\}$ and fixed-parameter tractable relative to parameter sets $\{|A|, |A|\}$, $\{corr, |A|\}$, $\{|A|, a_{max}\}$, and $\{corr, a_{max}\}$.

WEIGHTED COHERENCE
Input: A graph $N = (P, C)$, with $C = C^- \cup C^+$ and $C^- \cap C^+ = \emptyset$, a positive weight $w(p, q) > 0$ for each $(p, q) \in C$, and positive integers c.
Question: Is there a partition of P into accepted A and rejected R vertices such that the total weight of satisfied constraints $\sum_{(p,q) \in S(p,q)} w(p, q) \geq c$ and the total weight of unsatisfied constraints $\sum_{(p,q) \in (C^+ \cup C^-) - S(p,q)} w(p, q) \leq i$? Here the set of satisfied constraints is defined by $S(p, q) = \{(p, q) \in C^+ | p, q \in A \text{ or } p, q \in R\} \cup \{(p, q) \in C^- | p \in A \text{ and } q \in R\}$.

Math domains: Graph, Proposition formulas, Value function, Function optimization
Cognitive domains: Perception, Reasoning, Judgement, Analogy
Modeling framework: Symbolic, Connectionist

Remarks: WEIGHTED COHERENCE is known to be equivalent to HARMONY MAXIMIZATION, the problem of finding a harmony maximum (or energy minimum) activation pattern in Hopfield neural networks (van Rooij and Wareham, 2008; Thagard and Verbeurgt, 1998), van Rooij (2012) has furthermore considered the problem as a formalization of self-organization as conceived by dynamical systems approaches to embodied cognition.

Classical complexity: NP-hard by reduction from MAX CUT (Thagard and Verbeurgt, 1998), both for the general weighted case and the unweighted special case (i.e., where all weights $w(p, q)$ are set to "1"). van Rooij (2003) considered several generalizations of the problem incorporating what Thagard (2000) called the "data priority principle." (see also Chapter 10 in this book).

Parameterized complexity: The following parameters have been considered:

- The number of positive constraints ($|C^+|$)
- The number of negative constraints ($|C^-|$)
- The lower bound on the total weight of satisfied constraints (c)
- The upper bound on the total weight of unsatisfied constraints (u)

It was shown by van Rooij (2003) that this problem is fixed-parameter intractable relative to parameter set $\{|C^+|\}$ and fixed-parameter tractable relative to parameter sets $\{|C^-|\}$ and $\{c\}$. It is known that the problem is also fixed-parameter tractable for parameter u by reduction from k-EDGE BIPARTIZATION (unpublished result, see Practice 10.3.8 in Chapter 10).

References

Abdelbar, A. M., and Hedetniemi, S. M. 1998. Approximating MAPS for belief networks is NP-hard and other theorems. *Artificial Intelligence*, **102**(1), 21–38.

Abrahamson, K. A., Ellis, J., Fellows, M. R., and Mata, M. 1989. On the complexity of fixed-parameter problems [Extended abstract]. Pages 210–215 of: *Proceedings of the 30th Annual IEEE Symposium on the Foundations of Computer Science (FOCS '89)*. Los Alamitos, CA: IEEE Press.

Anderson, J. R. 1987. Methodologies for studying human knowledge. *Behavioral and Brain Sciences*, **10**(3), 467–477.

Anderson, J. R. 1990. *The Adaptive Character of Thought*. London: Psychology Press.

Arora, S. 1998. The approximability of NP-hard problems. Pages 337–348 of: *Proceedings of the 30th Annual ACM Symposium on Theory of Computing (STOC '98)*. New York: ACM.

Arora, S., and Barak, B. 2009. *Computational Complexity: A Modern Approach*. Cambridge/New York: Cambridge University Press.

Aucher, G., and Schwarzentruber, F. 2013. On the complexity of dynamic epistemic logic. Pages 19–38 of: *Proceedings of the 14th Conference on Theoretical Aspects of Rationality and Knowledge (TARK)*. Chennai, India: Institute of Mathematical Sciences.

Ausiello, G., D'Atri, A., and Protasi, M. 1981. Structure preserving reductions among convex optimization problems. *Journal of Computer and System Sciences*, **21**, 136–153.

Baker, C. L., Saxe, R., and Tenenbaum, J. B. 2009. Action understanding as inverse planning. *Cognition*, **113**(3), 329–349.

Balasubramanian, R., Fellows, M. R., and Raman, V. 1998. An improved fixed-parameter algorithm for Vertex Cover. *Information Processing Letters*, **65**(3), 163–168.

Berwick, R. C., Barton Jr., G. E., and Ristad, E. S. 1987. *Computational Complexity and Natural Language*. Cambridge, MA: MIT Press.

Blokpoel, M., Kwisthout, J., van der Weide, T. P., Wareham, T., and van Rooij, I. 2013. A computational-level explanation of the speed of goal inference. *Journal of Mathematical Psychology*, **57**(3), 117–133.

Blokpoel, M., van Kesteren, M., Stolk, A., Haselager, P., Toni, I., and van Rooij, I. 2012. Recipient design in human communication: Simple heuristics or perspective taking? *Frontiers in Human Neuroscience*, **6**(September), 253.

Blum, A. L., and Rivest, R. L. 1989. Training a 3-node neural network is NP-complete. Pages 494–501 of: *Advances in Neural Information Processing Systems*. San Francisco, CA: Morgan Kaufmann.

Blum, A. L., and Rivest, R. L. 1992. Training a 3-node neural network is NP-complete. *Neural Networks*, **5**(1), 117–127.

Blum, A. L., and Rivest, R. L. 1993. Training a 3-node neural network is NP-complete. Pages 9–28 of: *Machine Learning: From Theory to Applications*. Lecture Notes in Computer Science. Berlin/Heidelberg: Springer.

Bodlaender, H. L., van den Eijkhof, F., and van der Gaag, L. C. 2002. On the complexity of the MPA problem in probabilistic networks. Pages 675–679 of: van Harmelen, F. (ed.), *Proceedings of the 15th European Conference on Artificial Intelligence*. Amsterdam, The Netherlands: IOS Press.

Bolander, T., Jensen, M. H., and Schwarzentruber, F. 2015. Complexity results in epistemic planning. In: *Proceedings of the 24th International Joint Conference on Artificial Intelligence (IJCAI)*. AAAI Press/IJCAI.

Bruck, J., and Goodman, J. W. 1990. On the power of neural networks for solving hard problems. *Journal of Complexity*, **6**(2), 129–135.

Buss, J. F., and Goldsmith, J. 1993. Nondeterminism within P. *SIAM Journal on Computing*, **22**(3), 560–572.

Bylander, T. 1994. The computational complexity of propositional STRIPS planning. *Artificial Intelligence*, **69**(1), 165–204.

Bylander, T., Allemang, D., Tanner, M. C., and Josephson, J. R. 1991. The computational complexity of abduction. *Artificial Intelligence*, **49**(1–3), 25–60.

Cai, L., Chen, J., Downey, R. G., and Fellows, M. R. 1997. Advice classes of parameterized tractability. *Annals of Pure and Applied Logic*, **84**, 119–138.

Carruthers, P. 2005. Simple heuristics meet massive modularity. Page 24 of: Carruthers, P., Laurence, S., and Stich, S. (eds.), *Culture and Cognition*: The innate mind, vol. 2. Oxford, UK: Oxford University Press.

Cesati, M., and Wareham, T. 1995. Parameterized complexity analysis in robot motion planning. Pages 880–885 of: *Proceedings of the 25th IEEE International Conference on Systems, Man and Cybernetics*, vol. 1. Los Alamitos, CA: IEEE Press.

Chalmers, D. J. 2011. A computational foundation for the study of cognition. *Journal of Cognitive Science*, **12**(4), 323–357.

Chater, N., and Oaksford, M. 2000. The rational analysis of mind and behavior. *Synthese*, **122**(1-2), 93–131.

Chater, N., Oaksford, M., Nakisa, R., and Redington, M. 2003. Fast, frugal, and rational: How rational norms explain behavior. *Organizational Behavior and Human Decision Processes*, **90**(1), 63–86.

Chater, N., Tenenbaum, J. B., and Yuille, A. 2006. Probabilistic models of cognition: Conceptual foundations. *Trends in Cognitive Sciences*, **10**(7), 287–291.

Chen, J., Kanj, I. A., and Jia, W. 2001. Vertex Cover: Further observations and further improvements. *Journal of Algorithms*, **41**(2), 280–301.

Chen, J., Kanj, I. A., and Xia, G. 2010. Improved upper bounds for Vertex Cover. *Theoretical Computer Science*, **411**(40–42), 3736–3756.

Cherniak, C. 1986. *Minimal Rationality*. Cambridge, MA: MIT Press.

Chickering, D. M. 1996. Learning Bayesian networks is NP-Complete. Pages 121–130 of: *Learning from Data: AI and Statistics V*. Heidelberg: Springer.

Church, A. 1936. An unsolvable problem of elementary number theory. *American Journal of Mathematics*, **58**(2), 345–363.

Clark, H. H. 1996. *Using Language*. vol. 4. Cambridge, UK: Cambridge University Press.

Cobham, A. 1965. The intrinsic computational difficulty of functions. Pages 24–30 of: Bar-Hillel, Y. (ed.), *Logic, Methodology and Philosophy of Science: Proceedings of the 1964 International Congress (Studies in Logic and the Foundations of Mathematics)*. Amsterdam, The Netherlands: North-Holland Publishing.

Cockshott, P., and Michaelson, G. 2007. Are there new models of computation? Reply to Wegner and Eberbach. *The Computer Journal*, **50**(2), 232–247.

Cook, S. 1971. The complexity of theorem-proving procedures. Pages 151–158 of: *Proceedings of the Third Annual ACM Symposium on Theory of Computing*.

Cooper, G. F. 1984. *NESTOR: A Computer-based Medical Diagnostic Aid that Integrates Causal and Probabilistic Knowledge*. Tech. rept. HPP-84-48. Stanford University.

Cooper, G. F. 1990. The computational complexity of probabilistic inference using Bayesian belief networks. *Artificial Intelligence*, **42**(2), 393–405.

Cooper, R. P., and Peebles, D. 2017. On the relation between Marr's levels: A response to Blokpoel. *Topics in Cognitive Science*, **9**(2).

Cormen, T. H., Leiserson, C. E., Rivest, R. L., and Stein, C. 2009. *Introduction to Algorithms*. Cambridge, MA: MIT Press.

Cosmides, L., and Tooby, J. 1994. Origins of domain specificity: The evolution of functional organization. Pages 85–116 of: Hirschfeld, L. A., and Gelman, S. A. (eds.), *Mapping the Mind*. Cambridge, UK: Cambridge University Press.

Cummins, R. C. 2000. "How does it work" versus "what are the laws?": Two conceptions of psychological explanation. In: Keil, F., and Wilson, R. A. (eds.), *Explanation and Cognition, 117–145*. Cambridge, MA: MIT Press.

Cygan, M., Fomin, F. V., Kowalik, L., Lokshtanov, D., Marx, D., Pilipczuk, M., Pilipczuk, M., and Saurabh, S. 2015. *Parameterized Algorithms*. Berlin: Springer.

Dagum, P., and Luby, M. 1993. Approximating probabilistic inference in Bayesian belief networks is NP-hard. *Artificial Intelligence*, **60**(1), 141–153.

de Haan, R. 2016. *Parameterized Complexity in the Polynomial Hierarchy*. Ph.D. thesis, Technische Universität Wien.

Dennett, D. C. 1995. Cognitive science as reverse engineering several meanings of Top-down and Bottom-up. Pages 679–689 of: Prawitz, D., Skyrms, B., and Westerståhl, D. (eds.), *Logic, Methodology and Philosophy of Science IX*. Studies in Logic and the Foundations of Mathematics, vol. 134. Amsterdam, the Netherlands: Elsevier.

Deutsch, D. 1985. Quantum theory, the Church–Turing principle and the universal quantum computer. *Proceedings of the Royal Society of London, Series A*, **400**(1818), 97–117.

Downey, R. G., and Fellows, M. R. 1999. *Parameterized Complexity*. Berlin: Springer.

Downey, R. G., and Fellows, M. R. 2013. *Fundamentals of Parameterized Complexity*. Berlin: Springer.

Downey, R. G., and Fellows, M. R. 1995. Parameterized computational feasibility. Pages 219–244 of: *Feasible Mathematics II*. Berlin: Springer.

Downey, R. G., Fellows, M. R., and Stege, U. 1999. Parameterized complexity: A framework for systematically confronting computational intractability. Pages 49–99 of: *Contemporary Trends in Discrete Mathematics: From DIMACS and DIMATIA to the Future*. AMS-DIMACS Series in Discrete Mathematics and Theoretical Computer Science, vol. 49. Providence, RI: American Mathematical Society.

Dry, M., Lee, M. D., Vickers, D., and Hughes, P. 2006. Human performance on visually presented Traveling Salesperson problems with varying numbers of nodes. *The Journal of Problem Solving*, **1**(1), 20–32.

Dunne, P. E., Laurence, M., and Wooldridge, M. 2003. Complexity results for agent design problems. *Annals of Mathematics, Computing & Teleinformatics*, **1**(1), 18.

Edmonds, J. 1965. Paths, Trees, and Flowers. Pages 361–379 of: *Classic Papers in Combinatorics*. Boston: Modern Birkhäuser Classics.

Eisner, J. 1997. Efficient generation in primitive Optimality Theory. Pages 313–320 of: *Proceedings of the 35th Annual Meeting of the Association for Computational Linguistics and Eighth Conference of the European Chapter of the Association for Computational Linguistics*. Association for Computational Linguistics.

Eiter, T., and Gottlob, G. 1995. The complexity of logic-based abduction. *Journal of the ACM*, **42**(1), 3–42.

Falkenhainer, B., Forbus, K. D., and Gentner, D. 1989. The structure-mapping engine: Algorithm and examples. *Artificial Intelligence*, **41**, 1–63.

Fellows, M. R., and Langston, M. A. 1988. Nonconstructive tools for proving polynomial-time decidability. *Journal of the ACM*, **35**(3), 727–739.

Fellows, M. R., Pfandler, A., Rosamond, F. A., and Rümmele, S. 2012. The parameterized complexity of abduction. Pages 743–749 of: *Proceedings of the 26th AAAI Conference on Artificial Intelligence*. AAAI.

Fishburn, P. C., and LaValle, I. H. 1993. Subset preferences in linear and nonlinear utility theory. *Journal of Mathematical Psychology*, **37**(4), 611–623.

Fishburn, P. C., and LaValle, I. H. 1996. Binary interactions and subset choice. *European Journal of Operational Research*, **92**(1), 182–192.

Flum, J., and Grohe, M. 2006. *Parameterized Complexity Theory*. Berlin: Springer.

Fodor, Jerry A. 1987. *Psychosemantics: The Problem of Meaning in the Philosophy of Mind*. Cambridge, MA: MIT Press.

Forbus, K. D., Gentner, D., and Law, K. 1994. MAC/FAC: A model of similarity-based retrieval. *Cognitive Science*, **19**, 141–205.

Forbus, K. D., Gentner, D., Everett, J. O., and Wu, M. 1997. Towards a computational model of evaluating and using analogical inferences. Pages 229–234 of: *Proceedings of the 19th Annual Conference of the Cognitive Science Society*. Hillsdale, NJ: Lawrence Erlbaum Associates.

Forbus, K. D., and Hinrichs, T. 2006. Companion cognitive systems: A step towards human-level AI. *AI Magazine*, **27**(2), 83–95.

Forbus, K. D., and Oblinger, D. 1990. Making *SME* greedy and pragmatic. Pages 61–68 of: *Proceedings of the 12th Annual Conference of the Cognitive Science Society*. Mahweh, NJ: Lawrence Erlbaum Associates.

Fortnow, L. 2003. One complexity theorist's view of quantum computing. *Theoretical Computer Science*, **292**(3), 597–610.

Foulds, L. R. 1994. *Graph Theory Applications*. Berlin: Springer Science & Business Media.

Fraenkel, A., and Lichtenstein, D. 1981. Computing a perfect strategy for $n \times n$ chess requires time exponential in n. *Journal of Combinatorial Theory, Series A*, **31**, 199–214.

Frank, S. L., Haselager, W. F. G., and van Rooij, I. 2009. Connectionist semantic systematicity. *Cognition*, **110**(3), 358–379.

Frixione, M. 2001. Tractable competence. *Minds and Machines*, **11**(3), 379–397.

Garey, M. R., and Johnson, D. S. 1979. *Computers and Intractability: A Guide to the Theory of NP-Completeness*. New York: W.H. Freeman.

Gentner, D. 1983. Structure-mapping: A theoretical framework for analogy. *Cognitive Science*, **7**, 155–170.

Gentner, D. 2003. Why we're so smart. Pages 195–235 of: Gentner, D., and Goldin-Meadow, S. (eds.), *Language in Mind: Advances in the Study of Language and Thought*. Cambridge, MA: MIT Press.

Gentner, D., Lowenstein, J., Thompson, L., and Forbus, K. D. 2009. Reviving inert knowledge: Analogical abstraction supports relational retrieval of past events. *Cognitive Science*, **33**(6), 1343–1382.

Gentner, D., and Forbus, K. D. 2011. Computational models of analogy. *Wiley Interdisciplinary Reviews: Cognitive Science*, **2**(3), 266–276.

Gibbons, A., and Rytter, W. 1988. *Efficient Parallel Algorithms*. New York: Cambridge University Press.

Gigerenzer, G. 2008. Why heuristics work. *Perspectives on Psychological Science*, **3**(1), 20–29.

Gigerenzer, G., and Goldstein, D. G. 1996. Reasoning the fast and frugal way: Models of bounded rationality. *Psychological Review*, **103**(4), 650–669.

Gigerenzer, G., Hoffrage, U., and Goldstein, D. G. 2008. Fast and frugal heuristics are plausible models of cognition: Reply to Dougherty, Franco-Watkins, and Thomas (2008). *Psychological Review*, **115**(1), 230–239.

Gigerenzer, G., and Todd, P. M. 1999. *Simple Heuristics that Make Us Smart*. Oxford, UK: Oxford University Press.

Gigerenzer, G., Todd, P. M., and ABC Research Group. 2000. *Simple Heuristics that Make Us Smart*. Evolution and Cognition. Oxford/New York: Oxford University Press.

Gould, R. 1988. *Graph Theory*. San Francisco, CA: Benjamin/Cummings Publishing Co.

Grice, H. P. 1989. *Studies in the Way of Words*. Boston, MA: Harvard University Press.

Grootswagers, T. 2013. *Having Your Cake and Eating It Too: Towards a Fast and Optimal Method for Analogy Derivation*. MSc Thesis, Radboud University Nijmegen.

Gross, J. L., and Yellen, J. 1990. *Graph Theory and Its Applications*. London: Chapman and Hall.

Grush, R., and Churchland, P. S. 1995. Gaps in Penrose's toilings. *Journal of Consciousness Studies*, **2**(1), 10–29.

Hahn, U., Chater, N., and Richardson, L. B. 2003. Similarity as transformation. *Cognition*, **87**(1), 1–32.

Halford, G. S., Wilson, W. H., and Phillips, W. 1998. Processing capacity defined by relational complexity. *Behavioral & Brain Sciences*, 803–831.

Hamilton, R., and Wareham, T. 2012. Practical optimal-solution algorithms for schema-based analogy mapping. Pages 311–312 of: Rußwinkel, N., Drewitz, Uwe U., and van Rijn, H. (eds.), *Proceedings of ICCM 2012: 11th International Conference on Cognitive Modeling*. TU Berlin.

Haselager, P., van Dijk, J., and van Rooij, I. 2008. A lazy brain? Embodied embedded cognition and cognitive neuroscience. Pages 273–290 of: Calvo, P., and Gomila, A. (eds.), *Handbook of Cognitive Science. Perspectives on Cognitive Science*. San Diego, CA: Elsevier.

Haselager, W. F. G. 1997. *Cognitive Science and Folk Psychology: The Right Frame of Mind*. London: Sage Publications.

Horgan, T., and Tienson, J. 1996. *Connectionism and the Philosophy of Psychology*. Cambridge, MA: MIT Press.

Hüffner, F., Niedermeier, R., and Wernicke, S. 2008. Techniques for practical fixed-parameter algorithms. *The Computer Journal*, **51**(1), 7–25.

Jaja, J. 1992. *An Introduction to Parallel Algorithms*. Reading, MA: Addison-Wesley.

Jensen, F. V., and Nielsen, T. D. 2007. *Bayesian Networks and Decision Graphs*. Second edn. New York: Springer Verlag.

Joseph, D. A., and Plantings, W. H. 1985. On the complexity of reachability and motion planning questions. Pages 62–66 of: *Proceedings of the First Annual Symposium on Computational Geometry*. ACM.

Judd, J. S. 1987. Learning in networks is hard. Pages 685–692 of: *Proceedings of IEEE International Conference on Neural Networks, 1987*, vol. 2. Los Alamitos, CA: IEEE Computer Society Press.

Judd, J. S. 1990. *Neural Network Design and the Complexity of Learning*. Cambridge, MA: MIT Press.

Judd, J. S. 1988. On the complexity of loading shallow neural networks. *Journal of Complexity*, **4**(3), 177–192.

Kak, S. 2000. Active agents, intelligence and quantum computing. *Information Sciences*, **128**(1), 1–17.

Karp, R. M. 1972. Reducibility among combinatorial problems. Pages 85–103 of: Miller, R. E., and Thatcher, J. W. (eds.), *Complexity of Computer Computations*. New York: Plenum.

Kaye, R. 2000. Minesweeper is NP-complete. *The Mathematical Intelligencer*, **22**(4), 9–15.

Klapper, A., Dotsch, R., van Rooij, I., and Wigboldus, D. H. J. 2018. Social categorization in connectionist models: A conceptual integration. *Social Cognition*, **36**(2), 221–246.

Kleene, S. C. 1936. General recursive functions of natural numbers. *Mathematische Annalen*, **112**, 727–742.

Knuth, D. E. 1968. *The Art of Computer Programming: Fundamental Algorithms*. Reading, MA: Addison-Wesley.

Knuth, D. E. 1974. A terminological proposal. *SIGACT News*, 12–18.

Krueger, L. E., and Tsav, C. Y. 1990. Analyzing vision at the complexity level: Misplaced complexity? *Behavioral and Brain Sciences*, **13**(3), 449–450.

Kruskal, J. B. 1956. On the shortest spanning subtree of a graph and the Traveling Salesman Problem. *Proceedings of the American Mathematical Society*, **7**, 48–50.

Kube, P. R. 1991. Unbounded visual search is not both biologically plausible and NP-Complete. *Behavioral and Brain Sciences*, **14**(4), 768–770.

Kuehne, S. E., Forbus, K. D., Gentner, D., and Quinn, B. 2000. SEQL: Category learning as progressive abstraction using structure mapping. Pages 770–775 of: *Proceedings of the 22nd Annual Conference of the Cognitive Science Society.* Mahweh, NJ: Lawrence Erlbaum Associates.

Kwisthout, J. 2009. *The Computational Complexity of Probabilistic Networks*. Ph.D. thesis, Faculty of Science, Utrecht University, The Netherlands.

Kwisthout, J. 2011a. Most probable explanations in Bayesian networks: Complexity and tractability. *International Journal of Approximate Reasoning*, **52**(9), 1452–1469.

Kwisthout, J. 2011b. *The Computational Complexity of Probabilistic Inference*. Tech. rept. ICIS–R11003. Radboud University Nijmegen.

Kwisthout, J. 2012a. Relevancy in problem solving: A computational framework. *The Journal of Problem Solving*, **5**(1), 18–33.

Kwisthout, J. 2012b. Structure approximation of most probable explanations in Bayesian networks. Pages 131–138 of: Uiterwijk, J. W. H. M., Roos, N., and Winands, M. H. M. (eds.), *Proceedings of the 24th Benelux Conference on Artificial Intelligence (BNAIC'12).* The Netherlands: Department of Knowledge Maastricht University.

Kwisthout, J. 2015. Tree-width and the computational complexity of MAP approximations in Bayesian networks. *Journal of Artificial Intelligence Research*, **53**, 699–720.

Kwisthout, J. 2018. Approximate inference in Bayesian networks: Parameterized complexity results. *International Journal of Approximate Reasoning*, **93**(Feb.), 119–131.

Kwisthout, J., Bodlaender, H. L., and van der Gaag, L. C. 2011a. The Complexity of finding kth most probable explanations in probabilistic networks. Pages 356–367 of: *Proceedings of the 37th International Conference on Current Trends in Theory and Practice of Computer Science (SOFSEM 2011)*, vol. LNCS 6543. Dordrecht: Springer.

Kwisthout, J., and van Rooij, I. 2013. Bridging the gap between theory and practice of approximate Bayesian inference. *Cognitive Systems Research*, **24**(Sept.), 2–8.

Kwisthout, J., and van Rooij, I. 2018 (June). *Computational resource demands of a predictive Bayesian brain*. PsyArxiv preprint.

Kwisthout, J., Wareham, T., and van Rooij, I. 2011b. Bayesian intractability is not an ailment that approximation can cure. *Cognitive Science*, **35**(5), 779–784.

Kwisthout, J., Wareham, T., Haselager, P., Toni, I., and van Rooij, I. (2011). The computational costs of recipient design and intention recognition in communication. Pages 465–470 of: Carlson, L., Holscher, C., & T. Shipley, T. (Eds.), *Proceedings of the 33rd Annual Conference of the Cognitive Science Society*. Austin, TX: Cognitive Science Society.

Ladner, R. 1975. On the structure of polynomial time reducibility. *Journal of the ACM*, **22**(1), 155–171.

Lauritzen, S. L., and Spiegelhalter, D. J. 1988. Local computations with probabilities on graphical structures and their application to expert systems. *Journal of the Royal Statistical Society*, **50**(2), 157–224.

Levesque, H. J. 1989. Logic and the complexity of reasoning. Pages 73–107 of: *Philosophical Logic and Artificial Intelligence*. Dordrecht: Springer.

Levinson, S. C. 2006. The human interactional engine. Pages 39–69 of: *Roots of Human Sociality. Culture, Cognition and Human Interaction*. Oxford, UK: Berg Publishers.

Lewis, H. R., and Papadimitriou, C. H. 1997. *Elements of the Theory of Computation*. 2nd edn. Upper Saddle River, NJ: Prentice Hall.

Litt, A., Eliasmith, C., Kroon, F. W., Weinstein, S., and Thagard, P. 2006. Is the brain a quantum computer? *Cognitive Science*, **30**(3), 593–603.

Markman, A. B., and Gentner, D. 2000. Structure mapping in the comparison process. *The American Journal of Psychology*, **113**(4), 501.

Marr, D. 1977. Artificial intelligence: A personal view. *Artificial Intelligence*, **9**(1), 37–48.

Marr, D. 1981. *Vision: A Computational Investigation into the Human Representation and Processing Visual Information*. San Francisco, CA: W. H. Freeman.

Martignon, L., and Hoffrage, U. 2002. Fast, frugal, and fit: Simple heuristics for paired comparison. *Theory and Decision*, **52**(1), 29–71.

Martignon, L., and Schmitt, M. 1999. Simplicity and robustness of fast and frugal heuristics. *Minds and Machines*, **9**(4), 565–593.

McClelland, J. L. 2009. The place of modeling in cognitive science. *Topics in Cognitive Science*, **1**(1), 11–38.

Millgram, E. 2000. Coherence: The price of the ticket. *The Journal of Philosophy*, **97**(2), 82–93.

Montoya, J. A., and Mller, M. 2013. Parameterized random complexity. *Theory of Computing Systems*, **52**(2), 221–270.

Müller, M., van Rooij, I., and Wareham, T. 2009. Similarity as tractable transformation. Pages 50–55 of: *Proceedings of the 31st Annual Conference of the Cognitive Science Society*.

Narayanan, A. 1999. *Quantum computing for beginners*. Pages 2231–2238 in: *Evolutionary Computation*. Proceedings of the 1999 Congress, vol. 3. Los Alamitos, CA: IEEE Computer Society Press.

Newell, A., and Simon, H. A. 1961. *Computer Simulation of Human Thinking*. Santa Monica, CA: Rand Corporation.

Newell, A., and Simon, H. A. 1988a. GPS, a program that simulates human thought. Pages 453–460 of: Collins, A. M., and Smith, E. E. (eds.), *Readings in Cognitive Science: A Perspective from Psychology and Artificial Intelligence*. San Francisco, CA: Kaufmann.

Newell, A., and Simon, H. A. 1988b. The theory of human problem solving. Pages 453–460 of: Collins, A. M., and Smith, E. E. (eds.), *Readings in Cognitive Science: A Perspective from Psychology and Artificial Intelligence*. San Francisco, CA: Kaufmann.

Niedermeier, R. 2006. *Invitation to Fixed-Parameter Algorithms*. Oxford, UK: Oxford University Press.

Niedermeier, Invi, and Rossmanith, P. 1999. Upper bounds for Vertex Cover further improved. Pages 561–570 of: *STACS 99*. Lecture Notes in Computer Science. Berlin/Heidelberg: Springer.

Niedermeier, Invi, and Rossmanith, P. 2000. A general method to speed up fixed-parameter-tractable algorithms. *Information Processing Letters*, **73**(3–4), 125–129.

Niedermeier, Invi, and Rossmanith, P. 2003. On efficient fixed-parameter algorithms for Weighted Vertex Cover. *Journal of Algorithms*, **47**(2), 63–77.

Nordh, G., and Zanuttini, B. 2008. What makes propositional abduction tractable. *Artificial Intelligence*, **172**(10), 1245–1284.

Oaksford, M., and Chater, N. 1998. *Rationality in an Uncertain World: Essays on the Cognitive Science of Human Reasoning*. Abingdon-on-Park, UK: Psychology Press.

Oaksford, M., and Chater, N. 1993. Reasoning theories and bounded rationality. Pages 31–60 of: *Rationality: Psychological and philosophical perspectives*. London: Routledge.

Öllinger, M., Jones, G., and Knoblich, G. 2014. The dynamics of search, impasse, and representational change provide a coherent explanation of difficulty in the nine-dot problem. *Psychological Research*, **78**(2), 266–275.

Ordyniak, S., and Szeider, S. 2012. Algorithms and complexity results for exact Bayesian structure learning. *arXiv preprint arXiv:1203.3501*.

Orponen, P. 1994. Computational complexity of neural networks: A survey. *Nordic Journal of Computing*, **1**(1), 94–110.

Otworowska, M., Blokpoel, M., Sweers, M., Wareham, T., and van Rooij, I. 2018. Demons of ecological rationality. *Cognitive Science*, **42**(3), 1057–1066.

Parberry, I. 1994. *Circuit Complexity and Neural Networks*. Cambridge, MA: MIT Press.

Parberry, I. 1997. Knowledge, understanding, and computational complexity. Pages 125–144 of: Levine, Daniel S., and Elsberry, Wesley R. (eds.), *Optimality in Biological and Artificial Networks?* New York: Routledge.

Park, J. D., and Darwiche, A. 2004. Complexity results and approximation settings for MAP explanations. *Journal of Artificial Intelligence Research*, **21**, 101–133.

Paz, A., and Moran, S. 1981. Nondeterministic polynomial optimization problems and their approximations. *Theoretical Computer science*, **15**, 251–277.

Pearl, J. 1988. *Probabilistic Reasoning in Intelligent Systems: Networks of Plausible Inference*. Palo Alto, CA: Morgan Kaufmann.

Penrose, R. 1994. *Shadows of the Mind: A Search for the Missing Science of Consciousness*. 1st edn. New York: Oxford University Press.

Penrose, R. 1997. Physics and the mind. Pages 93–143 of: Longair, M. (ed.), *The Large, the Small and the Human Mind*. Cambridge, UK: Cambridge University Press.

Pizlo, Z., Stefanov, E., Saalweachter, J., Li, Z., Haxhimusa, Y., and Kropatsch, W. G. 2006. Traveling salesman problem: A foveating pyramid model. *The Journal of Problem Solving*, **1**(1).

Port, R. F., and van Gelder, T. 1995. *Mind as Motion: Explorations in the Dynamics of Cognition*. Cambridge, MA: MIT Press.

Post, E. L. 1936. Finite combinatory processes: Formulation. *Journal of Symbolic Logic*, **1**(3), 103–105.

Prasse, M., and Rittgen, P. 1998. Why Church's thesis still holds. Some notes on Peter Wegner's tracts on interaction and computability. *The Computer Journal*, **41**(6), 357–362.

Prim, R. C. 1957. Shortest connection networks and some generalizations. *The Bell System Technical Journal*, **36**(6), 1389–1401.

Pylyshyn, Z. W. 1991. The role of cognitive architectures in the theory of cognition. Pages 189–223 of: VanLehn, K (ed.), *Architectures for Intelligence*. Hillsdale, NJ: Lawrence Erlbaum Associates.

Reif, J. H. 1987. Complexity of the generalized mover's problem. In: Schwartz, J. T., Sharis, M., and Hopcroft, J. E. (eds.), *Planning, Geometry, and Complexity in Robot Motion*. Norwood, NJ: Ablex Publishing.

Reiter, R. 1980. A logic for default reasoning. *Artificial Intelligence*, **13**(1), 81–132.

Ristad, E. S. 1990. *Computational structure of human language*. Ph.D. thesis, Massachusetts Institute of Technology, Cambridge, MA.

Ristad, E. S. 1992. *Complexity of the simplified segmental phonology*. Tech. Rept. CS-TR-388-92. Department of Computer Science, Princeton University.

Ristad, E. S. 1993. *The Language Complexity Game*. Cambridge, MA: MIT Press.

Robere, R., and Besold, T. R. 2012. Complex analogies: Remarks on the complexity of HDTP. Pages 530–542 of: Thielscher, M., and Zhang, D. (eds.), *Australasian Joint Conference on Artificial Intelligence (AI 2012)*. Lecture notes in Computer Science, no. 7691. Berlin: Springer.

Rosch, E. H. 1973. On the internal structure of perceptual and semantic categories. Pages 111–144 of: Moore, T. E. (ed.), *Cognitive Development and the Acquisition of Language*. New York: Academic Press.

Sanborn, A. N., Griffiths, T. L., and Navarro, D. J. 2010. Rational approximations to rational models: Alternative algorithms for category learning. *Psychological Review*, **117**(4), 1144–1167.

Schmitt, M., and Martignon, L. 2006. On the complexity of learning lexicographic strategies. *Journal of Machine Learning Research*, **7**(Jan.), 55–83.

Schöning, U. 1990. Complexity cores and hard problem instances. Pages 232–240 of: *Algorithms, International Symposium SIGAL '90, Tokyo, Japan, August 16-18, 1990, Proceedings*.

Schwering, A., Krumnack, U., Kühnberger, K. -U., and Gust, H. 2009. Syntactic principles of heuristic-driven theory projection. *Cognitive Systems Research*, **10**(3), 251–269.

Scott, A., Stege, U., and van Rooij, I. 2011. Minesweeper may not be NP-complete but is hard nonetheless. *The Mathematical Intelligencer*, **33**(4), 5–17.

Selman, B., and Levesque, H. J. 1990. Abductive and default reasoning: A computational core. Pages 343–348 of: *Proceedings of the 8th National Conference on Artificial Intelligence (AAAI 1990)*.

Shafto, P., and Goodman, N. 2008. Teaching games: Statistical sampling assumptions for learning in pedagogical situations. Pages 1632–1637 of: *Proceedings of the Thirtieth Annual Conference of the Cognitive Science Society*. Austin, TX: Cognitive Science Society.

Shimony, S. E. 1994. Finding MAPs for belief networks is NP-hard. *Artificial Intelligence*, **68**(2), 399–410.

Shor, P. 1997. Polynomial-time algorithms for prime factorization and discrete logarithms on a quantum computer. *SIAM Journal on Computing*, **26**(5), 1484–1509.

Siegel, R. M. 1990. Is it really that complex? After all, there are no green elephants. *Behavioral and Brain Sciences*, **13**(3), 453–453.

Siegelmann, H. T., and Sontag, E. D. 1994. Analog computation via neural networks. *Theoretical Computer Science*, **131**(2), 331–360.

Šíma, J. 1994. Loading deep networks is hard. *Neural Computation*, **6**(5), 842–850.

Šíma, J. 1996. Back-propagation is not Efficient. *Neural Networks*, **9**(6), 1017–1023.

Šíma, J and Orponen, P. 2003. General-purpose computation with neural networks: A survey of complexity theoretic results. *Neural Computation*, **15**(12), 2727–2778.

Simon, H. A. 1955. A behavioral model of rational choice. *The Quarterly Journal of Economics*, **69**(1), 99–118.

Simon, H. A. 1988. Rationality as process and as product of thought. Pages 58–77 of: Bell, D. E., Raiffa, H., and Tversky, A. (eds.), *Decision making: Descriptive, Normative, and Prescriptive Interactions*. Cambridge, UK: Cambridge University Press.

Simon, H. A. 1990. Invariants of human behavior. *Annual Review of Psychology*, **41**(1), 1–20.

Sloper, C., and Telle, J. 2008. An overview of techniques for designing parameterized algorithms. *The Computer Journal*, **51**(1), 122–136.

Sperber, D., and Wilson, D. 1996. *Relevance: Communication and Cognition*. 2nd edn. Hoboken, NJ: Wiley-Blackwell.

Sperber D., and Wilson D. 2002. Pragmatics, modularity and mind-reading. *Mind & Language*, **17**(1-2), 3–23.

Stege, U., and Fellows, M. 1999. *An improved fixed-parameter-tractable algorithm for Vertex Cover*. Tech. Rept. 318. Department of Computer Science, ETH Zurich.

Sweers, M. 2015. *Adapting the adaptive toolbox: The computational cost of building rational behaviour*. MSc thesis, Radboud University Nijmegen.

Sy, B. K. 1992. Reasoning MPE to multiply connected belief networks using message-passing. Pages 570–576 of: Rosenbloom, P., and Szolovits, P. (eds.), *Proceedings of the Tenth National Conference on Artificial Intelligence*. Arlington, VA: AAAI Press.

Thagard, P. 1993. Computational tractability and conceptual coherence: Why do computer scientists believe that P≠NP? *Canadian Journal of Philosophy*, **23**(3), 349–363.

Thagard, P. 2000. *Coherence in Thought and Action*. Reprint edn. Cambridge, MA: MIT Press.

Thagard, P. 2003. Why wasn't O.J. convicted? Emotional coherence in legal inference. *Cognition and Emotion*, **17**(3), 361–383. PMID: 29715748.

Thagard, P. 2006. *Hot Thought: Mechanisms and Applications of Emotional Cognition*. Cambridge, MA: MIT Press.

Thagard, P. 2012. Coherence: The price is right. *The Southern Journal of Philosophy*, **50**(1), 42–49.

Thagard, P., and Findlay, S. 2011. Changing minds about climate change: Belief Revision, Coherence, and Emotion. Pages 329–345 of: Olsson, E. and Enqvist, S. (ed.), *Belief Revision Meets Philosophy of Science*. Berlin: Springer.

Thagard, P., and Verbeurgt, K. 1998. Coherence as constraint satisfaction. *Cognitive Science*, **22**(1), 1–24.

Thelen, E., and Smith, L. 1994. *A Dynamic Systems Approach to the Development of Cognition and Action*. Cambridge, MA: MIT Press.

Todd, P. M., and Gigerenzer, G. 2000. Prices of simple heuristics that make us smart. *Behavioral and Brain Sciences*, **23**(5), 727–741.

Todd, P. M., and Gigerenzer, G. 2012. *Ecological Rationality: Intelligence in the World*. Oxford/New York: Oxford University Press.

Tsotsos, J. K. 1989. The complexity of perceptual search tasks. Pages 1571–1577 of: Sridharan, N.S. (ed.), *Proceedings of the International Joint Conference on Artificial Intelligence*. San Francisco, CA: Morgan Kaufmann Publishers.

Tsotsos, J. K. 1990. Analyzing vision at the complexity level. *Behavioral and Brain Sciences*, **13**(3), 423–445.

Tsotsos, J. K. 2001. Complexity, vision, and attention. Pages 105–128 of: Harris, L., and Jenkin, M. (eds.), *Vision and Attention*. New York: Springer.

Turing, A. M. 1936. On computable numbers, with an application to the entscheidungsproblem. *Proceedings of the London Mathematical Society*, **42**(2), 230–265.

van de Pol, I., van Rooij, I., and Szymanik, J. 2018. Parameterized complexity of theory of mind reasoning in dynamic epistemic logic. *Journal of Logic, Language and Information*, 27(3), 255–294.

van Eijck, J., and Schwarzentruber, F. 2014. Epistemic probability logic simplified. Pages 158–177 of: Gore, R., Kool, B., and Kurucz, A. (eds.), *Advances in Modal Logic*. London: College Publications.

van Emde Boas, P. 1990. Algorithms and complexity. Pages 1–66 of: van Leeuwen, Jan (ed.), *Handbook of Theoretical Computer Science*, vol. A. Cambridge, MA: MIT Press.

van Gelder, T. 1998. The dynamical hypothesis in cognitive science. *Behavioral and Brain Sciences*, **21**(5), 615–628.

van Gelder, T. 1999. Defending the dynamic hypothesis. Pages 13–22 of: Tschacher, W., and Dauwalder, J. P. (eds.), *Dynamics, Synergetics, Autonomous Agents: Nonlinear Systems Approaches to Cognitive Psychology and Cognitive Science*. Singapore: World.

van Gelder, T. 1995. What might cognition be, if not computation? *Journal of Philosophy*, **92**(7), 345–381.

van Rooij, I. 2003. *Tractable Cognition: Complexity Theory in Cognitive Psychology*. Ph.D. thesis, Department of Psychology, University of Victoria.

van Rooij, I. 2007. Review of Paul Thagard (2006) "Hot thought: Mechanisms and applications of emotional coherence." *Philosophical Psychology*, **20**(5), 659–665.

van Rooij, I. 2008. The tractable cognition thesis. *Cognitive Science*, **32**, 939–984.

van Rooij, I. 2012. Self-organization takes time too: Topics in cognitive science. *Topics in Cognitive Science*, 4(1), 63–71.

van Rooij, I. (2015). How the curse of intractability can be cognitive science's blessing. In: Noelle, D. C., Dale, R., Warlaumont, A. S., Yoshimi, J., Matlock, T., Jennings, C. D., & Maglio, P. P. (Eds.) (2015). *Proceedings of the 37th Annual Meeting of the Cognitive Science Society*. Austin, TX: Cognitive Science Society.

van Rooij, I., Evans, P., Müller, M., Gedge, J., and Wareham, T. 2008. Identifying sources of intractability in cognitive models: An illustration using analogical structure mapping. Pages 915–920 of: *Proceedings of the 30th Annual Conference of the Cognitive Science Society*. Austin, TX: Cognitive Science Society.

van Rooij, I., Kwisthout, J., Blokpoel, M., Szymanik, J., Wareham, T., and Toni, I. 2011. Intentional communication: Computationally easy or difficult? *Frontiers in Human Neuroscience*, **5**(52), 1–18.

van Rooij, I., Stege, U., and Kadlec, H. 2005. Sources of complexity in subset choice. *Journal of Mathematical Psychology*, **49**(2), 160–187.

van Rooij, I., and Wareham, T. 2008. Parameterized complexity in cognitive modeling: Foundations, applications, and opportunities. *Computer Journal*, **51**(3), 385–404.

van Rooij, I., and Wareham, T. 2012. Intractability and approximation of optimization theories of cognition. *Journal of Mathematical Psychology*, **56**(4), 232–247.

van Rooij, I., Wright, C. D., and Wareham, T. 2012. Intractability and the use of heuristics in psychological explanations. *Synthese*, **187**(2), 471–487.

van Rooij, I., Wright, C. D., Kwisthout, J., and Wareham, T. 2018. Rational analysis, intractability, and the prospects of 'as if-explanations. *Synthese*, **195**(2), 491–510.

Veale, T., and Keane, M. T. 1997. The competence of sub-optimal theories of structure mapping on hard analogies. Pages 232–237 of: *Proceedings of the 15th International Joint Conference on Artificial Intelligence (IJCAI'97)*, vol. 1. San Mateo, CA: Morgan Kaufmann.

Wareham, T. 1999. *Systematic Parameterized Complexity Analysis in Computational Phonology*. Ph.D. thesis, University of Victoria.

Wareham, T. 2001. The parameterized complexity of intersection and composition operations on sets of finite-state automata. Pages 302–310 of: *Proceedings of the Fifth International Conference on Implementation and Application of Automata*. Lecture Notes in Computer Science, vol. 2088. Berlin: Springer.

Wareham, T. 2017. The roles of internal representation and processing in problem solving involving insight: A computational complexity perspective. *Journal of Problem Solving*, **10**(1), 3.

Wareham, T., Evans, P., and van Rooij, I. 2011a. What does (and doesn't) make analogical problem solving easy? A complexity-theoretic investigation. *Journal of Problem Solving*, **3**(2), 30–71.

Wareham, T., Kwisthout, J., Haselager, P., and van Rooij, I. 2011b. Ignorance is bliss: A complexity perspective on adapting reactive architectures. Pages 1–5 of: *Proceedings of the 2011 IEEE International Conference on Development and Learning (ICDL)*. Los Alamitos, CA: IEEE Computer Society Press.

Wareham, T., Robere, R., and van Rooij, I. 2012. A change for the better? Assessing the computational cost of re-representation. Pages 111–116 of: Rußwinkel, N., Drewitz, U., and van Rijn, H. (eds.), *Proceedings of ICCM 2012: 11th International Conference on Cognitive Modeling*. TU Berlin.

Wareham, T., and van Rooij, I. 2011. On the computational challenges of analogy-based generalization. *Cognitive Systems Research*, **12**(3), 266–280.

Wegner, P. 1997. Why interaction is more powerful than algorithms. *Communications of the ACM*, **40**(5), 80–91.

Wooldridge, M., and Dunne, P. E. 2005. The complexity of agent design problems: Determinism and history dependence. *Annals of Mathematics and Artificial Intelligence*, **45**(3–4), 343–371.

Xu, Z. -B., Hu, G. -Q., and Kwong, C. -P. 1996. Asymmetric Hopfield-type networks: Theory and applications. *Neural Networks*, **9**(3), 483–501.

Yao, X. 1992. Finding approximate solutions to NP-hard problems by neural networks is hard. *Information Processing Letters*, **41**(2), 93–98.

Index